IMPROVING EDUCATION FOR ENGLISH LEARNERS:

Research-Based Approaches

CALIFORNIA DEPARTMENT OF EDUCATION
SACRAMENTO, 2010

Publishing Information

The *Improving Education for English Learners: Research-Based Approaches* was developed by the Standards, Curriculum Frameworks, and Instructional Resources Division, California Department of Education. It was edited by Faye Ong, working in cooperation with Veronica Aguila, Administrator, Instructional Resources Unit. It was prepared for printing by the staff of CDE Press; the cover and interior design were created and prepared by Tuyet Truong; typesetting was done by Jeannette Reyes. It was published by the Department, 1430 N Street, Sacramento, CA 95814-5901. It was distributed under the provisions of the Library Distribution Act and *Government Code* Section 11096.

Ordering Information

Copies of this publication are available for sale from the California Department of Education. For prices and ordering information, please visit the Department Web site at http://www.cde.ca.gov/re/pn or call the CDE Press Sales Office at 1-800-995-4099. An illustrated *Educational Resource Catalog* describing publications, videos, and other instructional media available from the Department can be obtained without charge by writing to the CDE Press Sales Office, California Department of Education, 1430 N Street, Suite 3207, Sacramento, CA 95814-5901; faxing to 916-323-0823; or calling the CDE Press Sales Office at the telephone number shown above.

Notice

The guidance in *Improving Education for English Learners: Research-Based Approaches* is not binding on local educational agencies or other entities. Except for the statutes, regulations, and court decisions that are referenced herein, the document is exemplary, and compliance with it is not mandatory. (See *Education Code* Section 33308.5.)

Contents

Message from the State Superintendent of Public Instruction

Throughout the modern history of the American public school system, social scientists have documented a pernicious achievement gap between ethno-linguistic minority students and their mainstream counterparts. Although correlated with poverty, this gap persists even among populations of higher socioeconomic status, suggesting that the causes of this chronic condition in our schools are strongly influenced by sociocultural and political factors in our society. Adequate solutions to this problem are long overdue, and for that reason I have asked educators across the state and colleagues across the country to commit to efforts to better understand and address the minority-student achievement gap. I am therefore pleased that the California Department of Education has commissioned a group of nationally recognized scholars to synthesize the best available scientific research on improving educational outcomes for English learners—those students whose primary language is other than English and who are limited in the English language skills needed to effectively participate in our classrooms.

Federal and state laws are explicit in defining the responsibilities of schools to educate English learners. Regardless of programmatic approach, schools are required to design, implement, and evaluate instructional programs that result in all students reaching English language proficiency and grade-level academic achievement. In California, this means that English learners must meet state academic standards in English–language arts and other core curriculum such as mathematics, science, and social studies.

This publication is a progress report. It offers a comprehensive, user-friendly review and analysis of the strongest research evidence currently available to inform instructional practices for English learners. The research reported in this publication does not purport to offer recipes for perfect programs with perfect outcomes, nor does it answer every important question on second-language and academic development. Indeed, it highlights where there are significant gaps in the research. But taken collectively, the chapters form a foundation for planning and improving instructional programs for English learners, who currently constitute one in four of California's K–12 public school children.

We at the California Department of Education view this report as an indication of the substantial progress in the field of English learner education. We are encouraged by the practical implications of the research presented in this publication. We invite other researchers, teacher trainers, and school district personnel to not only reflect on the findings and put into practice the recommendations presented here, but to also improve upon and expand them until our schools fully meet all the educational needs of every English learner. To that end, we believe that a thorough examination of the evidence, ideas, and proposals contained in this publication is a worthwhile step in the right direction.

Jack O'Connell
State Superintendent of Public Instruction

Acknowledgments

The development of this publication began in 2006 and from the beginning was a uniquely collaborative effort that involved the participation of many individuals and the perseverance of a committed group of concerned educators who believe in the importance of addressing the educational needs of English learners.

First and foremost, the authors of the six chapters deserve special recognition for their perseverance and patience during the preparation of this publication: **William Saunders** and **Claude Goldenberg, Marguerite Ann Snow** and **Anne Katz, Susana Dutro** and **Kate Kinsella, Diane August** and **Timothy Shanahan, Jana Echevarria** and **Deborah Short,** and **Kathryn Lindholm-Leary** and **Fred Genesee.** They met on several occasions to fuse their outlines and drafts into an integrated and coordinated whole. They reviewed each other's drafts and negotiated revisions. We also recognize Adel Nadeau for her assistance with various aspects in the initial development of the chapter "English Language Development: Foundations and Implementation in Kindergarten Through Grade Five."

Development of the volume was supported indispensably by a team of reviewers who analyzed outlines and drafts and provided comprehensive input to the authors. In some cases, the reviewers even wrote additional or alternative text for consideration. The members of the field review team were **Norm Gold, Shelly Spiegel Coleman, Robert Linquanti, Katie Riggs,** and **Elise Trumbull.** At the final stages of development, we realized that the volume could benefit from an editorial effort focused on forging a coherent whole from the individual chapters. To that end, **Elise Trumbull** was asked to undertake content editing for the entire publication.

Many dedicated staff members at the California Department of Education (CDE) assisted in the development of this publication. Special thanks are extended to **David Dolson** and **Lauri Burnham-Massey,** who served as coordinators of the project and provided the day-to-day guidance and communication to the authors, reviewers, and other staff involved in the project.

Special appreciation is given to **Jack O'Connell,** State Superintendent of Public Instruction, for his leadership and commitment to closing the achievement gap. The California Department of Education staff who provided administrative support for the project were **Deborah V. H. Sigman,** Deputy Superintendent, Curriculum, Learning, and Accountability Branch; **Sue Stickel,** former Deputy Superintendent, Curriculum and Instruction Branch; **Anthony Monreal,** former Deputy Superintendent, Curriculm and Instruction Branch; **Tom Adams,** Director, Standards, Curriculum Frameworks, and Instructional Resources Division; **Phil Lafontaine,** Director, English Learner and Curriculum Support Division; **Hector Rico,** Director, Categorical Compliance Division; and **Veronica Aguila,** Administrator, Instructional Resources Unit, and former Administrator, Language Policy and Leadership Office.

Other staff members from the Language Policy and Leadership Office who assisted at various stages of this project were **Marcela Rodriguez,** and **Irma Hernandez-Larin,** Education Program Consultants; and **James Shields** and **Julia Agostinelli,** Program Analysts. Support was provided also by staff from the Standards and Assessment Division: **Dianna Gutierrez, Miguel Cordova,** and **Jamie Contreras,** Education Program Consultants.

Special appreciation is due to CDE Press for its editorial work on the publication and to WestEd for its partnership in the development of this publication. Liaisons at WestEd were **Fred Tempes** and **Robert Linquanti.**

Note: The titles and affiliations of the persons named in this section were current at the time the document was developed.

Biographical Sketches

Veronica Aguila, Ed.D., is the administrator of the Instructional Resources Office in the Standards, Curriculum Frameworks, and Instructional Resources Division at the California Department of Education. The division oversees the development of curriculum frameworks and the adoption of instructional materials. Previously, she served as the Title III state director and administrator for the Language Policy and Leadership Office for four years. As administrator of that office, she administered the Bilingual Teacher Training Program, the English Language Acquisition Program, the Community-Based English Tutoring Program, the Refugee Children's Grant, and the Title III program for limited-English-proficient and immigrant students. Her career includes 24 years in the California public school system as a bilingual and English language development (ELD) teacher, as a school district administrator, and as lecturer for the California State University system, where she taught methods of second-language acquisition and supervised student teachers. Her passion for addressing the needs of English learners comes from her personal experience as an immigrant and English learner.

Diane August, Ph.D., is currently a senior research scientist at the Center for Applied Linguistics as well as a consultant located in Washington, D.C. She is the principal investigator for a large federally funded study on the development of literacy in English-language learners, coprincipal investigator for a federally funded evaluation of English immersion and transitional bilingual programs, and coprincipal investigator at the National Research and Development Center on English-Language Learners.

She was staff director for the National Literacy Panel on Language Minority Children and Youth. She has been a senior program officer at the National Academy of Sciences where she was study director for the Committee on Developing a Research Agenda on the Education of Limited English Proficient and Bilingual Students.

Dr. August has worked as a teacher, school administrator, legislative assistant, grants officer for the Carnegie Corporation, and was director of education for the Children's Defense Fund. She received her Ph.D. in education from Stanford University and completed a postdoctoral fellowship in psychology, also at Stanford.

Susana Dutro is a founding partner of E. L. Achieve, an organization dedicated to assisting educators in equipping English learners for academic achievement. She has been a bilingual classroom teacher, district and county office administrator, director of English learner initiatives for the California Reading and Literature Project, and adjunct education faculty. She developed *A Focused Approach: Instruction for English Learners,* a framework for explicit language instruction on which her subsequent professional development handbooks are based.

Her articles include "Rethinking English Language Instruction: An Architectural Approach" and "What's Language Got to Do with It? Considerations for Secondary English Learner Programs." She speaks and consults nationally with school districts and other educational organizations, working with teachers and administrators to design effective programs for English learners.

Jana Echevarria, Ph.D., is professor of education at California State University, Long Beach (CSULB) and is coprincipal investigator with the Center for Research on the Educational Achievement and Teaching of English Language Learners (CREATE). Dr. Echevarria has taught in general education, special education, English-as-a-second-language (ESL), and bilingual programs. She has lived in Taiwan and Mexico where she taught ESL and second-language acquisition courses at the university level, as well as in Spain where she conducted research on immigrant students. Her research and publications focus on effective instruction for English learners, including those with learning disabilities. She has coauthored nine books, including *Making Content Comprehensible for English Language Learners: The SIOP Model* and *Sheltered Content Instruction: Teaching English Language Learners with Diverse Abilities,* both published by Allyn & Bacon. In 2005, Dr. Echevarria was selected as Outstanding Professor at CSULB.

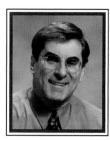

Fred Genesee, Ph.D., is a professor in the psychology department at McGill University, Montreal. He has conducted extensive research on alternative forms of bilingual and immersion education. His current research interests include language acquisition in preschool bilingual children, cross-language adopted children, and the language and academic development of at-risk students in bilingual programs. He is the author of numerous professional and scientific research reports and books, including *Literacy Instruction for English Language Learners* (2008), *Educating Second Language Children* (1994), *Classroom Based Evaluation in Second Language Education* (1996), *Beyond Bilingualism: Multilingualism and Multilingual Education* (1998), *Dual Language Instruction: A Handbook for Enriched Education (2000), Trends in Bilingual Acquisition* (2000), and *Dual Language Development and Disorders* (2004).

He has served as a consultant on second-/foreign-language and bilingual education in Estonia, Germany, Hong Kong, Italy, Japan, Latvia, Russia, Spain, and Switzerland.

Claude Goldenberg, Ph.D., is professor of education at Stanford University. He was formerly executive director of the Center for Language Minority Education and Research (CLMER) at California State University, Long Beach, and has taught junior high school in San Antonio, Texas, and first grade in a bilingual elementary school in Los Angeles. Dr. Goldenberg is the author of *Successful School Change: Creating Settings to Improve Teaching and Learning* (2004) and is completing a book, coauthored with Rhoda Coleman (Corwin Press), on the education of English learners. He was on the National Research Council's Committee for the Prevention of Early Reading Difficulties in Young Children and the National Literacy Panel, which synthesized research on literacy development among English-language learners.

Anne Katz, Ph.D., has worked for over 20 years as a researcher and evaluator with educational projects involving linguistically and culturally diverse students. In collaboration with school site personnel, she has provided and supported in-service professional development in districts throughout California. As a lecturer at the School for International Training in Brattleboro, Vermont, she teaches courses in curriculum and assessment. She has also worked as a teacher educator in Brazil and Egypt.

She led the Teachers of English to Speakers of Other Languages (TESOL)-sponsored team that developed assessment guidelines for the pre-K–12 ESL standards and was a member of the author team for TESOL's *PreK–12 English-Language Proficiency Standards.*

Kate Kinsella, Ed.D., is currently an adjunct faculty member in secondary education at San Francisco State University and provides consultation nationally to school districts regarding instruction of adolescent English learners. Her career has been devoted to ELD scholarship and classroom practice, including extensive experience teaching high school English learners and first-generation bilingual college students. As a teacher educator, she has maintained active involvement in upper elementary to high school classrooms by regularly coaching and coteaching while also teaching academic literacy skills to high school English learners in San Francisco State University's Step to College Program.

Dr. Kinsella is coauthor of Scholastic's (2006) *Read 180* literacy intervention program and is the (2008) author of the companion ELD curricula to *Read 180,* the *LBook*. She was coeditor of the CATESOL Journal from 2000 to 2005 and served on the editorial board of the *TESOL Journal* from 1999 to 2003. Dr. Kinsella led the development of the *Longman Study Dictionary* (2007) for adolescent English learners and is the author of Pearson's *Reading in the Content Areas: Strategies for Reading Success* (2000).

Kathryn Lindholm-Leary, Ph.D., is a professor in the College of Education at San Jose State University and has worked with children in immersion or bilingual programs for the past 30 years. She has evaluated over 30 programs and helped to establish programs in over 54 school districts in 11 states. She has authored or coauthored four books and many chapters and journal articles on the topics of dual-language education and child bilingualism.

She serves on several advisory boards in language education and preschool programs. She has been recognized for her teaching and research with the San Jose State Teacher-Scholar award, as a Distinguished Faculty Mentor, and as a finalist for the President's Scholar award. Dr. Lindholm-Leary received the California Association of Bilingual Education (CABE) Outstanding Contributions in Research and Two-Way CABE's Promoting Bilingualism Award.

William Saunders, Ph.D., is currently a senior research fellow at California State University, Long Beach; an associate researcher psychologist at the University of California, Los Angeles; and directs all research and implementation of the Learning Teams Programs at Pearson Achievement Solutions. He is currently engaged in research on school improvement and research on instruction for English learners.

Formerly a high school teacher and director of the Writing Project at the University of Southern California, Dr. Saunders was a coprincipal investigator for a large-scale study of the literacy and language development of Spanish-speaking English learners; a researcher at the Center for Research on Education, Diversity, and Excellence (CREDE); and both researcher and evaluator of several federally funded school and district-based projects for English learners. He received his Ph.D. in education in 1993 from U.C.L.A.

Timothy Shanahan, Ph.D., is professor of urban education at the University of Illinois, Chicago, where he is director of the Center for Literacy. He was director of reading for the Chicago public schools and has authored or edited more than 150 publications including *Developing Literacy in Second-Language Learners, Multidisciplinary Perspectives on Literacy: Reading and Writing Together,* and *Understanding Research in Reading and Writing.* His research emphasizes reading-writing relationships, reading assessment, and improving reading achievement.

Dr. Shanahan is past president of the International Reading Association, and he serves on the Advisory Board of the National Institute for Literacy. He served on the National Reading Panel and chaired the National Literacy Panel on Language Minority Children and Youth and the National Institute for Literacy. He codeveloped Project FLAME, a family literacy program for Latino immigrants, which received an Academic Excellence Award from the U.S. Department of Education.

Deborah J. Short, Ph.D., directs the Academic Language Research & Training, LLC, and consults in the United States and abroad on professional development and curriculum design for sheltered instruction and academic literacy. She is a senior research associate at the Center for Applied Linguistics where she codeveloped the research-validated Sheltered Instruction Observation Protocol (SIOP) Model. She has directed studies on English-language learner achievement and newcomer programs for the Carnegie Corporation of New York, the Rockefeller Foundation, and the U.S. Department of Education.

She is currently coprincipal investigator for an experimental study examining the SIOP Model's impact on science and language learning for the National Center for Research on the Educational Achievement and Teaching of English Language Learners. She chaired an expert panel on adolescent English learner literacy, coauthoring *Double the Work*. Her publications include books on the SIOP Model and several Hampton-Brown ESL series: *Edge, Inside, High Point,* and *Avenues.* Her research articles appear in numerous professional journals and books. She has taught English as a second language and foreign-language courses in New York, California, Virginia, and the Democratic Republic of Congo.

Marguerite Ann Snow, Ph.D., is a professor in the Charter College of Education at California State University, Los Angeles, where she teaches in the TESOL master's program. She is coauthor of *Content-based Second Language Instruction* (1989; 2003), and coeditor of *The Multicultural Classroom: Readings for Content-Area Teachers* (1992), and *The Content-Based Classroom: Perspectives on Integrating Language and Content* (1997). She is also editor of *Implementing the ESL Standards for PreK–12 Students in Teacher Education* (2000) and coeditor of *Academic Success: Strategies for K–12 Mainstream Teachers* (2005) and *Developing a New Course for Adult Learners* (2006).

She has published in *TESOL Quarterly, Applied Linguistics,* and *The Modern Language Journal.* She was a Fulbright scholar in Hong Kong and Cyprus. In 2006, she received the President's Distinguished Professor award at California State University, Los Angeles. In addition to working closely with ESL and mainstream public school teachers in the United States, she has trained teachers of English as a foreign language in settings such as Argentina, Brazil, Egypt, Japan, Morocco, Pakistan, and Turkey. Her main interests are integrated content and language instruction, English for academic purposes, and standards for English teaching and learning.

Foreword

It has been almost 30 years since the publication of *Schooling and Language-Minority Students: A Theoretical Framework* by the California State Department of Education, in 1981. That book provided a cornerstone on which the understanding of the education of language-minority students, still in its infancy, was built. Ideas that we presently take for granted, including academic language, sheltered academic content instruction, bilingual instruction, effective instruction, and appropriate assessment can all find their roots in that volume.

With that said, much has changed. We are in an era bearing the marks of standards-based reform, Proposition 227, No Child Left Behind, and the charter school movement, among other reforms. The knowledge base in educational research and the science of learning has expanded considerably. There is also a more positivistic approach to generating research knowledge—the federal office that funds research, once the National Institute of Education, was renamed the Office of Educational Research and Improvement. It was further renamed the Institute for Education Sciences to signal the importance of scientifically generated knowledge (and it is now up again for reauthorization).

This book represents work by a fabulous pooling of talent from the researcher and practitioner communities. This observation in itself is remarkable, as the very idea of usable knowledge—the underlying intent of this book—has undergone change in recent years. We no longer accept the trickle-down mode as optimal for knowledge dissemination and, instead, look to collaborative models that engage researchers and practitioners. The chapters in this publication are written by researchers and practitioners to address critical questions for educators—both teachers as well as educational leaders—about optimizing English language development, literacy development, and content instruction.

Thankfully, the papers are balanced with respect to the source of educational knowledge. They pay a proper amount of respect to knowledge based on the "gold standard" of randomized controlled studies. Yet they also understand that professional practice in many areas (even in medicine) include a rich macramé that interweaves various forms of systematic data-gathering as well as sound professional judgment.

The topic of the education of immigrants and language minorities in this country has almost always been accompanied by controversy. Particularly under such circumstances, the professional community must put its best foot forward, stating as clearly as possible the knowledge from research and practice in improving the educational prospects of English-language learner students. I believe this book does just that and hope it will be widely used for programmatic and professional development.

Kenji Hakuta
Lee L. Jacks Professor of Education
Stanford University

Introduction

Schooling English Learners: Contexts and Challenges

Veronica Aguila, California Department of Education

State Superintendent of Public Instruction Jack O'Connell has suggested that the academic achievement gap between ethno-linguistic minority students and other students, as represented by test scores, dropout rates, and college admissions and completion rates, is the most persistent and pressing challenge facing public schools nationwide (O'Connell 2008). Although the achievement gap exists everywhere in the United States, in California it affects a population of so-called "minority" students who together now have become the new numerical majority.

One of the largest segments of minority pupils consists of those students who are not fully proficient in English. The United States Department of Education estimates that 4,512,560 English learners are enrolled in public schools across the United States. California's proportion is approximately 34 percent of the national total, and California has more English learners than the next six states combined. With one of every four students being an English learner, no state has a greater stake in the education of these students than California. But California is not the only state that has a large English learner population and whose educators may benefit from this publication. Table A displays enrollment information for the top seven states in the nation having the highest enrollments of English learners.

> **With one of every four students being an English learner, no state has a greater stake in the education of these students than California.**

Table A. English Learner Enrollments in the U.S., 2009

State	English learner enrollment	Total enrollment	Percentage of English learners
California	1,553,091	6,275,469	24.7
Texas	693,031	4,674,832	14.8
Florida	231,403	2,666,811	8.7
New York	210,359	2,765,435	7.6
Illinois	189,926	2,112,805	9.0
Arizona	149,721	1,087,447	13.8
Colorado	85,323	801,867	10.6

Source: July 2009 EDFacts state profiles http://www.ed.gov/about/inits/ed/edfacts/state-profiles/index.html.

In school, English learners face a formidable challenge. Not only must they acquire English to levels comparable to that of native speakers of English of the same age and grade level, but they must also meet the same challenging grade-level standards and graduation requirements. In addition, the majority of English learners are racial and ethnic minorities; often come from lower-socioeconomic groups; and many have immigrant and/or migrant backgrounds. All these factors put them at risk academically in mainstream U.S. schools, which are often not prepared to differentiate instruction to meet the unique and varied needs of students with this range of needs.

Purpose and Audience

This publication is intended to assist school districts in the design, implementation, and evaluation of programs for English learners over the coming years. It is also intended to assist educators in addressing the instructional needs of

In school, English learners face a formidable challenge.

English learners and to support the implementation of the English language development (ELD) standards as well as the subject-matter standards and frameworks. The chapters are directed to an audience of classroom teachers, resource teachers, administrators, teacher educators, and providers of professional development. Program designers and policymakers are also likely to find the publication useful.

Features of This Publication

Some of the unique aspects of this publication are as follows:

⊙ Each chapter is the result of a paper commissioned by the California Department of Education (CDE) and written by a team of two scholars. The authors are well known and respected experts in their fields with substantial research, teacher education, and previous writing experience. Biographical sketches of the authors are included in this publication.

⊙ The publication is based on research. Recommendations are supported by research studies that meet the standards of contemporary research such as those promoted by the No Child Left Behind Act of 2001 (NCLB) and those advanced by the National Panel on Literacy Instruction commissioned by the U.S. Department of Education.

⊙ The authors were asked to respond to a series of questions commonly posed by practitioners. The questions ensure that the information in this publication is of practical value to those working in the field.

⊙ Development of the publication involved close coordination between the authors and practitioners. First, a panel of field and CDE advisers read drafts of the papers and provided feedback to the authors at two seminars held during the development of the papers. The feedback encouraged the authors to craft explanations of complex issues in a manner that would be understood readily by practitioners.

⊙ Second, the authors provided feedback to each other during the development of the papers. These efforts focused on articulation among and between the papers and challenged all of the teams to adhere to rigorous, research-based standards.

⊙ Third, a content editor was asked to read the publication to ensure that the papers functioned as a set of coherent chapters, maintained an appropriate level of redundancy, and were thorough and up to date in research-based representations of recommended practice.

Assessment—whether of language ability or academic progress—is a topic that is not addressed in depth in this publication. The focus on instruction kept the publication a reasonable length. However, that is not to say that it is absent (see, for example, Snow and Katz, August and Shanahan in this publication). Echevarria and Short (in this publication) address classroom-based assessment as part of the implementation of the sheltered content-based instruction model they describe.

History of Programs for English Learners

California has provided specialized programs for English learners since the late 1960s. State efforts have been bolstered by federal funding from various programs operated under the umbrella of the Elementary and Secondary Schools Act, as reauthorized by NCLB. Title I of NCLB addresses assistance for the educational needs of low-achieving children in our nation's highest-poverty schools, limited-English-proficient children (LEP), migrant children, children with disabilities, Native American children, neglected or delinquent children, and young children in need of assistance in reading. Title III targets limited-English-proficient and immigrant students. Notably however, California's first major program for English learners was provided for by Assembly Bill (AB) 2284 of 1972; however, participation was voluntary on the part of individual school districts. In 1976, the Legislature passed the Chacon-Moscone Bilingual Bicultural Education Act of 1976 (AB 1329), which mandated the establishment of organized programs of bilingual and English-as-a-second language (ESL) instruction. AB 1329 was replaced by the Bilingual-Bicultural Education Reform and Improvement Act of 1980 (AB 507) which expired in September 1987. In 1998, voters passed Proposition 227, codified as California *Education Code (EC)* 300–311, which required students enrolled in public schools to be taught "overwhelmingly" in English. Consequently, this shift in instruction remains the current legal framework for English learner education in California.

Nevertheless, the nature of specialized programs of instruction and the extent to which English learners should have access to them have been and continue to be subjects of significant educational, social, and political controversy.

Academic Performance of English Learners

Each time the legal framework that governs programs for English learners in California has been altered, there has been a corresponding expectation that student performance would improve substantially. Unfortunately, there is no clear evidence that this transformation has occurred on any significant scale. For example, a major evaluation study of Proposition 227 (Parrish et al. 2006) concluded that although the rate at which English learners are acquiring English seems to have improved, several factors associated with demographics of the English learner subgroup and changes in the English proficiency assessment process make this finding subject to question. Although there has been a slight decrease in the academic performance gap between English learners and native speakers of English, it has remained virtually constant in most subject areas for most grades (Parrish et al. 2006, viii).

The study does indicate optimism in that during the period of the investigation, the percentage of English learners participating in the statewide assessments increased

substantially. On the other hand, the Proposition 227 evaluation study (Parrish et al. 2006) also points out that along with changes in the program for English learners, in the late 1990s and early 2000s schools in California were affected simultaneously by other policies and initiatives, such as class size reduction, a move to standards-based education, and the establishment of state and federal accountability systems. In fact, educators interviewed as part of the study identified those factors as having a greater influence on English learner performance than the change in the legal framework (Parrish et al. 2006).

The findings of the evaluation study of Proposition 227 (Parrish et al. 2006) are supported by data from other sources, such as the 2005 National Assessment of Educational Progress, also known as the "Nation's Report Card." These data show that approximately half of all English learners at the elementary school level and nearly three-quarters of the English learners in middle school score below the basic level in reading and mathematics (Fry 2007).

Even more revealing is an analysis conducted by the University of California Linguistic Minority Research Institute (Rumberger 2007) of data collected on nearly 10,000 students as part of the Early Childhood Longitudinal Study (2007). The study was a national investigation designed to examine the progress of linguistic-minority students during elementary school. In this study, student achievement is expressed in terms of standard deviation (SD) units, a measure of the dispersion of data from a national mean of zero. The analysis shows that at the kindergarten level in the 1998-99 school year, the achievement gap between Spanish-speaking English learners and native speakers of English is 1.22 in California and .91 in the rest of the United States. Data on language achievement from this analysis are displayed in Table B.

Table B. Language Skills Measured at Kindergarten and Grade Five in California and the U.S., by Language Characteristics

	California		U.S.	
	Kindergarten	Grade 5	Kindergarten	Grade 5
All students	-0.21	-0.11	0.00	0.00
English-only	0.10	0.21	0.13	0.09
Hispanic students	-0.50	-0.41	-0.35	-0.20
English-dominant	-0.19	0.05	-0.16	0.02
Spanish-dominant	-0.71	-0.75	-0.19	0.18

Source: University of California Linguistic Minority Institute Newsletter, Vol. 16, No. 2 (Winter 2007), 2. Data are expressed in standard deviation units from a normalized national mean of zero. Students were kindergarteners in 1998-99 ($n = 9,796$) and fifth-graders in 2004-05.

These data indicate that Spanish-speaking English learners begin school at a considerable disadvantage compared with native speakers of English. Over a five-year period, the gap in language skills is reduced only slightly for the Spanish-dominant pupils at the national level, whereas in California the gap widens even further.

The results of the California Standards Test in English–language arts for English learners and English-only students over a five-year period are displayed in Table C. Although both groups of students demonstrated modest improvement, the gap between English learners and their native English-speaking peers grew at each of the four grade levels reported over the five-year period between 2003 and 2009.

Table C. Achievement of English-Only Students and English Learners California Standards Test, English–Language Arts Battery, 2003–09

	Percentage of English-only students deemed proficient or advanced in 2003	Percentage of English-only Students deemed proficient or advanced in 2009	Change	Percentage of English learners deemed proficient or advanced in 2003	Percentage of English learners deemed proficient or advanced in 2009	Change	Gap in 2003	Gap in 2009
3rd grade	42	53	+11	13	20	+7	29	33
5th grade	44	62	+18	9	19	+10	35	43
8th grade	38	57	+19	4	8	+4	34	49
10th grade	41	50	+9	4	6	+2	37	44

Source: http://dq.cde.ca.gov/dataquest/.

These and other studies point to the fact that while English learners may be making some gains in closing the academic gap that separates them from language-majority students, improvements in most cases tend to be modest. It is clear that more effective approaches are needed to improve the services provided to the English learner population and close the achievement gap between English learners and their English-only peers.

Need for Technical Assistance

Under the provisions of Title III of the NCLB Act, state educational agencies are required to provide general technical assistance to all local educational agencies (LEAs) that participate in the program. State educational agencies must also provide additional and specialized technical assistance to LEAs regarding three specific annual measurable achievement objectives (AMAOs):

- ⊙ The percentage of English learners who will meet ELD growth targets

- ⊙ The percentage of English learners at advanced ELD levels who will attain or maintain fluent English proficiency

- ⊙ The percentage of English learners and former English learners who will meet English–language arts and mathematics grade-level standards

Many school districts are having difficulty in meeting these initial benchmarks. Table D contains an overview of the performance of individual English learners enrolled in Title III LEAs and consortia on each of the three AMAOs as of the 2008-09 school year.

Table D. Title III Performance on Annual Measurable Achievement Objectives
Students and Subgrantees Meeting Targets in 2008-09

Objectives	Percentage of English learners	Percentage of school districts
ELD progress (AMAO 1)	58	82
English fluency (AMAO 2)	38	81
Proficient or above in English–language arts (AMAO 3)	34	44
Proficient or above in mathematics (AMAO 3)	43	56

Source: Data derived from the 2008-09 Title III research file and the state AYP report.

In Table D, percentages have been rounded to the nearest whole number. All Title III school districts in the state that enroll a statistically significant concentration of English learners are expected to meet these AMAOs. School districts that fail to meet their AMAOs must take corrective actions within a specified period of time.

In the coming years as the performance targets for participating Title III LEAs and consortia increase, predictably, more LEAs and consortia will encounter difficulty in meeting their AMAOs. In the 2008-09 school year, 138 LEAs failed to meet one or more of their AMAOs for four or more consecutive years; 59 LEAs and consortia failed to meet them for three consecutive years; and 135 failed for two consecutive years.

The development of this publication coincides with an important statewide initiative that stands to affect the education of English learners. California Superintendent O'Connell established a statewide group, known as the P-16 Council, to address the achievement gap experienced by minority students from prekindergarten through grade sixteen. The council's work focus on four major themes to address the challenges of closing the achievement gap:

(1) Access—the extent to which all students, including English learners, have equitable access to core conditions, such as qualified, effective teachers; rigorous, standards-aligned curriculum; and effective interventions.

(2) Culture and Climate—how schools can offer the best environment for promoting learning and a sense of belonging for students, parents, and school staff.

(3) Expectations—ways to foster high expectations for all who are involved with education.

(4) Strategies—proven effective or promising practices the state can promote for closing the achievement gap (O'Connell 2008).

The council issued 14 recommendations, and this publication focuses on recommendations 4 and 12. The council found that collecting and disseminating a high-quality, comprehensive body of knowledge, expertise, resources, and research on effective and successful practices is key to narrowing the achievement gap. This publication provides culturally relevant information that can be used as part of professional development for all school personnel. Most importantly, this publication has compiled effective and promising practices available to serve English learners.

Research on School Effectiveness

Educators should consider that even an optimally designed program for English learners is not likely to succeed unless it is implemented within the framework of an "effective" school. The *Effects of Implementation of Proposition 227* report (Parrish et. al 2006) states that school effectiveness research conducted over the past several decades consistently points to five institutional characteristics that correlate with superior student achievement:

1. A positive school climate focused on identified academic outcomes

2. A shared vision by a highly qualified staff

3. Strategic monitoring of student performance and the use of data in making instructional and programmatic decisions

4. Strong community involvement and support

5. Superior instructional leadership

Upon conducting a review of related studies on the effective features of English learner programs, Parrish and others (2006) identified in their report *Effects of Implementation of Proposition 227* several overlapping characteristics associated with positive program outcomes:

1. Adoption of a well-defined plan of standards-based instruction aligned with the language, academic needs, and cultural background of the students

2. Maintenance of high expectations for performance while attending to the specific language, academic, and cultural needs of English learners through ongoing assessment that is used to inform instruction

3. Cultivation of schoolwide accountability for English learner instruction and achievement through strong leadership, highly qualified staff, district support, and community involvement.

Lindholm-Leary and Genesee in Chapter 6 report that high-quality dual language programs share many of the same characteristics as high-quality mainstream programs (Lindholm-Leary and Borsato 2001). The common features of effectiveness include elements such as:

⊙ A cohesive schoolwide vision

⊙ Shared goals that define expectations for achievement

⊙ A clear instructional focus on and commitment to achievement

⊙ High expectations (Lindholm-Leary 2007)

In this publication, Lindholm-Leary and Genesee expand their analysis of effective schools to include the unique characteristics of effective dual language programs such as those reported previously in Howard and others (2007).

In an extensive review of the research on effective programs for at-risk students (Slavin and Calderón 2001), the principal investigators identified several conditions that were present in almost all of the programs supported by adequate research evidence:

1. Clear goals with methods and materials linked to these goals

2. Ongoing assessment of student progress

3. Well-specified instructional components

4. Comprehensive professional development

5. Full and high-quality implementation of the program design

The consistent findings of the school effectiveness research have important implications for English learner programs. Williams and others (2007) summarize the body of research in the following manner:

> . . . when school practices and policies aligned with California's academic standards are intensively implemented—with regard to curriculum, instruction, assessment, and monitoring progress—they contribute to higher school performance for English learners as they do for all students (page 22).

The researchers go on to add that effective schools are also characterized by the provision of adequate material resources and highly qualified and enthusiastic teachers. Those resources are found most frequently in schools that have strong, proactive leadership by a competent and supportive principal and adequate, timely support from the school district (Williams et al. 2007).

Research on effective schools highlights the importance of strong leadership and a strong vision to implement curriculum provided by highly qualified teachers to affect positively the school performance of English learners.

Importance of Professional Development

Designing programs according to scientifically based research is only the beginning of the challenge. Schools need to see that research can be used to inform and guide educational practice in ways that improve student learning. Opportunities for effective professional development are essential.

The goal of this publication is to provide a useful tool for teacher-preparation and educational agencies' staff development programs. Teacher-education faculties may decide to adopt the publication as a text in their programs. Similarly, county offices of education and staff development units in school districts may consider this publication as one of their central readings and make it an integral part of their in-service education programs.

Many U.S. teachers begin their careers in lower-socioeconomic areas where schools serve large populations of immigrant, English learner, and minority students. Unfortunately, new teachers often are given those demanding assignments without adequate training and support. After several years of struggle, some of these teachers leave minority schools or the profession, while others learn to cope rather than to teach effectively. Many teachers are still expected to know everything they need in their career or are left to pick up what they can on their own in occasional workshops. Few structured opportunities are offered as part of a comprehensive professional development program (Darling-Hammond 1998). If schools are serious in the desire to see research translated into practice and for professional development to result in improved student learning, they must focus on effective staff development approaches and embrace research-based practices.

In addition to the professional development practices that are effective for everyone yet focused on the needs of English learners, Snow and Katz, in this publication, outline the specific and general content that should be addressed in teacher preservice preparation and professional development related to English language development as the particular focus. Echevarria and Short, in this publication, draw upon research associated with professional development (Joyce and Showers 2002; National Staff Development Council 2001; Valli and Hawley 2002) and describe how this body of knowledge can be applied to staff development opportunities for educators who work in programs for English learners. Echevarria and Short identify eight critical elements of effective teacher training:

1. **Theoretical knowledge:** The theoretical underpinnings of instruction for English learners including the rationale behind various teaching techniques, strategies, and practices, are provided.

2. **Specific strategies:** Instructional strategies address anticipated problems or issues that English learners might confront in learning the content.

3. **Lesson planning:** Teachers receive opportunities to plan lessons or instructional units collaboratively, including engagement in inquiry around practice, student needs, and assessment of the impact of lessons on student learning (Chrispeels 2003).

4. **Modeling:** Opportunities to observe classrooms are organized for effective teaching of English learners and demonstration lessons by mentor teachers or coaches.

5. **Practice:** Features of effective instruction are implemented with guidance and support.

6. **Feedback and in-class coaching:** Coaches or peers observe classrooms and provide constructive feedback on lesson delivery.

7. **Independent application and analysis:** Teachers use targeted practices, usually through independent lesson planning and teaching. In collaborative groups with colleagues, teachers evaluate their lessons and analyze the instructional features, adjusting and refining as needed. They may go back and relearn a feature if necessary.

8. **Program coherence:** Teachers "speak" the same language by having consistent messages and practices through agreed-upon understandings (Garet et al. 2001; Goldenberg 2004).

There is still a place in professional development for conventional practices such as lectures and demonstrations. But it is becoming apparent that the use of these more traditional elements must be measured judiciously and augmented by other practices such as the use of local experts, mentoring, peer coaching, study groups, and a variety of innovative procedures such as those identified by Darling-Hammond and McLaughlin (1995) and Sparks (2002). In fact, other specialists in the field are now observing how some of these innovative research-based practices are being used in local schools as reported in teachers' dialogue journals, professional development portfolios, and participatory practitioner research (Diaz-Maggioli 2004).

Approaches to staff development in which staff and teachers are provided with random, disconnected workshops are not in themselves sufficient to develop competent teachers and administrators who are able to translate research into practice. What is needed is a comprehensive professional development program that is itself research-based and data-driven.

Importance of Sociocultural Factors

The papers in this publication focus primarily on the language and related academic variables associated with the education of English learners. However, several teams of authors, most notably Snow and Katz, Lindholm-Leary and Genesee, and August and Shanahan, also point out that there is substantial and compelling research to support the notion that powerful sociocultural factors strongly influence the outcomes of programs for English learners and other minority students and students of low socioeconomic status. Those factors have also been recognized by California Superintendent O'Connell. He has directed his statewide commission on closing the achievement gap to make every effort to integrate culturally responsive instruction into California's teacher preservice and professional development programs (O'Connell 2008).

As early as the mid-1980s, the California Department of Education recognized the importance of this research and published *Beyond Language: Social and Cultural Factors in Schooling Language Minority Students* (1986). That publication addressed a number of sociocultural variables, including ethnic identity, minority status, cross-cultural adjustment, cooperative learning, and—uniquely for an educational publication of the time—the response patterns of minority group members to the racism, prejudice, and discrimination they experience in schools and the wider society.

Since the 1980s, significant contributions have been made to an area of research that has been labeled traditionally as "multicultural education" (Banks 2005; Banks and Banks 2003). Building on these foundations, insightful and committed scholars such as Kathryn Au, Roland Tharp, Gary Howard, Sonia Nieto, Lisa Delpit, Carlos Cortes, and Gloria Ladson-Billings, among others, have collectively advanced a theory of culturally responsive pedagogy (Gay 2000). This theory postulates that sociocultural differences between the school and minority communities often contribute to scholastic underachievement. The theory also assumes that the academic performance of minority students will improve if schools and teaching are transformed in ways that reflect and draw upon the cultural and language strengths of minority populations (Gay 2000).

In response to the growing awareness of the importance of sociocultural issues, in 2003 the California Legislature (AB 54, Chapter 817) directed the Commission for Teacher Credentialing, in concert with the Department, to commission an evaluation study of the availability and effectiveness of practices associated with cultural competency. For the purposes of the study, cultural competency was defined as the capacity of a school system to respond positively and effectively to student and family differences. Culturally competent schools were said to:

- Value diversity.
- Have the capacity for cultural self-assessment,
- Be conscious of the dynamics of cultures in contact.
- Internalize cultural knowledge.
- Be able to adapt to diversity between and within cultures (Rockman et al. and WestEd 2005).

A growing number of educators believe that culturally competent schools and teachers have the potential to reduce, eliminate, and even reverse many of the sociocultural shortcomings of traditional school programs (see, for example, Derman-Sparks et al. 1998; Ladson-Billings 2000; Nieto 2005; West-Olatunji et al. 2008; and Lindholm-Leary and Genesee, this publication). In a recent annual State of

Education message, California Superintendent of Public Instruction Jack O'Connell explicitly acknowledged the importance of culturally competent schools when he pledged to collaborate with the deans of schools of education to embed culturally responsive instruction in all of California's teacher-training programs (Rockman et al. and WestEd 2005).

Issues Regarding Terminology

Terms such as *English learner, structured English immersion, English language development, dual language, sheltered content, and academic language,* among others, are used to refer to some of the most important concepts described in the publication. Although most of these terms are used commonly in the field of English learner education, the underlying meaning of the terms can vary significantly depending on the context. Researchers often have in mind precise operational or "scientific" definitions; while school district staff may refer to the constructs in broader, less specific, and more practical ways.

When describing research reports associated with language acquisition, scholars commonly employ the terms *L1* and *L2* as shorthand for the primary and the second language, respectively. L1 invariably refers to an English learner's first or home language, which is a language other than English. L2 represents the second language being acquired by English learners, which in the U.S. is English.

In some cases, constructs are defined statutorily, and such definitions may or may not be aligned with usage in contemporary research. For example, the term *English learner* is codified in California law but has the same general definition as "student of limited English proficiency," statutorily defined in the federal No Child Left Behind Act. On the other hand, many researchers and educators use the term *English language learners* to refer to those students. In most cases, the three terms refer to the same or similar cohort of students: those who have a primary language other than English and who, on the basis of some objective criteria, have been found to be limited in English proficiency.

On the other hand, the definitions of some terms can vary significantly. For example, in California, the *Education Code* defines *structured English immersion* simply as a "language acquisition process" for English learners. However, in most of the research literature, structured English immersion represents an English-based or English-only program model contrasted with bilingual education as an approach to address the language and academic needs of English learners.

The problem associated with terminology persists even in scholarly works. For example, *structured English immersion* is a label that has been used to refer to very different forms of instruction. For example, Cummins (1999) identifies research reports in which "structured English immersion" is used to describe:

- English-only sheltered content programs for English learners
- French immersion programs in Canada
- Bilingual instructional approaches

He points out that readers in some cases may be misled to think that the findings of the studies on structured English immersion are based consistently on the implementation of monolingual instructional approaches when, in fact in several key instances, the researchers actually investigated programs in which as much as one-third of the instruction was delivered in and through the primary language.

The variable use of terminology can be confusing for researchers and practitioners alike and presents a very real obstacle to understanding the research literature. In this publication, the authors have been asked to "operationalize" key terms by providing working definitions. Because terminology is used differently in various settings and, in most cases, there are no standard or universal definitions, our best advice is that readers be aware of the possible differences in meaning of the same terms as used in different sources and the possible misunderstanding that can result.

Summary

The intent of this publication is to provide a deeper understanding of key research-based insights. Accordingly, the authors were asked to highlight what they determined to be the most important points. Predictably, each team approached this task differently. Some sections of some chapters will require not only careful reading but also rereading and contemplation.

Collectively, the chapters in this publication provide a rich grounding in the issues, research, and recommended practice related to the education of English learners. Research by no means provides unequivocal guidelines for all aspects of practice; at times, the same research lends itself to different conclusions. Yet familiarity with the dialogue surrounding questions of instruction and student learning is valuable itself and should be part of the professional preparation of every educator involved in programs for English learners.

Collectively, the chapters in this publication provide a rich grounding in the issues, research, and recommended practice related to the education of English learners.

References

Banks, James A. 2005. *Cultural diversity and education: foundations, curriculum, and teaching.* 5th ed. Boston: Allyn & Bacon Publishers.

Banks, James A., and Cherry A. *McGee Banks,* eds. 2003. *Handbook of research on multicultural education.* 2nd ed. New York: Macmillan Publishers.

Beyond language: social and cultural factors in schooling language minority students. 1986. Los Angeles: Evaluation, Dissemination and Assessment Center, California State University. Developed by the Bilingual Education Office, California State Department of Education, Sacramento.

California Department o Education. 2009. Dataquest STAR Test Results. http://dq.cade.ca.gov/dataquest (accessed May 17, 2010).

Chrispeels, Janet H. 2003. Improving instruction through teacher collaboration in grade-level meetings. *Linguistic Minority Research Institute Newsletter* 12(2): 1–2.

Cortes, Carlos. 2002. *The making and remaking of a multiculturalist.* New York: Teachers College Press.

Cummins, James. 1999. Research, ethics, and public discourse: The debate on bilingual education. Presentation at the National Conference of the American Association of Higher Education, Washington, DC, March 22.

Darling-Hammond, Linda. 1998. Teacher learning that supports student learning. *Educational Leadership* 55(5): 6–11.

Delpit, Lisa. 1996. *Other people's children.* New York: The New Press.

Derman-Sparks, Louise, Sharon Cronin, Sharon Henry, Cirecie Olatunji, and Stacy York. 1998. *Future vision, present work.* Minneapolis, MN: Redleaf Press.

Diaz-Maggioli, Gabriel. 2004. *Teacher-centered professional development.* Alexandria, VA: Association for Supervision and Curriculum Development.

Early childhood longitudinal study, birth cohort (ECLS-B) *9 month–2 year residential zip code restricted-use data file.* 2007. (CD-ROM). (NCES 2008-038). Washington, DC: National Center for Education Statistics, United States Department of Education.

Fry, Richard. 2007. *How far behind in math and reading are English language learners?* Washington, DC: Report of the Pew Hispanic Center.

Garet, Michael S., Andrew C. Porter, Laura Desimone, Beatrice F. Birman, and Kwang Suk Yoon. 2001. What makes professional development effective?

Results from a national sample of teachers. *American Educational Research Journal* 38(4): 915–45.

Gay, Geneva. 2000. *Culturally responsive teaching: Theory, research, and practices.* New York: Teachers College Press.

Goldenberg, Claude. 2004. *Successful school change: Creating settings to improve teaching and learning.* New York: Teachers College Press.

Howard, Elizabeth, and others. 2005. *Guiding principles for dual language education.* Washington, DC: U.S. Department of Education and National Clearinghouse for English Language Acquisition. http://www.cal.org.

Joyce, Bruce, and Beverly Showers. 2002. *Student achievement through staff development.* 3rd ed. Alexandria, VA: Association for Supervision and Curriculum Development.

Ladson-Billings, Gloria. 1995. But that's just good teaching! The case for culturally relevant pedagogy. *Theory into Practice* 34(3): 159–65.

Ladson-Billings, Gloria. 2000. Fighting for our lives: Preparing teachers to teach African American students. *Journal of Teacher Education* 51(3), 206–14.

Ladson-Billings, Gloria and William F. Tate, eds. 2006. *Education research in the public interest: social justice, action, and policy.* New York: Teachers College Press.

Lindholm-Leary, Kathryn. 2007. Effective features of dual language education programs: A review of research and best practices. 2nd ed. Washington, DC: Center for Applied Linguistics.

Lindholm-Leary, Kathryn, and Graciela Borsato. 2001. Impact of two-way bilingual elementary programs on students' attitudes toward school and college. Research Report 10. University of California, Santa Cruz: Center for Research on Education, Diversity & Excellence.

Margolin, Jonathan, and Beth Buchler. 2004. *Critical Issue: Using scientifically based research to guide educational decisions.* Chicago: North Central Regional Educational Laboratory, Learning Point Associates.

National Staff Development Council. *NSDC standards for staff development.* 2001. http://www.nsdc.org/standards/index.cfm (accessed July 17, 2008.)

Nieto, Sonia. 2005. Schools for a new majority: The role of teacher education in hard times. *The New Educator* 1(1): 27–43.

Nieto, Sonia. 1999. *The light in their eyes: Creating multicultural learning communities.* New York: Teachers College Press.

O'Connell, Jack. 2008. Together we can close the achievement gap. *California Schools* 9–11.

Parrish, Thomas B., Robert Linquanti, Amy Merikel, Heather Quick, Jennifer Laird, and Phil Esra. 2006. *Effects of the implementation of Proposition 227 on the education of English learners, K–12: Findings from a five-year evaluation.* Submitted to the California Department of Education, Sacramento, CA. San Francisco: American Institutes for Research and WestEd.

Rockman et al., and WestEd. 2005. *Study of availability and effectiveness of cultural competency training for teachers in California: Final report.* San Francisco.

Rumberger, Russell. 2007. Lagging behind: Linguistic minorities' education progress during elementary school. *University of California Linguistic Minority Research Institute Newsletter* 16(2): 1–3.

Slavin, Robert, and Margarita Calderon. 2001. *Effective programs for Latino learners.* Mahwah, NJ: Lawrence Erlbaum Associates.

Slavin, Robert, and Alan Cheung. 2005. A synthesis of research on reading instruction for English language learners. *Review of Educational Research* 75: 247–84.

Tharp, Roland G., Peggy Estrada, Stephanie Dalton, and Lois Yamauchi. *2000. Teaching transformed: Achieving excellence, fairness, inclusion, and harmony.* Jackson, Tenn.: Westview Press.

Valli, Linda, and Willis Hawley. 2002. Designing and implementing school-based professional development. In *The Keys to Effective Schools,* ed. Willis Hawley. Thousands Oaks, CA: Corwin Press.

West-Olatunji, Cirecie A., Linda Behar-Horenstein, Jeffrey Rant, and Lakechia N. Cohen-Phillips. 2008. Enhancing cultural competence among teachers of African American children using mediated lesson study. *The Journal of Negro Education* 77 (Winter): 27–38.

Williams, Trish, Kenji Hakuta, Edward Haertel, Michael Kirst, Jesse Levin, Mary Perry, Isabel Oregón, and Noli Brazil. 2007. *Similar English learner students, different results: Why do some schools do better?* Mountain View, CA: EdSource. http://www.edsource.org/ (accessed March 26, 2008).

Chapter 1

Research to Guide English Language Development Instruction

William Saunders, U.C.L.A.
Claude Goldenberg, Stanford University

This chapter synthesizes existing research that provides direction for English language development (ELD) instruction. Many sources and resources might guide the direction of ELD instruction, including theory, research, ELD standards, practitioner experience, and published programs. The chapter focuses on studies and research syntheses that help identify guidelines for effective ELD instruction, that is, instruction delivered in a portion of the school day separately from English–language arts and other content areas (e.g., math, social studies) and that focuses specifically on helping English learners develop English language skills.

Currently, existing research to identify effective guidelines for ELD instruction is problematic. There is little that focuses specifically on kindergarten through grade twelve (K–12) ELD instruction for the population of U.S. students examined in this publication: "English language learners" (formerly "limited English proficient," or LEP, students). The scarcity of research directly based on the population of interest leads to some interesting questions, such as whether it is better to use research based on different types of students (e.g., adults learning a second language) or to say there is no research on a particular issue (e.g., whether it is effective to teach specific grammatical forms).

Note: Norm Gold, Shelly Spiegel-Coleman, and Elise Trumbull provided many helpful suggestions on this chapter. We are also indebted to Elise Trumbull for suggesting several passages that have helped clarify and extend our discussion and analysis. All errors or misstatements remain strictly our own.

In the absence of a comprehensive body of research, the field of second-language teaching (or more specifically in this case, ELD instruction) has been driven mostly by theory. The result is a large body of accepted practice based on theory that has yet to be fully supported by research. It is probably safe to say that the current, dominant theoretical perspective of teachers is that of "communicative language teaching." There are two primary tenets of communicative language teaching:

(1) The goal of second-language education is to develop learners' communicative competence.

(2) Communication is both a goal and means for developing language (Alcón 2004, 175).

From this perspective, second-language learning is a social process: language develops largely as a result of meaningful interaction with others (Long 1985), much as a first language does (cf. Krashen 1982). Language use is emphasized more than language knowledge. Acquisition of the forms and rules for combining them is seen to be an implicit process not appreciably affected by explicit instruction.

Many current conceptualizations of language learning may be characterized as "cognitive." They emphasize the processes by which learners construct language knowledge (e.g., DeKeyser and Juffs 2005). Certainly, language learning is both social and cognitive, and all language learning takes place within a sociocultural context. As Watson-Gegeo and Nielsen (2003, 157) observe, "All activities in which children participate with adults and other children (whether in the family, community, or classroom) are by definition socially organized and embedded in cultural meaning systems."

In this chapter we offer guidelines for instructional practice on the basis of existing research. For that reason teachers will likely observe that some of the practices they have come to accept as standard—or even exemplary—might not be represented. This, of course, does not necessarily mean that teachers are engaged in "wrong" practices, but rather that the standard wisdom of the field needs to be examined further through the lens of research. Second-language acquisition teachers, theorists, and researchers have realized that exposure and interaction might help promote fluency and communicative competence, but they are not sufficient for native-like accuracy (see Lyster 2007). Advanced English proficiency—ideally, to the point of native-like proficiency—is imperative for English learners in the U.S., indeed for any language-minority student whose future and livelihood will be influenced by his or her competence in the dominant social language. We have therefore seen a renewed focus on form as a critical element of second-language instruction.

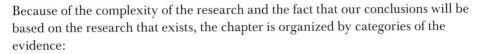

Because of the complexity of the research and the fact that our conclusions will be based on the research that exists, the chapter is organized by categories of the evidence:

⊙ Guidelines based on relatively strong supporting evidence from English learner research

⊙ Guidelines based on hypotheses emerging from recent English learner research

⊙ Guidelines applicable to ELD but grounded in non-English learner research

The chapter begins with an explanation and discussion of ELD instruction: what it is and what it is not. We then provide a brief description of the research base for ELD instruction and why it is so small. Subsequently, we report research related to 14 guidelines relevant to ELD instruction. The 14 guidelines are grouped in the three categories listed above and covered in the same order.

English Language Development Instruction

English language development (ELD) instruction is designed specifically to advance English learners' knowledge and use of English in increasingly sophisticated ways. In the context of the larger effort to help English learners succeed in school, ELD instruction is designed to help them learn and acquire English to a level of proficiency (e.g., advanced) that maximizes their capacity to engage successfully in academic studies taught in English. To put it another way, ELD instruction is designed to help English learners learn and acquire English to a level that minimizes the language barriers they face when engaging in academic studies in mainstream English classrooms. Clearly, one would hope that ELD instruction also helps students learn and acquire English sufficiently to engage successfully in social interactions with peers and adults inside and outside of school and in other kinds of pursuits requiring English proficiency, such as shopping, banking, obtaining news, and locating and using information. However, although there might be multiple goals for ELD instruction, we would argue that preparation for academic studies taught in English remains the top priority because of its relevance to school success. Helping English learners succeed in academic contexts is no doubt the most challenging goal and most likely the greatest need to emerge in recent English learner research.

> **English language development (ELD) instruction is designed specifically to advance English learners' knowledge and use of English in increasingly sophisticated ways.**

ELD instruction should not be confused with sheltered instruction or specially designed academic instruction in English (SDAIE; see Short and Echevarria, this publication). The primary goal of ELD instruction is learning and acquiring English; in California, this means mastering the ELD standards. Another goal of ELD instruction may be content-related. In fact, such a goal might actually contribute to the teaching and learning of English (Lyster 2007). But the primary goal of ELD instruction—as we are attempting to examine it here—is the learning and acquisition of English. If we were to evaluate the effects of ELD instruction, we would look first at the progress students make on the California English Language Development Test (CELDT), which assesses English learners' proficiency in listening, speaking, reading, and writing English. We might also look at student performance on the California Standards Tests (CSTs) for literacy, math, and various content areas to determine the extent to which ELD instruction supports content area learning, but that would be subordinate to evaluating the effects of ELD instruction on English language acquisition.

> **The primary goal of sheltered instruction is academic success in the content areas.**

In contrast to ELD instruction, the primary purpose of sheltered English instruction is teaching skills and knowledge in the content areas, more specifically (in California) the content identified in standards for English–language arts, math, science, social studies, physical education, and the arts. A second goal of sheltered instruction can and should be promoting language development, particularly what is called *academic language* (see Guideline 10 for more on *academic language*). This is the essence of sheltered instruction: Where use of the primary language is not possible, instruction is "sheltered" (or adjusted) in order to help students learn skills and concepts taught in a language they do not fully comprehend. In doing so, sheltered instruction ideally also supports ongoing learning and acquisition of English, specifically as it pertains to the content areas (math, science, social studies, etc.). But the primary goal of sheltered instruction is academic success in the content areas. (See Echevarria and Short, this publication, for further description of the distinction between ELD and sheltered instruction.)

If we were to evaluate the effects of sheltered instruction, we would look first at the progress students make on measures of content area learning, such as the subtests of the California Standards Tests (math, science, Algebra I, etc.). The principal question for sheltered instruction is the extent to which it is helping English learners master the content standards. We might also look at CELDT results to examine the extent to which sheltered instruction is supporting students' acquisition of English, but that would be secondary to evaluating content area learning.

In truth, the distinctions we are making here might appear somewhat contrived and artificial, since so much of academic content learning is highly language-dependent. It is particularly hard to know where the dividing line is between English *language arts* (content area) and English *language development*. But although the distinction between ELD and sheltered instruction can get blurred, our assumption is that it is better to keep them distinct and for teachers to be clear in their thinking when they are planning, delivering, and evaluating ELD instruction and when they are planning, delivering, and evaluating sheltered instruction. As we discuss below, clarity about objectives contributes to effective instruction. In ELD instruction, language is the primary objective and content is secondary. In sheltered instruction, content is primary and language is secondary.

The Research Base for ELD Instruction and Why It Is Small

This chapter draws heavily on six syntheses and/or meta-analyses: Ellis 2005a; Genesee et al. 2006; Keck et al. 2006; Lyster 2007; Norris and Ortega 2000; Russell and Spada 2006. We also discuss relevant individual studies.

Ellis (2005a) provides a review of empirical studies and theoretical views; based on his review, he posits 10 principles of instructed language learning (see the principles at the end of this chapter). Ellis notes that ". . . research and theory do not afford a uniform account of how instruction can best facilitate language learning," and he calls these principles "'provisional specifications' that might serve as the basis for language teacher education" (p. 210). From Genesee and others (2006) we draw mainly from the chapter that reviews oral language research (Chapter 2, Saunders and O'Brien) since oral English proficiency is an important goal of ELD instruction. Saunders and O'Brien are also cautious about the conclusions they reach, noting the near-absence of research on the effects of ELD instruction on English learners in the U.S. Keck and others (2006) present a meta-analysis of 14 studies that focused on task-based interaction, another topic relevant to ELD instruction. Lyster (2007) reviews both primary studies and syntheses that focused on the effects of content-based immersion programs. Norris and Ortega (2000) present a meta-analysis of 79 studies that focused on the effectiveness of second-language instruction. Russell and Spada (2006) analyzed 15 studies to estimate the effectiveness of corrective feedback on the acquisition of L2 (second language) grammar. We also draw on a few studies relevant to ELD instruction that were published subsequent to these six syntheses and meta-analyses, as well as on other broader syntheses that while not focused specifically on EL populations are applicable to ELD instruction (e.g., Slavin's [1987] review of research on grouping).

Admittedly, the six major syntheses and meta-analyses represent divergent populations and contexts. Ellis (2005a) casts a wide net across the entire field of second-language acquisition theory and research. Genesee and others (2006), specifically in the oral language chapter, synthesize across 50 K–12 studies, all of which were conducted within the U.S., and most of which involved Spanish-speaking English learners. Keck and others (2006) address U.S. and international studies involving primarily foreign-language contexts at the university level and a variety of primary and second languages (nine of the 14 studies involved university students and 10 of the 14 were foreign-language contexts). Russell and Spada (2006) analyze both classroom and laboratory studies involving foreign-language, second-language, and ESL contexts and populations. Lyster (2007) focuses on studies of immersion, primarily French immersion programs implemented in Canada. And finally, Norris and Ortega (2000) draw upon U.S. and international studies involving primarily college (51 of 79) or adult education contexts (11 of 79); only some studies in the sample involved K–12 contexts (five high school, 10 junior high, and one elementary). Moreover, only 28 percent of the studies analyzed by Norris and Ortega (2000) involved students learning English as a second language; most of the sample includes studies of foreign language instruction.

We have a relatively small body of research to guide the design and delivery of K–12 ELD instruction.

In sum, we have a relatively small body of research to guide the design and delivery of K–12 ELD instruction. Even among the 50 oral language studies synthesized in Genesee et al. (2006), very few focused on the effects of instruction. Many of those 50 studies are relevant to ELD instruction (e.g., language use, peer interaction, rates of proficiency attainment), but few actually focus on instruction explicitly. As mentioned, most of the other research that exists involved college-age and adult learners, primarily studying a foreign language. Even when we consider what we know about instructing language learning beyond a K–12 ELD context, we must recall Ellis's conclusion: "[R]esearch and theory do not afford a uniform account of how instruction can best facilitate language learning" (2005a, 210). Given the small research base, we have chosen to be inclusive. Rather than rule out studies and meta-analyses involving widely different populations and contexts (e.g., college-age and adult learners), we have chosen to review them and interpret them as best we can for their relevance to K–12 ELD instruction.

There is a growing U.S. literature base on educating English learners. However, very few studies from that literature actually examine the effects of instruction on language learning. Much of the research on English learners conducted in the U.S. over the last 25 to 30 years has focused on programs involving the use of different amounts of students' primary language (see Genesee and Lindholm-Leary, this publication). Indeed, since the *Lau v. Nichols* decision of 1974, which affirmed that English learners were guaranteed a "meaningful education," the majority of English learner studies conducted in the U.S.—at least those that measured student outcomes—focused primarily on evaluating some form of bilingual or English immersion programs. In many cases, the explicit or implicit intent of many of these studies was to estimate the extent to which programs of a specific design could produce achievement levels among English learners that matched native English-speaking students—typically as measured by nationally normed standardized tests of reading and mathematics. Many of the programs involved in these studies included ELD instruction, but the evaluation and research of these programs sought to measure the effects of the program overall rather than estimate the effects of the ELD instructional component on English language acquisition (for example, see Saunders 1999).

Guidelines

From existing research, we identified guidelines relevant to ELD instruction and categorized them based on the nature of the evidence. We begin with guidelines for which there is relatively strong supporting evidence, followed by findings that are emerging hypotheses. We then turn to guidelines applicable to ELD instruction but grounded in research with non-English learner populations. Table 1.1 displays the guidelines.

Table 1.1. Guidelines for ELD Instruction

Guidelines Based on Relatively Strong Supporting Evidence from English Learner Research

1. Providing ELD instruction is better than not providing it.

2. ELD instruction should include interactive activities among students, but they must be carefully planned and carried out.

Guidelines Based on Hypotheses Emerging from Recent English Learner Research

3. A separate block of time should be devoted daily to ELD instruction.

4. ELD instruction should emphasize listening and speaking although it can incorporate reading and writing.

5. ELD instruction should explicitly teach elements of English (e.g., vocabulary, syntax, grammar, functions, and conventions).

Table 1.1 *(continued)*

> 6. ELD instruction should integrate meaning and communication to support explicit teaching of language.
>
> 7. ELD instruction should provide students with corrective feedback on form.
>
> 8. Use of English during ELD instruction should be maximized; the primary language should be used strategically.
>
> 9. Teachers should attend to communication and language-learning strategies and incorporate them into ELD instruction.
>
> 10. ELD instruction should emphasize academic language as well as conversational language.
>
> 11. ELD instruction should continue at least until students reach level 4 (early advanced) and possibly through level 5 (advanced).
>
> **Guidelines Applicable to ELD but Grounded in Non-English Learner Research**
>
> 12. ELD instruction should be planned and delivered with specific language objectives in mind.
>
> 13. English learners should be carefully grouped by language proficiency for ELD instruction; for other portions of the school day they should be in mixed classrooms and not in classrooms segregated by language proficiency.
>
> 14. The likelihood of establishing and/or sustaining an effective ELD instructional program increases when schools and districts make it a priority.

At the end of this chapter, there are two tables. Table 1.2 lists the studies cited for each guideline categorized by the nature of the study: primary study, synthesis, or meta-analysis. Table 1.3 displays the evidence cited for each practice or guideline in terms of three factors: population relevance of the available studies, outcome relevance of the available studies, and reliability of the findings from the studies in relation to the number of studies. Ideally, we would want to base policy and practice on a research base containing studies that are high on all three factors; that is, they were conducted on the relevant population (in this case, K–12 English learners in the U.S.), use relevant outcomes (meaningful measures of English language proficiency or development), and are reliable (findings have been replicated over several independent studies). It should surprise no one to learn that no such research base exists. We must therefore carefully weigh the existing evidence and make judgments

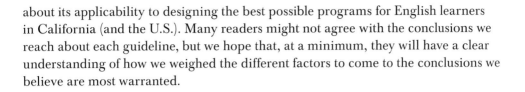

about its applicability to designing the best possible programs for English learners in California (and the U.S.). Many readers might not agree with the conclusions we reach about each guideline, but we hope that, at a minimum, they will have a clear understanding of how we weighed the different factors to come to the conclusions we believe are most warranted.

Guidelines Based on Relatively Strong Supporting Evidence from English Learner Research

1. Providing ELD instruction is better than not providing it.

Although existing research does not provide sufficient basis for determining the most effective methods of ELD instruction with total confidence, there is ample evidence that providing ELD instruction, in some form, is more beneficial than not providing it. Contemporary audiences may perhaps find it difficult to conceive, but 25 years ago "Does second-language instruction make a difference?" (Long 1983) was a viable question. A dominant view (then and for sometime after) was Krashen's (1982) "monitor" hypothesis, which proposed that formal instruction is of limited utility for second-language acquisition; instead, large amounts of exposure to comprehensible input in authentic communicative contexts is critical. Although second-language instruction might help learners learn some rules, language forms, and the like, Krashen proposed that this type of learning is not very useful for *language acquisition*—that is, being able to speak and understand a language in natural conversations and authentic contexts. However, in his review of available studies comparing second-language *instruction* to second-language *exposure,* Long (1983) concluded that instruction indeed aided second-language learning. This finding was true for young as well as older learners and at intermediate and advanced as well as beginning levels. There are certainly benefits to exposure—that is, living, working, and going to school with English speakers (or speakers of a target language)—as well as access to sheltered instruction that seeks to make academic subjects comprehensible. But second-language instruction clearly has added benefits.

> **There is ample evidence that providing ELD instruction, in some form, is more beneficial than not providing it.**

Norris and Ortega (2000) revisited this question in their meta-analysis and asked: How effective is second-language instruction overall and in comparison to exposure and communication with speakers of a second language? Norris and Ortega found that focused second-language instruction (designed to teach specific aspects of the second language) is more effective than conditions that do not provide focused second-language instruction (including exposure only, minimally focused instruction, minimal exposure). In the studies reviewed by Norris and Ortega, students who received focused second-language instruction made more than five times the gains that students who did not receive focused second-language instruction made (Norris and Ortega 2000, 468)

A recent and important study by Tong and her colleagues (2008) found that providing kindergarten and first-grade students with an "English-oracy intervention" resulted in more accelerated ELD growth (as measured by tests of vocabulary and listening comprehension), compared with students in control schools who received typical "ESL instruction." Schools using English immersion (i.e., receiving all-English instruction) and/or transitional bilingual education were randomly assigned to experimental or control conditions. The ELD intervention, which was equally effective with students in either English immersion or bilingual education, comprised:

   (a) daily tutorials with a published ELD program;

   (b) storytelling and retelling with authentic, culturally relevant literature and leveled questions from easy to difficult; and

   (c) an academic oral language activity using "Question of the Day."

Students who received the experimental treatment received more ELD instruction than students in the control schools (75–90 minutes/day for the experimental versus 45 minutes/day for the controls); moreover, "the very lowest performing students" (p. 1023) received 10–20 minutes of additional instruction provided by trained paraprofessionals. It is therefore impossible to rule out the effects of additional time, independent of the particular curriculum and instruction used. Nonetheless, the study is important in demonstrating the possibility of accelerating ELD in the early grade levels through intensive, organized instruction.

Although there are very few studies that have isolated the effects of ELD instruction, studies that compare outcomes for English learners receiving some form of accommodation for limited English proficiency (ELD and/or primary language instruction) to outcomes for English learners simply placed in mainstream classes and receiving no accommodation for their limited English yield consistent results: the former is more beneficial than the latter (August and Shanahan, this publication; Genesee et al. 2006; Thomas and Collier 2002). Even studies of content-based approaches to language learning, where content is taught in the second language, find that students learn more language when instruction includes strong elements of language teaching in contrast to approaches where students are simply placed in mainstream classes; that is, they simply receive exposure to the second language (see Lyster 2007 and Echevarria and Short, this publication).

2. **ELD instruction should include interactive activities, but they must be carefully planned and carried out.**

One might assume that providing English learners with opportunities to interact with more-proficient English learners and with native speakers or speakers of fluent English would be beneficial because such opportunities would provide English learners with models of proficient or at least more-proficient English-language speakers. But as Saunders and O'Brien (in Genesee et al. 2006) found in their synthesis of studies that focused on oral English language outcomes, creating such opportunities resulting in actual gains in proficiency involves more than simply pairing English learners with native speakers of English or more-proficient English learners. For instance, it may be

Interactive activities that effectively mix English learners and more-proficient English learners or native speakers of English typically involve carefully structured tasks.

assumed that in situations where the language input is slightly beyond English learners' level of understanding, they will work with their conversational partners to negotiate for meaning (cf. Long 1996, cited in Foster and Ohta 2005). However, a recent study showed that young adult second-language learners (who were observed for long stretches of time during shared classroom activities) focused more on "supportive and friendly discourse" than on negotiation of meaning or efforts to elicit "comprehensible input" (Foster and Ohta 2005). In such cases, it is fair to ask whether any language-proficiency gains are likely to occur. If interactive activities are to benefit English learners, careful consideration must be given to the following factors:

⊙ The design of the tasks students engage in

⊙ The training of the more-proficient-English speakers who interact with English learners

⊙ The language proficiency of the English learners themselves (August 1987; Johnson 1983; Peck 1987)

If attention is not paid to these factors, such interactive activities tend not to yield language-learning opportunities at all (Cathcart-Strong 1986; Jacob et al. 1996). Gersten and others (2007) drew a similar conclusion based on their review of English learner studies that focused on reading outcomes: Interactive activities that effectively mix English learners and more-proficient English learners or native speakers of English typically involve carefully structured tasks.

This guideline regarding interactive activities is supported by research on older second-language learners. Keck and others (2006) conducted a meta-analysis of 14 studies carried out in high school ($n = 2$), university ($n = 10$), and adult school institutions ($n = 2$) and in foreign-language ($n = 10$) and second-language ($n = 4$) contexts. The pivotal feature in their analysis is the nature of the interactive tasks. Although several research questions could not be definitively answered mainly because of the small number of studies and complexities related to control and comparison groups, the overall finding and the task components examined are relevant to K–12 ELD instruction. The overall finding is that treatments with interactive tasks produced a significant and substantial effect on language-learning outcomes. Most of the studies tested hypotheses about whether interactive tasks produced stronger effects on the targeted language form, compared with not using interactive tasks. As such, most studies did not include a true control group that received no treatment. Instead, the typical comparison group received a treatment without the interactive task and or without certain features designed to prompt learners to use the targeted language form as part of their interaction. Keck and others' (2006) findings can thus be interpreted to indicate that interactive tasks intentionally designed to produce learner use of the targeted language help second-language learners accomplish the objective.

The overall finding is that treatments with interactive tasks produced a significant and substantial effect on language-learning outcomes.

Keck and others (2006) examined two critical features of interactive tasks: "essentialness" and output. Essentialness has to do with the extent to which the targeted language form is essential to the task the group is trying to complete: does successful completion of the task *require* or is it at least *facilitated* by correct oral comprehension or production of the meaning of certain target words(e.g., modes of transportation: cars, trucks, trains, etc.) or language constructions (e.g., if-then, before-after)? Keck and others (2006) found that tasks whose successful completion either required or were facilitated by accurate use of the targeted language form produced stronger learning outcomes than tasks that did not require or were not facilitated by correct use of the language form. Interestingly enough, tasks that required and tasks that were facilitated by accurate use produced fairly similar effects on immediate post-test; however, tasks that *required* accurate use produced much stronger effects on delayed post-tests than tasks that were *facilitated* by accurate use. In other words, learning outcomes were stronger when learners had to learn language forms or rules that were necessary for successful completion of a group task. A second analysis with the same studies focused on interactive tasks that required attempts to actually produce the language form, for example, tasks that required students to produce oral utterances using the target words such as modes of transportation (cars, trucks, trains) or the target construction such as an if-then construction. Interactive tasks that required learners to attempt to produce the language form—in contrast to tasks that did not require learners to produce the language form—more consistently yielded stronger effects, both on immediate and delayed post-tests.

Reviewing five quasi-experimental studies involving students ages seven to fourteen, Lyster (2004a) arrived at the following conclusions:

(a) To be effective in supporting language development, interactive tasks need to be designed so that learners must *use* specified language forms in order to communicate successfully.

(b) Students' ability to make use of a task to improve their language depends on their level of language skill with the target of instruction.

Guidelines Based on Hypotheses Emerging from Recent English Learner Research

The following guidelines are based on hypotheses emerging from research on English learners.

3. A separate block of time should be devoted daily to ELD instruction.

Two studies provide guidance on whether there is any advantage to ELD instruction being provided during a separate time of the school day, as typically happens with reading, math, and the like. Saunders, Foorman, and Carlson (2006) found small positive but significant effects on oral language proficiency among Spanish-speaking kindergarteners who received ELD instruction during a separate block of time. Compared with kindergarteners whose teachers integrated ELD instruction in their larger language arts block, kindergarteners from ELD block classrooms made greater gains on end-of-year measures of oral English proficiency and also word identification (see Guideline 4 for discussion of word-identification effects). The study included more than 1,200 students from 85 classrooms and 35 schools located in Southern California and Texas. Students were in different types of language programs, including both bilingual and English immersion. In both bilingual and English immersion programs, some teachers used a separate block of time and others integrated ELD into their language arts block. In both the bilingual and English immersion classrooms, 58 percent had a separate block of time for ELD; 42 percent did not. The positive effects of an ELD block emerged in both English immersion and bilingual education programs. Even in the English immersion classrooms, where instruction was delivered almost exclusively in English, English learners provided with a separate ELD instructional block outperformed English learners whose teachers tried to integrate ELD in the language arts block.

What explains this effect? It is hard to know for sure. Saunders, Foorman, and Carlson (2006) also found that most of the ELD block time was devoted not to systematic, explicit vocabulary and language teaching but rather to oral English language *activities,* such as sharing personal experiences, identifying and naming colors, describing picture cards, naming the children in the class, and sing-alongs. Saunders, Foorman, and Carlson (2006) conjecture that while outcomes were significant, the magnitude of the effects may have been small because of the lack of explicit language teaching. In other words, establishing a separate block of time for ELD instruction is probably beneficial—perhaps in part because it helps teachers focus on English language itself and promotes both listening and speaking in English—but the size of the benefit might have more to do with what teachers actually do within the ELD block.

A recent dissertation addresses the question of whether a separate ELD block is beneficial for English learners' oral language development. O'Brien (2007) conducted a study designed to:

(a) Evaluate the effects of an ELD instructional program on oral language outcomes among first-grade Spanish-speaking English learners.

(b) Identify instructional practices associated with positive outcomes.

The study included nine classrooms representing three conditions:

1. Classrooms with a separate ELD block taught by teachers delivering the ELD program being evaluated

2. Classrooms with a separate ELD block taught by teachers delivering ELD derived from various components the individual teachers culled from published sources

3. Classrooms without a separate ELD block taught by teachers who were integrating ELD during their language arts time (where they used a published reading program)

The three conditions were evaluated based on the beginning level of first-grade and of second-grade California English Language Development Test (CELDT) listening and speaking scores.

Students in all three conditions made statistically significant gains over the year. But the gains were not equivalent. Students in Condition 2 (separate ELD block using materials that teachers themselves pulled together), on average, scored higher than students in Condition 3 (ELD integrated with language arts), although the difference was not statistically significant. Students in Condition 1 (separate ELD block using the ELD program being evaluated), however, scored significantly higher than did students in Conditions 2 and 3. The study also examined videotaped lessons from each condition to identify instructional features that distinguished the three conditions from one another in order to provide an account of the CELDT results.

Among other distinguishing features, Condition 1 was unique in that lessons involved attention to grammar (e.g., using prepositions), function (e.g., asking and responding to questions), and vocabulary (e.g., geography terms, such as *map, ocean, continent, world*). On average, teachers in Condition 1 spent 52 percent of lesson time in teacher-led interactive tasks that focused on grammar, language function, and content-related vocabulary. Teachers in Conditions 2 and 3 spent no time whatsoever on grammar or language function. Most of the lesson time in Conditions 2 and 3 was devoted to either discrete vocabulary (Condition 2: 86 percent) or content-related vocabulary (Condition 3: 84 percent).

These results support the conjecture of Saunders, Foorman, and Carlson (2006) that more attention to explicit language teaching (e.g., grammar and function) will make ELD instruction even more productive in terms of improved oral language development (see Guideline 5 for further discussion).

Tong and others (2008) also used a separate instructional block for their ELD intervention, but since the control schools also did (albeit a shorter one), we cannot infer that the separate block per se made a difference. A plausible hypothesis is that, as with the O'Brien (2007) and Saunders, Foorman, and Carlson (2006) study, the longer ELD block combined with focused, systematic language instruction helped accelerate children's oral language growth.

4. **ELD instruction should emphasize listening and speaking although it can incorporate reading and writing.**

As described in this publication, programs for English learners should include literacy instruction (see August and Shanahan, this publication); sheltered content area instruction (see Echevarria and Short, this publication); where possible, primary language support or instruction (see Genesee and Lindholm-Leary, this publication); and explicit ELD instruction (see Snow and Katz as well as Dutro and Kinsella, this publication). In such a comprehensive program, it would seem most beneficial to emphasize speaking and listening during ELD instruction. Although speaking and listening are emphasized in other parts of the instructional day, the textual demands of literacy and content area instruction no doubt need to be given priority during those instruction times. It is likely that time allotted for ELD is the one opportunity to make speaking and listening a priority. Two sources of evidence support this guideline as a promising hypothesis. First, there is evidence about the importance of oral language proficiency. Second, two studies support an emphasis on listening and speaking during ELD instruction.

The importance of oral English proficiency for English learners is well established in the research literature. With increasing oral English proficiency, English learners are more likely to use English, and more frequent use of English tends to be correlated with subsequent gains in oral English proficiency (Chesterfield et al. 1983; Saville-Troike 1984). In addition, with increasing oral proficiency in English, English learners are more likely to interact and establish relationships with native English-speaking peers, leading to more opportunities to use English (Strong 1983, 1984). With increasing oral English proficiency, English learners also tend to use more complex language-learning strategies, specifically strategies that allow them to monitor their own language use and the language use of others and thereby to interact more effectively with others (Chesterfield and Chesterfield 1985a). Finally, as English learners' oral English proficiency develops, they demonstrate a wider range of language skills, including skills associated with more academic uses of language, specifically higher-level question forms (Lindholm 1987; Rodriguez-Brown 1987) and the capacity to define what words mean (Carlisle et al. 1999; Snow et al. 1987).

Several studies have documented a positive relationship between oral English proficiency and English reading achievement (Carlisle et al. 1999; Garcia-Vázquez et al. 1997; Goldstein, Harris, and Klein 1993; Royer and Carlo 1991; Saville-Troike 1984; Snow et al. 1987; Ulibarri, Spencer, and Rivas 1981). This relationship has been established across grades one through nine and is based on various measures of oral proficiency and standardized measures of reading achievement. Moreover, the relationship between oral English proficiency and English reading achievement is stronger for measures that are associated with more academic aspects of oral language proficiency. For example, the number of different words English learners use during an interview correlates more strongly with reading achievement than the total number of words they use ($r = .63$ and $r = .40$, respectively; Saville-Troike 1984). The relationship between oral English proficiency and English literacy seems to strengthen substantially across the grades, arguably because both are similarly influenced by schooling and both are indicative of academic success. For example, in one study (Snow et al. 1987), correlations between English reading achievement and quality measures of English learners' word definitions goes from .16 in grade two to .50 in grade five.

The importance of oral English proficiency for English learners is well established in the research literature.

Two studies provide evidence suggesting that devoting more instructional time to listening and speaking yields significantly higher levels of oral language proficiency. The kindergarten study by Saunders, Foorman, and Carlson (2006) discussed above indicated that more time spent on oral English language instruction leads to stronger oral language outcomes without compromising literacy outcomes. That study found small but positive and significant effects on oral English proficiency and *also* English word identification. On average, teachers with an ELD block devoted 57 percent of the block time to instructional activities that focused exclusively on oral language (without text) and 32–39 percent on instructional activities that involved some form of reading or writing of text (average daily time allotment for ELD = 37–40 minutes). This evidence is only suggestive of proportions of time that should be devoted to listening and speaking within the ELD block because the study did not include a true comparison group, for example, a sample of classrooms with an ELD block that devoted most of the time to reading and less time to oral language. The comparison group in this study included classrooms in which ELD was reportedly embedded within the larger language arts block.

Results from O'Brien (2007) also suggest that an emphasis on listening and speaking during the ELD block might be beneficial. Although a relatively small-scale study, O'Brien (2007) allows for more direct comparisons of what teachers did in the two conditions that involved an explicit ELD block. Condition 1 included two teachers who were implementing a specific program that was being evaluated and that was designed to emphasize speaking, listening, and specific language objectives. Condition 2 included four teachers who were carefully selected to represent conscientious and fully credentialed (CLAD: cross-cultural, language, and academic development) teachers who consistently delivered a daily block of ELD instruction using published materials each teacher culled from various sources. As described earlier, students in Condition 1 scored significantly higher than did students in Conditions 2 and 3 (which contained no separate ELD block) on CELDT listening and speaking measures at the beginning of second grade. Instruction in Condition 1 focused at least half the time on grammar and language functions, which were completely absent from instruction in Condition 2. Moreover, teachers in Condition 1 carried out this focus on grammar and language functions almost exclusively through listening and speaking tasks: 96 percent of the ELD block was devoted to listening and speaking rather than tasks that involved some form of reading or writing or some other type of activity. Teachers in Condition 2 devoted only 55 percent of the ELD block to listening and speaking, with the remaining time devoted to tasks involving reading, writing, or something else.

The studies noted above found that more effective ELD approaches focused on oral language more than half of the time, with literacy activities comprising between one-third and slightly less than half of ELD instruction. A description of the intervention by Tong and others (2008), combined with data on fidelity of implementation, suggests that the ELD block in that study fell within the same general framework, with more than half of the instructional time devoted to oral language activities and instruction.

5. ELD instruction should explicitly teach elements of English (e.g., vocabulary, syntax, grammar, functions, and conventions).

In a recent review, Spada and Lightbown (2008) have pointed out that exposure to a second language in meaning-based school programs designed to promote second-language learning (e.g., content-based second-language instruction) can lead to the development of comprehension skills, oral fluency, self-confidence, and communicative abilities in a second language. However, second-language learners can still experience difficulties with pronunciation and morphological, syntactic, and pragmatic features (Spada and Lightbown 2008). Spada and Lighbown conclude that explicit instructional attention to those features (referred to as "forms" in the second-language literature) is likely to facilitate students' second-language learning in a way that relying solely on meaning- and communication-oriented instruction will not.

The essential body of evidence on teaching language elements explicitly is Norris and Ortega (2000). We discussed earlier the limitations of this meta-analysis in terms of its applicability to K–12 ELD contexts: of their sample of 79 studies, 78 percent involved college-age or adult learners; only 6 percent involved high school, 13 percent middle or junior high school, and 1 percent—just one study—involved elementary school. Moreover, most (59 percent) were conducted in foreign-language instructional contexts, and fewer than a third (29 percent) were conducted in second-language instructional contexts. Despite a lack of relevant research among English learners in grades K–12, however, findings from the Norris and Ortega analyses (2000) should not be dismissed or ignored. In these primarily college and adult-level foreign-language contexts, explicit instruction consistently produced stronger results than implicit instruction. Here, explicit instruction means either:

(a) instructors present or explain a language element (a rule or a form) to the students and then provide opportunities for them to study or practice the element with many examples (Norris and Ortega call this a "deductive" approach); or

(b) instructors engage students in tasks containing many examples of a particular form or rule and then direct students' attention to the language element so that students arrive at the rule by themselves or with the teacher's guidance (called "inductive" approach).

Explicit instruction included both approaches to studying features of the second language. Instructional treatments were classified as implicit in cases where instructors did not present or explain the language element and did not direct students' attention to the language form. On average, explicit instructional approaches were more than twice as effective—in terms of student learning—as implicit approaches, that is, where teachers did not draw students' attention to targeted language features.

This finding is important and possibly applicable to K–12 ELD instruction, although we are lacking studies that test it directly. The interventions studied by O'Brien (2007) and Tong and others (2008) involved explicit teaching of language, but there is not enough information about the degree of explicitness involved in teaching specific elements of English and how this explicitness contrasted with comparison conditions. We thus suggest some caveats in applying this guideline to younger learners.

As we have already pointed out, most of the research supporting this guideline was conducted with college and adult students. In addition, the great majority of the studies were of short duration. The average "treatment" lasted just over four hours and was more laboratory-like than long-term, classroom-like—which, of course, would be more relevant for drawing conclusions about what should happen in classrooms (rather than laboratory settings). Moreover, most of the studies were quite narrow in scope—teaching a specific feature of language (for example, verb tense, adverb placement, relative pronouns, or wh- questions) and then measuring the extent to which students learned that feature. Thus, whereas we can conclude that the most effective way to help older second-language learners learn a language form or rule is to teach it explicitly, we do not know empirically whether a semester or a year or multiple years of such instruction on a scope and sequence of language forms and rules would actually produce higher levels of second-language proficiency in young learners than some other approach sustained over time. Despite these caveats, the best available information points to the value of teaching language explicitly. Analogies between language instruction and literacy instruction must be offered cautiously, but similar findings have emerged about the value to English learners of explicit instruction in English reading skills and strategies (see August and Shanahan, this publication, and Genesee et al. 2006).

Explicit instruction is often associated with direct instruction.

Explicit instruction is often associated with direct instruction. Indeed, direct instruction is, by definition, explicit. However, it is not the only form of explicit instruction. Most models of direct instruction (see Slavin 2006) typically involve an explanation, demonstration, or presentation of the concept or skill in the early part of the lesson, followed by various forms of practice, feedback, and assessment. As such, direct instruction generally takes a deductive approach to teaching and learning—teachers teach students a skill or concept and then provide numerous examples followed by having students practice its application. In the Norris and Ortega analysis (2000), studies classified as explicit included not just deductive approaches but inductive as well. In other words, explicit instruction also included approaches where learners received a certain amount of experience with a language form (e.g., possessives or interrogatives), then were directed to attend to the form or to focus on deriving the underlying rule or nature of the form. Students were guided in "inducing" the rule or form rather than having been taught it directly before applying it. Thus it would not be accurate to interpret the Norris and Ortega "explicitness" finding as recommending only a direct-instruction approach, as direct instruction is typically defined. The key point in their finding is that instruction that explicitly focuses students' attention on the targeted language element, or form, produces higher levels of second-language learning than instruction that does not. Focusing the learners' attention is a central concept in Ellis's (2005a) principles of instructed language learning (see also Lyster 2007; Nassaji and Fotos 2004).

6. ELD instruction should integrate meaning and communication to support explicit teaching of language.

Meaning obviously plays a central role in language use. We use language to express and comprehend meaningful communication with others and to help build understanding for ourselves. Meaning also plays a central role in language learning insofar as being able to express and comprehend meaningful communication in the language being learned probably motivates and compels language learning. Although there is little controversy about the role of meaning and communication in language use—and by *communication* we mean both receiving and sending messages—their role in language *instruction* is more complicated. Should authentic, meaningful communication drive instruction? That is, should it be assigned top priority in second-language instruction? Or, alternatively, should explicit teaching of language forms drive instruction? Research on second-language learning and acquisition has advanced over the last two decades in coming to understand that instructed language learning must involve meaning and communication, but it also must direct students' attention to elements and functions of the language being learned. No doubt the interplay between meaning-making and conscious attention to language vary for different aspects of language, levels of second-language proficiency, the age of the learner, the learner's first language, and other factors (Spada and Lightbown 2008). Unfortunately, we do not have sufficient empirical evidence to understand this dynamic interplay fully, although Spada and Lightbown (2008) offer some useful hypotheses for second-language educators.

We constructed the wording of the guideline based on our review of the literature relative to the focus of this chapter: *ELD instruction should integrate meaning and communication to support explicit teaching of language.* Communicating meaning and providing explicit teaching are both important. However, we propose that communication and meaning should support explicit teaching of language, not necessarily drive ELD instruction. In the explanation of Guideline 4 (ELD instruction should incorporate reading and writing although it can incorporate listening and speaking), we argued that ELD instruction might be the one instructional block in the day wherein oral language, as opposed to reading and writing, could be afforded greater priority. We make a similar argument here for integrating meaning to support explicit teaching of the language rather than making meaning the driver of ELD instruction. The ELD block (or course) is likely the one portion of the day when explicit teaching of English can be afforded greater priority, insofar as the remainder of the instructional day will, ideally, have other content-specific objectives or communicative functions.

Lyster's review (2007) of primarily second-language immersion studies provides one source of evidence supporting the importance of incorporating meaning and communication in language-learning contexts, but also the need to better understand how best to balance meaning and communication with explicit language teaching. Drawing primarily from French immersion studies (K–12 and older), Lyster notes both the success and limitations of such programs: students instructed through carefully designed programs that immerse students in content study and language study consistently produce levels of second-language proficiency that exceed the levels achieved by students who study a second language simply as one more school subject. The content emphasis of the French immersion studies that Lyster reviews are examples of consciously incorporating communicating meaning—in this case, the meaning and communication associated with studying academic content.

Meaning obviously plays a central role in language use.

But Lyster also highlights another set of findings from French immersion studies: "What emerges from these studies is that immersion students are second language speakers who are relatively fluent and effective communicators, but non-target-like in terms of grammatical structure and non-idiomatic in the lexical choices and pragmatic expression—in comparison to native speakers of the same age" (p. 16). Lyster concludes that language immersion programs are likely to improve language learning by using enhanced instructional approaches that "counterbalance" content and form, that is, by more strategically and systematically teaching and helping students explicitly attend to language forms without compromising the effects of content-based, meaning-oriented pedagogy.

In his principles of instructed language learning (see page 73), derived from his review of both the theoretical and empirical literature, Ellis (2005a) emphasizes both meaning and form (principles 2 and 3, respectively, of the 10 principles) but clearly places more emphasis on meaning: "Instruction needs to ensure that learners focus predominantly on meaning" (Principle 2) and "Instruction needs to ensure that learners *also* focus on form" (Principle 3; pp. 211–12; emphasis added). In his discussion of meaning, Ellis draws a distinction between "semantic" meaning—where teacher and students focus on the meanings of words and constructions in the second language—and "pragmatic" meaning—where the second language is used as vehicle for communication, not the object of study per se. "Pragmatic meaning," in other words, is where learners "view the L2 as a tool for communicating and to function as communicators" (pp. 211–12). Although both types of meaning in second-language acquisition are important, Ellis says, "arguably . . . it is pragmatic meaning that is crucial to language learning" (p. 211).

Findings from Norris and Ortega's (2000) meta-analysis provide an interesting contrast to Ellis's (2005a) principles. Norris and Ortega found significant, positive effects for instructional treatments that (a) focused on form and integrated meaning and (b) focused solely on forms without integration of meaning: ". . . the current state of empirical findings indicates that explicit instruction is more effective than implicit instruction and that focus on form [which integrates communication and meaning] and a focus on forms [which does not] are equally effective." Norris and Ortega's (2000) analyses suggest that explicit instruction on language forms is central to language learning. Incorporating meaning would contribute to language learning only to the extent that students are provided with explicit presentations and explanations on the "rule-governed nature of L2 structures" (p. 483), whether through inductive or deductive approaches (both were represented in Norris and Ortega's sample, as previously discussed).

The contrast between Ellis's analysis (2005b) and Norris and Ortega's (2000) findings raises the following question: *If instruction needs to ensure that learners focus predominantly on meaning but also on form, why didn't the effects of treatments that focused on form and integrated meaning produce stronger results than those focused solely on form?* One possibility is that Ellis's strong emphasis on meaning might be less critical for adult learners. After all, most of the studies in the Norris and Ortega (2000) meta-analysis involved university students and adults. Recall that Ellis's principles are intended for language pedagogy ("provisional specifications") applicable to language learners of all ages. It is quite likely that university students and adults are more likely to engage in instructional activities (both lessons and drills) that do not integrate meaning.

Norris and Ortega classified treatments that integrate meaning when learners had the opportunity to engage with meaning-focused tasks prior to the introduction of the language form, or when treatments were designed specifically around the naturalness of the instructional tasks relative to the language form. At least for older populations, we can conclude that such integration of meaning neither significantly contributes to nor detracts from the learning of discrete language elements.

Another possibility is that the nature of the studies in the Norris and Ortega meta-analysis do not provide a good test of the role of meaning. The vast majority of the studies were focused, short-term tests of particular methods applied to the teaching of discrete language elements and involving the measurement of primarily just those discrete elements that were taught, rather than broader measures of language proficiency. Perhaps integrating meaning is less critical when the focus of what is taught and tested is very discrete.

The O'Brien (2007) study discussed earlier in this chapter is the only one with which we are familiar that explicitly tested the proposition underlying this guideline: meaning and communication can support explicit teaching of language during ELD instruction. The study was conducted with young English learners in U.S. classrooms, so its population relevance is extremely high. As previously reported, all three conditions in the study involved meaning and meaning-making, primarily by focusing on content, concepts, and vocabulary that students were studying in their English–language arts units and reading selections. However, the meaning or meaning-making aspects of the lessons from Condition 1 were utilized *to support* the learning of the language elements. No such connection existed for Condition 2 or 3. (See Guidelines 3 and 4 for further description of the conditions.) One-year oral proficiency gains for the first-graders in the study were significantly greater for students in Condition 1 than they were in Conditions 2 and 3.

For example, in Condition 1 there was clearly a targeted language form (*Where did XX sail? XX sailed to YY*), and the teacher's modeling and explanation about how to use the form and the practice students engaged in were supported by at least three dimensions that involved meaning and meaning-making. First, the lesson was broadly contextualized by the story students had read (about a character that sailed to different parts of the world). Second, the lesson was contextualized by a map of the world and a figurine students held and maneuvered as they constructed their responses (*Max sailed to Europe*). Third, students eventually took over the role of asking one another the general question (*Where did Max sail?*), and the respondent could construct his or her own answer, choosing the location on the map (showing where they had Max sail) and uttering the corresponding response.

The caveat here with the illustration from Condition 1 is that we do not know empirically the unique effects of those three meaning dimensions (story, map/figurine, and interactions) apart from the focus on form (*Where* question and response). Moreover, neither of the two other conditions provides a contrast that would allow us to conjecture about the contribution of the meaning dimensions to the focus on form: both had their own meaning dimensions, but neither focused on form. At best then, we can hypothesize that these meaning dimensions contribute to language learning and explicit language teaching. Unlike the older learners in many of the Norris and Ortega studies (2000), where meaning seemed not to make significant contribution to explicit language teaching, perhaps integrating meaning is more important and beneficial for younger learners.

The intervention by Tong and her colleagues (2008) also illustrates this guideline. As part of the ELD intervention, students listened to, answered questions about, and re-told stories; role-played conversations; and worked collaboratively with partners on workbook assignments. The study's design, however, does not permit any firm conclusions about the role of meaning and communication to support explicit language teaching, since Tong and others did not compare explicit language teaching with and without a communicative context.

7. ELD instruction should provide students with corrective feedback on form.

Providing English learners with feedback on form is probably not a matter of whether to do it, but how best to do it. During ELD instruction wherein the primary objective is studying and learning language, corrective feedback can be beneficial. Russell and Spada (2006) conducted a meta-analysis of 15 experimental and quasi-experimental studies that examined the effects of corrective feedback specifically on grammar. The studies include a mixture of foreign-language, second-language, and ESL contexts, some of which were conducted in classrooms and some conducted under laboratory conditions. Unfortunately, Russell and Spada do not report the age or grade level of the students involved in the studies, which makes it difficult to gauge the relevance of their findings to K–12 ELD contexts. Despite that limitation, all 15 studies involved (1) a treatment group that received some form of grammar-focused corrective feedback, (2) a comparison group that did not receive corrective feedback, and (c) a measure of language learning. In all 15 studies, the treatment group outperformed the comparison group, and in most cases (10 of 15) effects were large (> .8). The sample of studies varied in terms of other important instructional factors: Was feedback explicit or implicit? Was feedback provided by a teacher or a peer? Did feedback focus on oral or written production? Was feedback general or specific? The number of studies that focused on any of these instructional factors was too small to analyze quantitatively, but Russell and Spada's categorization of studies by those factors provides some insight into how best to deliver corrective feedback.

Lyster (2007) reviewed studies published since the time of Russell and Spada's meta-analysis. Ellis, Lowen, and Erlam (2006) involved adult ESL learners; Lyster (2004b) focused on fifth-grade immersion classrooms; and Ammar and Spada (2006) included sixth-grade ESL classrooms. All three studies tested the effects of implicit and explicit forms of corrective feedback, more specifically, recasts versus prompts. When teachers recast a student's utterance, they rearticulate what the student was trying to say with an utterance that includes corrections of one or more errors evident

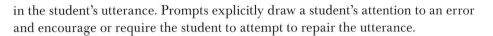

in the student's utterance. Prompts explicitly draw a student's attention to an error and encourage or require the student to attempt to repair the utterance.

As demonstrated by previous studies (Lyster and Ranta 1997), recasts are less likely to interrupt communication between the teacher and student, but students may not notice the correction and therefore may not benefit from it. Prompts, on the other hand, may momentarily interrupt communication between the teacher and student, but students are more likely to register the error and attempt to repair it. All three studies reviewed by Lyster (2007) had a treatment group that received prompts as feedback, a treatment group that received recasts as feedback, and a comparison group that received no feedback. In all studies, all treatment groups also received form-focused instruction. Ellis, Loewen, and Erlam (2006) found positive effects on students' use of the past tense for those students receiving prompts rather than recasts. On both oral and written measures administered immediately following the treatment and again two months later, Lyster (2004b) found positive effects

> **Prompts explicitly draw a student's attention to an error and encourage or require the student to attempt to repair the utterance.**

for both prompts and recasts (both treatment groups outperformed the comparison group) but stronger effects for prompts than recasts. On immediate and delayed post-tests of oral and written tasks, Ammar and Spada (2006) also found positive effects of both prompts and recasts and stronger effects for prompts in comparison with recasts. Ammar and Spada (2006) also found a differential effect: whereas higher-proficiency learners seemed to benefit equally from prompts and recasts, lower-proficiency learners seemed to benefit more from prompts.

The research interest in prompts and recasts as forms of more and less explicit feedback relates to a relatively new but important construct in second-language acquisition theory and research that focuses on *learner attention,* more specifically, what learners attend to during communication and language instruction. Lyster and Ranta (1997) studied teachers' interactions with students learning French as a second language. They found that teachers used several feedback strategies in responding to student errors during oral communication. The most frequent strategy was recasting. However, recasts were the least likely (31 percent of instances) feedback strategy to produce student "uptake," that is, an utterance by the student indicating an attempt to do something with the teacher's feedback. In contrast, "elicitations" (a form of "prompts"), where teachers directly elicited the correct form from students, produced uptake in 100 percent of instances. "Metalinguistic feedback" (information or questions related to the student's utterance, without explicitly providing the correct form) and "clarification requests" also provided high levels of student uptake,

86 percent and 88 percent, respectively. Interestingly, "explicit correction" produced uptake only 50 percent of time, suggesting too much explicitness might be counter-productive (but still better than implicit feedback, that is, recasts).

Lyster (2007) also provides an analysis of how feedback provided through more and less explicit forms might function differentially depending on teachers' relative emphasis on form versus meaning. Based on a review of studies that looked at recasts and prompts in French and Japanese immersion classes (Lyster and Mori 2006), Lyster concludes that the general classroom orientation influences the potential benefits of either recasts or prompts. In form-focused classrooms where teachers spend some time engaging students in oral drills and repetition of correct forms, the more subtle or implicit recast can serve as meaningful feedback, yielding student repairs, because the students are used to attending to form and repetition of teacher utterances. Recasts are less effective in meaning-oriented classrooms where students are more accustomed to attending to communication and more likely not to attend to corrections imbedded in teacher utterances. In meaning-oriented classrooms, prompts may be more effective because they explicitly mark the need for the repair of an utterance and therefore purposefully redirect students' attention, at least momentarily, away from meaning to the language itself.

The feedback guideline represents an important hypothesis for ELD instruction. First and foremost, feedback should not be taken for granted. We should not assume that students necessarily attend to and register corrective feedback delivered more implicitly. Where and when implicit feedback, such as recasts, seem to be relevant, ELD teachers will want to help students recognize them and understand their function, mostly likely as a broader orientation to the instruction block. ELD teachers will want to provide similar orientation to interactional activities and lessons that involve explicit feedback, so as to alert students to the fact that interactions will be momentarily interrupted to provide students with feedback intended to help them refine their language use. Most important, the evidence suggests that ELD teachers should not avoid or hesitate about providing corrective feedback. Rather, the central matter regarding corrective feedback is how to do it effectively so that students respond to it and benefit from it.

8. Use of English should be maximized during ELD instruction; the primary language should be used strategically.

This guideline does not negate the fact that many studies have shown the advantages of maintenance and development of English learners' home languages, in particular the benefit for second-language literacy of teaching English learners literacy skills in their primary language (Goldenberg 2008 reviews this research). We do not know

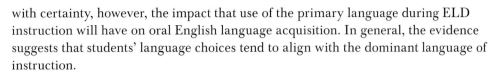

with certainty, however, the impact that use of the primary language during ELD instruction will have on oral English language acquisition. In general, the evidence suggests that students' language choices tend to align with the dominant language of instruction.

Chesterfield and others (1983) investigated the language choices of Spanish-speaking English learners in bilingual preschool classes. In classes where teachers tended to use more English for instruction, English learners tended to use more English with their peers. In classes where teachers tended to use more Spanish, learners tended to use more Spanish. Chesterfield and Chesterfield (1985b) also report language-use data for first-grade Mexican American English learners, half of whom were enrolled in "English" classes, and half of whom enrolled in Spanish bilingual classes. In the English classes, English learners used English during peer interactions most of the time. English learners in the bilingual classes used Spanish most of the time. Among second-grade English learners in Spanish bilingual programs where at least most instruction was delivered in Spanish, both Milk (1982) and Malave (1989) found that English learners were more likely to use Spanish during peer interactions; in fact, Malave found students using Spanish over English by a ratio of 6:1. Finally, among fourth-grade English learners who had participated in Spanish bilingual classrooms through grade three and were then placed in an "English-only" class, Pease-Alvarez and Winsler (1994) found a substantial increase from the beginning to the end of the year in students' use of English in their classroom interactions (53–83 percent).

Based on these studies, we would conclude the following: If a practical goal of ELD instruction is increased use of English, that goal will be served best by instruction delivered and tasks carried out primarily in English. However, we can imagine using the primary language in a limited but strategic manner during ELD instruction in order to ensure that students understand task directions, pay attention to cognates, and master language learning and metacognitive strategies.

9. **Teachers should attend to communication and language-learning strategies and incorporate them in ELD instruction.**

Genesee and others (2006) found that more-proficient English learners demonstrate a wider repertoire of language-learning strategies than less-proficient English learners. These strategies appear to emerge in the same order—from less to more sophisticated— and are correlated with levels of language proficiency. Second-language learners first use and rely most heavily on fairly simple receptive strategies, such as repetition and memorization, as they learn words and phrases. As they progress to the middle levels of language development, English learners begin to use more interactive strategies, such as verbal attention-getters and elaboration to engage in and sustain interactions with others. Finally, at more advanced levels English learners use language and communication-monitoring strategies, such as requesting clarification and appealing for assistance, in order to maintain and, as needed, repair communication with others.

In addition to the relevance of these findings for designing instructional strategies, in more general terms we view them as important information for ELD teachers. As students develop increasing proficiency, their capacity to use English increases, but so does their strategy use, which seems to undergo significant qualitative changes: from heavy reliance on receptive strategies to increased use of interactive strategies and eventually to more sophisticated communication-monitoring strategies.

Reviewing the literature on language-learning strategies, Chamot (2005, 115) states:

> Taken together, these studies identified the good language learner as one who is a mentally active learner, monitors language comprehension and production, practices communicating in the language, makes use of prior linguistic and general knowledge, uses various memorization techniques, and asks questions for clarification.

One study suggests that explicit instruction on how to use strategies effectively, especially metacognitive strategies, might be beneficial for English learners' oral language development. O'Malley and others (1985) conducted a study to test the effects of an eight-day (50 minutes per day) intervention designed to train high school English learners to use metacognitive and cognitive strategies in the context of integrative tasks: listening to lectures and making oral presentations. The training did not produce significant effects for listening, but it did produce significant effects for speaking. The authors' analyses of the strengths and limitations of their training modules suggest that listening outcomes could have been improved with stronger curricula and instruction. Although this is only one study, it yields a noteworthy hypothesis. The authors' previous observational and self-report investigations determined that students were less likely to apply strategies, particularly metacognitive strategies, to more challenging integrative tasks. Their subsequent experiment demonstrated that this weakness (or need) was amenable to instruction, at least for high school level English learners.

Several other studies have shown positive effects of teaching or priming listening comprehension strategies to English learners (e.g., Carrier 2003; Thompson and Rubin 1996 [cited in Chamot 2005]; Vandergrift 2002). Carrier conducted a study with seven intermediate-level ESL high school students that entailed 20 to 30 minutes of listening instruction for 10 sessions. Some of the strategies taught were how to listen to the rhythm and sounds of English, how to listen for specific information, and how to take notes (focusing on both form and meaning). Pretest and post-test comparisons showed statistically significant improvements in performance on discrete listening tasks and video listening and notetaking tasks.

Teachers may need to use students' primary language (when they can) to teach strategies for students at lower levels of second-language proficiency (Chamot, 2005, citing Macaro 2001)

Explicit instruction on how to use strategies effectively, especially metacognitive strategies, might be beneficial for English learners' oral language development.

10. ELD instruction should emphasize academic language as well as conversational language.

It is widely believed that successful performance in school requires proficiency in academic language and that a major objective of education for both language-majority and language-minority students is teaching the academic language skills they need to master the diverse subjects that make up the curriculum. For example, Snow and others (1991) found that performance on highly decontextualized tasks, such as providing a formal definition of words, predicted academic performance whereas performance on highly contextualized tasks, such as face-to-face communication, did not. In second-language literature, the concept of academic language was first proposed by Cummins (1984) in his distinction between "basic interpersonal communicative skills," or BICS, and "cognitive academic language proficiency," or CALP. Since then, several writers have proposed definitions of *academic language* (e.g., Bailey and Butler 2002; Bailey 2007; Scarcella 2003; Short and Fitzsimmons 2007).

Prior to discussing the research related to this guideline and why we characterize it as a hypothesis, we provide an explanation of academic language (drafted first by Fred Genesee and reviewed by other authors of this publication). Indeed, there is no definition of or consensus on academic language (see Scarcella 2003, for contrasts of two major perspectives, and see Valdés 2004, for a description and critique of both definitions and sociopolitical contexts related to conceptualizing academic language). Although not intending to dismiss this complexity, the authors of this publication agreed that it would be best to provide a working definition and explanation of academic language.

Chamot and O'Malley (1994) give this succinct definition of academic language: ". . . the language that is used by teachers and students for the purposes of acquiring new knowledge and skills . . . imparting new information, describing abstract ideas, and developing students' conceptual understanding" (p. 40). If Chamot and O'Malley's definition is expanded, academic language refers to the specialized vocabulary, grammar, discourse/textual, and functional skills associated with academic instruction

and mastery of academic material and tasks. In the simplest terms, academic language is the language that is needed in academic situations such as those students encounter during classroom instruction. The excerpt below includes an example of academic language during a lesson on using graphs to represent change in the manufacturing industry in California.

T: *Many things are manufactured in California, from airplanes to computer chips. Suppose you wanted to find out how many people worked in manufacturing jobs in California for the last 25 years. A line graph could help you. Look at the line graph on page 51 and trace the line to see changes over time. Why would the line be expected to move up over time?*

S: *More jobs.*

T: *That's right. Because manufacturing had increased over time, the line indicates the related rise in the number of jobs. What happened around 1990?*

S: *It stays the same.*

T: *Yes, the job market stabilized so there was only a slight increase—hardly discernible—in the line. What might happen if there were not products to manufacture?*

S: *People lose their jobs.*

S: *Some would move away.*

T: *That's right, and the graph would then indicate a decline. The line would go down in that case.*

This example of a verbal exchange between students and their teacher illustrates an important feature of academic language: it may be oral or written language. There are **sentence patterns with complex grammatical constructions** (such as *"What might happen if there were not products to manufacture"*); technical **vocabulary** (*manufactured, line graph, trace, related rise*); use of **explicit reference** to what is being talked about (e.g., *". . . the graph would then indicate a decline. The line would go down . . ."*); and **specific background knowledge.** Without the necessary background knowledge that was part of this lesson, the language used in this exchange would be even more challenging.

The performance of academic tasks also requires that students be competent performing sophisticated *language functions,* such as those listed here:

⊙ To argue persuasively for or against a point of view

⊙ To analyze, compare, and contrast

⊙ To evaluate alternative points of view and factual information

⊙ To justify a point of view or to debate different points of view

- To synthesize and integrate information
- To follow or give complex directions
- To hypothesize about the causal relationship between events
- To justify a predication, as in a science experiment
- To present a logical argument
- To question an explanation

Academic language is thought to differ from one subject to another (e.g., mathematics, science, history). Certain subjects require knowledge of specific technical vocabulary; sometimes this means that students must learn alternative meanings of common words, such as the mathematical use of the word *table* or *times* versus the day-to-day meanings of these words. The specific academic language of one subject, such as science, can also differ from that associated with another subject, such as mathematics, with respect to the particular grammatical forms and discourse patterns that are typically used in talking or writing about these subjects.

Definitions of academic language often contrast it with language used in everyday social situations. Cummins (1980), for example, characterized academic language as decontextualized and cognitively demanding, whereas social language tends to be more contextualized and less cognitively demanding. As a result, academic language tends to draw on more specialized technical vocabulary, to use more complex grammatical constructions, and to be more explicit in its intended meaning. Others have highlighted the nature of the vocabulary that characterizes academic versus everyday language use—academic language tends to use less common, more technical, and highly specialized vocabulary in contrast to that which is used in everyday conversations (e.g., Stevens, Butler, and Castellon-Wellington 2000). Although it is useful to contrast academic and social uses of language, it is not the case that academic language is necessarily more sophisticated than social language (Bailey 2007). Different kinds of language use in and outside school distinguishes academic communication from social communication. All the language functions listed earlier can be part of conversational language use. The difference between academic and social language lies in the fact that, in school, these functions are linked to academic content and thus to information or ideas that are often complex and abstract. To express these functions in school settings, the learner requires well-developed vocabulary, grammatical, and discourse/textual skills as well knowledge of the content domains (e.g., math or science).

Although the concept of academic language has gained attention in English learner literature, there is very little research to draw upon to guide ELD instruction. The notion that English learners' language development will benefit from ELD instruction focused heavily on academic language is a compelling hypothesis—but a hypothesis nonetheless since no study that we know has put it to the test. The hypothesis emerges from at least two interrelated findings. First, studies consistently find that English learners require from five to seven years to achieve native-like proficiency in oral language and literacy (Genesee et al. 2006; Collier 1987). One question that arises from these findings is whether this rate of acquisition can be accelerated. More specifically, since academic language probably plays an increasingly important role in defining what actually constitutes language proficiency as students go up the grade levels, it is reasonable to hypothesize that a focus on academic language might help students to attain advanced language proficiency more quickly. The second finding is that the rate at which students acquire proficiency tends to slow as they move to higher levels of proficiency (Genesee et al. 2006). Since higher levels of proficiency tend to be characterized by more academic uses of language, the question again arises as to whether higher levels of proficiency might be promoted by instruction that focuses more extensively on academic language.

It seems appropriate to put forward as a strong hypothesis that teaching academic language will help promote English learners' language development.

At this point, we do not have robust empirical answers to these questions, although a recent study demonstrated that English oral language development, at least in kindergarten and grade one, could be accelerated by providing 90 minutes or more of structured, organized ELD instruction (Tong et al. 2008). We also do not have a good empirical understanding of the kind of instruction that would reliably promote the development of academic language. The study by Tong and others (2008) provides an example of how academic language can be incorporated into kindergarten and first-grade ELD curricula, but it does not inform us about its long-term effects nor how it can help English learners progress beyond intermediate English proficiency. A recent volume of "practice guidelines" from the Institute of Education Sciences provides an indication of the state of research on academic language instruction (Gersten et al. 2007). From a review of the research, the authors put forth recommendations for effective literacy and language instruction for English learners at elementary grade levels. All recommendations were rated by the authors as having strong empirical evidence except for "Develop academic English," for which the panel found only two relevant studies, both of which focused on narrow aspects of academic English (quality of oral narrative and syntax) and did not explicitly test an instructional approach.

The authors retained the "Develop academic English" recommendation on the grounds of expert opinion. They observed the same phenomenon as we have: numerous scholars in the field of English learner education (Bailey 2007; Scarcella

2003), especially those synthesizing and meta-analyzing the research literature (August and Shanahan 2006; Genesee et al. 2006) and/or reviewing those syntheses and meta-analyses (Goldenberg 2008) are calling for attention to academic language or academic language proficiency, specifically because of its absence in the research literature and its apparent importance. Thus it seems appropriate to put forward as a strong hypothesis that teaching academic language will help promote English learners' language development.

From a practical standpoint, although we support the current emphasis on academic language and the call for instruction that effectively develops academic language among English learners, we must also acknowledge that this emphasis runs ahead of actual pedagogy, curriculum, and professional development that schools might use to answer the call. As Gersten and others (2007, 16) note: "The Panel feels the best way to promote the development of academic English is to use a curriculum with a scope and sequence aimed at building academic English. Unfortunately, the Panel knows of no existing curricular materials that have solid empirical support for this purpose."

Chapter 2 on kindergarten through grade five and Chapter 3 on grades six through twelve ELD instruction in this publication are intended to provide concrete examples of ELD instruction and curriculum that emphasize academic language. Although not yet systematically evaluated, the work in both chapters is informed by research related to ELD instruction and specific conceptualizations of academic language.

11. ELD instruction should continue at least until students reach level 4 (early advanced) and possibly through level 5 (advanced).

This guideline is consistent with California statute and federal law that require English learners to receive ELD instruction until they are redesignated as fluent in English. From a research standpoint, this guideline—a hypothesis—emerges from evidence about the rate at which students achieve advanced levels of proficiency. Students' English proficiency—both oral language proficiency and literacy—develops over time (five or more years). The evidence regarding literacy development has been reported and debated and theorized about for at least the last two decades (Collier 1987; August and Shanahan 2006). The evidence regarding oral English development among English learners has received much less direct attention. However, the synthesis of research on oral language by Genesee and others (2006) provides estimates based on a compilation of a small number of K–12 U.S. studies that contained longitudinal or cross-sectional oral language outcomes.

Summarizing across the studies (primarily elementary grade levels) and the various measures, Genesee and others (2006) report the following:

1. English learners require four to six years to achieve what would be considered "early advanced" proficiency (level 4, where level 1 is beginning and level 5 is advanced).

2. Average oral English proficiency approached native-like proficiency (level 5, advanced) by grade five in fewer than half of the available studies.

3. Progress from beginning to middle levels of proficiency is fairly rapid (level 1 to 3), but progress from middle to upper levels of proficiency (level 3 to 5) slows considerably—in other words, there is evidence of a *plateau effect,* where many English learners reach a middle level of English proficiency and make little progress thereafter.

4. As evident in one study that allowed for comparisons to native-English speaker norms (Hakuta, Butler, and Witt 2000; Woodcock Language Proficiency Battery), the gap between English learners and native speaker norms increased across grade levels.

Genesee and others (2006) highlight the common patterns in rates that emerged across grades one through five for students from both bilingual education and all-English programs and also for students learning English and for native speakers of English learning Spanish in two-way bilingual programs. The consistent patterns that emerged across programs, however, should be interpreted with caution because the number of studies representing each program is small (one to three).

English learners require four to six years to achieve what would be considered "early advanced" proficiency.

The hypothesis, then, is as follows: If English learners continue to receive explicit ELD instruction once they reach middle levels of English proficiency and as they move into early advanced and advanced levels, they can more rapidly attain native-like levels of oral proficiency and avoid the plateau many experience before becoming advanced speakers of English. Two assumptions underlie this hypothesis, and it is important to make them explicit. First, the hypothesis implicitly assumes that:

(a) English learners typically do not receive ELD instruction once they get to middle proficiency levels and, even less so, as they move into early advanced and advanced levels;

(b) the lack of ELD instruction is perhaps one reason for the stagnation.

Our observations at school sites corroborate this assumption. We rarely find cases where the ELD block, or a pullout ELD program, or ESL course work is maintained for English learners once they pass middle proficiency levels. However, we do not have empirical evidence to verify that this is common practice. Second, the hypothesis

54

assumes that ELD instruction would accelerate students' language development from middle level proficiency to early advanced and on into advanced English proficiency. As we discussed in Guideline 8, however, it is probably the case that instruction for English learners at higher levels of proficiency requires considerable attention to academic language. However, again, and as reported in Guideline 8, we do not have models of ELD instruction shown to be effective in promoting English learners' academic language proficiency.

Guidelines Applicable to ELD but Grounded in Non-English Learner Research

12. **ELD instruction should be planned and delivered with specific language objectives in mind.**

The use of instructional objectives is often considered a centerpiece of effective instruction. Good objectives function as starting points and rudders to help keep lessons and activities focused and heading toward productive ends (Slavin 2000). Yet the use of objectives can generate controversy. In their classic educational psychology textbook, Gage and Berliner (1975) identify and address some arguments against instructional (sometimes called "behavioral") objectives: for example, only trivial learning outcomes can be put in behavioral terms, certain types of learning do not lend themselves to stipulating objectives, and behavioral objectives lead to mechanistic teaching. Gage and Berliner refute each argument but acknowledge that educators do not universally subscribe to the use of instructional objectives. Moreover, the case for instructional objectives is not ironclad, and the evidence for the effects on achievement is mixed.

For example, DuChastel and Merrill (1973) found in their review that some studies report positive effects of instructional objectives on student learning while other studies do not. Similarly, Duell (1974) reviewed eight studies, four showing positive effects and four showing negative effects of instructional objectives. On the other hand, White and Tisher (1986) reviewed several studies, including a meta-analysis, in science teaching and concluded that although results are mixed, "general support for the use of objectives is available" (p. 876). White and Tisher (1986) cite a meta-analysis by Boulanger that found, "Among the strongest contributors to the large effect [of using preinstructional strategies] were the five studies on the use of behavioral objectives" (p. 876). Gage and Berliner (1975), despite the mixed evidence, come down strongly on the side of using instructional objectives because of the evidence suggesting that teaching will be more focused and purposeful when teachers use explicit objectives. In a more contemporary text in educational psychology, Slavin (2000) makes a similar point, citing a study by Cooley and Leinhardt showing that the strongest predictor of student reading and math scores was the extent to which students were actually taught the skills that were tested. Although this might seem mundane common sense, Slavin draws the conclusion that instructional objectives enhance learning outcomes "to the degree to which objectives, teaching, and assessment are coordinated with one another" (p. 465).

What we do not know empirically is the degree to which what seems to be generally true for other academic subjects also holds true for ELD instruction. However, we would like to elaborate on a potential connection between the more general research on instructional objectives and evidence on second-language instruction reported earlier. Norris and Ortega (2000) found strong effects for explicit instruction of targeted language forms. As defined by Norris and Ortega, explicit instruction constituted lessons wherein students were provided with an explanation or presentation of the rule or language form or specific directions to attend to a particular language form. A subset of the studies analyzed by Norris and Ortega included direct contrasts between treatments that specifically focused students' attention on the targeted language form and comparison conditions that involved simple exposure to or experience with the same language form. Such comparisons showed that explicit instruction focusing student attention on the targeted language form can substantially increase the success of such lessons. It is quite possible that formulating clear language objectives would support teachers' efforts to effectively direct students' attention to the targeted language form. Thus our hypothesis is that instructional objectives will be as useful for ELD instruction as it is for other types of academic instruction. California's ELD standards should serve as the foundation of ELD instructional objectives.

> Our hypothesis is that instructional objectives will be as useful for ELD instruction as it is for other types of academic instruction.

13. **English learners should be carefully grouped by language proficiency for ELD instruction; for other portions of the school day they should be in mixed classrooms and not in classrooms segregated by language proficiency.**

Should English learners be grouped with other English learners or kept with English speakers? If grouped with other English learners, should they be with others at similar language levels, or should they be in mixed-language-level groups? If they are grouped with others at similar language levels, for what purposes and for how much of the school day? We know of no research to answer these questions directly. However, as is the case for instructional objectives, many studies have examined the pros and cons of different types of grouping arrangements in other content areas, primarily, reading and mathematics. This research, which has been synthesized by Slavin (1987, 1989), suggests the following findings:

1. Keeping students of different achievement/ability levels in entirely separate ("homogeneous") classes for the entire school day (and throughout the school year) leads to depressed achievement among lower-achieving students with little to no benefit for average and higher-achieving students. A possible exception is for extremely high-achieving students (sometimes referred to as "gifted"), whose achievement can be significantly enhanced in homogeneous classes with other extremely high-achieving students. Unfortunately, we have found no studies that have looked at grouping practices for extremely high-achieving English learners.

> **English learners should be in mixed-ability (heterogeneous) classrooms but then grouped by English language proficiency specifically for ELD instruction.**

2. Students in mixed ("heterogeneous") classrooms can be productively grouped by achievement level for instruction in certain subjects (e.g., math or reading). Grouping can be done with students in the same classroom or students in different classrooms (the latter is sometimes called "Joplin plans"). In contrast to keeping students in homogeneous classes throughout the day (#1, above), grouping students by achievement level in certain subjects will result in enhanced achievement at all ability levels if:

   (a) instruction is tailored to students' instructional level; and

   (b) students are frequently assessed and regrouped as needed to maintain optimal match with their instructional needs (that is, students are taught what they need to know to make continual progress).

There are many ways in which second-language learning might be very different from learning school subjects such as reading and mathematics. Consequently, it is difficult to know if we can apply findings based on reading and mathematics to ELD instruction. On the other hand, and to the extent that second-language learning is analogous to learning in other curriculum areas, findings from the ability-grouping literature serve as a useful starting place to make decisions about how to group English learners.

These findings suggest that English learners should not be segregated into all-English-learner classrooms, much less into classrooms consisting of all high-achieving English learners or all low-achieving English learners. Instead, English learners should be in mixed-ability (heterogeneous) classrooms but then grouped by English language proficiency specifically for ELD instruction. Moreover, they should be regularly assessed to monitor their progress and to make certain that instruction and group placement are well suited to their language-learning needs. Presumably, as English learners attain proficiency in English, they can and should receive increasing amounts of instruction with students who are already proficient in English. (For further discussion of grouping, see, in this publication, Genesee and Lindholm-Leary for dual language programs.)

14. The likelihood of establishing and/or sustaining an effective ELD instructional program increases when schools and districts make it a priority.

Much literature suggests that a sustained and coherent focus on academic goals in schools and districts is associated with higher levels of student achievement. However, because of the near-absence of experimental research and detailed case studies in this area, it is difficult to draw firm conclusions about cause and effect. Moreover, some researchers have concluded that "distal" factors such as school and district policies are too removed from students' daily experience to have much impact on their achievement (Wang, Haertel, and Walberg 1993). Nonetheless, there is at least some consensus in the published literature that what gets emphasized in schools and districts can influence what teachers do and what students learn. Numerous dimensions of school and district functioning—leadership, common goals and curricula, professional development, ongoing support and supervision, regular assessments that inform instruction—are levers that school and district administrators can use to help shape the academic experiences of students (e.g., Edmonds 1979; Fullan 2007; Good and Brophy 1986; Joyce and Showers 1983; Goldenberg 2004; McDougall, Saunders, and Goldenberg 2007).

A recent study suggests the same holds true for English learners: what school and district leadership emphasizes has an influence on what students learn. Parrish and others (2006) found that relatively high-achieving California schools with high concentrations of English learners shared various characteristics that converged on their making academic achievement a priority. At the school level, according to principals, there was a schoolwide focus on ELD and standards-based instruction; shared priorities and expectations regarding the education of English learners; and curriculum, instruction, and resources targeted at them. District administrators cited a shared vision and plan for English learner achievement and professional development, resources, and school and classroom organization to support achievement. It is important to bear in mind that "high achieving" in this study was defined as high levels of academic achievement (literacy and other content areas), *not* necessarily high levels of English language development. Parrish and others (2006, iv–10) note, however, that inclusion of CELDT scores as a criterion for the selection of high-achieving schools "seemed to have little to no impact on the lists of top-ranked schools that were generated," suggesting that among the high-achieving schools, English learners tended to perform well on both English language development tests (CELDT) and academic achievement tests (California Standards Test).

Although far from definitive, available research suggests that one way to promote higher levels of English language development among English learners is to make sure it is a school- and districtwide priority. As is true in other areas of academic achievement, the direction set by school and district leadership is likely to influence what is emphasized in classrooms. Without the other factors considered in this chapter and volume, school or district priorities alone are unlikely to have an effect. But, together with curriculum and instruction based on the best research currently available, a high priority placed on ELD instruction by schools and districts is likely to contribute to promoting higher levels of English acquisition by English learners.

> **Available research suggests that one way to promote higher levels of English language development among English learners is to make sure it is a school- and district-wide priority.**

Summary

In this final section, we attempt to offer a synthesis of the research summarized in the chapter. Our goal is to provide a set of implications for practice and policy that are as clear as possible, given the tenuous nature of many of the findings. (See the tables at the end of this chapter.)

Our review of the research suggests there is good evidence for the following guidelines:

1. Providing ELD instruction is better than not providing it.

2. ELD instruction should include interactive activities, but they must be carefully planned and carried out.

Both guidelines are quite reliable because they are based on a number of studies, many of them experiments, that converge on those findings. Both guidelines also have adequate support from studies conducted with English learners in the U.S. and from studies that use measures of language proficiency. The research supporting Guideline 2 provides direction about the design of effective interactive activities, including the nature and structure of interactive tasks, the level of proficiency of the English learners, and the various ways in which they might be paired together during interactive tasks.

We consider the following guidelines to be hypotheses. That is, there are insufficient studies to constitute strong, reliable findings, and the studies that do exist have been conducted with only a small portion of the U.S. English learner population, thus limiting their generalizability. Although enough evidence exists to consider these "best guesses" at the moment, future research might well cause us to revise these guidelines:

---

3. A separate block of time should be devoted daily to ELD instruction.

4. ELD instruction should emphasize listening and speaking although it can incorporate reading and writing.*

5. ELD instruction should explicitly teach elements of English (e.g., vocabulary, syntax, grammar, functions, and conventions).

6. ELD instruction should integrate meaning and communication to support explicit teaching of language.

7. ELD instruction should provide students with corrective feedback on form.

8. Use of English should be maximized during ELD instruction; the primary language should be used strategically.

9. Teachers should attend to communication and language-learning strategies and incorporate them into ELD instruction.

10. ELD instruction should emphasize academic language as well as conversational language.*

11. ELD instruction should continue at least until students reach level 4 (early advanced) and possibly through level 5 (advanced).*

Of these eight guidelines, the strongest hypotheses (indicated by *) are Guidelines 4 (ELD instruction should emphasize listening and speaking), 10 (ELD instruction should emphasize academic language as well as conversational language), and 11 (ELD instruction should continue at least until students reach level 4 [early advanced] and possibly through level 5 [advanced]). However, with the exception of O'Brien (2007) and Saunders, Foorman, and Carlson (2006) for Guideline 3, there are no experimental or quasi-experimental studies (comparing specific instructional approaches) supporting any of these hypotheses, so they have not been tested directly. The studies that exist provide circumstantial evidence suggesting differences in student language development as a result of different types of instruction, but the evidence is not as strong as it is in the first group of practice guidelines. In addition,

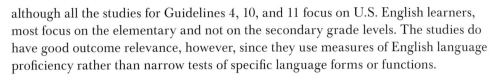

although all the studies for Guidelines 4, 10, and 11 focus on U.S. English learners, most focus on the elementary and not on the secondary grade levels. The studies do have good outcome relevance, however, since they use measures of English language proficiency rather than narrow tests of specific language forms or functions.

Guideline 5 (ELD instruction should explicitly teach elements of English [e.g., vocabulary, syntax, grammar, functions, and conventions]) has a strong supportive body of evidence, but few of the studies were conducted with U.S. English learners in K–12 or use outcome measures that are good gauges of language proficiency; instead, most use narrow assessments that measure specific language features, such as word order, verb conjugation, relative clauses, complements, and question forms. Nonetheless, we still believe that Guideline 5 is probably valid for English learners in the U.S. There is considerable evidence from literacy instruction that teaching specific components of literacy makes a contribution to literacy development (see August and Shanahan, this publication). Although there are limits to the analogy between literacy development and oral language development, it is plausible that both respond to comparable instructional approaches. The study by O'Brien (2007) with California first-graders suggested that an ELD program that included teaching elements of English grammar and functions produced more growth in language development than approaches that did not.

Guideline 6 brings together critical elements that are debatable: explicit instruction of language forms and the role of meaning, communication, and authentic and functional language use in the service of language learning. The truth is that there is no definitive empirical answer about the appropriate balance and exact relationships among these elements. Recall Ellis's statement cited near the beginning of this chapter: ". . . research and theory do not afford a uniform account of how instruction can best facilitate language learning." We know, empirically, that it is probably detrimental to language learning to leave explicit instruction out of the equation, but how—in an ELD instructional context—meaning and authentic and functional use complement explicit instruction is just not known at this time.

We concluded, based on our review of the literature, that all those elements are important for ELD instruction. The major challenge for instructional design and subsequent research is determining the right balance among these elements. With such subsequent work in mind, we would add one other observation. The construct of "meaning" can and should remain a central topic in subsequent research. Most first- and second-language acquisition theories posit a role for meaning-making in the acquisition process. Ellis (2005b) further specifies "pragmatic meaning," where language is used for communication rather than being the target of study, as particularly critical. Our review of current research, however, suggests that meaning—as an element of an instructional approach or intervention—is typically not sufficiently defined to study and understand its nature and/or contribution to language acquisition and learning.

The other four guidelines in this group—3 (A separate block of time should be devoted daily to ELD instruction), 7 (ELD instruction should provide students with corrective feedback on form), 8 (Use of English should be maximized during ELD instruction), and 9 (Teachers should attend to communication and language-learning strategies and incorporate them in ELD instruction)—either have very few studies and/or have examined only a tiny fraction of the K–12 English learner population. There is compelling evidence for Guideline 7 insofar as the effects of corrective feedback (either implicit or explicit) have been successfully replicated in both classroom and laboratory contexts but not with U.S. English learner populations. In the case of Guidelines 8 and 9, only one study supporting each guideline actually used measures of student English-language proficiency as an outcome variable; thus we know very little about the effect of maximizing English use during ELD instruction (Guideline 8) or incorporating communication and language-learning strategies (Guideline 9) on students' English language development. Guideline 3 (A separate block of time should be devoted daily to ELD instruction) had the most valid outcome measures, but there are only two studies, and they were conducted with kindergarten and grade one students.

Our third category of guidelines draws from the broader educational literature, not from research on English learners per se:

> 12. ELD instruction should be planned and delivered with specific language objectives in mind.
>
> 13. English learners should be carefully grouped by language proficiency for ELD instruction; for other portions of the school day they should be in mixed classrooms and not in classrooms segregated by language proficiency.
>
> 14. The likelihood of establishing and/or sustaining an effective ELD instructional program increases when schools and districts make it a priority.

These guidelines are not definitive in the context of ELD instruction for English learners, but they are generally accepted as meaningful and reliable within education research more broadly defined. The issue for ELD instruction is generalizability. Do these guidelines apply to schools and classroom contexts serving English learner populations and specifically with regard to ELD instruction? This is clearly an empirical question, although our experience leads us to believe they do. Although we have not tested these specific guidelines in our own English learner and school improvement studies, they are consistent with what we have observed in our work trying to help schools with large numbers of English learners become more effective schools.

Clearly, much work remains to be done to develop an empirical research base on which to build effective ELD instructional programs. As we said at the beginning of the chapter, however, many sources and resources might guide the direction of ELD instruction, including theory, research, ELD standards, practitioner experience, and published programs. Our experience in schools throughout California suggests attention to ELD instruction is growing, and important efforts are underway to develop effective ELD programs for both elementary and secondary school students. Attention to the matter of academic language proficiency is also growing. It is imperative to complement those efforts and interest with careful research and evaluation. We are encouraged by efforts such as those by Tong and others (2008) that bring together a number of elements and guidelines discussed here. Clearly no single practice or principle will be sufficient to help English learners gain access to high-level, mainstream academic curriculum. Instead, we must not only test individual components and guidelines; we must also construct comprehensive ELD programs and test the proposition that they help students acquire high levels of English language proficiency as rapidly as possible and regardless of whether they are in bilingual or in English-only programs. From our experience, strong opinion too often trumps careful weighing of evidence in this highly volatile and politically charged field.

> **Our experience in schools throughout California suggests attention to ELD instruction is growing, and important efforts are underway to develop effective ELD programs for both elementary and secondary school students.**

Current accountability practices shine a bright spotlight on academic progress—or lack of progress—among English learners. Accountability may be a good thing for schools and English learners, or it may be problematic. It may produce a strong and long-term commitment toward building effective programs for English learners; or it might result in a frenzied search for the next "quick fix." The major theme of this entire volume is that success for English learners likely requires comprehensive programs and approaches that incorporate ELD instruction, strong English literacy instruction, effective sheltered instruction in the content areas, and—ideally—effective use of students' primary language. We have a lot to learn about what constitutes effective ELD instruction. Nothing in this chapter or this publication suggests there are quick fixes waiting around the corner for schools and districts trying to meet next year's accountability criteria. For ELD instruction in particular and educating English learners in general, success is going to require a sustained effort informed by attention to both evidence and thoughtful practice.

References

Alcón, Eva. 2004. Research on language and learning: Implications for language teaching. *International Journal of English Studies* 4: 173–96.

Ammar, Ahlem, and Nina Spada. 2006. One size fits all? Recasts, prompts, and L2 learning. *Studies in Second Language Acquisition* 28 (December): 543–74.

August, Diane. 1987. Effects of peer tutoring on the second language acquisition of Mexican-American children in elementary school. *TESOL Quarterly* 21 (December): 717–36.

August, Diane, and Timothy Shanahan. 2006. *Developing literacy in second-language learners: Report of the national literacy panel on language-minority children and youth.* Mahwah, NJ: Lawrence Erlbaum.

Bailey, Alison. 2007. *The language of school: Putting academic English to the test.* New Haven, CT: Yale University Press.

Bailey, Alison L., and Frances A. Butler. 2002. *An evidentiary framework for operationalizing academic language for broad application to K–12 education: A design document.* Los Angeles: University of Californi. (National Center for Research on Evaluation, Standards, and Student Testing (CRESST).

Carlisle, Joanne, Margaret Beeman, Lyle Hull Davis, and Galila Spharim. 1999. Relationship of metalinguistic capabilities and reading achievement for children who are becoming bilingual. *Applied Psycholinguistics* 20 (December): 459–78.

Carrier, Karen. 2003. Improving high school English language learners' second language listening through strategy instruction. *Bilingual Research Journal* 27 (Fall): 383–408.

Cathcart-Strong, Ruth. 1986. Input generation by young second language learners. *TESOL Quarterly* 20 (September): 515–29.

Chamot, Anna. 2005. Language learning strategy instruction: Current issues and research. *Annual Review of Applied Linguistics* 25 (July): 112–30.

Chamot, Anna, and J. Michael O'Malley, comp. 1994. *CALLA handbook: Implementing the cognitive academic language learning approach.* Reading, MA: Addison-Wesley.

Chesterfield, Ray, and Kathleen Barrows Chesterfield. 1985a. Natural order in children's use of second language learning strategies. *Applied Linguistics* 6: 45–59.

Chesterfield, Ray, and Kathleen Barrows Chesterfield. 1985b. Hoja's with the H: Spontaneous peer teaching in bilingual classrooms. *Bilingual Review* 12 (September–December): 198–208.

Chesterfield, Ray, Kathleen Barrows Chesterfield, Katherine Hayes-Latimer, and Regino Chavez. 1983. The influence of teachers and peers on second language acquisition in bilingual preschool programs. *TESOL Quarterly* 17 (September): 401–19.

Collier, Virginia. 1987. Age and rate of acquisition of second language for academic purposes. *TESOL Quarterly* 21: 617–41.

Cummins, James. 1980. The construct of language proficiency in bilingual education. In *Georgetown University round table on languages and linguistics,* ed. James E. Alatis. Washington, DC: Georgetown University Press.

Cummins, James. 1984. Wanted: A theoretical framework for relating language proficiency to academic achievement among bilingual students. In *Language proficiency and academic achievement,* ed. Charlene Rivera. Clevedon, England: Multilingual Matters.

DeKeyser, Robert, and Alan Juffs. 2005. Cognitive considerations in L2 learning. In *The handbook of research in second language teaching and learning,* ed. Eli Hinkel, 437–54. Mahwah, NJ: Lawrence Erlbaum.

DuChastel, Phillipe, and Paul Merrill. 1973. The effects of behavioral objectives on learning: A review of empirical studies. *Review of Educational Research* 43: 53–69.

Duell, Orpha. 1974. Effect of type of objective, level of test questions, and the judged importance of tested materials upon test performance. *Journal of Educational Psychology* 66 (April): 225–32.

Edmonds, Ronald. 1979. Effective schools for the urban poor. *Educational Leadership* 37 (October): 15–27.

Ellis, Rod. 2005a. Principles of instructed language learning. *System* 33 (June): 209–24.

Ellis, Rod. 2005b. Communicative language teaching: Strategies and goals. In *The handbook of research in second language teaching and learning,* ed. Eli Hinkel, 635–51. Mahwah, NJ: Lawrence Erlbaum.

Ellis, Rod, Shawn Loewen, and Rosemary Erlam. 2006. Implicit and explicit corrective feedback and the acquisition of L2 grammar. *Studies in Second Language Acquisition* 28 (June): 339–68.

Foster, Pauline, and Amy Snyder Ohta. 2005. Negotiation for meaning and peer assistance in second language classrooms. *Applied Linguistics* 26 (September): 402–30.

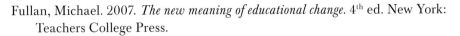
Fullan, Michael. 2007. *The new meaning of educational change.* 4th ed. New York: Teachers College Press.

Gage, Nathaniel, and David Berliner. 1975. *Educational psychology.* Chicago: Rand McNally.

Garcia-Vázquez, Enedina, Luis A. Vasquez, Isabel C. Lopez, and Wendy Ward. 1997. Language proficiency and academic success: Relationships between proficiency in two languages and achievement among Mexican-American students. *Bilingual Research Journal* 21 (Fall): 395–408.

Genesee, Fred. 1999. *Program alternatives for linguistically diverse students (Educational practice report 1).* Santa Cruz, CA, and Washington, DC: Center for Research on Education, Diversity, and Excellence.

Genesee, Fred, Kathryn Lindholm-Leary, William Saunders, and Donna Christian. 2006. *Educating English language learners: A synthesis of research evidence.* New York: Cambridge University Press.

Gersten, Russell, and others. 2007. *Effective literacy and English language instruction for English learners in the elementary grades.* NCEE 2007-4001. Washington, DC: National Center for Education Evaluation and Regional Assistance, Institute of Educational Sciences, U.S. Department of Education. http://ies.ed.gov/ncee

Goldenberg, Claude. 2004. *Successful school change: Creating settings to improve teaching and learning.* New York: Teachers College Press.

Goldenberg, Claude. 2008. Teaching English language learners: What the research does—and does not—say. *American Educator* 32 (Summer): 8–23, 42–44.

Goldstein, Barbara Comoe, Kathleen Harris, and M. Diane Klein. 1993. Assessment of oral storytelling abilities of Latino junior high school students with learning handicaps. *Journal of Learning Disabilities* 26 (February): 138–43.

Good, Tom, and Jerry Brophy. 1986. School effects, In *The handbook of research on teaching* 3rd ed., ed. Merlin Wittrock, 570–602. New York: Macmillan.

Hakuta, Kenji, Yuko Goto Butler, and Daria Witt. 2000. *How long does it take English learners to attain proficiency?* Linguistic Minority Research Institute. (ERIC Document Reproduction Service No. FL 026 180). http://www.lmri.ucsb.edu/publications/00-hakuta.pdf.

Howard, Elizabeth, Donna Christian, and Fred Genesee. 2003. *The development of bilingualism and biliteracy from grade 3 to 5: A summary of findings from the Cal/CREDE study of two-way immersion education.* Santa Cruz, CA, and Washington, DC: Center for Research on Education, Diversity, and Excellence.

Jacob, Evelyn, Lori Rottenberg, Sondra Patrick, and Edyth Wheeler. 1996. Cooperative learning: Context and opportunities for acquiring academic English. *TESOL Quarterly* 30 (Summer): 253–80.

Johnson, Donna M. 1983. Natural language learning by design: A classroom experiment in social interaction and second language acquisition. *TESOL Quarterly* 17 (March): 55–68.

Johnson, Karen. 1995. *Understanding communication in second language classrooms.* Cambridge: Cambridge University Press.

Joyce, Bruce, and Beverly Showers. 1983. *Power in staff development through research on training.* Alexandria, VA: Association for Supervision and Curriculum Development.

Joyce, Bruce, Beverly Showers, and Carol Rolheiser-Bennett. 1987. Staff development and student learning: A synthesis of research on models of teaching. *Educational Leadership* 45 (October): 11–23.

Keck, Casey, Gina Iberri-Shea, Nicole Tracy-Ventura, and Safary Wa-Mbaleka. 2006. Investigating the empirical link between task-based interaction and acquisition: A meta-analysis. In *Synthesizing research on language learning and teaching,* ed. John M. Norris and Lourdes Ortega, 91–131. Philadelphia: John Benjamins.

Krashen, Stephen. 1982. *Principles and practice in second language acquisition.* Oxford: Pergamon Press.

Lindholm, Kathryn. 1987. English question use in Spanish-speaking ESL children: Changes with English language proficiency. *Research in the teaching of English* 21 (February): 64–91.

Lindholm-Leary, Kathryn. 2001. *Dual language education.* Clevedon, England: Multilingual Matters.

Loban, Walter. *Language development: Kindergarten through grade twelve* (Research Report No. 18). Urbana, IL: National Council of Teachers of English.

Long, Michael. 1983. Does second language instruction make a difference? A review of research. *TESOL Quarterly* 17 (September): 359–82.

Long, Michael. 1985. *Input and second language acquisition,* ed. Susan Gass and Carolyn Madden, 377–93. Rowley, MA: Newberry House.

Long, Michael. 1996. The role of the linguistic environment in second language acquisition. In *Handbook of research on language acquisition: Second language acquisition,* ed. W. C. Ritchie and T. K. Bahtia, 413–68. New York: Academic Press.

Lyster, Roy. 2004a. Research on form-focused instruction in immersion classrooms: Implications for theory and practice. *Journal of French Language Studies* 14 (November): 321–41.

Lyster, Roy. 2004b. Differential effects of prompts and recasts in form-focused instruction. *Studies in Second Language Acquisition* 26 (September): 399–432.

Lyster, Roy. 2007. *Learning and teaching languages through content: A counterbalanced approach.* Philadelphia: John Benjamins.

Lyster, Roy, and Hirohide Mori. 2006. Interactional feedback and instructional counterbalance. *Studies in Second Language Acquisition* 28: 321–41.

Lyster, Roy, and Leila Ranta. 1997. Corrective feedback and learner uptake: Negotiation of form in communicative classrooms. *Studies in Second Language Acquisition* 19 (March): 37–66.

Malave, Lilliam. 1989. Contextual elements in a bilingual cooperative setting: The experiences of early childhood LEP learners. *NABE Journal* 13: 96–122.

McDougall, Dennis, William Saunders, and Claude Goldenberg. 2007. Inside the black box of school reform: Explaining the how and why of change at getting results schools. *International Journal of Disability, Development and Education* 54 (March): 51–89.

Medina, Marcello, and Kathy Escamilla. 1992. English acquisition by fluent- and limited-Spanish-proficient Mexican-Americans in a 3-year maintenance bilingual program. *Hispanic Journal of Behavioral Sciences* 14 (May): 252–67.

Milk, Roberto. 1982. *Language use in bilingual classrooms: Two case studies.* In On TESOL '81, ed. M. Hines and W. Rutherford, 181–91. Washington, DC: TESOL.

Nassaji, Hossein, and Sandra Fotos. 2004. Current developments in research on the teaching of grammar. *Annual Review of Applied Linguistics* 24 (March): 126–45.

Norris, John M., and Lourdes Ortega. 2000. Effectiveness of L2 instruction: A research synthesis and quantitative meta-analysis. *Language Learning* 50 (September): 417–528.

O'Brien, Gisela. 2007. The instructional features across three different approaches to oral English language development instruction. PhD diss., University of Southern California.

O'Malley, J. Michael, Anna Uhl Chamot, Gloria Stewner-Manzanares, Rocco P. Russo, and Lisa Kupper. 1985. Learning strategy applications with students of English as a second language. *TESOL Quarterly* 19 (September): 557–84.

Parrish, Thomas B., Robert Linquanti, Amy Merikel, Heather Quick, Jennifer Laird, and Phil Esra. 2006. *Effects of the implementation of proposition 227 on the education of English learners, K–12: Findings from a five-year evaluation.* Final Report for AB 56 and AB 1116. San Francisco: American Institutes for Research & WestEd.

Pease-Alvarez, Lucinda, and Adam Winsler. 1994. Cuando el maestro no habla español: Children's bilingual language practices in the classroom. *TESOL Quarterly* 28 (Fall): 507–35.

Peck, Sabrina. 1987. Signs of learning: Child nonnative speakers in tutoring sessions with a child native speaker. *Language Learning* 37 (December): 545–71.

Public Agenda. 2008. *A mission of the heart: Leaders in high-needs districts talk about what it takes to transform a school.* New York: Public Agenda. http://www.publicagenda.org/research/research_reports_details.cfm?list=118

Rodriguez-Brown, Flora. 1987. Questioning patterns and language proficiency in bilingual students. *NABE Journal* 13: 217–33.

Royer, James, and Maria Carlo. 1991. Transfer of comprehension skills from native to second language. *Journal of Reading* 34 (March): 450–55.

Russell, Jane, and Nina Spada. 2006. The effectiveness of corrective feedback for the acquisition of L2 grammar. In *Synthesizing research on language learning and teaching,* ed. John M. Norris and Lourdes Ortega, 133–64. Philadelphia: John Benjamins.

Saunders, William. 1999. Improving literacy achievement for English learners in transitional bilingual programs. *Educational Research and Evaluation* 5 (December): 345–81.

Saunders, William, Barbara Foorman, and Coleen Carlson. 2006. Is a separate block of time for oral English language development in programs of English learners needed? *Elementary School Journal* 107 (November): 181–98.

Saville-Troike, Muriel. 1984. What really matters in second language learning for academic achievement? *TESOL Quarterly* 18 (June): 199–219.

Scarcella, Robin. 2003. *Accelerating academic English: A focus on the English learner.* Oakland: Regents of the University of California.

Short, Deborah, and Shannon Fitzsimmons. 2007. *Double the work: Challenges and solutions to acquiring language and academic literacy for adolescent English language learners.* A report to the Carnegie Corporation of New York. Washington, DC: Alliance for Excellent Education.

Slavin, Robert. 1987. Ability grouping and student achievement in elementary schools: A best-evidence synthesis. *Review of Educational Research* 57 (Fall): 293–336.

Slavin, Robert. 1989. *School and classroom organization*. Hillsdale, NJ: Erlbaum.

Slavin, Robert. 2000. *Educational psychology*. Boston: Allyn & Bacon.

Snow, Catherine E., Herlinda Cancino, Jeanne De Temple, and Sara Schley. 1991. Giving formal definitions: A linguistic or metalinguistic skill? In *Language processing in bilingual children,* ed. Ellen Bialystok, 90–113. Cambridge: Cambridge University Press.

Snow, Catherine, and others. 1987. *Second language learners' formal definitions: An oral language correlate of school literacy* (Tech. Rep. No. 5). Los Angeles: University of California, Center for Language Education and Research.

Spada, Nina, and Patsy Lightbown. 2008. Form-focused instruction: Isolated or integrated? *TESOL Quarterly* 42 (June): 181–207.

Squire, James. 1991. The history of the profession. In *The handbook of research on teaching the English language arts,* ed. James Flood and others, 3–17. New York: Macmillan.

Stevens, Robin, Frances Butler, and Martha Castellon-Wellington. 2000. *Academic English and content assessment: Measuring the progress of ELLs.* (CSE Tec. Rep. No. 552). Los Angeles: University of California, National Center for Research on Evaluation, Standards, and Student Testing (CRESST).

Strong, Michael. 1983. Social styles and the second language acquisition of Spanish-speaking kindergartners. *TESOL Quarterly* 17 (June): 241–58.

Strong, Michael. 1984. Integrative motivation: Cause or result of successful second language acquisition? *Language Learning* 34 (September): 1–13.

Thomas, Wayne, and Virginia Collier. 2002. *A national study of school effectiveness for language minority students' long-term academic achievement final report: Project 1.1.* Santa Cruz, CA, and Washington, DC: Center for Research on Education, Diversity, and Excellence.

Tong, Fuhui, Rafael Lara-Alecio, Beverly Irby, Patricia Mathes, and Oi-man Kwok. 2008. Accelerating early academic oral English development in transitional bilingual and structured English immersion programs. *American Educational Research Journal* 45 (December): 1011–44.

Ulibarri, D. M., M. L. Spencer, and G. A. Rivas. 1981. Language proficiency and academic achievement: A study of language proficiency tests and their relationship to school ratings as predictors of academic achievement. *NABE Journal* 5 (Spring): 47–79.

Valdés, Guadalupe. 2004. Between support and marginalization: The development of academic language in linguistic minority children. *Bilingual Education and Bilingualism* 7: 102–32.

Vandergrift, Larry. 2002. It was nice to see that our predictions were right: Developing metacognition in L2 listening comprehension. *Canadian Modern Language Review/La revue canadienne des langues vivants* 58 (June): 555–75.

Vygotsky, Lev. 1962. *Thought and language.* Cambridge, MA: M.I.T. Press.

Wang, Margaret, Geneva Haertel, and Herbert Walberg. 1993. Toward a knowledge base for school learning. *Review of Educational Research* 63 (Fall): 249–94.

Watson-Gegeo, Karen, and Sarah Nielsen. 2003. Language socialization in SLA. In *The handbook of second language acquisition,* ed. Catherine J. Doughty and Michael H. Long, 155–77. Malden, MA: Blackwell.

Weslander, Darrell, and Gene V. Stephany. 1983. Evaluation of an English as a second language program for southeast Asian students. *TESOL Quarterly* 17 (September): 473–80.

White, Richard, and Richard Tisher. 1986. Research on natural sciences. In *The handbook of research on teaching.* 3rd ed., ed. Merlin Wittrock, 874–905. New York: Macmillan.

Principles of Instructed Language Learning

Principle 1:   Instruction needs to ensure that learners develop both a rich repertoire of formulaic expressions and a rule-based competence.

Principle 2:   Instruction needs to ensure that learners focus predominantly on meaning.

Principle 3:   Instruction needs to ensure that learners also focus on form.

Principle 4:   Instruction needs to be predominantly directed at developing implicit knowledge of the L2 while not neglecting explicit knowledge.

Principle 5:   Instruction needs to take into account the learner's "built-in syllabus."

Principle 6:   Successful instructed language learning requires extensive L2 input.

Principle 7:   Successful instructed language learning also requires opportunities for output.

Principle 8:   The opportunity to interact in the L2 is central to developing L2 proficiency.

Principle 9:   Instruction needs to take account of individual differences in learners.

Principle 10: In assessment of learners' L2 proficiency it is important to examine free as well as controlled production.

Source: Ellis 2005a.

Table 1.2. Studies, Syntheses, and Meta-analyses Cited

	Studies	Syntheses	Meta-analyses
Guidelines Based on Relatively Strong Supporting Evidence from English Learner Research			
1. Providing ELD instruction is better than not providing it.	Thomas and Collier (2002), Tong et al. (2008)	Genesee et al. (2006), Long (1983)	Norris and Ortega (2000)
2. ELD instruction should include interactive activities, but they must be carefully planned and carried out.	August (1987), Johnson (1983), Peck (1987), Cathcart-Strong (1986), Jacob et al. (1996), Tong et al. (2008)	Except for Tong et al. (2008), studies listed to the left are synthesized in Genesee et al. (2006), Lyster (2004a).	Keck et al. (2006), Gersten et al.(2007)[†]
Guidelines Based on Hypotheses Emerging from Recent English Learner Research			
3. A separate block of time should be devoted daily to ELD instruction.	Saunders et al. (2006), O'Brien (2007),Tong et al. (2008)		
4. ELD instruction should emphasize listening and speaking although it can incorporate reading and writing.	Carlisle et al. (1999), Chesterfield et al. (1983), Chesterfield and Chesterfield (1985a), Garcia-Vázquez et al. (1997), Goldstein et al. (1993), Lindholm (1987), Rodriguez-Brown (1987), Royer and Carlo (1991), Saville-Troike (1984), Strong (1983, 1984), Snow et al. (1987), Ulibarri, Spencer, and Rivas (1981)	Studies listed to the left are synthesized in Genesee et al. (2006).	
Importance of oral English proficiency Studies of ELD instruction	Saunders et al. (2006), O'Brien (2007), Tong et al. (2008)		

Note: Citations designated by a dagger symbol indicate analyses that support the practice or guideline for ELD instruction from another domain (e.g., literacy instruction).

Table 1.2 *(continued)*

	Studies	Syntheses	Meta-analyses
5. ELD instruction should explicitly teach elements of English (e.g., vocabulary, syntax, grammar, functions, and conventions).		Genesee et al. (2006)[†]	Norris and Ortega (2000) August and Shanahan, this publication[†]
6. ELD instruction should integrate meaning and communication to support explicit teaching of language.	O'Brien (2007), Tong et al. (2008)	Lyster (2007)	Norris and Ortega (2000)
7. ELD instruction should provide students with corrective feedback on form.	Ammar and Spada (2006); Ellis, Lowen, and Erlam (2006); Lyster (2004b); Lyster and Mori (2006); Lyster and Ranta (1997)	Studies listed to the left are synthesized in Lyster (2007).	Russell and Spada (2006)
8. Use of English during ELD instruction should be maximized; the primary language should be used strategically.	Chesterfield and Chesterfield (1985b); Chesterfield et al. (1983); Malave (1989); Milk (1982); Pease-Alvarez and Winsler (1994)	Studies listed to the left are synthesized in Genesee et al. (2006).	
9. Teachers should attend to communication and language-learning strategies and incorporate them into ELD instruction	Chesterfield and Chesterfield (1985a), O'Malley et al. (1985), and Carrier (2003)	With the exception of Carrier (2003), studies listed to the left are synthesized in Genesee et al. (2006).	

Table 1.2 *(continued)*

	Studies	Syntheses	Meta-analyses
Guidelines Applicable to ELD but Grounded in Non-English Learner Research			
10. ELD instruction should emphasize academic language as well as conversational language. 11. ELD instruction should continue at least until students reach level 4 (early advanced) and possibly through level 5 (advanced).	Hakuta, Butler, and Witt (2000), Howard et al. (2003), Lindholm-Leary (2001), Medina and Escamilla (1992), Thomas and Collier (2002), Weslander and Stephany (1983)	Studies listed to the left are synthesized in Genesee et al. (2006).	
12. ELD instruction should be planned and delivered with specific language objectives in mind.		DuChastel and Merrill (1973), Duell (1974), Gage and Berliner (1975), Slavin (2000)	Norris and Ortega (2000)
13. English learners should be carefully grouped by language proficiency for ELD instruction; for other portions of the school day they should be in mixed classrooms and not in classrooms segregated by language proficiency.		Slavin (1987, 1989)	
14. The likelihood of establishing and/or sustaining an effective ELD instructional program increases when schools and districts make it a priority.	Goldenberg (2004); Good and Brophy (1986); McDougall, Saunders, and Goldenberg (2007); Parrish et al. (2006)	Edmonds (1979), Fullan (2007), Joyce and Showers (1983)	Wang, Haertel, and Walberg (1993)

Note: The studies reviewed for Guidelines 10 and 11 document the plateau effect for oral English proficiency, from which the hypotheses emerge: Explicit ELD instruction should emphasize academic language and should continue through level 4 and possibly 5. There are no studies that actually test these hypotheses.

Table 1.3. Assessments of Relevance and Reliability

	Population relevance of the available studies	Outcome relevance of available studies	Reliability of findings (number of studies)
Guidelines Based on Relatively Strong Supporting Evidence from English Learner Research			
1. Providing ELD instruction is better than not providing it.	**Medium. Includes grades K–12 in Long (1983), Thomas and Collier (2002), and Genesee et al. (2006); Tong et al. (2008) is K and grade 1.	**Medium. Studies listed under population relevance used language proficiency measures. Could not rate higher given the distinctly discrete measures that characterize the studies in Norris and Ortega (2000).	*** High. Includes all studies listed under population relevance, plus the 79 studies from the Norris and Ortega (2000) meta-analysis.
2. ELD instruction should include interactive activities, but they must be carefully planned and carried out.	**Medium. Six K–8 studies with U.S. EL populations, and five studies of students ages 7–14 in immersion programs. Unfortunately, no studies of students in grades 9–12 were conducted.	**Medium. Most of the studies included measures of language proficiency or language use within tasks.	***High. All studies listed under population relevance plus 14 studies of mostly college and adult populations from the Keck et al. (2006) meta-analysis, all converging on the same finding.
Guidelines Based on Hypotheses Emerging from Recent English Learner Research			
3. A separate, daily block of time should be devoted to ELD instruction.	*Low. Saunders et al. (2006), O'Brien (2007), and Tong et al. (2008) focus on K or grade 1 or both with U.S. EL populations, thus covering only a small portion of the K–12 grade span.	***High. All three studies include measures of English language proficiency (CELDT or Woodcock Language Proficiency Battery).	**Medium. Three studies, although they are limited to K and grade 1.

Population: K–12 ELs conducted in the U.S.; **Outcomes:** Progress through ELD levels, or at least achievement along dimensions that map onto English language proficiency (e.g, vocabulary, use of syntax, listening comprehension). **Reliability of findings:** Sufficient number of studies to provide some degree of confidence; * to *** = low to high in relevance or reliability.

Table 1.3 *(continued)*

	Population relevance of the available studies	Outcome relevance of available studies	Reliability of findings (number of studies)
4. ELD instruction should emphasize listening and speaking although it can incorporate reading and writing. *Importance of English oral proficiency* *Studies of ELD instruction*	**Medium. About a dozen studies, mostly involving U.S. EL populations spanning grades K–6. Only two include students in grades 8–12.	***High. All studies use measures of English language proficiency.	**Medium. Sufficient number of studies producing consistent results at least across grades 1–6.
	*Low. Saunders et al. (2006), O'Brien (2007), and Tong et al. (2008) focus on K and/or grade 1 with U.S. EL populations, thus covering only a small portion of the K–12 grade span.	***High. All three studies include measures of English language proficiency (CELDT or Woodcock Language Proficiency Battery).	**Medium. Three studies, although limited to K and grade 1.
5. ELD instruction should explicitly teach elements of English (e.g., vocabulary, syntax, grammar, functions, and conventions).	*Low. Few studies with K–12 U.S. EL population.	*Low. Few studies use broad measures of language proficiency; rather, used discrete measures of the language skill taught.	***High. Based on 79 studies from Norris and Ortega (2000) and also similar findings found for reading (Genesee et al. 2006 and Shanahan and August, this publication).
6. ELD instruction should integrate meaning and communication to support explicit teaching of language.	*Low. O'Brien (2007) and Tong et al. (2008) integrate meaning to support language learning but focuses only on K and grade 1. Very few studies in the Norris and Ortega meta-analysis and studies reviewed by Lyster include K–12 U.S. EL populations.	**Medium. O'Brien (2007) and Tong et al. (2008) measured language proficiency (CELDT, Woodcock), and many of the French immersion studies reviewed by Lyster measured multiple aspects of proficiency and communicative competence. Very few of the studies in the Norris and Ortega meta-analysis used broader measures of language proficiency.	**Medium. With college-age students and adults, Norris and Ortega (2000) found similar effect sizes for integration of meaning (focus on form) and its absence (focus on forms). Based on his review of studies of Immersion contexts, Lyster (2007) concluded that integrating meaning through the study of content positively contributes to language learning but also has some limitations.

Table 1.3 *(continued)*

	Population relevance of the available studies	Outcome relevance of available studies	Reliability of findings (number of studies)
7. ELD instruction should provide students with corrective feedback on form.	*Low. Only one of the studies reviewed by Lyster (2006) includes a relevant population: Ammar and Spada (2006), grade 6 ESL. Others are adult or French immersion. Russell and Spada (2006) do not report the age or grade level of the subjects in their studies.	*Low. Two of the three studies reviewed by Lyster (2006) measured multiple aspects of proficiency (Ammar and Spada 2006 and Lyster 2004). Unfortunately, Russell and Spada do not report the nature of the measures used in their studies.	***High. All 15 studies meta-analyzed by Russell and Spada (2006) favored corrective feedback over no corrective feedback; 10 of the 15 studies produced high effect sizes.
8. Use of English during ELD instruction should be maximized; the primary language should be used strategically.	*Low. The five studies reviewed all include U.S. EL populations but include only preK through grade 4 contexts, and not specifically ELD instructional contexts but more generally classroom context studies.	*Low. Only one of the studies actually measured English proficiency. The other four measured language choice of teacher and students—which is relevant to the guideline as a mediating variable (more English use) but not actually an outcome variable (higher proficiency).	*Low. Five studies all found that the dominant language of the classroom influences students' language choices, but only one study documented a positive relationship between English language use and increases in English proficiency.
9. Teachers should attend to communication and language-learning strategies and incorporate them into ELD instruction	*Low. Both studies include U.S. EL populations but covered only portions of the K–12 span: preK–1 (Chesterfield and Chesterfield, 1985a) and high school (O'Malley et al. 1985; Carrier 2003).	*Low. Chesterfield and Chesterfield (1985a) document the hierarchical nature of strategies which is relevant; but only O'Malley et al. (1985) and Carrier (2003) measured facets of proficiency as outcomes of teaching language-learning strategies	*Low. Only two studies demonstrate positive effects of teaching language-learning strategies (O'Malley et al. 1985; Carrier 2003).

Table 1.3 *(continued)*

	Population relevance of the available studies	Outcome relevance of available studies	Reliability of findings (number of studies)
10. ELD instruction should emphasize academic language as well as conversational language. 11. ELD instruction should continue at least until students reach level 4 (early advanced) and possibly through level 5 (advanced).	**Medium. All six studies include U.S. EL populations; however, five of the six include K–5 students and only one includes secondary school students.	**Medium. All include measures of English language proficiency, albeit, oral English proficiency.	**Medium. All six studies support the finding for K–5 students and oral proficiency that ELs tend to plateau and progress is slower moving from levels 3 to 4 and 5; only one study demonstrates the same for secondary-level students.
	Note: The studies reviewed for Guidelines 10 and 11 document the plateau effect for oral English proficiency, from which the hypotheses emerge: ELD instruction should emphasize academic language, and ELD instruction should continue through level 4 and possibly 5. There are no studies that actually test these hypotheses.		

Guidelines Applicable to ELD but Grounded in Non-English Learner Research

	Population relevance of the available studies	Outcome relevance of available studies	Reliability of findings (number of studies)
12. ELD instruction should be planned and delivered with specific language objectives in mind.	*Low. Most of the syntheses are based on studies of non-EL populations or non K–12 EL populations.	*Low. None of the studies or syntheses cited focused on English language proficiency.	**Medium. There were many studies in the four syntheses and one meta-analysis, but they produce mixed results that generally favor the use of objectives but not definitively.
13. English learners should be carefully grouped by language proficiency for ELD instruction; for other portions of the school day they should be in mixed classrooms and not in classrooms segregated by language proficiency.	* Low. All syntheses are based on studies of non-EL populations.	* Low. None of the studies or syntheses cited focused on English language proficiency.	** Medium. There were two syntheses of several studies.

Table 1.3 *(continued)*

	Population relevance of the available studies	Outcome relevance of available studies	Reliability of findings (number of studies)
14. The likelihood of establishing and/or sustaining an effective ELD instructional program increases when schools and districts make it a priority.	**Medium. Most syntheses are based on studies of non-EL populations; three studies include U.S. EL populations (Goldenberg 2004; McDougall et al. 2007; Parrish et al. 2006)	*Low. None of the studies or syntheses cited focused on English language proficiency.	***High. Large number of syntheses and studies producing fairly consistent results.

All sources used for this chapter are empirical studies (primary studies) or included syntheses and meta-analyses that analyzed the effects of specific independent variables on measured dependent variables.

Chapter 2

English Language Development: Foundations and Implementation in Kindergarten Through Grade Five

Marguerite Ann Snow, California State University, Los Angeles
Anne Katz, School for International Training

This chapter addresses instruction for English learners in kindergarten through grade five (K–5) who are in the process of acquiring English as a second language in school. These young learners need to develop English language proficiency—the ability to use English for all their communicative purposes—in listening, speaking, reading, and writing. For successful functioning in each of those domains, students require proficiency with vocabulary, syntax (grammar), phonology (sounds and sound patterns), and morphology (or how prefixes and suffixes indicate word meanings and grammatical roles). Students also must develop the skills to participate effectively in oral and written discourse of many kinds, including narrating experiences; engaging in conversation; interacting appropriately in discussions and argumentation; and using language to seek and represent new information.

> The main goal of English language development (ELD) in school is to ensure that students develop the levels of English proficiency required to succeed academically.

The main goal of English language development (ELD) in school is to ensure that students develop the levels of English proficiency required to succeed academically. Whereas the focus of ELD is on academic language development, proficiency also includes the social and pragmatic uses of language that enable learners to use English to meet their communicative needs. The challenge for these learners is tremendous. They must simultaneously acquire all aspects of English while concurrently learning grade-level subject matter usually taught through the medium of English.[1] Because they are also young learners, language development is intertwined with cognitive and social development.

This chapter provides a picture of both the foundations undergirding ELD instruction in K–5 (hereafter referred to as ELD K–5) and the many challenging facets of implementation. In the foundations section that follows, we discuss the roles of primary language and sociocultural factors in school success. We then draw on relevant research in second-language acquisition and its implications for ELD K–5. Moving on to implementation, we provide a rationale for standards-based instruction and assessment in ELD and English–language arts; briefly examine an approach to weaving academic language into other areas of elementary instruction; and provide many examples of strategies for teaching ELD in each skill area. Next, we present excerpts from actual lesson plans that demonstrate how standards and instructional strategies are applied in ELD K–5. We close the chapter with a discussion of the implications for professional development.

The term *instructed* ELD will be used throughout this chapter to describe the systematic, explicit instruction of English that takes place during designated ELD time periods in organized, regularly scheduled time blocks as part of the English learner program. Hence, the focus here is on instruction in English language skills per se for the express purpose of preparing students for the myriad uses of language requisite for full transition to English–language arts (ELA) and mainstream content instruction. From this perspective, ELD is its own content area, guided by standards and mandated assessments, and focusing on the aspects of English not typically covered at home or in subject-matter instruction (cf. Table 1.1, Chapter 1). The school day offers many potentially rich environments for English learners to learn English—on the playground, in a science lesson, at the school library. However, ELD time focuses specifically and formally on language development. (See Saunders and Goldenberg, this publication, for a detailed discussion of the research base for ELD.)

Although we focus on instructed ELD, we also discuss what constitutes an overall approach to instruction of English learners because we believe that successful learning—of English and academics—depends upon an integrated program that reflects an understanding of how many factors interact to promote or deter students' progress in both realms (see also the discussion by Dutro and Kinsella, this publication).

ELD instruction can be configured in many ways. It generally takes place during a designated ELD time block (for example, 20 minutes in kindergarten and up to an

---

1. Ten percent of California's English learners are enrolled in alternative bilingual programs and about 35 percent in English-medium programs that claim to provide primary language support.

hour in grade five). It may occur during the time allotted to ELA; in this case, English learners are grouped for separate ELD instruction. ELD instruction also takes place in structured English immersion classes, during sheltered content instruction, in bilingual classrooms, or in mainstream classes. Students may be grouped by proficiency levels within a grade level so that a teacher instructs one or two levels of students for the ELD period. In some schools, ELD instruction takes the form of a pullout program where English learners leave the regular classroom for a specified period of time. Finally, it may take place in the regular classroom, where teachers "team" to cover certain subjects or during the ELD portion of a dual-language program. Regardless of the instructional configuration, a specified ELD time allows teachers to deliver explicit English instruction designed specifically for English learners' levels of proficiency. Instructed ELD complements informal instruction that happens throughout the school day in spontaneous situations where the skillful teacher takes full advantage of every opportunity for teachable moments. (See Guideline 1 in Saunders and Goldenberg, this publication.) Because English learners enter school with a wide range of backgrounds, instructed ELD of necessity requires that students be grouped according to English language proficiency levels and that teachers tailor instruction appropriate to those levels. In California, proficiency levels are aligned with those specified by the California English Language Development Test (CELDT): beginning to advanced. The five proficiency levels are described below.

> **Regardless of the instructional configuration, a specified ELD time allows teachers to deliver explicit English instruction designed specifically for English learners' levels of proficiency.**

CELDT Proficiency Levels

Beginning: Students performing at this level may demonstrate little or no receptive or productive English skills. They are beginning to understand a few concrete details during unmodified instruction. They may be able to respond to some communication and learning demands but with many errors. Oral and written production is usually limited to disconnected words and memorized statements and questions. Frequent errors make communication difficult.

Early Intermediate: Students performing at this level continue to develop receptive and productive English skills. They are able to identify and understand more concrete details during unmodified instruction. They may be able to respond with increasing ease to more varied communication and learning demands with a reduced number of errors. Oral and written production is usually limited to phrases and memorized statements and questions. Frequent errors still reduce communication.

Intermediate: Students performing at this level begin to tailor their English language skills to meet communication and learning demands with increasing accuracy. They are able to identify and understand more concrete details and some major abstract concepts during unmodified instruction. They are able to respond with increasing ease to more varied communication and learning demands with a reduced number of errors. Oral and written production has usually expanded to sentences, paragraphs, and original statements and questions. Errors still complicate communication.

Early Advanced: Students performing at this level begin to combine the elements of the English language in complex, cognitively demanding situations and are able to use English as a means for learning in the content areas. They are able to identify and summarize most concrete details and abstract concepts during unmodified instruction in most content areas. Oral and written production is characterized by more elaborate discourse and fully developed paragraphs and compositions. Errors are less frequent and rarely complicate communication.

Advanced: Students performing at this level communicate effectively with various audiences in a wide range of familiar and new topics to meet social and learning demands. For students at this level to attain the English proficiency of their native English-speaking peers, further linguistic enhancement and refinement are still necessary. Students at this level are able to identify and summarize concrete details and abstract concepts during unmodified instruction in all content areas. Oral and written production reflects discourse appropriate for content areas. Errors are infrequent and do not reduce communication (CELDT Assistance Packet 2008).

Foundations of ELD Instruction for Young Learners

In this section, we discuss three areas of research and theory on instruction for English learners: primary language, sociocultural background, and the second-language acquisition process itself. As acknowledged in Chapter 1 (Saunders and Goldenberg), a considerable amount of recommended practice rests on theory more than on research; however, there is research that points to the importance of these three areas.

Primary Language

Young English learners entering U.S. schools bring with them knowledge and skills learned in their primary language and linked to their home communities (Genesee et al. 2006; Miramontes, Nadeau, and Commins 1997). As Saunders and Goldenberg (this publication) note, students' primary languages are intellectual, social, and personal resources. Concepts and words learned in the primary language can form a foundation for parallel learning in the second language (cf. Genesee et al. 2006).

Knowledge of word formation (e.g., compounding by combining two words, such as *blue* and *berry* to form *blueberry*) may be applicable across languages—as it is for English, Cantonese, Mandarin, and Korean (McBride-Chang et al. 2008). And students who maintain and develop their primary or home language also benefit from the continued ability to communicate with parents and other family members whose English may not be fully developed (see Wong Fillmore 1991).

Young English learners entering U.S. schools bring with them knowledge and skills learned in their primary language and linked to their home communities.

Students' sense of identity and self is embedded in the language learned as infants in the familiar surroundings of family and home (Ricento 2005). Teachers' attitudes toward students' primary language can affect students' motivation to learn English or to maintain the primary language (Lee and Oxelson 2006). The school community, including teachers, school staff, and site administrators, can create a climate in which students' primary languages and cultures are valued and viewed as resources. Members of the school community can demonstrate an openness to differences and empathy for students and their families adjusting to the new environment; the school can also communicate a sense that English learners and their families are full-fledged members of the school community (Trumbull et al. 2001).

In addition, classroom teachers can serve as cultural brokers, assisting English learners and their families as they integrate into a new or unfamiliar school system (Cooper, Denner, and Lopez 1999). Those efforts can contribute to creating a safe and supportive learning environment for young learners, a place where they can take risks as they learn a new language and understand how to interact appropriately and effectively.

To truly demonstrate that English learners' language and culture are valued, teachers can provide strategic opportunities for students to use their native languages at school even when English is the main language of instruction. Lucas and Katz (1994) found that, in exemplary programs, students are encouraged to use their primary language to assist one another, tutor other students, interact socially, ask/answer questions, write in the primary language, and use bilingual dictionaries. Teachers who speak the students' primary language use it to check comprehension, translate terms, and interact socially with students. In the larger school context, exemplary schools provide instruction in the students' native culture and history, libraries maintain collections of native language books, teachers encourage parents to read to their children in the native language at home and to be actively involved in school activities, and schools communicate with parents in the first language. Through such activities, members of the entire school community serve as advocates for English learners and their families.

Since literacy development is a process that begins early in childhood before students attend school, it is affected by the primary-language foundation of English learners (see the discussion in August and Shanahan, this publication). Several factors have been shown to relate closely to school success in literacy development, among them literacy-related skills

The degree of children's native-language proficiency is a strong predictor of their English-language development.

at school entry, oral language skills including vocabulary, and background knowledge (Lesaux and Geva 2006). Umbel and Oller (1994) found that among Spanish-speaking students, those with better Spanish vocabularies also had better English vocabularies, highlighting the importance of encouraging language-minority parents to interact verbally and read to their children at home. August and Hakuta (1997), in their National Research Council report, underscored these findings: "the degree of children's native-language proficiency is a strong predictor of their English-language development" (p. 28). Bailey and others (2007) emphasize this important point for teachers of English learners: ". . . the closer a student's home language matches the language used in school, the less likely the schism between academic uses of language and everyday uses of language" (p. 110).

In other words, students' exposure to literate practices at home in their first language, especially ones that engage higher-order cognitive processes, facilitates the development of literacy; conversely, English learners who have limited exposure to literacy activities in their first language may need additional assistance in ELD.

Sociocultural Considerations and Parental and Community Support

Effective schooling for English learners begins with an understanding of their backgrounds. The English learner population in California's schools, indeed in U.S. schools in general, comes with a complex mosaic of languages, native countries and cultures, familial circumstances, and educational experiences. Other factors, such as socioeconomic status, family support and expectations, and social challenges, affect English learners and their chances for school success (Snow 2005a). In addition, students coming from rural, poor, or war-torn countries may have gaps in their education. In other cases, the high transiency rate of migrant worker families, the pressures of undocumented status, family situations such as living and child care arrangements, and the need to return to the home country during the school year can create serious challenges in school (Walqui 2000).

English learners can also differ in terms of age of arrival. They generally fall into three broad categories:

(1) early immigrants,

(2) recent immigrants, and

(3) U.S.-born students.

These three types of students differ along a number of dimensions, perhaps the most critical of which is the degree to which they have been exposed to literacy practices or have developed literacy skills in their native language. For example, U.S.-born children who speak a minority language may come to school with little prior schooling in their primary language and, if they live in ethnic communities, often have little exposure to English in their daily lives. By contrast, recent immigrants may have received schooling in their primary language, if they arrive in later elementary school.

Collier (1987) found that children who arrive in the U.S. between the ages of four and seven and are schooled exclusively in English may need up to five years to reach the same levels of academic achievement as older English learners who have had some instruction in their native languages. Indeed, ELD teachers in the K–5 setting will observe considerable variation among their students depending on age of arrival, grade placement, extent and types of literacy practices in the home, and amount of schooling in their native countries. (See Dutro and Kinsella, this publication, for a discussion of the different pathways English learners take in U.S. schools.)

Given this incredible diversity, what can be done in the K–5 context to ensure that English learners have access to excellent schools that are responsive to their particular needs? In a synthesis of studies on academic achievement among second-language learners, Lindholm-Leary and Borsato (2006) note that schools with high-quality programs have a cohesive schoolwide vision, shared goals with expectations for achievement, and a clear instructional focus on and commitment to achievement. Findings on effective programs for English learners are consistent with research on effective schools for mainstream students. In particular, studies of effective schools for English learner populations share the following finding: educational personnel hold the belief that all children can learn. Other findings were as follows: The school climate is orderly and safe; there is a warm, caring community; the curriculum is academically challenging; and the program model is informed by sound theory and best practices (Lindholm-Leary and Borsato 2006).

Research by Berman and others (1995) identified similar features of effective schools and also noted that effective schools for English learners make a

> ELD teachers in the K–5 setting will observe considerable variation among their students depending on age of arrival, grade placement, extent and types of literacy practices in the home, and amount of schooling in their native countries.

conscious effort to hire bilingual staff members, communicate with parents in their native language, and honor the multicultural quality of the student population. Miramontes, Nadeau, and Commins (1997) suggest further that outreach to the English learner community must include clear patterns of communication; strategies for making parents welcome in schools and involving them integrally in making decisions; appointment of liaisons to the community; and careful planning for ways to use minority languages at meetings that include parents. Research on involving immigrant parents in the schooling process supports the recommendations and points also to the importance of understanding families' goals and values from their own perspective (see Lott 2003; Ramirez 2003; Trumbull et al. 2007).

Second-Language Acquisition Processes

Second-language acquisition theory and research illuminate key processes that enhance our understanding of how learners acquire their second language. From these, we can draw implications for the teaching of young English learners in ELD K–5.

Developmental Stages. Studies of second-language learners reveal that they generally follow a common route in the acquisition of the second language. In other words, they generally learn grammatical forms in a fairly set order. The route of second-language acquisition parallels that identified by studies in which young children learning their first language exhibit a rather consistent order of acquisition of grammatical forms. Thus, just as children go through stages when they learn their first language (e.g., babbling, one-word and two-word utterances, questions, negatives), second-language learners work their way through a number of developmental stages from the use of very basic grammar and vocabulary in the earliest stages to progressively more elaborate versions of *interlanguage*—the language produced by a nonnative speaker, which is composed of elements of the learner's first language and the target language (e.g., English) (Selinker 1972). Early in acquisition, second-language learners use, for example, the *ing* form in verbs such as *running* or *writing*. They may use a word such as *many* to show more than one and produce phrases such as "many book" or "many girl" to indicate the plural before they apply the plural morpheme *s* with the noun to produce the correct forms *books* or *girls*.

Next in the developmental sequence might come the past tense verb forms such as *-ed* in *painted*. For a while, second-language learners may overgeneralize the regular past tense to all verbs in English, producing forms such as "goed" or "writed" before they master both regular and irregular verbs (Selinker, Swain, and Dumas 1975).

Research also reveals that, while the route of acquisition is quite consistent across second-language learners with different primary languages, the *rate,* or speed, at

The language faculty is said to be triggered by the input the young child receives from his or her caregivers. which learners progress varies greatly and may depend on factors such as age, motivation, exposure to input, aptitude, and learning style (Ellis 1994; Saunders and O'Brien 2006). As second-language learners advance through those developmental stages, they achieve closer and closer approximations of the second language (Gass and Selinker 2001), and thus their interlanguage bears closer resemblance to standard features of English. English learners, for example, might first express negation with a form such as "I no have paper" before producing "I don't have paper," as they internalize input they receive and make adjustments in their interlanguage system.

Implications for ELD instruction K–5. The notion of developmental stages has led to a variety of schemas for teachers that describe the typical stages that they might expect from their students and that can guide instruction and assessment. In the *English-Language Development Standards for California Public Schools* (2002), the stages of ELD are designated as follows: Beginning, Early Intermediate, Intermediate, Early Advanced, and Advanced. The California English Language Development Test (CELDT), previously described, utilizes the same basic schema for assessing English learners. Similarly, the *PreK–12 English Language Proficiency Standards* (2006) published by Teachers of English to Speakers of Other Languages has five levels: Level 1 (Starting), Level 2 (Emerging), Level 3 (Developing), Level 4 (Expanding), and Level 5 (Bridging). Whatever schema is used, the main implications for teachers of English learners are that their students will most likely move through stages, that the stages share certain characteristics, that the rate of development may vary, and that delivery of instruction and methods of assessment must take into account students' varying levels of proficiency in English. Thus, English learners are not always developmentally ready to perform the tasks expected of monolingual students during English–language arts instruction.

Age Factor. Common lore has it that children learn second languages more quickly and easily than adults. According to the Critical Period Hypothesis (Lenneberg 1967), children learn languages more quickly and easily than adults because their brains are more flexible—that is, the cortex of their brains is more plastic than that of adults. Lenneberg's theory was aligned with that of Chomsky (1957, 1965) and his followers, who posited that humans possess an innate language faculty, known popularly as the "language acquisition device." Chomsky and his followers have asserted that all children are born with access to a "universal grammar," a biological blueprint for language. The language faculty is said to be triggered by the input the young child receives from his or her caregivers. This perspective on language acquisition as a natural, biologically based process has had a powerful influence on views of second-language acquisition and instruction. Among second-language-acquisition theorists, debate has centered on whether adolescent and adult learners have full access to the innate blueprint that is readily accessible to children and young learners (Mitchell and Myles 2004).

Research in second-language acquisition has shown that young learners are not necessarily superior in language learning (Gass and Selinker 2001). McLaughlin (1992), in fact, labels this a myth in need of debunking, noting that experimental research in which children have been compared with adults in informal and formal settings has revealed that adolescents and adults perform better on many types of tasks (e.g., identifying correct morphological and grammatical structures) or tasks where they must use language to negotiate meaning. Older learners benefit from having a fully developed cognitive system; they are not learning to think while still learning both their first and second languages simultaneously as is the case with young learners. They, therefore, can bring to bear on second-language learning the cognitive and analytical skills they possess as more experienced learners in general.

> **Research in second-language acquisition has shown that young learners are not necessarily superior in language learning.**

However, young children have demonstrated consistent superiority in second-language learning in two areas: the ability to develop native-like pronunciation of the second language and to develop proficiency with grammatical structures (Johnson and Newport 1989; Munro and Mann 2005; Newport, Bavelier, and Neville 2001). This research supports the contention that the earlier a child is exposed to a new language, the more likely he or she is to develop proficiency with both the sound system and the grammatical system of that language. Many children have an accent in the new language if they begin to learn it past the age of seven (Munro and Mann 2005). It is important, however, to keep in mind that children who sound as though they possess native-like fluency may not actually be fully proficient in the range of skills in English needed to be successful in school.

Implications for EL instruction K–5. Teachers should not underestimate the task at hand for young English learners. Language learning is a complex process; learning a second language is a formidable undertaking. Further, as McLaughlin (1992) pointed out, children do not have access to the memory techniques and other analytical strategies that more experienced learners can apply to learning the required elements of language: phonology, morphology, syntax, semantics, and pragmatics. Children may be shy and embarrassed about making mistakes in front of peers. In fact, the so-called affective variables—attitudes, motivation, language anxiety—and

individual differences in personality and what researchers term "willingness to communicate" (MacIntyre et al. 2002) can affect children as well as adults learning a second language. Teachers of ELD K–5, therefore, have a critical, supportive role to play: encouraging students to communicate in English and guiding them through their linguistic stages while also recognizing the challenge of learning an additional language at any age.

Input, Output, and Interaction. Theorists hold different views on the relative contributions of *input* (language available to the learner through exposure), *output* (learner production of the language), and *interaction* (conversation in the language) for second-language acquisition. Research suggests, however, that all three play a key role (Ellis 2005a). Krashen (1985), in his "Input Hypothesis," coined the term *comprehensible input*—language input that is slightly ahead of the learner's current state of knowledge. Krashen's position is that only comprehensible input facilitates second-language acquisition. In other words, input containing structures that learners already know or structures well beyond the learner's current state of knowledge are not useful to the acquisition process.

Swain (1985) countered Krashen's input hypothesis with the notion of "comprehensible output," arguing that input alone is not sufficient for second-language acquisition. In her 2005 update, she outlined three functions of output:

    (1) Noticing or Triggering

    (2) Hypothesis Testing

    (3) Metalinguistic or Reflection

Long (1983) asserted with his Interaction Hypothesis the importance of interaction—the notion that interaction in the target language facilitates acquisition of that language. The work of Swain (1985, 2001) and Swain and Lapkin (1998, 2008) underscores the importance, for progress in acquisition, of giving students many opportunities to speak and write in the second language. Swain (1985) argued that when second-language learners listen or read, they concentrate on *semantic* analysis of the message (i.e., getting the meaning). However, when learners speak and write, they must engage in *syntactic* analysis of their intended message. In other words, they must make grammatical and lexical choices and are usually more aware of correctness.

In a series of investigations with English-speaking students studying in French immersion classes in the upper elementary through secondary levels, Swain and Lapkin designed collaborative tasks such as dictogloss, jigsaw, role play, and reformulation,[2] which required students to extend their language output. In these tasks, students had to *notice* the target language while attempting to produce it, use their output as a means of hypothesis formulation and testing, and then negotiate meaning around the task by engaging in "metatalk"—use their second language (French, in this case) to reflect on language use. Students were not only engaged with input and output but also interacting with each other. Tasks that require use of particular target language forms have been shown to be more effective in promoting acquisition of the forms (see Keck et al. 2006, cited in Saunders and Goldenberg, this publication).

From a psycholinguistic point of view, it is believed that interaction allows second-language learners to "fine-tune" the language they are receiving in order to progress toward target language (e.g., English) norms (Mitchell and Myles 2004). In this view, interaction serves the function of providing more input to the learner. Saunders and O'Brien (2006) cite studies showing that increased language use and interaction are associated with increased language development over a given period of time.

From the perspective of sociolinguistic views of interaction, learning is fundamentally a social process in which learners' identity and language knowledge are constructed collaboratively during the course of interaction (cf. Lantolf and Thorne 2007). Hall (1995) characterizes the learner as an apprentice of a range of language and cultural practices; others have investigated the interactions between expert and less-expert users to find instances of scaffolding—that is, how the expert user creates supports through interaction that assist the less-expert second-language learner in using the second language for communication.

Increasing research on second-language instruction points to the need to focus on form, sometimes very explicitly, not just incidentally or implicitly—in the way that Swain and Lapkin (1998, 2008) have discussed. There is a growing complaint that accuracy is being sacrificed for fluency in many ELD programs; of course, students need both (Alcón 2004). There is argument about whether teaching form in a meaningful activity is important or whether isolated form instruction is more effective (Spada and Lightbown 2008). It seems likely that younger students would be more responsive to an interesting, engaging set of activities that includes form instruction.

---

2. These collaborative tasks all require students to use the second language interactively in pairs or groups, take on specific roles (jigsaw and role play), and reflect on jointly produced language (dictogloss and reformulation). Dictoglass entails students' reconstructing what another person (usually the teacher) has said or read to the group (Rost 2005, 509). Jigsaw activities are ones in which students work cooperatively by taking on different portions of a larger task, then combining their solutions (Kagan 1989). Role play involves students in responding to a situational prompt, whether for the purpose of assessment or promoting language use between students (Kasper and Roever 2005).

Task-based instruction allows a focus on form (Ellis 2005b). Tasks can be designed to elicit particular grammatical forms: for example, a narrative versus an argumentative task will tend to call upon different grammatical forms (Ellis 2005b).

Ellis (2005b) cites research showing that a "structured input" approach has been shown to be effective, and it is one that appears to be more appropriate for young language learners than some others. "[Structured] [i]nstruction requires learners to process L2 data that has been specially designed to induce 'noticing' of the targeted form and that can only be comprehended if the targeted form has been processed" (Ellis 2005b, 716). Ellis contrasts this "discovery" approach to more "didactic" approaches that focus on rules or understanding a targeted form. This is parallel to what Saunders and Goldenberg (this publication) refer to as an "inductive" approach.

> A key component of successful language instruction is teacher feedback to students about the accuracy of their language.

Lyster (2004a), reporting his comparative analysis of five research studies with French immersion students in Canada ages seven to fourteen, concluded that form-focused instruction was most effective when it included "a balanced distribution of opportunities for noticing, language awareness and controlled practice with feedback" (p. 321).

A key component of successful language instruction is teacher feedback to students about the accuracy of their language (see Saunders and Goldenberg, this publication, Guideline 7). A meta-analysis of studies on the effectiveness of corrective feedback concluded that it is both beneficial and enduring in its impact (Russell and Spada 2006). The majority of the studies cited were conducted with high school and college students, not the population addressed in this chapter. However, Lyster's (2004b) findings in a study with 179 fifth-graders are consonant with Russell and Spada's conclusions (2006).

Feedback can be implicit, as is the case when the teacher recasts a student utterance (Student: "Mommy taked me to the doctor." Teacher: "Oh, your mommy took you to the doctor?"). But research suggests that many language learners do not notice such implied corrections (Lyster and Ranta 1997) without the teacher's making it clear that the recast is not simply to foster communication but, instead, to make a correction (Han and Kim 2008).

Other forms of feedback, such as elicitations of the correct form and metalinguistic cues (e.g., "How do we show it happened in the past?") have been shown to be more effective for both short-term and long-term language learning (Lyster 2004). (See Saunders and Goldenberg, this publication, for definitions and discussion of *recast, elicitation, metalinguistic feedback, clarification request, explicit correction,* and related research.) Many teachers hesitate to give direct feedback or to correct students, fearing that it will discourage or embarrass them. Seedhouse (2001, 368–69) observes:

> Teachers are avoiding direct and overt negative evaluation of learners' linguistic errors with the best intentions in the world, namely to avoid embarrassing and demotivating them. However, in doing so, they are interactionally marking linguistic errors as embarrassing and problematic. (Cited in Ellis 2005b, 719.)

Implications for ELD instruction K–5. One key implication of research on second-language acquisition is that some learners need a silent period in which they accept input before producing language. For young learners, the silent period may be a very important stage, allowing English learners to develop their new language system without pressure to use it right away. Teachers of English learners should not confuse this silent period with lack of progress. Just as children learning their native language have a silent period of about two years before beginning to talk, a silent period allows English learners to attend to the incoming input, formulate internal hypotheses about the target language, and ultimately prepare themselves to use the second language productively. During this period, teachers should provide as much rich language input as possible. When English learners begin to use their English, teachers can encourage oral language production, especially in the lower elementary grade levels. All four language skills can be taught in an integrated fashion as students progress in their language development; however, during dedicated ELD instruction, oral language should be emphasized (see Guideline 4 in Saunders and Goldberg, this publication).

> **One key implication of research on second-language acquisition is that some learners need a silent period in which they accept input before producing language.**

The major implication of input/output/interaction research for teachers of ELD K–5 is that English learners need rich language environments for second-language acquisition to take place. Learners need to be exposed to authentic input through multiple means (e.g., books, songs, pictures, charts, audiotapes and videotapes, shared reading, visual arts, storytelling) and given opportunities to attend to meaning as they expand their language system. However, input alone is not sufficient. English learners also need to use the language productively—to speak and write it—in order to extend their syntactic and morphological development. As discussed, English learners will exhibit stages in which they use formulaic patterns such as "I no go" or other fixed sequences of words that can be produced somewhat automatically (Ellis 2005a). With opportunities for extended input and output, learners will gradually begin to approximate correct target forms, though there may still be some variability

as they work out the new language system. Teachers should employ a variety of grouping strategies other than teaching to the whole group because participation in small groups and pairs increases the amount of input and output to which English learners are exposed (McGroarty and Calderón 2005).

Explicit Instruction. A prevailing belief in the last two decades is that second-language learners do not benefit from explicit instruction in language, that language learning is incidental, and that learners, especially young learners, will eventually work things out through implicit learning. Current research contradicts this position, finding that explicit instruction in language per se and tailored to students' ELD levels[3] may be beneficial, providing direction to teachers of ELD K–5 (Norris and Ortega 2006). (See Guidelines 1, 5, and 6 in Saunders and Goldenberg, this publication.)

Implications for ELD instruction K–5. Explicit instruction should consist of cycles of explanation and practice of language skills (listening, reading, speaking, writing) and other elements of language (e.g., grammar, vocabulary, language functions). As Saunders and Goldenberg (this publication) mention, explicit instruction can also take the form of presenting students with examples and supporting them to identify the rules/regularities represented. VanPatten and Williams (2007) theorize that learners process linguistic information unconsciously until they acquire the rules, at which point they need practice opportunities to apply the rules to new instances. Scarcella (2003) observes: "The most efficient way to teach English is to provide direct instruction with clear explanations, expose students to the language features being taught, provide students with multiple opportunities to practice the features, and give supportive feedback on errors" (p. 10). Sociocultural theories of second-language acquisition that rely heavily on Vygotsky's (1979) principles view explicit instruction as beneficial, especially if it involves instruction that fosters social connections between teachers and students and between English learners and more expert peers (Lantolf and Thorne 2007).

Dutro and Moran (2003) advocate "front-loading" of language that students need in language arts and other curricular subjects. Teachers first determine the language demands of the upcoming subject matter and use ELD time to teach grammar, vocabulary, and language functions so that students are prepared in advance to engage with the key concepts and class activities and assignments (see Dutro and Kinsella, this publication, for a more detailed discussion; cf. Saunders and Goldenberg Guidelines 5 and 12). Chen and Mora-Flores (2006) provide an example of explicit instruction of language. They advocate giving students frames that show them how

---

3. Some research has shown that even when grammar instruction is not perfectly matched to students' developmental levels but is beyond their current level, it can result in learning (Ellis 2005b).

language functions are expressed in English. For example, the teacher can introduce such language functions to English learners in the lower elementary grade levels as "It sounds like . . ." to talk about ways to identify objects, and "In the beginning . . . next . . . finally . . ." to show steps or events in a sequence. By the upper grade levels, students can learn more complex phrases for language functions such as ". . . belongs in this category because . . ." for classification, or "I believe the author is trying to say that . . ." for drawing inferences.

Designing ELD Instruction and Assessment

In designing instruction and assessment, teachers of ELD K–5–like all teachers–deal with certain key questions about how to design practice that meets the needs of their students:

⊙ What aspects of language do I teach?

⊙ How do I know if students are learning?

⊙ How can I integrate ELD with content learning?

⊙ How can I teach effectively?

This section addresses approaches to answering those questions in the context of instruction for English learners in elementary classrooms. Figure 2.1 provides an overview of how these questions will be addressed.

Figure 2.1. Overview of Instructional Design and Assessment

What aspects of language do I teach?	○⟶ **Standards**
How do I know if students are learning?	○⟶ **Standards-based assessments**
How can I integrate ELD with content learning?	○⟶ **The role of academic language**
How can I teach effectively?	○⟶ **Strategies for ELD instruction**

Standards-Based Instruction and Assessment

The context for designing instruction and assessment for English learners has been shaped by the standards reform movement, an initiative that has had an effect on education not only in California but also throughout the U.S. Any plan for instruction must take into account relevant standards, for they outline the core content of instruction–what students must know and be able to do as a result of instruction.

The standards-based reform model operates as a system with several key components. Challenging *standards* for all students provide high expectations for learner performance, ones that are transparent for all members of the educational community—students, teachers, administrators, and parents. *Assessments* linked to the standards provide a means for students to demonstrate

> Any plan for instruction must take into account relevant standards, for they outline the core content of instruction.

the knowledge and skills they have learned. School *accountability* is tied to the results of these assessments, which help to answer the question "Have schools allocated their resources appropriately so that students meet the targeted high standards?" Accountability is also intended to create incentives to work harder and to focus instruction and curriculum on the targeted standards. Professional development and other resources provide support for improving teaching and, thus, higher levels of learning. A model of the theory of standards-based reform can be seen in Figure 2.2.

Figure 2.2 Standards-based Reform Model

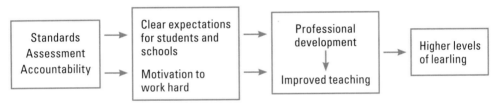

Source: National Research Council 1999.

In 1999, the State Board of Education adopted California's ELD standards, *English Language Development Standards for California Public School: Kindergarten Through Grade Twelve*. Those standards define what English learners in California schools are expected to know and be able to do. The standards are designed so that as students develop English proficiency, they have access to the mainstream English–language arts (ELA) curriculum. Thus, the standards are intended as a pathway to supporting students as they develop both English proficiency and the knowledge and skills defined in the *English–Language Arts Content Standards for California Public Schools: Kindergarten Through Grade Twelve* (1998) in place for monolingual students. In fact, the skills described in the ELD standards at more advanced levels are very much like the ELA standards for that topic area. The link between ELD and ELA standards is even more pronounced in the standards related to phonemic awareness, decoding, vocabulary development, and concepts of print for grade levels K–2. Within that grade span, grade-level ELA standards can be found alongside related ELD standards at all levels of proficiency. An example drawn from the ELD standards, grades K–2, beginning level is shown.

> **ELD Standard:**
> Read aloud simple words (e.g., nouns and adjectives) in stories or poems.
>
> **ELA Content Standards, Kindergarten:**
> 1.17 Identify and sort common words in basic categories (e.g., colors, shapes, foods).

The ELD standards describe language learning within the skill areas or "domains" of listening, speaking, reading, and writing. The box below provides an outline of topics addressed by the ELD standards within each of these areas, which are the same for ELA.

Listening and Speaking

⊙ Strategies and Applications
   Comprehension
   Organization and Delivery of Oral Communication
   Analysis and Evaluation of Oral and Media Communications

Reading

⊙ Word Analysis
   Concepts about Print
   Phonemic Awareness
   Vocabulary and Concept Development
   Decoding and Word Recognition

⊙ Fluency and Systematic Vocabulary Development
   Vocabulary and Concept Development
   Decoding and Word Recognition

⊙ Reading Comprehension
   Comprehension
   Analysis of Grade-Level-Appropriate Text
   Structural Features of Informational Materials
   Expository Critique

⊙ Literary Response and Analysis
   Narrative Analysis of Grade-Level-Appropriate Text
   Structural Features of Literature
   Literary Criticism

Writing
- ⊙ Strategies and Applications
  Penmanship
  Organization and Focus
  Evaluation and Revision
  Research and Technology

- ⊙ English-Language Conventions
  Capitalization
  Punctuation
  Spelling
  Sentence Structure and Grammar

The ELD standards extend over four grade spans: K–2, 3–5, 6–8, and 9–12 and five proficiency levels. Within each topic, descriptors geared to a specific grade span and proficiency level define what students must know and be able to do. Here is an example of a standard in reading under the topic Vocabulary and Concept Development. It is geared to grades 3–5 and for the beginning ELD level:

Demonstrate comprehension of simple vocabulary with an appropriate action.

The standard illustrates an observable and assessable behavior that students can perform in class to demonstrate learning and that can be monitored and assessed by their teacher.

As mentioned earlier, to determine whether students are progressing in the development of their English proficiency, schools assess English learners using the California English Language Development Test (CELDT). The results are used to identify learners requiring ELD instruction, determine their level of English proficiency, and assess their progress in acquiring English skills. The CELDT is aligned to the ELD standards and reports student performance for each skill area in terms of a five-level proficiency scale (see pages 85–86 for CELDT levels).

Using Standards to Plan ELD Instruction and Assessment

The ELD standards share the following characteristics:

- ⊙ *They define a range of competence* through the various topics across language domains that ensure instruction will encompass skills and knowledge identified as worth learning.

⊙ *They give teachers and students goals for achievement* by identifying observable and assessable behaviors.

⊙ *They provide a clear and consistent basis for assessment* by linking instruction to a system of targeted goals for learning on a continuum of language proficiency.

⊙ *They offer a coherent, shared vision for learning* through common, transparent learning targets that are articulated across grade and proficiency levels and that can form the basis of discussions among members of the school community.

Standards, however, are not a magic wand. Classrooms and learners still need high-quality teachers who are skilled in translating standards into sound classroom practices. Teachers can use the ELD standards in the following ways:

Planning standards-based instruction. Teachers draw on grade-level ELD standards to identify the content of those lessons, ensuring that those lessons cover the essential skills and knowledge their students must master in order to develop targeted oral and literacy competencies and be prepared to move on to the next grade. In addition to using the ELD standards, K–5 teachers also refer to the ELA standards when planning instruction. Those encapsulate the intended long-range targets for language learning. English learners use textbooks that are aligned with the ELD standards and incorporate information and tasks that will help them develop the skills and knowledge called for in the standards. Because the standards are geared to grade-level spans, they provide curriculum designers and program administrators with an articulated continuum for planning language development across the elementary school years. Teachers can use standards as a starting point and then delineate the specific language objectives for a lesson.

Planning standards-based assessment. ELD standards also inform the design and use of classroom assessments. When teachers plan assessment in standards-based classrooms, they have a clear sense of what needs to be measured, since the ELD standards describe observable language behaviors that English learners must demonstrate at each level of the language proficiency continuum. That continuum also provides a constant measure for helping teachers and learners determine whether students are making appropriate progress and for maintaining high expectations for learning. Schools use the data collected from classroom assessments to monitor student achievement, identify instructional gaps, and provide resources as needed to improve instruction and learning in light of the learning targets described in the standards.

Putting it all together. For many teachers, a curriculum is often perceived as a set of binders outlining grade-level expectations for learning in specific content areas. Graves (2006), however, drawing on a systems approach to curriculum design, envisions it as a dynamic set of processes—planning, enacting, and evaluating—influenced by specific contextual factors such as the institutional setting, teachers' beliefs, educational policies, cultural influences, and community expectations. Teachers' actions in creating instructional and assessment plans are situated within this dynamic framework.

To develop lessons for instructed ELD, teachers draw on a variety of resources to ensure that they utilize their time as effectively as possible. Figure 2.3 illustrates an approach that describes how to plan for, enact, and evaluate such instruction.

Figure 2.3. Planning, Enacting, and Evaluating Instructed ELD

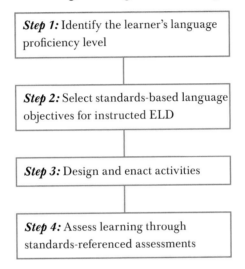

Step 1: Identify the learner's language proficiency level

Step 2: Select standards-based language objectives for instructed ELD

Step 3: Design and enact activities

Step 4: Assess learning through standards-referenced assessments

Step 1: Identify the learner's language proficiency level. For the first step in the process, teachers determine English learners' language needs. This information should be collected from multiple sources. One source, of course, will be student scores on the CELDT. Those scores will indicate a student's language proficiency level according to state ELD standards. Other means include the use of formative or ongoing assessments to gather samples of language performance as students engage in academic tasks in the classroom. The assessments should provide information about student language ability across all four domains: listening, speaking, reading, and writing; they may also include information about language performance collected from tasks in various content areas. Data gathered from student language performance on authentic tasks in a specific classroom provide rich and detailed information about student strengths and difficulties in each skill area (Bachman 2002). They can also provide additional insights about such things as students' learning processes, confidence in using language, participation in classroom tasks, and interaction patterns with other students—factors that can influence the design of instructional tasks.

Step 2: Select standards-based language objectives for instructed ELD. For this step, teachers draw on ELD and ELA standards to identify specific targets for language learning. They also use information collected in Step 1 to frame expected learning outcomes according to the language proficiency level(s) of students in the class. Because the ELD standards are organized by levels of proficiency, teachers can select standards that match their students' language-learning needs. After appropriate sets of standards are identified, teachers design language objectives geared to the levels of English proficiency of students in the class.

Step 3: Design and enact activities. For this step in the process, teachers design learning activities that will help students develop target language skills, drawing on a range of resources such as textbooks, additional reading texts, learning kits, and manipulatives. Because teachers have identified students' language learning needs, at this stage teachers can also differentiate instruction according to learners' levels of language proficiency. We will examine instructional strategies appropriate for this step in the next section of this chapter.

Step 4: Assess learning through standards-referenced assessments. In classrooms where assessment supports learning and teaching, teachers will want to collect information about what students have learned as a result of the activities and tasks in the unit of instruction. *Have students met the language objectives? Have they developed the language skills highlighted in the ELD and ELA standards? Are they ready to move on to the next lesson or unit? Do they need additional support or review? In addition, teachers may also want to examine the effectiveness of the instructional plan. Were resources used effectively? Were directions useful in directing student work? Did students engage in tasks actively and productively? Were they able to work collaboratively? Did instruction facilitate students' meeting targeted ELD and ELA standards? Were these outcomes in line with the teacher's expectations for learning and in line with students' language abilities?*

A detailed plan for assessment is beyond the scope of this chapter, but here are a few suggestions for planning assessment that will help teachers and students to monitor student progress in developing English-language skills.

- *Gather information frequently within the classroom.* One test at the end of a chapter or unit provides a single snapshot of students' developing skills. Multiple assessments, of various types, will help to create a more detailed and nuanced picture of what students know and can do with language (Shepard 2000).

- *Keep a written record of information collected and link the information to targeted standards.* Merely noticing student performances is not enough. Writing anecdotal notes or using a scoring guide of some sort to record student performances provides a means for teachers to monitor student growth. When that record is

linked to targeted standards, teachers can keep track of language development across learning objectives to ensure that instruction is covering the range of intended outcomes (see Barr 2000).

⊙ *Review the data to see patterns of growth or areas of difficulty.* Collecting assessment data alone will provide little guidance for understanding student learning. By examining patterns of growth or areas of difficulty that emerge from an analysis of assessment data, teachers can take the next step of using data to make decisions such as whether to provide additional support to learners, secure additional resources, or revise instruction.

⊙ *Engage students in monitoring their own learning.* When students are actively engaged in assessing their own learning, they become more aware of the intended learning targets and performance criteria, as well as the processes to achieve that learning. Learners at all levels of English-language proficiency can be involved in reflecting on their learning and charting their awareness of their language development (Anderson 2005; Gunn 2003).

The Role of Academic Language

In the previous section, we outline the basis for an approach to planning, enacting, and evaluating focused, explicit segments of ELD instruction based on ELD and ELA standards for English learners. We also recognize that K–5 teachers make their instructional decisions about learning and teaching in the context of broader requirements mandated by schools and districts. In addition to learning English during a daily block of ELD instruction, K–5 English learners are developing language skills and knowledge related to a range of content areas such as mathematics, science, and social studies. K–5 teachers need to be aware of the importance of assisting students with language learning in those content areas (see Echevarria and Short, this publication). To maximize student learning, teachers must consider the entire instructional day as they design ELD instruction for a curriculum appropriate to the student's grade level. This broader picture is necessary both for enlarging the scope of ELD so that students learn English throughout the instructional day and for ensuring that through their language learning, English learners have access to a rigorous, standards-aligned curriculum across content areas.

Since learning the language of school is the primary purpose of ELD K–5, teachers need to have a thorough understanding of the notion of **academic language.** (See also Guideline 10 and the discussion in Saunders and Goldberg, this publication.) Cummins (1980, 2000) first drew the well-known conceptual distinction between the type of language used in everyday conversation (basic interpersonal communicative skills) and that required in school (cognitive academic language proficiency).

As Saunders and Goldenberg (this publication) explain, academic language entails all aspects of language, from grammatical elements to vocabulary and discourse structures and conventions. It also involves using language for various functions, such as classifying, sequencing, and comparing. Yet many teachers may think almost solely in terms of the specialized vocabulary used on tests, in discussions, or associated with the content areas. Solomon and Rhodes (1996) conducted a survey of elementary, middle, and high school ESL teachers, graduate students training to become ESL professionals, ESL teacher trainers, and administrators to find out how they defined academic language. Their study revealed that these groups identified vocabulary as the most salient feature of academic language. Respondents gave examples of terms such as *triangle, habitat,* and *protein* from math, social studies, and science, respectively. Others contrasted academic language with social language, noting that *pick* would be used more typically in conversation, but *select* would appear in written form. Respondents also defined academic language in terms of typical classroom activities. For example, English learners need to use academic language to follow directions, present findings to classmates, participate in discussions in science labs, write in journals, and state opinions.

> Since learning the language of school is the primary purpose of ELD K–5, teachers need to have a thorough understanding of the notion of academic language.

Investigations of actual classrooms enhance our understanding of academic language functions. Bailey and others (2004), for example, observed fourth- and fifth-grade science classrooms to analyze the academic language functions used by both teachers and students. Teachers primarily used four language functions:

(1) Description: *"A sunflower has bright yellow petals and a long green stem."*

(2) Explanation: *"Clownfish will actually protect the sea anemone. That's a mutualistic relationship."*

(3) Comparison: *"Flowers have mechanisms of attraction like whales have echolocation."*

(4) Questioning: *"What did we learn in our last unit on water properties?"*

Student talk in those science classes consisted of five academic language functions: *description, explanation, comparison, questioning,* and *commenting.* Although contrasting types of language is useful for understanding the range of uses of language in school, conversational language and academic language should not be viewed as a dichotomy. Schleppegrell (2004) argues that interactional spoken language can be complex and cognitively demanding. Students, for example, would need to use complex language to debate the pros and cons of walking to school versus taking the school bus in a second-grade transportation unit. Bailey (2007) suggests that it is perhaps more accurate to speak of the differences between social and academic language as differences in the *frequency* of complex grammatical structures, specialized terminology, and academic language functions of the kinds exemplified above. Further, she argues that it is more helpful to consider whether the situation is primarily social or academic rather than the language per se.

There are tremendous expectations of young English learners at the lower primary grade levels to develop social language and nascent academic literacy in English. While English learners in grades K–5 generally benefit from an early start in the school compared with older English learners, teachers need to plan systematically for instruction that will help students, over the K–5 grade span, to develop the decontextualized language skills they need in cognitively demanding academic subjects in the upper elementary grade levels and beyond. And, as they progress through grades K–5, English learners must develop the multidimensional aspects of academic literacy described here and in Saunders and Goldenberg (this publication) in order to transition from ELD to ELA and to succeed academically in the content areas with specialized vocabularies and genres.[4] For teachers, the challenge is to teach the academic language needed and to teach it in a directed but interactive manner.

Here is an example of how academic language intersects with instruction in the classroom. Content tasks will have some academic language features that teachers will need to identify to prepare their students for access to the content. In a fourth-grade math unit on analyzing data in graphs or tables, a teacher might engage students in the task of writing an analysis in which they summarize the data and apply them to a new situation. Inherent in this task are certain academic language demands: the vocabulary of graphs and tables as well as the specific data represented in these graphic forms; sentence structures that shape the understanding and display of information; the features of the discourse genre required for writing the analysis. In preparing for the final writing task, students may work in groups, and so additional speaking and listening skills may be required.

Gibbons (2006) suggests that teachers create a "language inventory," or list of the academic language features that can be found in a unit of instruction, as part of the instructional design process. This language inventory can then be used to develop language objectives, to design learning activities that focus explicitly on the language connected to content tasks, and to guide the development of assessments to determine whether students are learning language while developing content knowledge and skills. K–5 classrooms are multifaceted learning environments. English learners

---

4. Gibbons (2002) defines *genres* as forms of writing that share certain characteristics, such as a specific purpose, a particular overall structure, and specific linguistic features.

must be engaged in all aspects of this environment if they are to have access to required grade-level content and to a rich array of opportunities to develop their language proficiency.

Strategies for ELD Instruction

This section addresses the last question: *How do I teach effectively?* As noted earlier in this chapter, second-language acquisition is a complex process. Young learners of English are simultaneously developing cognitively and acquiring English as they progress through the elementary grade levels. Gibbons (2006), like many theorists, believes that "language-based tasks must therefore be designed to provide appropriate intellectual and cognitive challenge, not simply to rehearse language" (p. 220). Tasks can also be designed to provide opportunities for specific language learning and practice (Ellis 2005b; Saunders and Goldenberg, this publication). Compared with older learners, English learners enrolled in elementary school have the advantage of time to acquire the language and academic skills needed for school success. Nevertheless, taking full advantage of the early school years requires a well-designed plan that integrates standards, appropriate instructional materials, and effective instruction and assessment strategies that focus on second-language development. Such a plan must address (a) dedicated ELD instruction in a specific time block and (b) instruction during the rest of the day.

Crabbe (2003) identifies six components of language learning and presents sample classroom activities for each in Table 2.1 (adapted by McGroarty and Calderón 2005).

Table 2.1. Six Components of Language Learning	
Components	**Sample classroom activities**
Input	Listening to a story or reading a dialogue
Output	Producing meaningful utterances in written or spoken form, either as a monologue or during interaction
Interaction	Speaking or writing with others in simulated or real communicative situations
Feedback	Receiving information, either directly or indirectly, about one's own use of the second language
Rehearsal	Improving specific aspects of one's second-language performance through any kind of deliberate repetition such as memorization of words or word patterns, repeated role plays, or pronunciation practice
Language Understanding	Conscious attention to one's language learning intended to lead to better cognitive control over learning, including awareness of tasks, strategies, and difficulties encountered

From the early grade levels, teachers of English learners can maximize opportunities for ELD by deliberate planning for instruction that incorporates the components noted above. At the earliest stages of language development (the stages of language proficiency presented earlier), teachers provide *input* during designated ELD instruction that is accessible to English learners. They focus extensively on oral language development, recognizing that research indicates it takes English learners several years to develop oral academic English skills and that native-like proficiency in oral skills does not generally appear until grade five (Saunders and O'Brien 2006). Teachers of ELD recognize that mere exposure to English is not sufficient. During ELD instruction teachers "scaffold" instruction in ways that extend students' comprehension (*input*) and production (*output*).

> As we consider how to use the components of language learning in designing second-language instruction, we must rely on strategies that are supported by research. . . .

Bruner (1966) used the term *scaffolding* to describe the way parents or caregivers of young children provide early support for child language acquisition. In the context of ELD, teachers play a similarly critical role. In a classroom, a teacher uses a scaffold to *support students' understanding* of a concept or skill (Rea and Mercuri 2006), offer *feedback,* or provide opportunities for *rehearsal.* The scaffold, however, is temporary, needed only until students master the material or skill and move on to more autonomous *language understanding* (Quiocho and Ulanoff 2008). One type of scaffold is conversational scaffolding in which the teacher supports and maintains a conversation so that English learners with limited proficiency can participate. Scaffolding in conversation means paying close attention to the speaker, repeating the scaffolding process until the learner indicates understanding, asking open-ended questions or making comments to encourage the learner to speak, and interpreting or expanding the learner's comments (Horwitz 2008).

As we consider how to use the components of language learning in designing second-language instruction, we must rely on strategies that are supported by research, so that teachers can be confident that instruction is effective in assisting ELD students to progress in second-language development. We now examine five strategies that teachers of ELD K–5 can implement as they design instruction for helping students at all levels of English proficiency. The suggestions that follow are based in some cases on a rather thin body of research. They have some support as useful strategies for all learners, but the implementation and the potential impact on achievement for English learners need to be explored through additional research.

1. **Protracted Language Events:** Téllez and Waxman (2006) concluded that effective language instruction must be built on lengthy interactions or what

they refer to as "protracted language events." Research with children learning their first language provides compelling evidence of how parents and caretakers routinely engage in extended speech events as a means of supporting and expanding children's language development (e.g., Brown and Bellugi 1964; Snow and Ferguson 1977). Bridges, Sinha, and Walkerdine (1981), in the same vein, urge teachers to create opportunities for English learners to be understood, for their speech acts to be valued, and occasions for language forms to be corrected as needed. Wells (1986) argues that the "co-construction of meaning" between the teacher and students and among students must be central to all instructional practices because protracted speech acts, in which students have plentiful opportunities to use language, forms the foundation on which all academic learning is built. Drawing on Crabbe's components of effective learning, we point out that it is during these protracted language events that English learners can be exposed to a variety of sources of linguistic *input,* can practice or *rehearse* language performances, can have multiple opportunities to produce *output,* can *interact* with other language users, and can receive *feedback* on their language performances.

2. **Communitarian Practices:** Téllez and Waxman (2006) use the term *communitarian practices* to describe approaches, such as cooperative learning, that have the potential to enhance learning opportunities. Téllez and Waxman (2006) cite research by Goatley, Brock, and Raphael (1995) in which a group of third-graders who varied in their language proficiency worked on the common task of creating a planet story. The researchers found that although the task did not necessarily offer each student in the group the same opportunities to learn, it allowed students varied ways to organize their own learning, thereby individualizing instruction. This practice could perhaps increase the likelihood of students' engaging in meaningful and productive interactions with peers.

    McGroarty and Calderón (2005) reviewed numerous studies showing that cooperative learning leads to improved oral language and literacy development on the part of English learners. They also cite research showing that cooperative learning can be used beneficially with students of beginning levels of second-language proficiency if mainstream students are trained to help English learners. They also underscore the positive effects of cooperative learning on the development of social skills. Students are taught strategies for turn-taking (e.g., "I'd like to say something here . . .") and language frames for enhanced task participation such as stating opinions ("In my opinion . . .") and praising ("That's a good point").

Although research has revealed the value of increasing students' opportunities to use the language through cooperative tasks and group activities, it has also revealed that communitarian tasks must be carefully designed and consistently implemented for students to reach full potential (Calderón, Hertz-Lazarowitz, and Slavin 1998; cf. Saunders and Goldenberg, Guideline 2, this publication). Otherwise, students may misuse the strategy, as reflected in the following example from Jacobs and others (1996) in which native English-speaking students and English learners limited their interactions in order to complete the cooperative task as reflected in a student's comment: "Just write that down. Who cares? Let's finish up" (p. 270). In summing up, Téllez and Waxman suggest that encouraging students who are learning English to engage in academic conversations with their peers connects them to a fundamental tool of language learning and, although the teacher should serve as a language model, students can also be effective models.

3. **Multiple Representations:** A third instructional strategy recommended by Téllez and Waxman (2006) is providing students with multiple representations in instruction. In other words, teachers should link oral and written language with other types of representations such as visuals, props, pictures, real objects, manipulatives, graphic organizers and semantic webs, music, film, and other multimedia forms (see also Gersten and Baker 2000).

4. **Building on Prior Knowledge:** The fourth instructional practice found to be significant in the metasynthesis was building on or activating prior knowledge. Garcia (1991) found that prior knowledge played a key role when Latino English learners had to demonstrate their understanding on literacy tests. Students' limited background knowledge of the content impacted their performance on questions that required use of prior knowledge, negatively affecting their understanding of vocabulary and interpretation of text. Similarly, Hornberger (1990) conducted a yearlong study of two classrooms: one that had several Spanish-speaking children and one that had only a few English learners from different native language backgrounds. She found that both teachers activated students' prior knowledge but in diverse ways and contexts. The teacher in the class with several Spanish-speaking students was more likely to use cultural knowledge as prior knowledge in making text comprehensible, whereas the teacher of the mixed group of English learners used more immediate instances of students' prior knowledge such as a story that the students had read earlier in the school year. In both cases, the teachers used *activation of prior knowledge* as an effective instructional tool.

111

Téllez and Waxman (2006) argue in favor of those strategies and emphasize the various ways that teachers may activate background knowledge, underscoring the complexity of this instructional practice. Thus, teachers may simply remind students what was covered in a previous lesson; they may employ instructional activities such as class or small-group discussion or a K-W-L chart (K=*what I already know,* W=*what I need to know,* L=*what I need to learn*); or they may also devise more elaborate applications of the practice such as identifying students' cultural values and incorporating them into a series of lessons or a unit. The key is for teachers to be mindful of activating prior knowledge in as many creative ways as possible.

5. **Learning-Strategy Instruction:** Current thinking within cognitive-social learning theory views learners as mentally active participants in the teaching-learning process (Chamot 2005; DeKeyser and Juffs 2005). Learning strategies are mental processes that students can learn to control consciously when they have a learning goal (Chamot 2005). According to a review of research (Anderson 2005), "[p]roficient L2 learners have been found to have a wider repertoire of strategies and draw on them to accomplish L2 tasks" (p. 762). Teaching learning strategies to English learners is one productive way to incorporate Crabbe's component *language understanding* and to assist students to regulate their own learning through active participation (cf. Guideline 9, Saunders and Goldenberg, this publication). In the earliest grade levels, students can be taught metacognitive strategies: to plan, organize, monitor, and evaluate their learning. By the second grade and beyond, they can apply such learning strategies as making inferences, using imagery, and summarizing. Teachers can modify the K-W-L technique to add a learning- strategy component as appropriate to the grade level (Richard-Amato and Snow 2005). See the box below for variations of this strategy. By teaching "learning-to-learn" strategies, teachers can equip students with skills they will use in all content areas and classes throughout their academic careers.

Variations of KWL Technique

⊙ K-W-H-L where "H" column is "*How* to learn"

⊙ K-W-L-S where "S" column corresponds to "What I *still* need to learn

---

Applying Instructional Strategies for Listening, Speaking, Reading, and Writing

Now we examine how to apply these strategies and components to the domains of listening, speaking, reading, and writing when designing lessons for English learners.

In doing so, we emphasize the importance of utilizing protracted language events, so that language is taught within a communication system consisting of extended interaction (e.g., more than one item or isolated utterances) situated within a context and for the construction of meaning. We also recognize the need to ensure that ELD instruction includes a focus on particular forms and patterns of their construction and use.

> Listening and speaking . . . are key foundations of second-language acquisition.

Listening/Speaking: In the early grade levels, English learners must learn to understand the English language and to produce it orally.[5] Listening and speaking, which are treated together in the California ELD standards, are key foundations of second-language acquisition. Listening is itself a highly complex cognitive process. For learners of a home language, listening ability develops naturally in tandem with cognition; however, successful listening in a second language may require more conscious strategies on the part of learners and interventions by teachers. Rost (2005) characterizes listening in terms of several tasks. Listening entails both bottom-up and top-down processes: the listener attends to the speech signal (bottom-up processing) and uses context and prior knowledge to help with comprehension (top-down processing). Knowledge of phonology, syntax, vocabulary, and discourse patterns must be brought to bear—all at the same time. Three processing phases of listening are described as "simultaneous and parallel":

(1) decoding (attention, perception, word recognition, syntactic parsing, use of visual and aural cues);

(2) comprehension (identifying salient information, activating schemata or "modules" of knowledge, making inferences); and

(3) interpretation (using pragmatic information about the speaker, topic, context, and so forth to orient to the speaker's meaning)

At the beginning and early intermediate levels, English learners benefit from listening to material before they are required to speak, read, or write about it (Peterson 2001). A variety of input, such as dialogues and stories read by teachers and classmates or recorded on audiotapes or CDs, can be used effectively for extensive listening instruction. Prelistening activities, such as discussion or advance organizers, activate students' background knowledge before listening and encourage "top down" processing of information (getting the gist) and, during listening activities, assist the learner to get the main idea, topic, situation, or setting (cf. Rost 2005). Selective listening, on

---

5. Listening and speaking are discussed together because they have been combined in the *English-Language Development Standards for California Public Schools* (2002).

the other hand, helps students pay attention to details such as names or dates, and to forms such as plural markers (*s*), irregular forms, and verb-tense endings (*ed, ing*).

A communicative approach to speaking instruction provides practice with authentic communication, not language as an object of analysis, but rather as a tool for students' social and academic needs (Peck 2001). However, there is a role for regarding language as an object of analysis (Ellis 2005b), and even very young children can engage in activities that allow them to do so. For instance, metalinguistic awareness of the sound patterns, word formations (morphology), and syntactic patterns of

> **At the beginning and low-intermediate levels, English learners benefit from listening to material before they are required to speak, read, or write about it.**

the second language is important to both oral and written language development (August and Shanahan, this publication; Durgunoglu and Öney 2000). One way to heighten metalinguistic awareness is through language play or games designed to focus on particular features of language (Cazden 1974). Young learners generally like to play with language, enjoying the sounds, rhythm, and repetition in songs, chants, and poems. Drama, role plays, and storytelling provide English learners with opportunities to rehearse the constituent skills of speaking, such as intonation and stress. Activities in which the teacher gives a series of physical commands, such as "Stand up" or "Bend over," provide practice with listening, then progress to include oral language as selected students give the commands while other students follow their instructions. In addition, carefully designed communitarian practices give students opportunities to interact in small groups to listen to their classmates' ideas and add their own to the discussion. An example of such an activity is Think-Pair-Share. Students *think* about a question or topic that has been posed, one student *pairs* with another student to discuss their ideas, and then student pairs *share* their ideas with the entire group.

Teachers often wonder whether to correct errors in oral language. There are two ways to tackle error correction. An indirect approach entails teacher modeling of correct usage. Teachers, especially at the early stages of proficiency, can recast students' sentences containing errors with the correct forms, thereby providing indirect feedback of correct forms. However, learners may be focused on meaning and not notice how a teacher has altered the form of an utterance. Teachers can help students develop language awareness by assisting them to "notice" mistakes in form and vocabulary and consciously drawing their attention to language, leading students gradually to correct their own errors. Several recent studies conducted with elementary-age students also point to the value of direct or explicit feedback for students' immediate and later use of correct forms. See, for example, Lyster (2004a), who reviewed five studies of students ages seven to fourteen in immersion classes. He concludes, "Less effective instructional options overemphasise negotiation for meaning in oral tasks where message comprehensibility and communication strategies circumvent the need for learners to move beyond the use of interlanguage forms" (p. 321).

Key constituent skills of listening and speaking are listed in the box below. Further, the *English Language Development Standards* (2002) is a resource regarding what students should know and be able to do in terms of listening and speaking skills.

Listening and Speaking Skills

⊙ At the beginning level, segment speech stream into word units and begin to recognize and use key vocabulary.

⊙ Begin with intelligible approximations of English pronunciation and gradually approximate native-like pronunciation.

⊙ Recognize the main idea and supporting details in a listening passage.

⊙ Listen for phonemes, morphological endings, and stress and intonation contours, and gradually use them fluently in spoken form.

⊙ Use context and background knowledge to build expectations and make predictions and then confirm predictions in speaking.

⊙ Use standard English grammatical forms.

⊙ Recognize contractions, sentence fillers, reduced forms, and the like that are typical of spoken English and use them orally.

⊙ Make inferences and figure out the speaker's intent.

⊙ Take notes from listening sources (e.g., CDs, mini-lectures).

Reading: Protracted language events provide opportunities for English learners to develop reading skills. English learners bring vastly different primary language and cultural backgrounds to the classroom. Those differences are particularly relevant to the teaching of reading in ELD instruction because, as noted earlier in this chapter, English learners who have some literacy development in their first language tend to transfer those skills to reading in English. (Literacy issues are discussed in much greater detail in the August and Shanahan chapter, this publication.) At beginning levels, English learners need to understand certain assumptions about the printed word:

(1) pictures go with text;

(2) in English, readers read from left to right, from front to back, from top to bottom;

(3) words are written separately from each other;

(4) quotation marks mean that someone is speaking (in the reading);

(5) punctuation marks separate notions or ideas from each other; and

(6) written language has different rules and conventions from oral language (Ediger 2001).

Many essential techniques for teaching reading are contained in the various ELD textbooks and ancillary materials adopted by school districts in California. Typically, ELD programs contain systematic approaches to teaching word-recognition skills through exposure to different genres of reading such as fiction and nonfiction. In addition, teachers of English learners are guided by the *English Language Development Standards* (2002) for reading. The standards describe the English reading skills students should know and be able to use. Teachers should provide as many authentic sources and purposes for reading as possible in addition to the required reading texts. They can label items in the classroom and have students read them and other types of print such as classroom chore lists, school announcements and notes to parents, and charts and graphs posted around the classroom. Students can read signs around the school and be asked to notice signs in their communities.

As students gain proficiency in English, teachers can introduce academic reading skills to prepare them for reading in the content areas. Such skills include how to preview a text using headings and text features, such as boldface and shading, to provide cues to the reading topic. Most textbooks contain helpful learning features, such as graphics, glossaries, and interim summaries, that students can learn to utilize to read strategically. Teachers can develop lesson plans using a three-stage approach:

(1) *Prereading*—Teachers activate students' background knowledge through prereading questions, previewing key vocabulary, a picture walk, or an anticipation guide such as the one presented in Figure 2.4, which sets the purpose for reading:[6]

(2) *During reading*—In this stage, teachers ask themselves, *What concepts do I want students to learn? How can I guide them in their comprehension?* They may plan a

---

6. This anticipation guide was developed by Maria Rebecca Cortez for use in her second-grade class at Camino Nuevo Charter Academy in Los Angeles.

Directed Reading-Thinking Activity[7] or have students complete a teacher-prepared reading guide or advance organizer such as a Venn diagram requiring students to indicate similarities and differences between two characters or two events;

(3) *Postreading*—In the final stage, the teacher may lead a whole-class discussion, for instance, after students have worked in small groups to answer questions, or students work on a reading-related activity such as a letter to the editor, a poem, a poster, or larger unit project.

These reading activities engage students in extended literacy events that require interaction with various kinds of print and with other students as part of developing their skills.

Figure 2.4. Story Structure and Elements

Title:	
Author(s): Illustrator:	
Main Characters (Who or what is this story about?) 	**Setting** (Where? When?) 
Problem (What is the main problem in the story?) 	**Solution** (How is the problem solved?) 

Sequence of Events

Event #1	Event #2	Event #3

---

7. DR-TA is a "stop-and-start" technique used in class to assist students with difficult text material (Dornan, Rosen, and Wilson 2005). The teacher divides the reading passages, asking students to predict upcoming passages and comment on the reading afterwards. The goal is to guide interpretation, foster prediction, and teach students how to make connections across a reading.

As English learners move through the elementary grade levels, teachers can also help them recognize the knowledge structures needed to read well (and write well) in the content areas. So, for example, students should be introduced to common discourse patterns in the content areas (for example, chronology in social studies or spatial relationships in mathematics). Listed in the box below are common discourse patterns found in science (Carr, Sexton, and Lagunoff 2006). Table 2.2 contains common function words typical of science discourse that signal text organization and provide cues to text comprehension (Carr, Sexton, and Lagunoff 2006). Both the discourse patterns and function words aid English learners in reading (and, of course, thinking, speaking, and writing) as scientists do.

Common Discourse Patterns in Science

⊙ Analyze	⊙ Measure
⊙ Classify	⊙ Observe
⊙ Compare	⊙ Predict
⊙ Conclude	⊙ Provide evidence/rationale
⊙ Demonstrate	⊙ Record
⊙ Distinguish cause from effect	⊙ Report
⊙ Formulate	⊙ Solve
⊙ Hypothesize	⊙ Strategize
⊙ Infer	⊙ Summarize

Table 2.2. Common Function Words in Science

Language Function	Words
Definition	*is equal to, means, refers to, is the same as, consists of, in fact, in other words*
Providing an example	*for example, for instance, including, such as, is like, to illustrate*
Sequencing	*first . . . second, initially, next, finally, preceding, following, not long after*
Showing cause and effect	*because, since, consequently, as a result, may be due to, this led to, so that, in order to, if. . . . then, for this reason*
Expressing an opinion or conclusion	*I think, I believe that, I suggest that, I conclude that In my opinion, I agree with . . . that*
Reporting findings or outcomes	*I/we found that, I/we learned that, I/we discovered that, I now realize that, I want to find out more about*

Writing: Protracted language events are also used for the skill of writing. The *English Language Development Standards* (2002) provide teachers of English learners with strategies and applications for teaching writing. The writing standards include teaching penmanship in the early grade levels and guiding English learners to write a few words about a story or character. As students progress, they will be able to write simple sentences. Table 2.3, for example, shows the sentence-starters used in a unit on elections for a third-grade class where a majority of the English learners were at CELDT levels 1–3.[8] As English learners move through the elementary grade levels, writing instruction focuses more explicitly on organization and introduces students to a variety of genres such as narrative, poetry, and expository writing (e.g., description, compare and contrast, cause and effect). Teachers who plan for the higher proficiency levels must be particularly mindful of preparing students for the kinds of writing requisite for the content areas. Although many of the common discourse patterns cross over content areas (e.g., compare and contrast), others pertain more specifically to a particular content area, such as some of the patterns listed previously for science. English learners will learn to recognize discourse patterns and expressions as a way to improve reading comprehension and writing. Thus, in reading instruction, teachers should draw attention to the patterns and then focus explicitly on them for production when teaching academic writing skills.

Table 2.3. Discourse Patterns Applied to Writing and Speaking

Directions to students:

1. Write as many sentences as you can about elections.

2. Write them the way you practiced them orally.

3. Look at the tree map to choose words and to check spelling.

4. Use capitals and periods correctly.

Sentence-Starters:

Let me tell you about . . .

During an election, voters . . .

Candidates . . .

I know about elections because . . .

---

8. The election unit was developed by Linda Marquez, Lorena Robles, Carmen Verduzco, and Hillary Hinkle for TESL 564, Teaching English for Academic Purposes, at California State University, Los Angeles.

Writing also offers an opportunity for students to focus on the conventions of writing, such as grammar, spelling, and mechanics (e.g., capitalization and punctuation). Recall Swain's notion of the output hypothesis. In her research with second-language learners, she found that students moved from semantic, or meaning-based learning, to syntactic processing when "pushed" to produce output—that is, to produce written or spoken language in which they have to pay attention to both meaning *and* form. Writing activities offer an excellent opportunity to raise students' awareness of grammatical structures in a contextualized and meaningful way. Teachers also find that the process approach to writing (prewriting, writing, sharing, revising, editing, and evaluating) is an excellent method for teaching writing that is both meaning-based and form-focused. English learners often feel insecure about their writing skills, especially in the upper grade levels. The writing process is particularly effective with these students because the process focuses on developing ideas, organizing those ideas, and communicating them fluently before being concerned with correctness (Richard-Amato and Snow 2005).

> **Writing activities offer an excellent opportunity to raise students' awareness of grammatical structures in a contextualized and meaningful way.**

Vocabulary: Underlying proficiency in listening, speaking, reading and writing, is vocabulary knowledge. In terms of lexical demands, Stevens, Butler, and Castellon-Wellington (2000) identified three categories of words:

(1 high-frequency general words used regularly in everyday contexts;

(2) nonspecialized academic words that are used across content areas and not specific to any content area; and

(3) specialized content-area words that are unique to specific disciplines (e.g., *atom, plot, protractor*).

It is critical in the early grade levels to develop a systematic program of vocabulary teaching, starting with the high-frequency general terms used in everyday contexts and moving toward the nonspecialized academic words across content areas. The ability to use a range of vocabulary and explicate word meanings marks the beginning of academic language use. Scarcella (2003) helps us realize the complexity associated with learning vocabulary. Knowing a word goes well beyond simply knowing what a word means. It also includes knowing its collocations (other words that commonly occur with it, e.g., nuclear ____; related to ____); register (is it formal or informal? academic or conversational?); and grammar (is the word transitive or intransitive or both? Can it have both animate and inanimate subjects? How is it that *unfriendly* is an adjective and not an adverb?). What form do derivations take? (Why do we say *unhappiness* but not *dishappiness*?) (See the box below for an expanded list of demands.)

What Does It Mean to Know a Word?

⊙ Understand a word's meaning (and shades of meaning).

⊙ Know its derivations and word families.

⊙ Know its collocations.

⊙ Know its register.

⊙ Know its part of speech.

⊙ Control its grammar.

⊙ Know its frequency.

⊙ Know its spelling.

⊙ Know its pronunciation.

Source: Scarcella 2003.

Teachers of English learners can use a multitude of techniques to create a systematic program of vocabulary instruction. These include direct vocabulary learning strategies such as word and wall charts; vocabulary flash cards; vocabulary journals and notebooks; work sheets on prefixes, roots, and suffixes; and indirect strategies such as extensive and narrow reading, listening activities, and strategies for guessing the meaning from the context (Coxhead 2006). There is also increasing recognition of the importance of capitalizing on students' native languages as a bridge to vocabulary development. Spanish-speaking students, for example, can benefit from highlighting cognates (i.e., words that share a common root in English and the student's first language). An example of academic and common words and their cognates in Spanish (Reiss 2005) is provided in Table 2.4.

Table 2.4. English Words and Spanish Cognates

Academic Word	Spanish Word	Common Word
encounter	*encontrar*	meet
observe	*observar*	watch
maintain	*mantener*	keep
ultimate	*último*	last
equal	*igual*	same
entire	*entero*	whole
quantity	*cantidad*	amount

As English learners progress through the grade levels, ELD instruction can help learners to expand their speaking and listening skills as they begin to develop reading and writing. Consequently, English learners have extended opportunities for output, interaction, feedback, and rehearsal. And while the individual component skills of listening, speaking, reading, and writing should be explicitly taught (e.g., listening for details, reading for the gist, notetaking, writing mechanics) and are tested separately on the CELDT, teachers can also design interactive instructional activities in ELD that integrate all four skills to prepare students for content-area learning. By the upper elementary grade levels, all aspects of vocabulary—basic everyday vocabulary, general academic vocabulary, and grade-appropriate specialized terminology—will also require systematic attention. The goal is to teach English learners all elements of language needed for academic success.

> **The goal is to teach English learners all elements of language needed for academic success.**

Examples of Effective ELD Instruction

This section provides examples of actual materials developed for two different ELD lessons. Our intent is to illustrate how teachers construct effective learning environments for English learners. With the model of planning, enacting, and evaluating instruction (see Figure 2.3) as a framework for describing lesson components, our discussion will focus on Step 3, *Design and enact activities.* It will draw on 10 elements of effective ELD instruction; these elements synthesize our review of the literature presented earlier in this chapter.

- ⊙ Recognition/use of the primary language and culture and linkages with students' families and community

- ⊙ A focus on academic language

- ⊙ A foundation in standards-based instruction and assessment

- ⊙ Use of prior knowledge

- ⊙ Exposure to authentic input through multiple means and representations of language

- ⊙ Exposure to correct language models and frames that show how language functions are expressed in English

- ⊙ Opportunities to use language both receptively (input: listening and reading) and productively (output: speaking and writing)

⊙ Cycles of explanation and practice of language skills and other elements of language that provide learners with opportunities to rehearse language within extended language events

⊙ A variety of grouping strategies to encourage and support extended interaction

⊙ Learning strategy instruction to lead to deeper language and cognitive understanding and to student autonomy

Classroom #1: This example is drawn from a unit focused on reading instruction for students in first grade who are at the early advanced ELD level.[9] Because the teacher must use district-required reading materials from *Open Court* (SRA-McGraw Hill) geared to the English–language arts (ELA) standards and curriculum, she has supplemented them with ELD lessons designed to meet the language development needs of her English learners. For this unit, students read the story of "Matthew and Tilly," written by Rebecca C. Jones, and learn about games and friendship. Although ELA learning objectives are woven throughout the unit, we focus on how the teacher shapes the lessons to incorporate the elements of effective instruction for ELD.

Table 2.5. "Matthew and Tilly" Unit Matrix

	Monday	Tuesday	Wednesday	Thursday	Friday
Lesson highlights to incorporate the standards	⊙ Blending ⊙ Accessing prior knowledge ⊙ Asking background questions ⊙ Engaging in picture talk ⊙ Listening to CD	⊙ Introducing key vocabulary ⊙ Reading story ⊙ Continuing picture talk	⊙ Filling out vocabulary chart ⊙ Practicing the five "W" questions	⊙ Comparing and contrasting two characters ⊙ Checking comprehension ⊙ Completing vocabulary sorting matrix	⊙ Testing comprehension ⊙ Writing response

---

9. This unit was developed by Esmeralda Brown, Kim Luong Barcenas, and Florence Nguyen-Quang for TESL 564, Teaching English for Academic Purposes, at California State University, Los Angeles.

Table 2.5 *(continued)*

	Monday	Tuesday	Wednesday	Thursday	Friday
ELA standard(s)	*Decoding and Word Recognition* 1.13: Read compound words and contractions. *Comprehension and Analysis of Grade-Level-Appropriate Text* 2.6: Relate prior knowledge to textual information.	*Reading Comprehension* 2.1: Identify text that uses sequence or other logical order. *Concepts about Print* 1.1: Match oral words to printed words. *Written and Oral English Language Conventions* 1.6: Use knowledge of the basic rules of punctuation and capitalization when writing.	*Reading Comprehension* 2.2: Respond to *who, what, when, where,* and *how [why]* questions. *Vocabulary and Concept Development* 1.17: Classify grade-appropriate categories of words (e.g., concrete collections of animals, foods, toys).	*Reading Comprehension* 2.0: Read and understand grade-level appropriate material. *Vocabulary and Concept Development* 1.17: Classify grade-appropriate categories of words (e.g., concrete collections of animals, foods, toys).	*Reading Comprehension* 2.0: Read and understand grade-level appropriate material. *Writing Strategies* 1.0: Write clear and coherent sentences and paragraphs that develop a central idea. *Writing Applications* 2.0: Write brief narratives (e.g., fictional, autobiographical) describing an experience.
ELD early advanced level	*Decoding and Word Recognition* 1.10: Generate the sounds from all the letters and letter patterns, including consonant blends and long- and short-vowel patterns and blend those sounds into recognizable words. *Strategies and Applications* Std EA1. Listen attentively to stories and information, and orally identify key details and concepts	*Word Analysis* 1.9: Blend vowel-consonant sounds orally to make words. *Fluency and Systematic Vocabulary Development* Std EA5. Use decoding skills and knowledge of academic, social vocabulary to begin independent reading. *Reading Comprehension* Std EA6. Read text, use detailed sentences to identify orally the main idea and use the idea to draw inferences about the text.	*Reading Comprehension* 1.10: Read stories and texts from content areas and respond orally to them by restating facts and details to clarify ideas. *Fluency and Systematic Vocabulary Development* Std EA3. Recognize simple antonyms and synonyms (e.g., good, bad; blend, mix) in stories or games	*Reading Comprehension* 10: Read stories and texts from content areas and respond orally to them by restating facts and details to clarify ideas. *Vocabulary Development* Std EA5. Use decoding skills and knowledge of academic and social vocabulary to begin independent reading.	*Vocabulary Development* 3: Use complex vocabulary and sentences appropriate for language arts and other content areas.

Source: Numbers for the standards (EA1, EA6) are derived from the ELA/ELD Standards Correlation Matrix at http://www.cde.ca.gov/ci/rl/im/documents/elaeldmtrxkjun07.doc.

The lesson highlights in Table 2.5 illustrate the teacher's attention to designing instructional activities that incorporate the standards and engage students in using oral and written language. They also reveal the careful planning required. Because the teacher already identified students' English level, she has included ELD standards appropriate to that level to help her create appropriate language objectives related to the ELA standards.

Each successive day's lesson builds on and extends student learning. For example, on Monday the teacher builds on students' prior knowledge about the topic of friends by asking background questions. In the lesson on Tuesday, the teacher introduces vocabulary related to the reading. On Wednesday, students complete a vocabulary chart by supplying a synonym and antonym for each word and drawing a picture to remind them of the word. The activity explicitly links the targeted ELD standard for that day's lesson: students will be able to "recognize simple antonyms and synonyms . . . in stories and games." On Thursday, with a partner, students will sort the words into conceptual categories, a task that requires extended interaction.

Throughout the week of literacy instruction, students will produce language across all skill areas: for example, they will listen to and speak with the teacher during Picture Talk on Monday and interact with other students as they engage in asking and answering questions about the story; they will read the story as well as accompanying handouts; and in a culminating writing task, they will demonstrate understanding of the story as well as their learning of vocabulary as the students work toward meeting the ELA standard: "write clear and coherent sentences and paragraphs that develop a central idea."

Lesson Plan for Day 4 of This Unit

Lesson Plan for Day 4
Theme/Topic: Character investigation
Grade/Language Level: first grade, ELD 4
Lesson Topic: Comparing characters in "Matthew and Tilly"
Content Objective
⊙ Students will describe the similarities and differences between the main characters of "Matthew and Tilly."
ELA State Standards
⊙ Reading Standard 2.1: Students will be able to read and understand grade-level appropriate material.

Lesson Plan for Day 4 of This Unit *(continued)*

Language Objectives

- ⊙ Students will use adjectives to describe the characters in the story.

ELD Standard Level 4, Grade 1

- ⊙ Standard 10 (early advanced): Students will be able to "read stories and texts from content areas and respond orally to them by restating facts and details to clarify ideas."

Learning Strategy Objective

- ⊙ Students will use a graphic organizer to compare and contrast two characters of the story.

Materials

- ⊙ Text from *Open Court:* "Matthew and Tilly"
- ⊙ Venn diagram

Preparation

Students have already read "Matthew and Tilly" and may reread it if time allows and if they choose to. The teacher will review the concept of compare and contrast, as they have been taught earlier in the year.

Students and teachers will review the rubric to be used to evaluate the Venn diagrams to make sure the assessment meets the ELA standard for describing similarities and differences with characterizations.

Presentation

Step 1

- ⊙ The teacher will elicit the meaning of *compare* (word that means identify what is the same about two things) from students.

- ⊙ The teacher will elicit the meaning of *contrast* (word that means identify what is different about two things) from students.

- ⊙ The teacher will explain that the Venn diagram chart has three parts: Compare/Same, Matthew, and Tilly

Step 2

- ⊙ The teacher will ask students to compare the characters, Matthew and Tilly
  - O "What is the same about Matthew and Tilly?"

    (The teacher records students' ideas on a big Venn diagram (in the "same" area) and writes the student's initials next to the idea.)

  - O Students will actively participate in describing aspects of the two characters that are the same.

Lesson Plan for Day 4 of This Unit *(continued)*

○ "What is different about Matthew and Tilly?"

(The teacher records students' ideas on a big Venn diagram (in the specific area "Matthew" or "Tilly") and writes the student's initials next to the idea.)

○ Students will actively participate in describing aspects of the two characters that are different.

○ The teacher will ask students to think about whether an idea belongs in the "same" area or in the "Matthew" or "Tilly" area.

Practice

After the first part of the guided lesson, students will work in pairs to fill out the Venn diagram work sheet.

Upon completion of the diagram, the pairs of students share their answers with the rest of the class. To prepare for their oral report, students will practice using these sentence-starters with their partners:

○ "I filled the Matthew area with this because . . ."

○ "I filled the Tilly area with this because . . ."

○ "I filled the Compare/Same area with this because . . ."

Self-Evaluation

Students will assess their own understanding of compare and contrast by comparing their work with the ideas shared during the class discussion.

Expansion

⊙ Students can use the compare/contrast discourse pattern with other subjects, including science, social studies, mathematics, and art.

⊙ Students can draw connections to the characters that were evaluated.

⊙ Students can use the ideas in their Venn diagram to write about how they are more like one character or both.

⊙ Students will gain better reading comprehension by reviewing the main characters and the events that took place.

Assessment

⊙ Using the standards-referenced rubric, the teacher will review each pair's Venn diagram as another form of assessment.

⊙ During a writers workshop, students can write in their journals describing how they are similar to or different from Matthew or Tilly.

The lesson is based on both content and language objectives that identify explicit learning targets, ones that are linked to state ELA and ELD standards, as well as learning strategy objectives designed to develop students' metacognitive awareness (see Guidelines 9 and 12 in Saunders and Goldberg, this publication). In preparing for the lesson, the teacher builds on students' prior learning from a previous lesson about the concept of "compare and contrast" to introduce the use of a Venn diagram graphic organizer. The sentence-starters given by the teacher offer students correct language frames to support them in practicing using appropriate language in their contributions to the lesson. Throughout this lesson, students are engaged in activities requiring input, output, and interaction.

Both the unit and sample lesson plan illustrate several elements of effective practice. Lesson objectives are based on both ELA and ELD standards. New learning is framed by prior knowledge; instruction focuses on all skill areas and provides opportunities for both structured practice and communicative output. The teacher plans a variety of grouping strategies so that students engage in extended interaction, and the focus is explicitly on the academic language of the lesson.

Classroom #2: This example comes from a 10-hour thematic unit on immigration designed for fifth-grade English learners.[10] In conjunction with Unit 8, "We the People" of *Avenues* (Schifini et al. 2004), students learn about immigration patterns from the early years until today and examine how their own experiences connect to these historical trends. The teacher has designed the unit with content, language, and strategy objectives in mind. Language objectives include learning the key vocabulary needed to understand the theme (e.g., *ancestors, descendants, relatives, resident, citizen*) and expanding their knowledge of word families using stems and affixes; features of nonfiction texts (e.g., maps, charts, graphs); using research skills to select a foreign-born American and find out about his or her accomplishments; using correct grammatical forms for "Wh" questions (e.g., *who, what, when, where, why, and how*); listening for specific information in class presentations by their peers; and writing and revising essays based on a peer editing checklist and rubric. The teacher based the unit on both the ELD and ELA standards, since many students at fifth grade are ready to transition. Culminating activities for the unit are a biographical essay and a poster presentation.

The lesson plan on the next page was designed for Day 8 of the unit on immigration. At this point in the unit, students have interviewed a family member or friend who immigrated to the U.S. and are drafting biographical essays based on their interview

---

10. The unit was designed by Molly Arevalo, Vruyer Malekian, Connie Quintero, and Sergio Quiroz for TESL 564, Teaching English for Academic Purposes, at California State University, Los Angeles.

notes. To meet the ELD standard for writing strategies and applications, students must write multiparagraph expository compositions with consistent use of standard grammatical forms. To meet the ELA writing strategies standard in their multi-paragraph expository compositions, students must establish a topic, present important ideas, sequence events in chronological order, and use transitions to link ideas. They must also write a conclusion that summarizes the key ideas in the essay.

Immigration Unit

Lesson Number: 8

Grade and Subject: Fifth-Grade Interdisciplinary English Language Development (ELD)

Time block: Approximately one hour

ELD Standards Addressed: Early advanced level for writing strategies and applications: Write multiparagraph narrative and expository compositions appropriate for content areas, with consistent use of standard grammatical forms.

ELA Writing Strategies: 1.2 Create multiple-paragraph expository compositions:

a. Establish a topic, important ideas, or events in sequence or chronological order.

b. Provide details and transitional expressions that link one paragraph to another in a clear line of thought.

c. Offer a concluding paragraph that summarizes important ideas and details.

Content Objective: Students will use what they learned about immigration patterns, applying it to the specific case of a family member or friend whom they have interviewed.

Language Objective: Students will draft a three-paragraph biographical essay with logical organization (chronological or main idea/details).

Learning Strategy Objective: Students will synthesize their notes to write a biographical essay about their interviewee.

Assessment Evidence: Peer editing checklist and essay rubric

Materials/Resources: Interview notes

Grouping patterns: Individual, pair work, whole class

Immigration Unit *(continued)*

Opening: Teacher starts by asking students to share their reactions to the interviews conducted. Several students share with whole class and then they break into groups of four to share their interview findings.

Direct Instruction: Teacher should help students organize their information to create three paragraphs. The first paragraph should introduce the interviewee and provide background information and history. In the second paragraph, the student should write about life in the interviewee's country of origin, reasons for immigrating, and how the interviewee arrived in the U.S. The final paragraph should inform the reader of what the interviewee's life is like now and include a reflection.

Guided Practice: For ELD students who need more structure, the work sheet below can be used to help students organize their essays. They can draft sentences on the work sheet to convert to essay format. The teacher assists ELD students to convert their interview notes to paragraphs.

Independent Practice: Students can begin working on their essays in class.

Closing: Teacher answers any questions students may have regarding the writing assignment and reminds them to use the rubric as they develop their essays.

Homework/Extension: Students should complete their essay and plan their poster layout, gathering pictures and/or other items they would like to put on their poster.

Work Sheet for a Biographical Essay

First Paragraph

What is your interviewee's name? Which country did he/she come from? How many languages does the person you interviewed speak? Which ones? What was his/her occupation in the former country? For what reasons did he/she leave the home country?

_____

_____

_____

_____

Second Paragraph

How and when did the person you interviewed travel to the United States? Did anyone else travel with him/her? Prior to coming to the United States did any family members already live here? If so, did they help arrange the trip? What was the most difficult part of coming to the United States?

_____

_____

_____

_____

Third Paragraph

How long has the person you interviewed been in the country? What does he/she do for a living now? Was it difficult to find employment? How is his/her life different in the United States? Does he/she miss anything from his/her country? Is the person you interviewed happy he/she immigrated to the United States? If he/she had to choose, would he/she do so again? What advice does he/she have for people who want to come to the United States?

_____

_____

_____

_____

The fifth-grade unit and lesson plan presented above reflect the elements of effective instruction listed at the beginning of this section of the chapter. The theme of immigration draws on students' culture, family, and community. Clearly, all activity focuses on academic language development through input, output, and interaction by a variety of means such as textbook reading, oral interviews, pair and group work, and whole-class discussion. Instruction is standards-based, addressing both ELD standards for students classified as English learners and ELA standards because teachers must teach and assess ELA standards at each grade level as required by the state and prepare all students, including English learners, for the California Standards Test. The unit exposes students to explicit instruction in the four language skills (with the emphasis on writing skills in the lesson plan) and includes systematic vocabulary and grammar instruction. It includes both content and language objectives and, in addition, assists students in developing learning strategies that lead to the development of effective study skills and critical thinking skills. The rubric below, as a peer editing tool and teacher assessment measure, reflects both the ELA and ELD writing standards in the lesson plan and is used by students individually as they develop their essays.

Biographical Essay Rubric

Criteria	Rating				Points Received
	4	**3**	**2**	**1**	
Organization	Very logical, clear, and direct; flows smoothly	Mostly logical, clear, and direct; some-what choppy	Logical but lacks clarity	No logical sequence	
Ideas	Information is accurate, interesting, and unique; all information is included.	Information is mostly accurate and interesting; most of the information is included.	Information is partially accurate; little information from the interview is included.	Information is inaccurate and incomplete.	
Conventions	No misspellings or grammatical errors	One or two misspellings or grammatical errors	Three or four misspellings or grammatical errors	Five or more misspellings and errors	
Presentation	Creative pictures, fonts, alignment with texts and visuals	Some creativity	Little creativity	No creativity	
				Total score	

The two lesson plans presented demonstrate how teachers of English learners in grades one and five can develop activities that meet standards for ELD students. In many classrooms, teachers will have to differentiate instruction for ELD students at many levels of English proficiency. In the grade one unit, beginning students would not have the language skills to compare and contrast two characters; they could, however, focus on learning some of the key adjectives for describing characters in the story "Matthew and Tilly" and, in pairs, use a vocabulary chart to sort words. By the early intermediate level, they can begin to ask and answer questions using phrases or simple sentences about the story and may be able to use a basic sentence-starter such as "Matthew and Tilly are the same because. . . ."

In the grade five unit on elections, while the upper intermediate students are learning to write multiparagraph essays, the teacher can assist beginning and early intermediate students to write two or three interview questions using the models in the work sheet. Students then write short simple sentences answering the questions. They could then practice in pairs asking and answering questions alternately. Grading must reflect how well these students demonstrate writing at ELD levels 1 and 2, recognizing that these students will not have control over all grammatical elements or spelling and punctuation conventions. By the same token, teachers need to provide more challenging tasks for English learners at the advanced levels in their classes with particular focus on the relevant ELA standards for the grade level. Advanced English learners, for instance, would be expected to write multiparagraph essays as required in the grade five lesson plan and also to revise their writing for appropriate word choice and organization, consistent point of view, and transitions.

Professional Development

"Examples of Effective ELD Instruction" began with a list of 10 elements of well-planned, research-based instruction for English learners in K–5 classrooms in California. Rather than serving as a checklist for practice, the elements indicate the complexity of creating and developing effective instructional plans for ELD. They also indicate that effective ELD instruction is more than just "good teaching." It is a multifaceted endeavor requiring teachers to understand second-language development, plan and deliver ELD instruction, and assess learning outcomes. To be prepared for these challenges, teachers of ELD K–5 need professional development. This section examines professional development in both pre- and in-service settings and emphasizes the need for ongoing teacher learning.

> . . . effective ELD instruction is more than just "good teaching." It is a multifaceted endeavor requiring teachers to understand second-language development, plan and deliver ELD instruction, and assess learning outcomes.

Preservice Education

With the burgeoning population of English learners in the U.S., preservice education for teachers of those students is increasingly in the spotlight. Wong Fillmore and Snow (2005) underscore this point, arguing that *all* teachers, not only those serving English learners, should have a thorough grounding in language and its role in education. Prospective educators need to know more about language in order to take on five functions as teachers:

(1) teacher as *communicator*—how teachers can structure their own language output for maximum clarity to work effectively with students from many different cultural, social, and linguistic backgrounds;

(2) teacher as *educator*—how teachers can help students learn and use aspects of language associated with the academic discourse of the various school subjects;

(3) teacher as *evaluator*—how teachers can make valid judgments about students' abilities by understanding variation in language use such as vernacular varieties of English, normal progress for second-language learners, or developmental delays or disorders;

(4) teacher as *educated human being*—how teachers can understand basic concepts about language and literacy to engage in public discussions and make informed decisions about issues underlying second-language learning and effective education for language-minority students; and

(5) teacher as *agent of socialization*—how teachers can help students learn the everyday practices, the system of values and beliefs, and the means and manners of communication of their cultural communities and, at the same time, how they can help students make the transition in ways that do not undermine the role played by parents and family members in their communities.

Wong Fillmore and Snow (2005) call for courses in educational linguistics in teacher-education programs. They maintain that teachers-to-be should learn about characteristics of oral language: the basic units of language such as phonemes and morphemes and larger units of language such as sentence and discourse structures. They need to know about written language, such as features of narrative and expository writing, and they need to know how vocabulary is acquired—what it means to really know words and how to apply their varied meanings appropriately and expressively.

Harper and de Jong (2004), however, claim that two basic assumptions guide many current teacher-preparation programs:

(1) that the needs of English learners do not differ significantly from those of other diverse learners; and

(2) that the discipline of ESL is primarily a menu of pedagogical adaptations appropriate for a variety of diverse learners.

These faulty assumptions, they note, are reflected in the following teacher's statement: "It's not all that different" (the process of second-language learning). Such assump-

tions lead to the beliefs that the learning of a second language simply requires exposure to and interaction in the target language and that all English learners will learn English in the same way. Instead, assisting teachers to formulate belief systems based on sound theory and practice must be a key objective of preservice preparation so that teachers in training learn to pay explicit attention to the special language needs of English learners and to understand the myriad factors that affect the learning of English (e.g., personality, motivation, attitude, cultural background, learning styles, etc.) (de Jong and Harper 2005, 2007).

To do this, effective preservice training must prepare prospective teachers to attend to the demands of language development and academic content of their English learners. To do so, teachers need to be knowledgeable about the process of second-language development; the role and interaction of learner variables; strategies for explicitly teaching second-language skills; and the language demands of the content areas. Teachers must become familiar with critical topics such as profiles of English learners and their parents so that they develop a sense of the background (e.g., literacy levels, family support, immigration status) accompanying English learners. Such training must also treat key concepts in second-language acquisition such as those presented in an earlier section of this chapter, and considerable time must be devoted to strategies for teaching listening, speaking, reading, writing, grammar, and vocabulary. The teachers-to-be also need to learn how to design lesson plans with language, strategy, and content objectives in mind and how to adapt materials and strategies appropriately for English learners of different proficiency levels. Finally, they need to learn about key issues in assessment, both for measuring classroom performance and for understanding large-scale standardized testing, including how to use assessment information as input in instructional decisions.

In-Service Professional Development

Even as the number of English learners in schools has increased, professional development for their teachers has not kept pace. A recent national survey found that in many states, even those with large English learner populations, less than 10 percent of the teachers surveyed had received more than eight hours of in-service training in ELD in the previous three years (United States Department of Education 2002). In California, Gándara, Maxwell-Jolly, and Driscoll (2005) documented the limited amount of professional development that teachers of English learners have received. Their survey of 5,300 California teachers revealed that half of those surveyed had up to 50 percent English learners in their classes; however, teachers had attended only one training session in bilingual or ESL methods—or none at all—in the past five years.

Preservice education should lay the foundation for a well-rounded and skilled teacher. In-service professional development, on the other hand, requires a focus on specific skills. Historically, at the K–5 grade level, in-service training for ELD instruction has included a set of bandage strategies and techniques. If the systematic process described in this chapter is to be implemented, then schools must adopt a focus for ELD instruction that is schoolwide and not left to individual teacher decisions or relegated to the level of strategies and ELD materials with little relevance to the regular curriculum.

> In the end, both preservice and in-service training must equip teachers with the knowledge, skills, and disposition to effectively teach English learners.

A focused plan for in-service that has as its goal standards-based, differentiated instruction needs intensive time allocation accompanied by in-house coaching (Joyce and Weil 1992). Teachers need time and ongoing support to shift paradigms from one in which ELD is seen as an additional demand during the school day to one in which it is seen as systematically permeating the curriculum and something for which all teachers take responsibility. To tell teachers that they must teach ELD without the training to accomplish such a task is to invite failure. The necessary components of such training are face-to-face, collaborative sessions conducted over time; in-house coaching; and calendared planning time (de Jong and Harper 2005). Coaching and planning are specific, targeted activities. They are centered on standards-based, differentiated lessons developed during the sessions. Time for continued planning at school is followed by coaching with regular follow-up support.

In the end, both preservice and in-service training must equip teachers with the knowledge, skills, and disposition to effectively teach English learners.[11] There are 10 competencies that teachers of English learners should possess (Merino 2007). The competencies should guide professional development, assisting teachers at all stages of their careers to teach all English learners well and to prepare them to be productive members of their school and home communities.

⊙ Knowledge of research on first- and second-language acquisition and how this research has informed instruction and assessment

---

11. Materials suitable for professional development of teachers of English learners in kindergarten through grade five have increased exponentially in the past few years. In addition to the teacher resources discussed in this chapter, other useful references are as follows: Carrasquillo and Rodriguez (2002), Freeman and Freeman (2002), Zainuddin et al. (2002), Dragan (2005), and Ariza (2006).

- Understanding of academic language in English, with experience in helping students make connections to the home language

- Knowledge of discipline-specific content and its cognitive and linguistic demands on English learners

- Deep understanding of instruction, both in practice and through research, on the implementation of curricula and strategies effective with English learners

- Understanding and implementation of assessment to inform instruction and monitor progress meaningfully and efficiently in response to English learner needs

- Understanding of how contextual factors in classrooms, schools, and communities influence learning and access to the curriculum for diverse learners

- Understanding of learners and their families, their strengths and their challenges—especially the impact of language and culture on communities living in poverty

- Knowledge and expertise in the use of approaches to involve families in extending classroom learning to diverse communities

- Knowledge and skill in conducting inquiry about teaching and learning in classrooms in ways that are responsive to English learner needs

- Skills and experience in working effectively and collaboratively within small communities of inquiry designed to advance learning for English learners. (Merino 2007, 6)

Throughout this chapter, our intent has been to provide teachers of ELD K–5 with the theoretical and research foundations for understanding the complex dynamics of second-language acquisition along with a set of practical instructional and assessment strategies for use in the classroom. Perhaps most important, it is our hope that teachers of ELD K–5 will become passionate advocates for English learners in their school communities.

References

Alcón, Eva. 2004. Research on language and learning: Implications for language teaching. *International Journal of English Studies* 4(1): 173–96.

Anderson, Neil. 2005. Learning strategies. In *Handbook of research in second language teaching and learning,* ed. Eli Hinkel, 757–71. Mahwah, NJ: Lawrence Erlbaum.

Ariza, Eileen N. 2006. *Not for ESOL teachers: What every classroom teacher needs to know about the linguistically, culturally, and ethnically diverse student.* Boston, MA: Allyn & Bacon.

August, Diane, and Kenji Hakuta. 1997. *Improving schooling for language minority children: A research agenda.* Washington, DC: National Research Council.

Bachman, Lyle F. 2002. Alternative interpretations of alternative assessments: Some validity issues in educational performance assessment. *Educational Measurement: Issues and Practices* 21(3): 5–19.

Bailey, Alison L., ed. 2007. Introduction: Teaching and assessing student learning English in school. In *The language demands of school: Putting academic English to the test,* ed. Alison L. Bailey, 1–26. New Haven, CT: Yale University Press.

Bailey, Alison L., Frances A. Butler, Charmien Laframenta, and Christine Ong. 2004. *Towards the characterization of academic language in upper elementary science classrooms.* (Final deliverable to OERI/OBEMLA, Contract No. R305b960002). University of California, Los Angeles: National Center for Research on Evaluation, Standards, and Student Testing (CRESST).

Bailey, Alison L., Frances A. Butler, Robin Stevens, and Carol Lord. 2007. Further specifying the language demands of school. In *The language demands of school: Putting academic English to the test,* ed. Alison L. Bailey, 103–56. New Haven, CT: Yale University Press.

Barr, Mary A. 2000. Looking at the learning record. *Educational Leadership* 57(5): 20–24.

Berman, Paul, Catherine Minicucci, Barry McLaughlin, Beryl Nelson, and Katrina Woodworth. 1995. *School reform and student diversity: Case studies of exemplary practices for LEP students.* Santa Cruz, CA: National Center for Research on Cultural Diversity and Second Language Learning, and B. W. Associates.

Bridges, Allayne, Chris G. Sinha, and Valerie Walkerdine. 1981. The development of comprehension. In *Learning through interaction: The study of language development,* ed. Gordon Wells, 116–56. Cambridge: Cambridge University Press.

Brown, Roger, and Ursula Bellugi. 1964. Three processes in the child's acquisition of syntax. *Harvard Educational Review* 34(2): 133–51.

Bruner, Jerome. 1966. On cognitive growth. In *Studies in cognitive growth,* ed. Jerome Bruner and R. R. Oliver. New York: John Wiley and Sons.

Bunch, George. 2006. Academic English in the 7th grade: Broadening the lens, expanding access. *Journal of English for Academic Purposes* 5(4): 284–301.

Calderón, Margarita, Rachel Hertz-Lazarowitz, and Robert E. Slavin. 1998. Effects of bilingual cooperative integrated reading and composition on students making the transition from Spanish to English reading. *Elementary School Journal* 99(2): 153–65.

Carr, John, Ursula Sexton, and Rachel Lagunoff. 2006. *Making science accessible to English learners: A guidebook for teachers.* San Francisco: WestEd.

Carrasquillo, Angela L., and Vivian Rodriguez. *2002. Language minority students in the mainstream classroom.* 2nd ed. Clevedon, England: Multilingual Matters.

Cazden, Courtney B. 1974. Play with language and metalinguistic awareness: One dimension of language experience. *The Urban Review* 1: 28–39.

CELDT Assistance Packet – California English Development Test. 2008. http://www.cde.ca.gov/ta/tg/el/documents/celdt08astpkt1.pdf

Chamot, Anna U. 2005. The cognitive academic language learning approach (CALLA): An update. In *Academic success for English language learners: Strategies for K–12 mainstream teachers,* ed. Patricia A. Richard-Amato and Marguerite A. Snow, 87–102. White Plains, NY: Longman.

Chen, Linda, and Eugenia Mora-Flores. 2006. *Balanced literacy for English language learners, K–2.* Portsmouth, NH: Heinemann.

Chomsky, Noam. 1957. *Syntactic structures.* The Hague: Mouton.

Chomsky, Noam. 1965. *Aspects of the theory of syntax.* Cambridge, MA: M.I.T. Press.

Collier, Virginia P. 1987. Age and rate of acquisition of second language for academic purposes. *TESOL Quarterly* 21(4) (December): 617–41.

Cooper, C. R., J. Denner, and E. M. Lopez. 1999. Cultural brokers: Helping Latino children on pathways toward success. *When School Is Out* 9 (2), 51–57. http://www.bridgingworlds.org/pdfs/culturalbrokers.pdf (accessed September 17, 2008).

Coxhead, Averil. 2006. *Essentials of teaching academic vocabulary.* Boston: Houghton Mifflin.

Crabbe, David. 2003. The quality of language learning opportunities. *TESOL Quarterly* 37 (Spring): 9–34.

Cummins, Jim. 1980. Psychological assessment of immigrant children: Logic or intuition? *Journal of Multilingual and Multicultural Development* 1: 97–111.

Cummins, Jim. 2000. *Language, power and pedagogy: Bilingual children in the crossfire.* Clevedon, England: Multilingual Matters.

de Jong, Ester J., and Candace A. Harper. 2005. Preparing mainstream teachers for English language learners: Is being a good teacher good enough? *Teacher Education Quarterly* 32: 101–24.

de Jong, Ester J., and Candace A. Harper. 2007. ESL is good teaching plus: Preparing standard curriculum teachers for all learners. In *Language, curriculum, & community in teacher education,* ed. Maria Estela Brisk, 101–24. Mahwah, NJ: Lawrence Erlbaum.

DeKeyser, Robert, and Alan Juffs. 2005. Cognitive considerations in L2 learning. In *Handbook of research in second language teaching and learning,* ed. Eli Hinkel, 437–54. Mahwah, NJ: Lawrence Erlbaum.

Dornan, Reade, Lois Matz Rosen, and Marilyn Wilson. 2005. Lesson designs for reading comprehension and vocabulary development. In *Academic success for English language learners: Strategies for K–12 mainstream teachers,* ed. Patricia A. Richard-Amato and Marguerite A. Snow, 248–74. White Plains, NY: Longman.

Dragan, Pat B. 2005. *A how-to guide for teaching English language learners in the primary classroom.* Portsmouth, NH: Heinemann.

Dulay, Heidi.C., and Marina K. Burt. 1973. Should we teach children syntax? *Language Learning* 23(2): 245–58.

Durgunoglu, Aydin Y., and Banu Öney. 2000. Literacy development in two languages: Cognitive and sociocultural dimensions of cross-language transfer. Proceedings of a Research Symposium on High Standards in Reading for Students from Diverse Language Groups: Research, Practice & Policy, 78–99. Washington, DC. April 19–20.

Dutro, Susana, and Carrol Moran. 2003. Rethinking English language instruction: An architectural approach. In *English learners: Reaching the highest levels of English literacy,* ed. Gilbert G. Garcia, 227–58. Newark, DE: International Reading Association.

Ediger, Anne. 2001. Teaching children literacy skills in a second language. In *Teaching English as a second or foreign language.* 3rd ed., ed. Marianne Celce-Murcia, 153–69. Boston, MA: Heinle & Heinle.

Ellis, Rod. 1994. *The study of second language acquisition.* Oxford, England: Oxford University Press.

Ellis, Rod. 2002. Does form-focused instruction affect the acquisition of implicit knowledge? *Studies in Second Language Acquisition* 24: 223–36.

Ellis, Rod. 2005a. Principles of instructed language learning. *System* 33: 209–24.

Ellis, Rod. 2005b. Instructed language learning and task-based teaching. In *Handbook of research in second language teaching and learning,* ed. Eli Hinkel, 713–28. Mahwah, NJ: Lawrence Erlbaum.

Ellis, Rod., S. Loewen, and R. Erlam. 2006. Implicit and explicit corrective feedback and the acquisition of L2 grammar. *Second Language Acquisition* 28: 339–68.

English–language arts content standards for California public schools: Kindergarten through grade twelve. 1998. Sacramento: California Department of Education.

English language development standards for California public schools: Kindergarten through grade twelve. 2002. Sacramento: California Department of Education.

Freeman, Yvonne S., and David E. Freeman (with Sandra Mercuri). 2002. *Closing the achievement gap: How to reach limited-formal-schooling and long term English learners.* Portsmouth, NH: Heinemann.

Gándara, Patricia, Julie Maxwell-Jolly, and Anne Driscoll. 2005. *Listening to teachers of language learners.* Santa Cruz, CA: Center for the Future of Teaching and Learning.

Garcia, Georgia E. 1991. Factors influencing the English reading test performance of Spanish-speaking Hispanic children. *Reading Research Quarterly* 26: 371–92.

Gass, Susan M., and Larry Selinker. 2001. *Second language acquisition: An introductory course.* 2nd ed. Mahwah, NJ: Lawrence Erlbaum.

Genesee, Fred, Kathryn Lindholm-Leary, William Saunders, and Donna Christian. 2006. *Educating English language learners: A synthesis of research evidence.* New York: Cambridge University Press.

Gersten, Russell, and Scott Baker. 2000. What we know about effective instructional practices for English-language learners. *Exceptional Children* 66(4): 454–70.

Gibbons, Pauline. 2002. *Scaffolding language, scaffolding learning: Teaching second language learners in the mainstream classroom.* Portsmouth, NH: Heinemann.

Gibbons, Pauline. 2006. Steps for planning an integrated program for ESL learners in mainstream classes. In *Planning and teaching creatively within a required curriculum for school-age learners,* ed. Penny McKay, 215–33. Alexandria, VA: Teachers of English to Speakers of Other Languages.

Goatley, Virginia J., Cynthia H. Brock, and Taffy E. Raphael. 1995. Diverse learners participating in regular education "Book Clubs." *Reading Research Quarterly* 30: 352–80.

Graves, Kathleen. 2006. Series editor's preface. In *Planning and teaching creatively within a required curriculum for school-age learners,* ed. Penny McKay, v-viii. Alexandria, VA: Teachers of English to Speakers of Other Languages.

Gunn, Cindy L. 2003. Exploring second language communicative competence. *Language Teaching Research* 7(2): 240–58.

Hall, Joan Kelly. 1995. (Re)creating our worlds with words: A sociohistorical perspective of face-to-face interaction. *Applied Linguistics* 16: 206–32.

Han, Zhao-Hong H., and J. H. Kim. 2008. Corrective recasts. What teachers might want to know. *Language Learning Journal* 36(1): 35–44.

Harper, Candace, and Ester de Jong. 2004. Misconceptions about teaching English-language learners. *Journal of Adolescent and Adult Literacy* 48 (October): 152–62.

Harrell, Adrienne L., and Michael Jordan. 2008. *Fifty strategies for teaching English language learners.* 3rd ed. Upper Saddle River, NJ: Pearson.

Hornberger, Nancy. 1990. Creating successful learning contexts for bilingual literacy. *Teachers College Record* 92: *212–29.*

Horwitz, Elaine K. 2008. *Becoming a language teacher: A practical guide to second language learning and teaching.* Boston, MA: Allyn & Bacon.

Jacobs, Evelyn, Lori Rottenberg, Sondra Patrick, and Edythe Wheeler. 1996. Cooperative learning: Context and opportunities for acquiring academic English. *TESOL Quarterly* 30(2) (Summer): 253–80.

Johnson, Jacqueline S., and Elissa L. Newport. 1989. Critical period effects in second language learning: The influence of maturational state on the acquisition of English as a second language. *Cognitive Psychology* 21: 60–99.

Joyce, Bruce B., and Marsha M. Weil. 1992. *Models of teaching.* 4th ed. Boston, MA: Allyn & Bacon.

Kagan, Spencer. 1989. *Cooperative learning: Resources for teachers.* Laguna Niguel, CA: Resources for Teachers.

Kasper, Gabriele, and Carsten Roever. 2005. Pragmatics in second language learning. In *Handbook of research in second language teaching and learning,* ed. Eli Hinkel, 317–35. Mahwah, NJ: Lawrence Erlbaum.

Kinsella, Kate. 1997. Moving from comprehensible input to "learning to learn" in content-based instruction. In *The content-based classroom: Perspectives on integrating language and content,* ed. Marguerite Ann Snow and Donna M. Brinton, 46–68. White Plains, NY: Longman.

Krashen, Stephen. 1985. *The input hypothesis: Issues and implications.* London: Longman.

Lantolf, James, and Steven L. Thorne. 2007. Sociocultural theory and second language learning. In *Theories in second language acquisition: An introduction,* ed. Bill VanPatten and Jessica Williams, 201–24. Mahwah, NJ: Lawrence Erlbaum.

Lee, Jin S., and Eva Oxelson. 2006. It's not my job: K–12 teacher attitudes toward students' heritage language maintenance. *Bilingual Research Journal* 30(2): 453–77.

Lenneberg, Eric. 1967. *Biological foundations of language.* New York: Wiley.

Lesaux, Nonie K., and Esther Geva. 2006. Synthesis: Development of literacy in language-minority students. In *Developing literacy in second-language learners: Report of the national literacy panel on language-minority children and youth,* ed. Diane August and Timothy Shanahan, 53–74. Mahwah: NJ: Lawrence Erlbaum.

Lightbown, Patsy, and Nina Spada. 2006. *How languages are learned.* 3rd ed. Oxford: Oxford University Press.

Lindholm-Leary, Kathryn, and Graciela Borsato. 2006. Academic achievement. In *Educating English language learners: A synthesis of research evidence,* ed. Fred Genesee, Kathryn Lindholm-Leary, William C. Saunders, and Donna Christian, 176–222. Cambridge: Cambridge University Press.

Long, Michael H. 1983. Linguistic and conversational adjustments to non-native speakers. *Studies in Second Language Acquisition* 5: 177–93.

Lott, B. 2003. Recognizing and welcoming the standpoint of low-income parents in the public schools. *Journal of Educational and Psychological Consultation* 14: 91–104.

Lucas, Tamara, and Anne Katz. 1994. Reframing the debate: The roles of native languages in English-only programs for language minority students. *TESOL Quarterly* 28(3) (Autumn): 537–61.

Lyster, Roy. 2004a. Research on form-focused instruction in immersion classrooms: Implications for theory and practice. *Journal of French Language Studies* 14: 321–41.

Lyster, Roy. 2004b. Differential effects of prompts and recasts in form-focused instruction. *Studies in Second Language Acquisition* 26: 399–432.

Lyster, Roy, and Leila Ranta. 1997. Corrective feedback and learner uptake: Negotiation of form in communicative classrooms. *Studies in Second Language Acquisition* 19: 37–66.

MacIntyre, Peter D., Susan C. Baker, Richard Clément, and Lesley A. Donovan. 2002. Sex and age effects on willingness to communicate, anxiety, perceived competence, and L2 motivation among junior high school French immersion students. *Language Learning* 52: 537–64.

Mayer, Jan. 2007. A conceptual framework of academic English language for broad application to education. In *The language demands of school: Putting academic English to the test,* ed. Alison L. Bailey, 68–102. New Haven, CT: Yale University Press.

McBride-Chang, Catherine, Twila Tardif, Jeung-Ryeul Cho, Hua Shu, Paul Fletcher, Stephanie F. Stokes, Anita Wong, and Kawai Leung. 2008. What's in a word? Morphological awareness and vocabulary knowledge in three languages. *Applied Psycholinguistics* 29: 437–62.

McGroarty, Mary, and Margarita Calderón. 2005. Cooperative learning for second language learners: Models, applications, and challenges. In *Academic success for English language learners: Strategies for K–12 mainstream teachers,* ed. Patricia A. Richard-Amato and Marguerite A. Snow, 174–94. White Plains, NY: Longman.

McLaughlin, Barry. 1992. *Myths and misconceptions about second language learning: What every teacher needs to unlearn.* Santa Cruz, CA: The National Center for Research in Cultural Diversity and Second Language Learning.

Merino, Barbara. 2007. Identifying critical competencies for teachers of English learners. *Newsletter of the University of California Linguistic Minority Research Institute* 16(4) (Summer): 1–7.

Miramontes, Ofelia B., Adel Nadeau, and Nancy L. Commins. 1997. *Restructuring schools for linguistic diversity: linking decision making to effective programs.* New York: Teachers College Press.

Mitchell, Rosamond, and Florence Myles. 2004. *Second language learning theories.* 2nd ed. London: Hodder Arnold.

Munro, Miles, and Virginia Mann. 2005. Age of immersion as a predictor of foreign accent. *Applied Psycholinguistics* 26: 311–41.

National Research Council. 1999. *Testing, teaching and learning: A guide for states and school districts,* ed. Richard F. Elmore and Robert Rothman. Board on Testing and Assessment, Commission on Behavioral and Social Sciences and Education. Washington, DC: National Academy Press.

Newport, Elissa L., Daphne Bavelier, and Helen J. Neville. 2001. Critical thinking about critical periods: Perspectives on a critical period for language acquisition. In *Language, brain and cognitive development: Essays in honor of Jacques Mehler,* ed. E. Dupoux, 481–502. Cambridge, MA: M.I.T. Press.

Norris, John M., and Lourdes Ortega, eds. 2006. *Synthesizing research on language learning and teaching.* Amsterdam: John Benjamins Publishing Co.

Peck, Sabrina. 2001. Developing children's listening and speaking in ESL. In *Teaching English as a second or foreign language.* 3rd ed., ed. Marianne Celce-Murcia, 139–49. Boston, MA: Heinle & Heinle.

Peterson Pat W. 2001. Skills and strategies for proficient listening. In *Teaching English as a second or foreign language,* 3rd ed., ed. Marianne Celce-Murcia, 87–100. Boston, MA: Heinle & Heinle.

PreK–12 English language proficiency standards. 2006. Alexandria, VA: Teachers of English to Speakers of Other Languages.

Quiocho, Alice L., and Sharon H. Ulanoff. 2008. *Differentiated literacy instruction for English language learners.* Boston, MA: Allyn & Bacon.

Ramirez, A. Y. Fred. 2003. Dismay and disappointment: Parental involvement of Latino immigrant parents. *The Urban Review* 35(2): 93–110.

Rea, Denise M., and Sandra P. Mercuri. 2006. *Research-based strategies for English language learners: How to reach goals and meet standards,* K–8. Portsmouth, NH: Heinemann.

Reiss, Jodi. 2005. *Teaching content to English language learners.* White Plains, NY: Longman.

Ricento, Tom. 2005. Considerations of identity in L2 learning. In *Handbook of research in second language teaching and learning,* ed. Eli Hinkel, 895–910. Mahwah, NJ: Lawrence Erlbaum.

Richard-Amato, Patricia A., and Marguerite Ann Snow. 2005. Instructional strategies for K–12 mainstream teachers. In *Academic success for English language learners: strategies for K–12 mainstream teachers,* ed. Patricia A. Richard-Amato and Marguerite A. Snow, 197–223. White Plains, NY: Longman.

Rost, Michael. 2005. L2 listening. In *Handbook of research in second language teaching and learning,* ed. Eli Hinkel, 503–27. Mahwah, NJ: Lawrence Erlbaum.

Russell, Jane Valezy, and Nina Spada. 2006 The effectiveness of corrective feedback for the acquisition of L2 grammar. In *Synthesizing research language on learning and teaching,* ed. John M. Norris and Lourdes Ortega, 133–64. Philadelphia: John Benjamins.

Saunders, William C., and Gisela O'Brien. 2006. Oral language. In *Educating English language learners: A synthesis of research evidence,* ed. Fred Genesee, Kathryn

Lindholm-Leary, William C. Saunders, and Donna Christian, 14–63. Cambridge: Cambridge University Press.

Scarcella, Robin C. 2003. *Accelerating academic English: A focus on the English learner.* Oakland, CA: Regents of the University of California.

Schifini, Alfredo, Deborah J. Short, Josefina Villamil Tinajero, Eugene E. Garcia, Erminda Garcia, Else Hamayan, and Lada Kratky. 2004. *Avenues.* Carmel, CA: Hampton Brown.

Schleppegrell, Mary. 2004. *The language of schooling: A functional linguistic perspective.* Mahwah, NJ: Lawrence Erlbaum.

Seedhouse, P. 2001. The case of the missing "no": The relationship between pedagogy and interaction. *Language Learning* 51 (Supplement 1): 347–85.

Selinker, Larry. 1972. Interlanguage. *International Review of Applied Linguistics* 10: 209–31.

Selinker, Larry, Merrill Swain, and Guy Dumas. 1975. The interlanguage hypothesis extended to children. *Language Learning* 25: 139–52.

Shepard, Lorrie A. 2000. *The role of classroom assessment in teaching and learning.* Washington, DC: Center for Research on Education, Diversity and Excellence/Center for Applied Linguistics.

Short, Deborah J. 1994. Expanding middle school horizons: Integrating language, culture, and social studies. *TESOL Quarterly* 28(3) (Autumn): 581–608.

Snow, Catherine E., and Charles Ferguson, eds. 1977. *Talking to children: Language input and acquisition.* Cambridge: Cambridge University Press.

Snow, Marguerite A. 2005a. Primary language instruction: A bridge to English language development. In *Schooling and language minority students: A theoretical framework.* 3rd ed., 119–60. Los Angeles: California State University, Evaluation, Dissemination and Assessment Center.

Snow, Marguerite A. 2005b. A model of academic literacy for integrated language and content instruction. In *Handbook of research in second language teaching and learning,* ed. Eli Hinkel, 693–712. Mahwah, NJ: Lawrence Erlbaum.

Solomon, Jeff, and Nancy Rhodes. 1996. Assessing academic language: Results of a survey. *TESOL Journal* 5 (Summer): 5–8.

Spada, Nina, and Patsy Lightbown. 2008. Form-focused instruction: Isolated or integrated? *TESOL Quarterly* 42(2) (June): 181–207.

Stevens, Robin A., Frances A. Butler, and Martha Castellon-Wellington. 2000. *Academic language and content assessment: Measuring the progress of ELLs.* University of California, Los Angeles: National Center for Research on Evaluation, Standards, and Student Testing (CRESST).

Swain, Merrill. 1985. Communicative competence: Some roles of comprehensible input and comprehensible output in its development. In *Input and second language acquisition,* ed. Susan Gass and Carolyn Madden, 235–53. Rowley, MA: Newbury House.

Swain, Merrill. 2001. Integrating language and content teaching through collaborative tasks. *Canadian Modern Language Review* 58(1): 44–63.

Swain, Merrrill. 2005. The output hypothesis: Theory and research. In *Handbook of research in second language teaching and learning,* ed. Eli Hinkel, 471–83. Mahwah, NJ: Lawrence Erlbaum.

Swain, Merrill, and Sharon Lapkin. 2008. Lexical learning through a multitask activity: The role of repetition. In *Pathways to multilingualism: Evolving perspectives on immersion education,* ed. Diane Tedick and Tara Fortune, 119–32. Clevedon, England: Multilingual Matters.

Swain, Merrill, and Sharon Lapkin. 1998. Interaction and second language learning: Two adolescent French immersion students working together. *Modern Language Journal* 83 (Autumn): 320–37.

Téllez, Kip, and Hersh C. Waxman. 2006. A meta-synthesis of qualitative research on effective teaching practices for English language learners. In *Synthesizing research on language learning and teaching,* ed. John M. Norris and Lourdes Ortega, 245–77. Amsterdam: John Benjamins Publishing Co.

Trumbull, Elise, Patricia M. Greenfield, Carrie Rothstein-Fisch, and Blanca Quiroz. 2007. Bridging cultures in parent conferences: Implications for school psychology. In *Handbook of multicultural school psychology: An interdisciplinary perspective,* ed. G. B. Esquivel, E. C. Lopez, and S. Nahari, 615–36. Mahwah, NJ: Lawrence Erlbaum.

Trumbull, Elise, Carrie Rothstein-Fisch, Patricia M. Greenfield, and Blanca Quiroz. 2001. *Bridging cultures between home and school: A guide for teachers.* Mahwah, NJ: Lawrence Erlbaum.

Umbel, Vivian M., and D. Kimbrough Oller. 1994. Developmental changes in receptive vocabulary in Hispanic bilingual school children. *Language Learning* 44(2): 221–42.

United States Department of Education. 2002. *Schools and staffing survey 1999–2000.* Washington, DC: U.S. Department of Education.

VanPatten, Bill, and Jessica Williams, eds. 2007. *Theories in second language acquisition: An introduction.* Mahwah, NJ: Lawrence Erlbaum.

Vygotsky, Lev. 1979. *Mind in society: The development of higher psychological processes,* ed. Michael Cole and others. Cambridge, MA: Harvard University Press.

Walqui, Aida. 2000. *Access and engagement: Program design and instructional approaches for immigrant students in secondary school.* McHenry, IL, and Washington, DC: Center for Applied Linguistics and Delta Systems.

Wells, Gordon. 1986. *The meaning makers: Children learning language and using language to learn.* Portsmouth, NH: Heinemann.

Wong Fillmore, Lily. 1991. *Second language learning in children: A model of language learning in social context. Language processing in bilingual children,* ed. Ellen Bialystok, 49–69. Cambridge: Cambridge University Press.

Wong Fillmore, Lily, and Catherine E. Snow. 2005. What teachers need to know about language. In *Academic success for English language learners: Strategies for K–12 mainstream teachers,* ed. Patricia A. Richard-Amato and Marguerite A. Snow, 47–75. White Plains, NY: Longman.

Wood, David., Jerome S. Bruner, and Gail Ross. 1976. The role of tutoring in problem-solving. *Journal of Child Psychology and Psychiatry* 17: 89–100.

Zainuddin, Hanizah, Noochaya Yahya, Carmen A. Morales-Jones, and Eileen W. Ariza. 2002. *Fundamentals of teaching English to speakers of other languages in K–12 mainstream classrooms.* Dubuque, IA: Kendall/Hunt.

Chapter 3

English Language Development: Issues and Implementation at Grades Six Through Twelve

Susana Dutro, E.L. Achieve
Kate Kinsella, San Francisco State University

Secondary education is a complex endeavor. Fast-paced schedules, specialized courses, rigorous content, high-stakes assessments, and a variety of instructional methods place a high demand on students. For English learners, who must navigate these complexities while acquiring English, the demands intensify significantly (Dutro and Levy 2008).

The teachers who serve these students deserve support to gain an understanding of second-language acquisition and clear guidance for providing the language instruction English learners require to participate in their schooling.

Secondary education is a complex endeavor.

In this chapter we advocate a comprehensive, standards-aligned English language development (ELD) curriculum taught during a dedicated course of study. We present an approach for rethinking English language instruction for adolescent English learners based on current research and promising practices. We do this by providing:

1. A discussion of the linguistic challenges adolescent English learners face

2. An overview of the diversity among English learners in grades six to twelve and standards-based English proficiency levels

3. A rationale for instructed ELD in the secondary school context

4. An analysis of common course placements for adolescent English learners and their potential shortcomings of those placements

5. A model for instructed ELD in the secondary school context. To illustrate the model, we include specific examples with corresponding tools to:

⊙ Identify high-yield cognitive functions and related functional language.

⊙ Explicitly teach vocabulary and develop expressive word knowledge, including a schema for identifying high-priority words.

⊙ Ensure ample opportunities for structured, contextualized language production with a focus on targeted language forms, along with teacher feedback.

Throughout this chapter, we will reference the key research detailed in Chapter 1, "Research to Guide English Language Development Instruction." Saunders and Goldenberg report on existing research related to instructed ELD through the 14 guidelines for practice. This research base supports the instructional framework outlined in this chapter and provides important background information.

We take a functional, communicative competence approach to second-language learning. Saunders and Goldenberg's Guideline 6 (this publication) states, "ELD instruction should integrate meaning and communication to support explicit teaching of language." However, they also note that the recommended relative emphasis on form or meaning as well as the degree to which form has to be addressed within a meaningful context have yet to be determined by research. When presenting instructional activities focused on language forms, we consistently couch them in meaningful contexts (Doughty and Williams 1998; Long 2007). In this regard, we are aligned with Ellis's conclusions (2005a) that "instructed language learning"—in this case, instructed ELD—provides purposes for paying attention to language, authentic and functional uses of the language being learned, and activities beyond students' current level of proficiency. We also agree with Norris and Ortega (2000), who assert that carefully planned and explicit instruction is more effective than ad hoc implicit instruction.

Linguistic Challenges for Adolescent English Learners

Language development, whether a first or second language, is a lifelong endeavor. However, learning to speak our primary language occurs mostly effortlessly, almost invisibly (Gleason 2005). It is only when we are learning to manipulate a new language (or the academic aspects of our first one) that many of these aspects of language become obvious; for example when we have difficulty sounding like native speakers (phonology), putting words in the correct order (syntax), or using the appropriate language in a particular context (pragmatics) (Dutro and Helman in press).

Adolescent English learners face a particularly daunting task. To succeed in schooling, they must gain a multifaceted knowledge of the English language. This complex linguistic knowledge comprises six aspects.

Figure 3.1. Language Competence

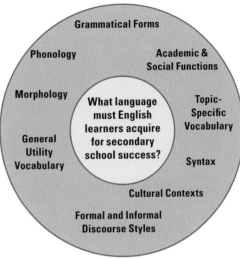

(Adapted from Dutro 2005a.)

1. Phonology—the individual sounds of a language (e.g., /th/ or subtle differences between long and short *i*)

2. Morphology—meaningful parts that make up a word (e.g., *un-, dis-, -able, -struc-, trans-*)

3. Vocabulary—knowing the meanings of both general utility (e.g., *characteristic, produce*) and topic-specific words (e.g., *integer, simile, plasma*)

4. Syntax—how words are ordered to generate sentences (e.g., subject-verb-object, dependent clauses)

5. Formal and informal discourse styles—language for different disciplines (e.g., scientific inquiry, literary analysis), genres (e.g., narrative, expository, proposition/support), and settings (e.g., formal social event, informal gathering with friends, classroom discussion, academic debate).

6. Academic and social functions—the cognitive task at hand (e.g., comparing a book and movie, giving directions or stating a position and supporting it with evidence).

Academic English

Proficiency in academic language is essential to achieving long-term success in school and beyond (see Guideline 10, Saunders and Goldenberg, this publication). The importance of academic English extends beyond academics to real-life situations. Informed consumers and citizens must problem-solve, weigh evidence, and think critically. Language knowledge is needed to perform the paperwork associated with such tasks as banking, health care, and property rental.

Although there are many definitions of academic English, there are agreed-upon commonalities. According to various sources cited by Saunders and Goldenberg (this publication), "Academic language refers to the specialized vocabulary, grammar, discourse/textual, and functional skills associated with academic instruction and mastery of academic material and tasks" (p. 58). Academic language is significantly different from the informal speech

Academic English requires sufficient background knowledge to apply general knowledge of words differently across subject areas.

students use outside the classroom. The language of schooling includes everyday words (e.g., *reason, understand*), general academic vocabulary that cuts across subject areas (e.g., *respond, category*) and specialized terms (e.g., *polygon, onomatopoeia*) (Feldman and Kinsella 2008). Written and spoken classroom discourse is also characterized by academic text structures and grammatical complexity (Bailey 2007; Scarcella 2003; Schlepegrell 2004; Wong Fillmore and Snow 2000).

Academic English requires sufficient background knowledge to apply general knowledge of words differently across subject areas. For example, *division* and *product* have strikingly different meanings in mathematics than they do in social studies or everyday use. Similarly, a student might encounter the term *factor* in a mathematics class (process) and later that same day in a discussion of economics (issue). Academic English also entails specialized knowledge of concepts in particular subject areas. Consider the background knowledge and vocabulary needed to understand the context for terms such as *proofread, edit, revise, rewrite,* and *recopy*. Knowledge of diverse academic text structures helps a reader follow the narrative in a biography of Lance Armstrong, identify bias in an editorial about the Tour de France, make sense of a physics text explaining how bicycle pedals and gears use torque, and follow instructions for assembling a bicycle.

Adolescent English learners do not have the luxury of listening and absorbing the forms and structures of academic English over an extended period of time. Instructional strategies to tap into prior knowledge, scaffold content instruction, and ensure student motivation and interaction—although critical—are not enough to ensure student learning. There is general agreement among educators that academic English must be continually developed and explicitly taught. We argue that to accelerate the language proficiency of English learners, teachers of all disciplines must make "visible" the otherwise "invisible" skills of content-specific academic language.

In an English class, instructed ELD may mean pointing out the distinctions in purpose and form between an informal written summary of a short story in a reading journal and a formal written summary of a journal article, including use of

expressions such as "According to the author" and "The author maintains." In a science class, ELD may mean teaching students how to explain the solution to a problem by sequencing a series of discrete steps. The teacher responsible for in- structed ELD lays a solid foundation of language knowledge that enables students to engage in a range of academic tasks.

They must tackle this formidable language-learning task while mastering demanding grade-level subject matter. Adolescent English learners must "get a handle" on every word and sentence pattern that native speakers of English have spent thousands of hours internalizing during their early childhoods and schooling. This arduous lin- guistic and cognitive task must be accomplished in a highly condensed time frame, often only during the hours a student is in school. In addition, English learners must learn the specialized language being taught in every subject area. This task includes mastery of the conceptual and concrete language taught in the current year and re- call of, and facility with, the foundational vocabulary taught in previous years. Short and Fitzsimmons (2007) contend that, with gaps in English language and literacy, adolescent English learners must strive to accomplish "double the work" of native English-speaking students while studying rigorous standards-based curricula and taking the same high-stakes assessments.

Gaps in Language Proficiency

Statistics regarding English proficiency in grades six through twelve for second- language learners are dismaying. A significant number of English learners achieve adequate oral fluency for face-to-face communication yet lag dramatically in measures of academic success and tasks requiring academic language proficiency. As noted by Gold and Maxwell-Jolly (2006) in the academic year 2005, 60 percent of tenth-grade English learners scored at the proficient level on California's assessment of English proficiency (CELDT), while only 3 percent scored proficient on the more rigorous California Standards Test in English that requires knowledge of complex language for abstract uses. This finding suggests that although a high number of adolescent English learners are gaining fluency in English as measured by the CELDT, a disturbingly high percentage of these same learners are demonstrating a limited command of the vocabulary and structures of academic English neces- sary for successful schooling. They are not yet equipped with sufficient knowledge of English to successfully engage in common academic tasks, such as inference, analysis, hypothesis, and summary.

> **A significant number of English learners achieve adequate oral fluency for face-to-face communication yet lag dramatically in . . . tasks requiring academic language proficiency.**

Diversity of Adolescent English Learners

Each student's path to the secondary classroom includes a unique range of experiences. Achieving a skillful command of English depends on several factors, including the level of language and literacy development in the primary language, amount of time in U.S. schools, type of instructional program, age, individual experiences, and—most important—*the quality of instruction* (Darling-Hammond 1997).

As Gold and Maxwell-Jolly (2006) note about adolescent English learners: "They share the English learner designation based on their language status. They arrive in our high schools via diverse paths, and with a wide range of skills and experiences" (p. 3). We cannot assume that adolescent English learners have seamlessly moved through the levels of English proficiency or acquired the expected prerequisite skills and content as they moved through the system. Neither can we assume that limited proficiency in English equates to limited content knowledge. English learners are not a monolithic group.

English learners who have previously studied English in a formal context, perhaps through courses in their home country, may be more competent in reading and writing English than speaking or understanding it. But for the majority of English learners who have been in American schools for multiple years, everyday oral proficiency develops more quickly than more formal oral and written language (Hakuta, Butler, and Witt 2000). Students glean a great deal of English knowledge from daily experiences in language learning. Therefore, it is common that while an English learner may have internalized certain complex verb forms, he or she may consistently misuse some common irregular verbs, incorrectly use certain pronouns, and periodically confuse basic prepositional phrases or common vocabulary.

Some adolescent English learners are newcomers who have had high-quality schooling in their home country. Their literacy and content knowledge may be at or above grade level. When provided with well-designed ELD instruction, they are able to make good or excellent progress in learning English. Course work may pose challenges depending on several factors, such as socioeconomic status, study skills, previous exposure to English, and quality of support in the new school environment (cf. Boyson and Short 2003; Ruiz-de-Velasco and Fix 2000). Other newly arrived English learners have had interrupted schooling and little opportunity to develop academic skills in their home country. Those students require intensive and targeted ELD instruction, additional instruction in literacy and content knowledge, and social support.

Many English learners have been in American schools for several years or are U.S.-born and are making good or adequate progress. They have moved (or are moving) through ELD courses and may be in mainstream or sheltered-content courses. Those students vary in levels of primary language knowledge: from full literacy to none at all and from having a full oral command of the language to limited oral proficiency. Most of those English learners have strong English language skills but have gaps in vocabulary or syntactic knowledge (Boyson and Short 2003; Scarcella 1996). They continue to benefit from a sheltered approach and targeted language support in rigorous content classes and instructed language appropriate to their English level to help them navigate the increasingly complex language demands of content learning in secondary school.

> A significant number of second-language learners are long-term . . . English learners, who have had most or all of their education in American schools and are not enjoying academic success.

A significant number of second-language learners are long-term—or protracted—English learners, who have had most or all of their education in American schools and are not enjoying academic success (Batalova 2006). The educational services they have received during their schooling vary dramatically due to program design and actual implementation (Short and Fitzsimmons 2007). The students are mostly fluent in everyday language, but they often struggle with reading and writing, have limited vocabulary and syntactical knowledge, and lack sufficient with academic English to accomplish academic tasks. This lack of language proficiency and achievement may cause parents, teachers, and the student to underestimate student's academic potential (Olsen, Romero, and Gold 2006).

In summary, because of the tremendous range of backgrounds and experiences of adolescent English learners, a "one-size-fits-all" approach is not feasible. To better understand the assets and potential challenges that impact English learners' academic readiness, it is helpful for the teacher to consider:

1. **Literacy and content knowledge in the primary language** (level of education in a native country, participation in a bilingual program, level of parent literacy, availability of books and other learning resources in the home and community, nonschool-based experiences)

2. **Previous experiences in American schools** (consistent or interrupted schooling, participation in a reading intervention program, attendance in extended-day classes or tutorials, sheltered content course work, quality and consistency of instruction, and so on)

3. **English language knowledge** (number of years in American schools, prior exposure to English, participation in instructed ELD/ESL courses, quality of previous English language instruction)

Levels of English Proficiency

The levels of English proficiency that follow here are adapted from *Systematic English Language Development* (Dutro 2005a). They reflect a common understanding in the field of ELD, agree with those in state and national standards documents, and are widely used by practitioners to guide instructional planning. These levels were introduced in Chapter 1. We reintroduce them and present mini-case studies for each level to illustrate student needs and effective instructional practices at secondary schools.

Beginning: Level 1

Early Intermediate: Level 2

Intermediate: Level 3

Early Advanced: Level 4

Advanced: Level 5

Terminology

The terminology used in describing levels of English proficiency can sometimes be confusing. For purposes of No Child Left Behind mandates, states determine **students' level of achievement** on standards-based assessments using the following terms: Far Below Basic, Below Basic, Basic, Proficient and Advanced. The term *advanced* in this context signifies achievement beyond the proficient level in a content area (mathematics, reading comprehension, science, or history) based on standardized measures, such as the California Standards Test (CST).

However, the terms used to describe English proficiency in the *English Language Development Standards for California Public Schools* (1999) indicate a **student's instructional level** along a continuum of English language skills. They are performance expectations that describe what students must internalize and learn to do independently, automatically, and in a variety of contexts. A student at the early advanced level of English needs to learn the competencies, vocabulary, and language forms described in the early advanced level. The student is not yet fully proficient in English to accomplish grade-level tasks without some level of targeted language support. Only upon exiting the advanced level of English proficiency is a student considered to be approximating grade-level and native-like proficiency.

English Language Development Standards

English language development (ELD) standards and descriptions of proficiency levels apply to all English learners regardless of program type. Each teacher of English learners is responsible for helping them develop full academic proficiency in English, whether in a mainstream or sheltered context. ELD standards are designed to serve as a pathway to reading/language arts and content area learning. In the *English Language Development Standards for California Public Schools* (1999), as in the standards of several other states, oral (listening and speaking) and written (reading and writing) language are integrated reciprocal processes.

> **English language development (ELD) standards and descriptions of proficiency levels apply to all English learners regardless of program type.**

1. Beginning Level

Jose Luis entered seventh grade with a beginning level of English proficiency. During the year, he progressed from having no receptive or productive English skills to possessing a basic use of English, which included many errors. He acquired comprehension of high-frequency words and everyday utterances that referred to his concrete surroundings.

Students new to English demonstrate dramatic growth as they gain familiarity with the sounds, rhythms, and patterns of English. They progress from having no receptive or productive English skills to possessing basic English for daily life, following directions, and survival tasks. Very early in the beginning level, students use gestures to communicate basic needs and quickly learn to comprehend high-frequency words and basic phrases in immediate physical surroundings. As they progress, they learn to produce words, phrases, and simple sentences using common nouns and verbs (e.g., *apple, red apple, ride. It is big. She is singing*). They often make many basic errors in speech and have minimal comprehension of general meaning.

Beginning-level students learn English letter/sound correspondence, interact with frequently used English print in a limited way, and learn to write newly learned language by, for example, completing a frame using an illustrated word bank to describe people, things, or actions: *I am _____ (happy, hungry, sitting); I need (help with math, a pencil); there is/are _____.*

Newcomers should be assessed in their primary language, whenever possible, and in content areas before determining course placement. For students who have been in American schools, teachers need to use all available data from previous schools, including local and standardized assessments.

2. Early Intermediate Level

Marisol is at the early intermediate level of English proficiency. She is demonstrating increased comprehension of oral and written English. She uses basic vocabulary in response to pictures and other visual prompts, uses routine expressions, and answers questions by using simple sentences with a subject and predicate in present and past tenses. Marisol responds to short pieces of text with structured support and, when provided with scaffolds such as sentence and paragraph frames, generates writing that includes the main idea and a description.

As students move into the early intermediate level, they learn to use routine expressions independently. They can respond orally and in writing using phrases and simple sentences. They continue to learn a great deal of vocabulary with an emphasis on expressing complete thoughts using:

- Present tense and present progressive

    Examples: "My brother is riding a bike," "The lion roars." "The lion roars loudly."

- Simple future and past progressive tenses in utterances

    Examples: "My brother is going to ride a bike," "Was the lion roaring?" and "No, the lion was eating."

- Past tense form of common verbs, such as *walked, ran, went, saw, ate, wanted* in sentences

    Examples: "I saw a train." "We went to the park." "I added the numbers."

Their comprehension of general meaning increases dramatically. They may grasp some specific meaning and write about concrete and/or familiar topics using frames or simple vignettes and word banks and compound sentences with support. Early intermediate English learners will continue to exhibit some basic errors in speech.

3. Intermediate Level

Phuong's English is at the intermediate level. She is able to comprehend information on familiar topics and produce sustained conversation with others on an expanding variety of general topics. Her vocabulary knowledge is deepening, becoming more precise and varied. Her speech and writing include varied verb forms, but the conditional form eludes her and she misuses some past-tense forms.

At this proficiency level, students are learning to combine known language in new ways to formulate and answer questions, retell, identify main points of a story, explain, predict, describe, and compare/contrast (e.g., *This story is just like the other one*). They write using compound sentences joining two independent clauses (e.g., *He studied hard, and he got a good grade*) and complex sentences with support. They are learning to use a variety of verb tenses and grammatical

structures (e.g., *I went to school yesterday. I didn't want to go because I felt sick, but we were having a test*). By using language patterns, such as signal words and phrases, and sentence and paragraph frames as a starting point, intermediate-level English learners can express ideas, describe events, and give information orally and in writing. There is tremendous vocabulary growth as students learn to use words more precisely. For example, they learn many synonyms (*large, giant, huge*), antonyms (*quick/slow, strong/weak, subtraction/addition*), and basic idioms (*cut it out, raining cats and dogs*).

Students at the intermediate level comprehend and discuss main ideas and basic concepts in content areas and write basic information and expanded responses. They demonstrate good comprehension of general meaning and increasing comprehension of specific meaning. They can read familiar below-grade-level text independently and grade-level text with scaffolds, the amount depending on the familiarity and difficulty of the text. Oral and written language may focus on forms and conventions such as pronoun usage and past-tense verb endings; language use may include reporting, dialogues, skits, and games.

As they respond and experiment with sentences using more detail and new vocabulary, they will continue to have some errors in speech.

4. Early Advanced Level

Ivan is able to use English in complex, cognitively demanding ways and communicate clearly about a range of topics using specific and varied vocabulary. When discussing the development of newborn mammals, he said, "After a few hours, the colt could stand up and the mare didn't have to help him." Although his meaning is clear, Ivan used circumlocution to communicate his point. As is typical of this level of proficiency, Ivan sometimes avoids using language he recognizes but has not yet internalized, such as the reflexive pronoun by itself in this example.

One of the characteristics of advanced English proficiency is that learners begin to initiate and sustain spontaneous interactions in English. They are able to comprehend increasingly complex oral and written material and learn new vocabulary usage through those interactions. Explicit and systematic ELD instruction currently is rare at either of the advanced levels, depriving students of the opportunity to master the academic language necessary to compete in higher-level academic contexts.

Students at the early advanced level of English proficiency exhibit consistent comprehension of general meaning and good understanding of implied meaning. They are able to sustain conversations and respond with detail in varied sentences using extensive vocabulary (*How can black bears survive in the forest if they can't find food there?*). These students can use language for a range of purposes and communicate with multiple audiences. Their vocabulary is specific and academic, and they can manipulate the English language to adequately represent their thinking. In general, early advanced students communicate using standard grammar with few random errors.

At this level, students learn to use the appropriate language to present, report, or identify a main idea, supporting details, and concepts; solicit information; hypothesize; and infer word meaning from context and affixes (*He was flipping through the pages of the book trying to find the picture he wanted to show me*). They are able to read most grade-level text with instructional support (handle vocabulary and sentence/text structure), write with support using complex sentences having at least one dependent clause, and compose an essay with the support of explicit teaching, samples, and scaffolds such as paragraph and essay formats, and vocabulary webs. Written language may be a bit stilted and lack common figurative devices or precise vocabulary.

5. Advanced Level

Elena participates fully in core content curriculum with minimal language support. She is able to read grade-level material about concrete and abstract topics with limited comprehension. She recognizes many subtleties in language and uses vivid vocabulary in a variety of communicative settings. She is still fine-tuning her understanding of shades of meaning. For instance, when choosing a synonym for move *she said, "The Museum of Modern Art has situated into a vast, new building."*

Students at the advanced level write to satisfy social and academic purposes by recombining previously learned vocabulary and structures. However, even at the advanced level, expression is sometimes stilted and occasionally inappropriate to the context. Explicit instruction in the finer points of usage is still needed at the advanced level in order to achieve standard native-like English production (See Guideline 11, Saunders and Goldenberg, this publication). Advanced students demonstrate comprehension of general and implied meaning, including an increased understanding of idiomatic and figurative language. They initiate and negotiate communication using complex sentence structures and vocabulary (*Black bears prefer to scavenge for food; whereas grizzlies hunt for small animals*). They have mastered language conventions for formal and informal use.

Explicit language instruction at the advanced level should focus on addressing persistent problem areas in grammar, working to develop fluency and automaticity, teaching idioms, figurative language, and the nuances of language use in

a variety of settings. At this level, students learn to debate and support point of view, persuade, and justify. They understand and use native-like speech, abstract and figurative language, idioms, jokes, and embedded and tag questions (*I wonder what time it is. You don't know what time it is, do you?*). They read grade-level text with light instructional support (vocabulary and sentence/text structure), compose with the support of explicit teaching, samples, and scaffolds using nearly native-like discourse and write using complex sentences with at least one dependent clause (without support).

Instruction Throughout the Day

In this section we place instructed ELD in the context of an adolescent English learner's school day.

A Rationale for Instructed ELD

To engage successfully in standards-based course work taught in English, adolescent English learners must operate from a competent second-language base. Many of them have limited exposure to English or opportunities for interaction outside the classroom. Without informed and systematic instruction in how English works—vocabulary, word usage, grammatical features, and syntactical

> To engage successfully in standards-based course work taught in English, adolescent English learners must operate from a competent second-language base.

structures—older school-age learners are not apt to develop a confident command of English for complex social and academic purposes. Further, even the most effective instructional support for rigorous content area learning in the academic mainstream may be woefully insufficient for students in simultaneous need of sophisticated discipline knowledge and linguistic knowledge. Academic achievement across the secondary school curricula will be accelerated only when students are truly proficient in English. This finding has led many to conclude that, like other complex learning, proficiency in English requires systematic and explicit instruction in a dedicated course of study (Saunders, Foorman, and Carlson 2006; Norris and Ortega 2006). Consistent, explicit, and purposeful language instruction with regular structured practice is necessary for adolescent English learners to develop a competent command of school-based terms and internalize the forms of academic language (see Saunders and Goldenberg's Guidelines 5 and 10, this publication).

There is widespread confusion, however, as to the appropriate time during the instructional day for language courses, their context in the rest of a student's course work, and the sacrifices to be made to integrate this critical course work (Short and Fitzsimmons 2007). The unfortunate consequence is that many adolescent English learners do not have a clear course of study to help them develop confidence in both social and academic English language use.

In tandem with Saunders and Goldenberg in this publication, we propose a compre-hensive approach as the most productive way of preparing adolescent second-language students to reach grade-level standards in English: explicit English language instruction throughout the instructional day. Figure 3.2 illustrates a comprehensive approach to instructing adolescent English learners, which includes a dedicated course for teaching English as its own content area (ESL/ELD), complemented by targeted academic English instruction across the subject areas (Dutro and Moran 2003). Such an approach maximizes the effectiveness of instruction by ensuring adolescent English learners are taught appropriately *through-out* the school day.

During instructed ELD, language learning is squarely in the foreground.

Content instruction is driven by the standards and compe-tencies of a particular discipline. The science, math, or social studies teacher's task is to identify the language that enables students to discuss, read, and write about the critical lesson concepts and processes at hand. Core content knowledge is understandably placed in the foreground, while language considerations are in the background. Whereas teachers from every subject area must shoulder responsibility for teaching the specific academic language necessary to construct and express meaning of content being taught, content learning is paramount. (See Echevarria and Short in this publication for a thorough discussion of sheltered content instruction.) The language taught during content instruction is in the service of content standards mastery rather than the English language skills outlined by ELD standards. That is, during content instruction, the content objective is in the foreground and language support in the background.

In contrast, during instructed ELD, language learning is squarely in the foreground; content is in the background, providing something viable and stimulating to discuss, read, and write about. The learning objectives are guided by ELD standards (*English-Language Development Standards for California Public Schools* 1999). The content used during instructed ELD engages students either with a topic of immediate relevance, such as recycling or cyber-bullying, or content that directly relates to some aspect of their academic course work. Whether introduced in a reading selection, video, or hands-on experience, the content in instructed ELD essentially serves as a vehicle to introduce, practice, and reinforce developmentally appropriate language targets (see Saunders and Goldenberg in this publication, Guidelines 5 and 12). Instructed ELD is a school's one dedicated opportunity to teach English learners the vocabulary,

Figure 3.2. Blueprint for Instruction of Adolescent English Learners

Instructed ELD	English Language Arts Instruction		Mathematics, Social Studies, Science, Physical Education, Arts
	Reading Intervention	Grade-Level ELA	

Instructed ELD

Goal
Develop a solid English language foundation needed to fully engage in academic and real-life situations.

Purpose
Teach students language necessary to move from one assessed English-proficiency level to the next. Language is in the foreground.

Content
⊙ English is taught in functional contexts following a scope and sequence of oral and written language skills, balancing focus on form and focus on meaning.
⊙ Determined by students' ELD levels and linked to ELD standards.
⊙ *Beginning/Early Int*—basic foundation, everyday topics
⊙ *Intermediate*—increasing specificity, building toward ELA standards
⊙ *Early Adv/Advanced*—increasing precision, in-depth genre work for meeting ELA standards.

Teachers Need
⊙ Knowledge of L2 levels, L2 learning, and pedagogy
⊙ Tools to assess and plan instruction
⊙ Collaboration time
⊙ Scheduled time to teach language

Reading Intervention

Goal
Gain literacy skills needed to accelerate achievement (for students currently performing below grade level)

Teachers Need
⊙ Understanding of how to diagnose and teach skills of reading and writing
⊙ Pedagogical knowledge for accelerating learning and achievement

Grade-Level ELA

Goal
Achieve grade-level content standards

Teachers Need
⊙ Understanding of how to assess and teach skills of reading and writing,
⊙ Pedagogical knowledge

Mathematics, Social Studies, Science, Physical Education, Arts

Goal
Achieve grade-level content standards

Teachers Need
⊙ Knowledge of content being taught
⊙ Pedagogical knowledge

Explicit Language Instruction for Content Learning

Purpose	Teach language needed to construct and express meaning of content concepts. Content learning is in the foreground.
Content	Determined by demands of lesson and students' knowledge of English.
Teachers Need	Tools to identify essential language demands of lesson
	Tools to plan language instruction for content learning
	Support through collaborative planning

Adapted from Dutro 2008.

sentence structure, and grammar that they did not learn outside school, that will not be taught in any other content class, and that they need to be able to use effectively every day—within both school and real-world contexts.

Common Student Placements and Potential Shortcomings

Secondary schools place English learners in a common array of courses with the intent of accelerating second-language proficiency and overall academic achievement. Those courses have distinct purposes and outcomes, not all of which are optimal for second-language students (Short and Fitzsimmons 2007; Olsen, Romero, and Gold 2006)

English language development (ELD). Courses dedicated to ELD have a primary goal of assisting second-language students in developing a solid English language foundation. This entails teaching the language that will not be taught adequately or reliably in other course work and that is needed for daily school-based communicative contexts, literacy tasks, content comprehension, and full access to the curriculum. In every other course of study throughout the academic year, content instruction invariably trumps language development. For adolescent English learners to develop a competent command of the English language for school-based purposes, they must be placed in a dedicated ELD class with students at similar proficiency levels with the sole intent of accelerating their English progress (cf. Saunders and Goldenberg, in this publication, Guidelines 5 and 13).

Secondary schools characteristically provide instructed ELD for English learners at the beginning, early intermediate, and intermediate levels. Schools generally use scores from standardized language assessments, such as California's English Language Development Test (CELDT) to determine placement in courses commonly labeled ELD or ESL 1, 2, or 3. Often both relatively new arrivals (students in American schools for less than five years) and protracted long-term English learners are placed in the same intermediate ELD 3 course. Long-term English learners may indeed have a comfortable command of conversational English yet display persistent and significant gaps in knowledge of English. Based on extensive work with secondary schools throughout the nation, the authors have found that few middle or high schools provide formal language instruction once students reach the upper-intermediate and advanced proficiency levels. Consequently, there is no set-aside course or dedicated time within a course for high intermediate and advanced English learners to receive specific support in developing a firm grasp of English critical to successful grade-appropriate academic interactions, reading comprehension, and writing tasks. Yet this is the stage of language development when English learners are ready to grapple with a deeper understanding of how English works and to learn to use increasingly complex language structures and sophisticated vocabulary. This is precisely when skilled language instruction is critical to help propel them out of intermediate limbo into the advanced levels of English proficiency.

Reading intervention. Another significant variable in the weak development of academic language for adolescent English learners is the high proportion of students placed in reading-intervention programs. The primary goal of reading intervention is to address basic knowledge and skills in English literacy that are posing challenges for striving readers. For students with the most acute basic literacy needs, reading intervention initially includes the foundational components of phonemic awareness and phonics (the sounds of a language and how to put sounds together to form words). For students who have mastered the basic decoding skills in English, reading-intervention course work includes work with advanced decoding of multisyllabic words, reading fluency, and text comprehension strategies.

Increasingly, ELD is being taught as part of a comprehensive reading-intervention block where the focus is on building decoding and fluency rather than explicitly teaching a well-thought-out scope and sequence of English language instruction. From our knowledge of secondary schools and reports from teachers and administrators, it appears that these placements are generally determined by scores on state assessments or the results of a single reading measure and do not consider students' English levels or literacy skills in their primary language. Similar to mainstream English classes, reading-intervention courses are not designed to provide instructed ELD; that is, explicit preparation in the language needed to construct meaning and express understanding of language for everyday and academic purposes.

Reliance on reading-intervention courses alone to address both comprehensive ELD standards and reading achievement is distressing in light of the pivotal role that oral language proficiency plays in reading comprehension. As Saunders and Goldenberg, as well as August and Shanahan, point out in this publication, there is ample evidence of the reciprocal relationship between oral English proficiency and reading achievement. In examining research on the reading performance of English learners, Genesee and colleagues (2006) found that students with well-developed oral English skills experience greater success in English reading. Similarly, the National Literacy Panel on Language Minority Children and Youth Report (August and Shanahan 2006) found that ". . . well-developed oral proficiency in English is associated with English reading comprehension and writing skills. . . . Specifically, English vocabulary knowledge, listening comprehension, syntactic skills, and the ability to handle metalinguistic aspects of language, such as providing definitions of words, are linked to English reading and writing proficiency." They also noted that despite this critical relationship between oral language proficiency and reading comprehension and writing competence, oral language is rarely systematically addressed in curricula or instructional practice.

In Chapter 4, August and Shanahan report "although instructional approaches that have worked with native speakers of English can be a good place to start, using these procedures slavishly *with no adjustment despite the very real differences that often exist between first- and second-language learners is less effective"* (p. 222, emphasis added). They go on to say, ". . . providing high-quality instruction in literacy skills alone may be insufficient to support equal academic success for language minority students. Sound reading strategy instruction (and instruction in other literacy basics) must be combined with efforts to increase the scope and sophistication of these students' oral language proficiency."

Despite intensive efforts in many of the nation's schools to provide targeted reading intervention for both native English-speaking students and English learners who struggle with reading, the achievement gap persists. The data and mounting research evidence suggest that reading-intervention courses by themselves are not likely to appropriately address the instructional needs of English learners (August and Shanahan, this publication; Genessee et al. 2006; Saunders and Goldenberg's Guidelines 3, 4, and 5, this publication; Short and Fitzsimmons 2007).

We believe that these disappointing outcomes result in part from a failure to infuse dedicated language development in reading-intervention programs. Dedicated ELD instruction focused on oral language is also required to equip students with both the language and literacy skills needed to navigate demanding course work in secondary school.

Sheltered content area instruction. Well-designed sheltered instruction (defined and discussed in Saunders and Goldenberg, this publication) uses an array of instructional techniques to render content comprehensible to English learners. The main goal is to provide English learners with meaningful access to grade-level content knowledge. Another goal of sheltered instruction is to equip students with the language needed for content learning (Echevarria, Vogt, and Short 2000). Because of time constraints and the demands of delivering challenging content, instructors must devote most of their instructional minutes to helping students grasp the fundamental concepts and processes. Optimally, the vocabulary and language structures taught are in the service of constructing and expressing meaning of core content knowledge. However, some researchers have observed that effective content teaching may not always be effective language teaching (Arreaga-Mayer and Perdomo Rivera 1996; Ramirez 1992; Swain 1988). In fact, during sheltered content instruction, time for language learning often becomes incidental to learning about the content or is omitted altogether and results in a "failure to systematically impart the skills students need in speaking and writing" (Gersten and Baker 2000). In this publication, Saunders and Goldenberg maintain that language instruction in the service of specialized content learning is insufficient to equip English learners with a solid command of English. (See Echevarria and Short in this publication for a detailed discussion of sheltered content instruction.)

Special education. Special education services are designed to provide academic support for students with diagnosed learning challenges, including native English-speaking students and English learners. At the secondary school level, this support is commonly geared to assisting students with basic task completion across the subject areas. Language knowledge plays a critical role in reading comprehension, and reading problems are central among students receiving special education services. Therefore, it makes sense to include language-proficiency goals and objectives in an individualized education program (IEP). Doing so helps to ensure that English learners with diagnosed learning needs receive the additional targeted and intensive language development necessary to comprehend and articulate understandings in academic English.

Description of Instructed ELD

Although research and theory do not present a uniform view of how to best teach English for academic purposes, there is ample evidence that providing carefully planned lessons explicitly addressing specific aspects of the second language is far more productive than merely exposing students to abundant English and incidentally addressing specific forms (Norris and Ortega 2006). Although Saunders, Foorman, and Carlson (2006) found that English learners provided with a separate ELD instructional period consistently outperformed English learners who primarily received ELD integrated during their language arts period, the researchers similarly noted that the students' gains in English would have been far more substantive had their teachers provided more explicit instruction of concrete language features and guided practice rather than primarily engaging students in an array of activities (Guidelines 2 and 5, Saunders and Goldenberg, this publication).

> There is ample evidence that providing carefully planned lessons explicitly addressing specific aspects of the second language is far more productive than merely exposing students to abundant English and incidentally addressing specific forms.

Meaning-focused exposure to a second language through communicative activities allows learners to develop greater oral fluency and confidence. However, without complementary form-focused instruction that intentionally draws students' attention to language elements and with structured analysis and application, students may never acquire many critical linguistic forms and have persistent difficulties with pronunciation as well as with morphological, syntactic, and pragmatic features of the second language (Long 1998; Harley and Swain 1984; Lyster 1987).

Because many adolescent English learners' exposure to English occurs primarily or exclusively in the classroom, those older students require meaningful yet form-focused instruction that enables them to make more efficient use of their limited exposure to the sounds, words, and sentence structures of English (Lightbown and Spada 2006; Long 1991). Explicit teaching helps learners to notice features in meaning-based context, making it more likely that they will master them (Doughty and Williams 1998; Lightbown 1998; Schmidt 1990). Spada and Lightbown (2008) maintain that the most compelling question in second-language pedagogy is no longer whether older second-language learners benefit from form-focused explicit instruction but how it can be most effectively delivered.

In instructed ELD, students are grouped by their assessed English level (see Chapter 1). Instructed ELD uses an organized method that does not leave the development of vocabulary knowledge or grammatical structures and patterns to random experiences or chance encounters. It follows a developmental scope and sequence of language skills identified in ELD standards, is explicitly taught, and includes substantive practice to ensure students develop in-depth understanding of how English works, fluency, and accurate command of the language. Instructed ELD puts language learning squarely in the forefront and:

- Explicitly teaches language by assessed proficiency level
- Emphasizes oral language development (listening and speaking) through carefully structured, purposeful, and engaging interactions
- Integrates reading and writing applications of taught language in authentic contexts
- Lays out a scope and sequence of grammatical forms necessary to communicate for a range of purposes (functions) by proficiency level
- Teaches vocabulary for social and academic purposes, moving from general to increasingly precise words
- Draws students' attention to a variety of aspects of English (e.g., rhythm and cadence, pronunciation, colloquial expressions, formal and informal registers)

A Model for Explicit Language Instruction

This section presents a model for instructed ELD, based on research, with a goal of equipping English learners with full English proficiency (see Figure 3.3). Each lesson must be designed to build fluent and accurate use of English for a range of academic and other real-life purposes. We will describe a process for determining:

> I. Purposeful uses of language identified in ELD standards (language functions)
>
> II. Language tools needed to accomplish these goals
>
> III. Robust and contextualized instruction that includes many opportunities to engage in language practice

Figure 3.3. Features of Explicit Language Instruction

I. Language Functions

Purposes of language
- To perform cognitive tasks
- To express thinking orally and in writing
- To inform text structure
- To engage in social and academic conversation

Relevance to EL instruction

What communicative purposes must English learners be able to navigate? What language functions do standards-based cognitive tasks require? What text structures must students comprehend?

- Participate in discussions
- Classify and compare/contrast
- Express social courtesies
- Describe, explain, and elaborate
- Give/follow directions
- Make generalizations
- Predict
- Summarize

- Express action and time relationships
- Sequence
- Express needs, likes and feelings
- Express cause/effect
- Draw conclusions
- Proposition/support
- Clarify

II. Language Tools

What language tools are needed to communicate for different purposes?
What language is needed to comprehend text and express thinking orally and in writing?

Figure 3.3 *(continued)*

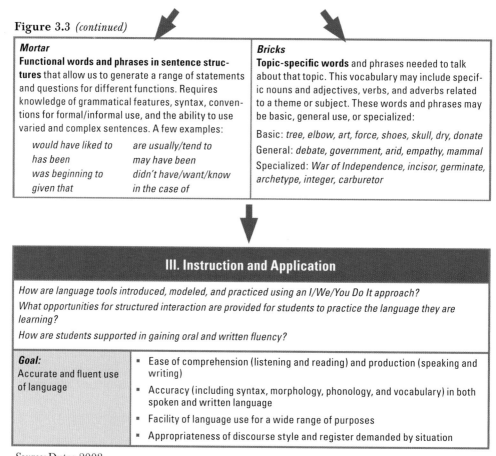

Mortar	Bricks
Functional words and phrases in sentence structures that allow us to generate a range of statements and questions for different functions. Requires knowledge of grammatical features, syntax, conventions for formal/informal use, and the ability to use varied and complex sentences. A few examples: *would have liked to* *are usually/tend to* *has been* *may have been* *was beginning to* *didn't have/want/know* *given that* *in the case of*	**Topic-specific words** and phrases needed to talk about that topic. This vocabulary may include specific nouns and adjectives, verbs, and adverbs related to a theme or subject. These words and phrases may be basic, general use, or specialized: Basic: *tree, elbow, art, force, shoes, skull, dry, donate* General: *debate, government, arid, empathy, mammal* Specialized: *War of Independence, incisor, germinate, archetype, integer, carburetor*

III. Instruction and Application

How are language tools introduced, modeled, and practiced using an I/We/You Do It approach?

What opportunities for structured interaction are provided for students to practice the language they are learning?

How are students supported in gaining oral and written fluency?

| **Goal:**
Accurate and fluent use of language | • Ease of comprehension (listening and reading) and production (speaking and writing)

• Accuracy (including syntax, morphology, phonology, and vocabulary) in both spoken and written language

• Facility of language use for a wide range of purposes

• Appropriateness of discourse style and register demanded by situation |

Source: Dutro 2008.

I. Language Functions (Cognitive Tasks)

We embark on the lesson-planning process by determining the communicative purposes, or language functions, essential for communicative competence in English. Language functions are the cognitive tasks that drive us to connect thought and language (Halliday 1973; Brown 1994). Language functions are used on a continuum from simple to complex, orally (express opinion, participate in a discussion) and in writing (persuasion, description), and are determined by the situation and by the content concept. The language function determines the required language forms and sentence structures, in addition to informing text structure. For example,

Language functions are the cognitive tasks that drive us to connect thought and language.

participation in everyday class discussion requires dexterity in a myriad of language functions, including contributing an opinion ("I don't believe that . . ."), asking for clarification ("So you are saying" . . . "Is that right?"), and reporting information ("We have concluded that . . .").

Throughout the course of the instructional day, students may be called upon to express time relationships ("Before the Civil War began"; "The year before last"), or identify cause-and-effect relationships ("I got detention because I forgot my home-work; "Due to the recent budget crisis . . ."). Our emphasis on language functions is echoed by Saunders and Goldenberg (this publication), who note that "performance of academic tasks also requires that students be competent performing sophisticated 'language functions'":

- ⊙ To argue persuasively for or against a point of view
- ⊙ To analyze, compare, and contrast
- ⊙ To evaluate alternative points of view and factual information
- ⊙ To justify one's point of view or to debate different points of view
- ⊙ To synthesize and integrate information
- ⊙ To follow or give complex directions
- ⊙ To hypothesize about the causal relationship between events
- ⊙ To justify a prediction, as in a science experiment
- ⊙ To present a logical argument
- ⊙ To question an explanation

We assert that identifying and teaching language functions for everyday and academic purposes is a cornerstone of effective language instruction for adolescent English learners. Those cognitive tasks reflect the demands of ELD, English-language arts, and other content area standards. Table 3.1 identifies an array of response frames that help English learners to engage successfully in a range of daily classroom language functions, whether collaborating with peers or contributing independently during a unified class discussion.

Table 3.1. Language Functions and Frames for Classroom Communication

Express an Opinion

I think/believe that . . .

In my opinion . . .

Based on my experience, I think . . .

Predict

I predict/imagine that . . .

Based on . . ., I infer that . . .

I hypothesize that . . .

Ask for Clarification

What do you mean?

Will you explain that again?

I have a question about that.

Paraphrase

So you are saying that . . .

In other words, you think . . .

What I hear you saying is . . .

Solicit a Response

What do you think?

We haven't heard from you yet.

Do you agree?

What answer did you get?

Acknowledge Ideas

My idea is similar to _'s idea.

I agree with (a person) that . . .

As _ already mentioned, . . .

My idea builds upon _'s idea.

Report a Partner's Idea

_indicated that . . .

_pointed out to me that . . .

_emphasized that . . .

_concluded that . . .

Report a Group's Idea

We decided/agreed that . . .

We concluded that . . .

Our group sees it differently.

We had a different approach.

Disagree

I don't agree with you because . . .

I have a different answer from you.

I see it another way.

Offer a Suggestion

Maybe we could . . .

What if we . . .

Here's something we might try.

Affirm

That's an interesting idea.

I hadn't thought of that.

I see what you mean.

Hold the Floor

As I was saying, . . .

If I could finish my thought . . .

What I was trying to say was . . .

II. Language Tools   (Adapted from Kinsella 2002.)

Language tools are determined by the need—the language function or purpose for communication, plus the topic at hand—and students' level of English proficiency. Communicative competence (e.g., Canale and Swain 1980) entails the ability to effectively use language for specific purposes in particular settings, such as those described in ELD standards. Competence includes knowing the appropriate words, grammatical features and sentence structures, and having the social knowledge and discourse competence to put all the linguistic information together for effective communication. Communicative competence requires the speaker, reader, or writer to have the ability to call on different linguistic tools depending on the task at hand. By unpacking the language demands of the cognitive tasks described in ELD standards, teachers can gain a better idea of what to teach. For example, a range of language skills is needed to give clear directions to the nearest bank, relate an amusing incident, discuss a recently read book, or write a paper on the social impact of the last decade's technological innovations.

> **To support students in acquiring this linguistic competence, we need clear guidance about what English language skills to teach.**

To support students in acquiring this linguistic competence, we need clear guidance about what English language skills to teach. The construction metaphor of "bricks" and "mortar" has been helpful in considering the type of language necessary for completing various communication tasks (Dutro and Moran 2003; Dutro and Levy 2008). In this metaphor, "bricks" refer to the vocabulary specific to the topic at hand, whether it be Romeo's decision to flee Verona, global warming, or the advantages of text messaging; it is ***what we are thinking, talking, reading, and writing about.*** The "mortar" is the functional language that is required to generate connected print and speech. It is grammar in action and binds together single words and phrases. "Mortar" is made up of functional words and phrases that connect "bricks" (words) to form ideas, such as making predictions, describing a process, or justifying a perspective. "Mortar" allows expression of ***what we are saying about the topic.*** Students must learn the ***meanings*** of "bricks" (words). In contrast, they must learn ***how to use*** "mortar."

For example, in addressing an ELD standard calling for students to clearly state a point of view with relevant examples—which is a high-priority linguistic task across content areas—an ELD teacher might begin with a topic relevant to adolescent learners, such as the advantages of keeping in touch with family and friends by telephone versus text messaging. The teacher might introduce the following topic-specific "brick" vocabulary words: *cell phone, call, texting, immediate, communicate, right away, easy, quick, difficult, message, advantage, convenient, inconvenient, interrupt, busy.*

But in order to compare the two methods of communication, we need functional "mortar":

> Both _____ and _____ are _____.
>
> However, _____ is better than _____ when _____.
> One advantage of _____ ing is _____.
> _____ is the _____ est way to _____ because _____.

175

Teaching students to combine "bricks" and "mortar" in varied ways enables students to generate language more adeptly:

Both *texting (text messaging)* and *calling* are *convenient.*

However, *text messaging* is better than *calling* when (*you are in a hurry/the other person is busy/you don't want to interrupt the person*).

One *advantage* of *calling* is that *you can hear the person's voice/discuss things in detail/ say more.*

An *advantage* of *texting* is that *you don't have to spend a lot of time talking/you don't have to leave a message.*

Texting is the *easiest* way to *communicate/get in touch with someone because it is quick and convenient.*

This topic could also be mined to teach the ELD standard calling for expressing time relationships using an interactive strategy for combining topic-specific brick vocabulary in sentence patterns, as illustrated in Figure 3.4.

Figure 3.4. Putting Vocabulary in Functional "Mortar"

_____ I	_____	_____.
When?	*did what?*	*for how long?*
Yesterday	texted my friend	for a few minutes.
Last week	talked on the phone	for two hours.
Last night	went shopping	most of the afternoon.
Over the weekend	studied for a test	for half an hour.
During vacation	read for two hours	all evening.

Once we decide what we want to communicate, we use our knowledge of grammar and syntax to construct sentences and paragraphs that convey our meaning. Table 3.2 provides examples of key words and phrases for common language functions demanded by secondary school content standards. The examples are organized by proficiency levels to assist the teacher in selecting appropriate language tools—or functional mortar—to accomplish the communication task at hand.

Table 3.2. Common Language Functions in the Secondary School Classroom

Function	Sample Tasks	Sample Words to Show Relationships		
		Beginning Level	Intermediate Level	Advanced Level
Elaborate/ Describe	Describe attributes, qualities, character- istics, and proper- ties. Explain relationship of objects in space.	*Has/have, is/are* *Next to, close to, above, under, behind*	*Usually, often* *Contain, consist, demonstrate* *Near, between, among, beside*	*Tend to* *Exhibit, associated with, defined by, con- sists of* *Adjacent, alongside, parallel to, in relation to*
Compare	Understand and express how two or more things are similar and how they are different.	*Like* *Are the same because . . .* *Both* *_er, _est*	*Just like* *Are similar because . . .* *Have in common* *Compared to*	*Just as* *Shared/common at- tributes* *By comparison*
Contrast	Understand and express how two or more things are different.	*But, however, unlike* *_er than*	*In contrast* *On the other hand* *Differences between*	*Whereas* *As opposed to* *A distinction between*
Identify Cause- and-Effect	Explain the cause of an outcome. Express why something occurred.	*Because* *Because of* *So*	*As a result of* *Therefore* *If . . . then* *The cause was*	*Consequently, thus* *Due to* *This led to (caused)*
Advance a Proposition and Support Present a Problem and Solution	Defend an opinion. Explain reasoning. Justify a position.	*I think/believe* *One reason that* *My (his, her) opinion* *My (his, her, our) idea*	*In my opinion* *Point of view* *Believes that* *In support of, against* *Provides evidence, make an argument*	*From the perspec- tive of* *Take a stand* *Express the view* *Thesis, position, claim, statement*
Describe a Sequence	Relate steps in a process Express time relationships and actions within a larger event	*First, second* *next, later, then* *before/ after*	*While, now, finally* *Earlier* *For the past*	*Prior to* *Previously* *Since* *Eventually* *Subsequently*
Summarize	Express main ideas and significant details	*The author (story) tells/says* *Important because*	*In summary* *Explains, discusses*	*Illustrates, mentions, concludes, explores, focuses on*

Source: Dutro and Levy 2008.

III. Instruction and Application to Develop Accurate Fluency

The literature on ELD and second-language acquisition uses the terms *accuracy* and *fluency* to refer, respectively, to instructional and developmental goals:

(1) error-free language and

(2) language that is produced easily.

Crafting instruction that results in both accuracy and fluency is challenging. No one knows the exact mix of strategies that will guarantee a balance of the two for every second-language learner. Most second-language scholars agree that one goal should not be sacrificed for the other (Alcón 2004; Celce-Murcia and Olshtain 2005; Long 1991; Lyster 2004; Spada and Lightbown 2008). For that reason, we use the term *accurate fluency* to characterize the primary goal of instructed ELD. From our perspective, *accurate fluency* entails not only grammatical and vocabulary appropriateness produced with ease, but also contextually appropriate production and interpretation of oral or written language.

> **Research on second-language acquisition indicates that English learners do not reliably develop ease and accuracy in using language required for academic tasks through passive listening or unstructured interactions.**

Research on second-language acquisition indicates that English learners do not reliably develop ease and accuracy in using language required for academic tasks through passive listening or unstructured interactions. (Several of Saunders and Goldenberg's guidelines in this publication address that fact.) We believe that students develop fluency best through authentic and engaging uses of language—both oral and written—and through carefully crafted opportunities to practice newly learned structures in different contexts.

Wong Fillmore and Snow (2000) contend that many teachers have been given misguided advice about what instructional practices are optimal for teaching English learners: from simply letting students acquire the language naturally, to simplifying the language use, to avoiding any formal grammatical explanation or error correction. Norris and Ortega (2006) explored the impact of specific instructional practices on school-age English learners learning a second language. attainment, In tandem with those research colleagues, Wong-Fillmore and Snow (2000) maintain that explicit teaching of language structures and vocabulary is frequently the most effective method of accelerating second-language proficiency.

Elements of explicit ELD instruction. In their analysis of 77 studies focused on the effectiveness of second-language instructional practices, Norris and Ortega (2006)

drew strong conclusions regarding the decided merits of explicit ELD for older English learners. In addition to clarifying the benefits of form-focused instruction, they defined three elements of explicit language teaching:

(1) conscientiously directing students' attention to a new word, language rule, or form; then

(2) clearly explaining and demonstrating that language element; and

(3) providing ample opportunities for use of the newly taught language.

In explicit, instructed ELD, focus on a linguistic form can and should be both conscientiously planned and incidental. Although most of the language features in focus should be anticipated and planned for by the teacher, some targeted language instruction can occur spontaneously during the course of a communicative task (cf. Ellis 2005b).

Students' introduction to the language feature may be either inductive or deductive, but their attention is clearly focused on learning a specific language element (Norris and Ortega 2006). The manner of introducing a new word or grammatical form is not as crucial as is channeling students' attention to the language feature. In an inductive presentation, a teacher might guide students in reading a brief paragraph about a student's daily morning routines that contains examples of third-person singular present-tense verb phrases, such as *wakes up, eats* breakfast, and *dresses* quickly. After completing the paragraph, the teacher might direct students to underline the verb in each sentence and then ask them what they notice about the verb endings. Once students have specified that they all end in *-s,* the teacher would clarify that we must put an *-s* at the end of a present-tense verb when we describe the actions that someone does often or always. In a deductive presentation, this process would be reversed. The teacher would begin with the rule and might follow with a task-based reading and highlighting of the paragraph that includes examples of the focal third-person singular verb forms. This calculated introduction and analysis, whether inductive or deductive, is immediately followed by guided meaningful opportunities to further study and apply the language feature.

In explicit ELD, students' interactions with the new language element are thus carefully orchestrated, moving from teacher modeling, to scaffolded practice with peers, to independent practice. There is a gradual release of responsibility in this scaffolded instructional model, moving from teacher delivery to class practice to peer collaboration (student-to-student interaction) to independent practice. Sometimes referred to in student-friendly terms as "I do it, we do it, you do it," this model of explicit instruction includes demonstration, explanation, guided practice, and independent practice.

Figure 3.5. Gradual Release of Responsibility Model

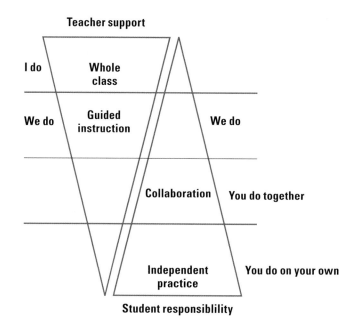

Permission granted by the National Council of Teachers of English.

Figure 3.5, from Fisher, Rothenberg, and Frey (2007), represents the mentoring relationship and two-way interaction between the teacher and student in explicit, scaffolded language development. At the beginning of a lesson or when new material is being introduced, the teacher has a prominent role in the delivery of the content. This is the "I do" phase. But as the students process and apply the new information and skills, the responsibility of learning shifts from teacher-directed instruction to student application. In the "We do" phase of learning, the teacher continues to model, question, prompt, and cue students; but as students move into the "You do" phase, they rely more on themselves and less on the teacher to complete the learning task.

Given the limitations of space, we do not provide guidelines for instructed ELD curriculum at all proficiency levels. Rather, our intention is to provide sufficient illustrative examples to begin to map a course for secondary schools interested in improving ELD instruction.

Determining the Language to Teach in Instructed ELD

The remainder of the chapter provides concrete examples of a model of instructed ELD. We do this first by providing guidance for selecting topic-specific "bricks" and functional "mortar" language by proficiency level. These examples of language tools are followed by practical illustrations of research-informed instructed ELD in action.

Building Vocabulary Knowledge

Word knowledge is critical to comprehension and effective writing. Numerous studies in K–12 contexts have documented the strong and reciprocal relationship between vocabulary knowledge and reading comprehension (Beck, McKeown, and Kucan 2002; Graves 2000; Stahl and Fairbanks 1986). For school-age English learners, vocabulary knowledge similarly correlates with reading comprehension and other indicators of school success, including writing and test scores (August et al. 2005). In fact, vocabulary knowledge proves to be a highly reliable predictor of English learner academic achievement across the subject area domains (Marzano 2004; Saville-Troike 1984).

Adolescent English learners must develop a broad and deep vocabulary to navigate the language they encounter in conversation, in content instruction, and in texts. They must learn thousands of words that native speakers of English have learned in the home, in school, and in daily life throughout their childhoods and do so in an accelerated time frame. Some of this vocabulary is specific to a topic, such as *photosynthesis, simile,* or *geometric.* For example, when students read about global warming, topic-specific "brick" vocabulary could include *carbon dioxide, greenhouse gases,* and *climate change.* Reading about American history calls for knowledge of the *constitution, mid-Atlantic states,* and *taxation,* while studying biology calls for knowledge of *cell, membrane, nucleus,* and so on. The responsibility for teaching this specific vocabulary belongs to credentialed content experts. Vocabulary and should be taught within the context of those disciplines.

> **Adolescent English learners must develop a broad and deep vocabulary to navigate the language they encounter in conversation, in content instruction, and in texts.**

However, many high-frequency vocabulary words span multiple disciplines, such as the words *accurate, analyze, significant, environment, consume, issue, temperature,* and *produce.* These words appear in a wide array of academic contexts, but they are not regularly used in day-to-day communication. Nor are they generally taught in content courses as they are inaccurately presumed to be common knowledge. Therefore, it is absolutely essential to teach this high-utility vocabulary in instructed ELD.

Instruction must address not only grade-level appropriate terms but also fill gaps in foundational word knowledge that can prevent English learners from fully participating in schooling.

As students develop English proficiency, the vocabulary that they learn and practice becomes increasingly sophisticated, growing from words needed to discuss here-and-now, concrete and observable experiences at early stages; to past and future experiences at more intermediate levels; to events not in students' experience; and abstractions at the advanced levels. This lexical progression moves from:

⊙ Basic words (*rules, promise, water, air, city*) to

⊙ More specific general utility words and phrases (*laws, pledge, liquid, gas, suburb*) to

⊙ Increasingly precise terms (*judicial system, allegiance, properties, solid matter, rural community*)

Table 3.3 illustrates the progression in lexical complexity and precision demanded of English learners as they tackle increasingly challenging communication and literacy tasks in their second language. ELD teachers must be mindful of their students' current level of English proficiency and give them a reasonable amount of preparation in a responsible manner for the vocabulary challenges of their lessons. Table 3.3 follows.

Table 3.3. Sample Progression of Vocabulary to Be Taught Across Proficiency Levels

	Beginning/Early Intermediate Level	Intermediate Level	Early Advanced/ Advanced Level
Nouns	paper	tissue paper, construction paper	cardstock, cellophane
	blue, light/dark blue	sky blue, turquoise, navy	indigo, cobalt, baby blue, aqua
	forest	woods	woodland
	flowers, trees, plants	bushes, garden, branches, stem	vegetation, hedge, twig
	leg, feet, toes	knees, thighs, ankles	calves, shins, muscles, joints
	rule	law	judicial system
	city	suburb	rural community
	storm, rain, snow	thunderstorm, rainstorm	blizzard, gale force wind
	problem	calculation	computation
	story, poem	novel, biography, short story	narrative, historical fiction

Table 3.3 *(continued)*

	Beginning/Early Intermediate Level	Intermediate Level	Early Advanced/ Advanced Level
Adjectives	**Sound:** *loud, quiet, soft* **Movement:** *fast, slow* **Texture:** *soft, rough, smooth*	*blaring, muted* *elegant, peaceful, calm* *bumpy, silky, stiff*	*deafening, ear-splitting, faint* *fluid, agile, light-footed, swift* *serrated, jagged, coarse, textured*
	States of being: *hungry, thirsty, tired* **Space:** *full, empty, crowded*	*starving, so hungry I could eat a horse, exhausted* *overcrowded, vacant, busy*	*dying of thirst, parched, famished, worn-out, drowsy* *deserted, occupied/un occupied*
	Taste: *sweet, salty, sour*	*chocolaty, tangy, mint-flavored*	*bitter, nutty, rancid*
	Complexity: *hard, easy*	*difficult, simple*	*challenging, a "breeze"*
Verbs	*walk, run, sit, kick* *grow* *read, look at* *write, redo* *ask, answer, tell* *promise* *help*	*walk fast, race, squat, kneel* *develop, get ripe, bloom* *skim, study* *jot, edit, revise* *explain, respond, request* *pledge* *help out*	*stroll, saunter, sprint* *mature, age, ripen, blossom* *peruse, analyze* *outline, proofread* *elaborate, pose a question, inquire* *vow, promise allegiance* *support, assist*
Adverbs	*slowly, fast (adjective)* *now, soon* *every day*	*quickly, suddenly, bit by bit* *right away* *often, usually, at ten o'clock, on time*	*rapidly, steadily, abruptly* *immediately, in a moment* *frequently, weekly, regularly, at times*

(Adapted from Dutro 2005a.)

Vocabulary to Teach Within Instructed ELD

Determining the "language" to teach during instructed ELD begins with the proficiency level of the students in the course grouping. Teachers should consider the specific communicative tasks students will be expected to perform and the lesson topic. To assist teachers in making practical word-choice decisions, researchers have proposed various criteria (Beck, McKeown,

Determining the "language" to teach during instructed ELD begins with the proficiency level of the students in the course grouping.

and Kucan 2002; Calderón 2005; Nation 2001). These criteria tend to focus on two principal considerations:

- ⊙ Words that are important to understanding a particular lesson concept or reading selection

- ⊙ Words that are generally useful for students to know and that they are likely to encounter fairly regularly in academic settings.

Feldman and Kinsella (2008) offer the following guidelines for choosing words that have practical and wide use in ELD classrooms in secondary schools:

- ⊙ Choose words that name or relate to the central concepts addressed in lesson materials (e.g., *peer pressure, global warming, technology, cultural traditions, journey*).

- ⊙ Choose general academic words that students are likely to encounter in various materials across subject areas (e.g., *consequence, significant, analyze, respond*).

- ⊙ Choose words that are members of a high-frequency academic word family, words that have derivations or "word cousins" utilized regularly across disciplines and that secondary and college-bound students need to master for school and professional reading and communication (e.g., *assume/assumption; predict/prediction/predictable* (see Coxhead 2000). In presenting such sets of words, teachers can take the opportunity to highlight patterns of roots and affixes (Nation 2005).

- ⊙ Choose *polysemous* (multiple-meaning) words that have a new academic meaning in the lesson in addition to a more familiar everyday or academic meaning (e.g., *factor* meaning one of several things that affect a situation or decision versus a number that divides evenly into another number).

- ⊙ Choose additional words, not included in the lesson materials, that students will need to know to be competent in written and spoken discourse about the central lesson concepts, theme, issues, or characters. This step is particularly essential when narrative texts are used as the central lesson materials. Literature tends to be laden with potentially interesting yet low-incidence words that do not necessarily facilitate comprehension and discussion of the most critical content.

For example, the highly anthologized short story *Raymond's Run,* by Toni Cade Bambara, explores the ways in which the main character demonstrates respect to her sibling and peers in a challenging context. In so doing the protagonist gains greater respect from her peers while also developing self-respect. Students will clearly benefit from learning conceptual vocabulary such as the nouns *respect, self-respect, relationship, sibling,* and *peer* as well as general, high-frequency academic verbs such as *demonstrate, obtain, gain,* and *develop.* The essential vocabulary for articulate

discourse about the theme and character development is not contained in the actual story. The brief word list typically identified for targeted instruction by publishers includes these low-utility choices: *periscope, ventriloquist,* and *prodigy.* These words warrant a brief clarification but not a significant amount of instructional time. Instead, devoting instructional attention to the story's thematic language will equip English learners with vocabulary that will serve them for this assignment and others.

Building Functional Language

In addition to deepening vocabulary knowledge, instructed ELD must support English learners in understanding how English works and enable them to combine vocabulary (or "bricks") in connected language to express their thinking. The functional "mortar" is the language that connects individual words into sentences that communicate thinking. This functional language requires word knowledge and knowledge of grammatical features, such as subject/verb agreement, use of conjunctions to make complex and compound sentences, and word order (syntax). Highly proficient English speakers are able to combine words and phrases into seemingly endless sentence combinations with agility.

Mastery of language and syntactic features allows students' full participation in academics by enabling them to put ideas together in a wide range of ways. Mastery includes learning a breadth of language patterns to communicate relationships between ideas: to explain, describe, compare, and contrast, summarize, generalize, express cause-and-effect relationships, sequence, and so on. The intentional teaching of language structures—the "mortar"—enables English learners to internalize the patterns needed to express concepts, ideas, and thinking. This approach to language development draws on Long's *Focus on Form* (1991) and does not practice isolated language features. Rather, it focuses on form in a meaning-based context (Doughty and Williams 1998) and uses communicative functions relevant to academic purposes (e.g., using past-tense verbs to retell a series of events; using the conditional to express possible outcomes of events). As the conceptual demands of academic content increase, the learner is called upon to know and be able to use increasingly complex language structures.

> **In addition to deepening vocabulary knowledge, instructed ELD must support English learners in understanding how English works and enable them to combine vocabulary in connected language to express their thinking.**

Building Language with "Bricks" and "Mortar"

Table 3.4 depicts several functions of language and examples across levels of English proficiency. These examples serve to illustrate the relationship among:

185

(1) the communicative task or function,

(2) the variation by proficiency level, and

(3) the topic vocabulary, or "bricks" (italicized in Table 3.4), and functional linguistic "mortar" needed to generate connected language.

Other topic vocabulary may be substituted for the italicized words and phrases to create novel statements with the same communicative function or purpose. For example, if intermediate English learners have learned the structure "Texting is an easy way to communicate," they can easily replace the topic words *texting* and *communicate* with *microwaving* and *cook* or heat food to express a new thought.

Table 3.4. Progression of Functional Language to Be Taught Across Proficiency Levels

	Beginning/Early Intermediate Level	Intermediate Level	Early Advanced/ Advanced Level
Describe #1	*Texting* is easy.	*Texting* is an easy way to com-municate. One example of *communicating* quickly *is text messaging.*	One *convenient way to communicate* is *texting.* *Text messaging is a convenient method/means of communication.*
Describe #2	*Sleep* is important. *Students* need *sleep* *because* it is important.	*Students* need enough *sleep* to be able to *stay awake in class.*	*Students* require sufficient/adequate *sleep* to *be alert in class.*
Express Cause & Effect	*Students stay up late.* They are *tired.* *Students watch TV.* They *go to bed late.*	If *students stay up too late,* they don't get enough *sleep.* Without enough *sleep, students are tired during class.* When *students stay up late watching TV,* they are *tired in the morning.*	*Lack of sleep often makes students tired in class.* *Students can't concentrate in class* as a result of *sleep loss.* *Significant sleep loss* results in/ leads to a *variety of health problems.*
Sequence	First, *Elena was worried.* She had *a new step-father.* Then *the family moved.* Now *Elena feels better.*	At first, *Elena was worried about moving to a house with her new stepfather.* After a few weeks, *she* started to get/become comfortable. Now she is *trying to be positive.*	In the beginning, *she was concerned about moving into a new home with her stepfather.* During the next few weeks, *things changed drastically.* Gradually, *Elena became accus-tomed to her new home and daily routines.* Currently, *she is trying to be optimistic about the changes in her life.*

Teaching English language skills from the perspective of language functions helps to identify the language demands of a specific academic task (describing, sequencing events, comparing attributes) and content concept (methods of communication, narrative events). The benefits of learning to use a language function such as *comparing,* for example, extend beyond a given task because once English learners know how to compare, they can apply that skill to a range of contexts across content areas. Students practice and extend their language skills for comparing by applying it in different ways. Increasing competence in any language function obligates the speaker or writer to use increasingly complex sentence structures.

Using this approach, learning interesting content—and how to talk and write about that interesting content—is not delayed until more advanced levels of proficiency are reached. Academic language is developed from the beginning stages of second-language learning. Competence in a range of functions equips students to participate in content instruction and supports academic language proficiency. Language becomes a vehicle, rather than a barrier, to learning.

Instructed ELD in Action

Following are detailed discussions of explicit vocabulary instruction and structured oral language development in a secondary school context.

Explicit Vocabulary Development in ELD Classrooms

Explicit vocabulary instruction that enables adolescents English learners to develop in-depth knowledge of important words should follow consistent routines. In that way, students can devote their intellectual capital and attention span to comprehending the word rather than to adjusting to a constantly fluctuating array of steps. Explicit instructional routines should encourage English learners to notice, gain control of, and develop fluency in using the word (Coxhead 2006). Explicit instruction of vocabulary engages students in the pronunciation and meaning of new words and their spelling and grammatical patterns. This instruction should enable them to know the words well enough to gain meaning about them from memory as they read or as they hear them used in discussion. It should go an important step further in equipping students with enough structural knowledge of the word to use it appropriately in a sentence.

Nation (1990) and Scarcella (2003) detail the complexities of expressive word knowledge, what is involved consciously or subconsciously in "knowing a word." As an illustration, the example below shows what it means to truly "know" the high-utility academic word *accurate.*

- ⊙ **Pronunciation:** ák•kyu•rit

- ⊙ **Meaning(s):** correct or exact in every detail

- ⊙ **Spelling:** a-c-c-u-r-a-t-e

- ⊙ **Part of speech:** an adjective (describing word)

- ⊙ **The word's register:** It is primarily used in relatively formal writing and speaking for academic or professional purposes.

- ⊙ **The word's frequency:** It is not commonly used in casual conversation or correspondence but frequently used in formal academic and professional contexts.

- ⊙ **The word's grammar:** It modifies and precedes a noun: *The school board anticipates an accurate report from the superintendent.*

- ⊙ **The word's collocations:** It is regularly used to describe information, data, measurements, and reports.

- ⊙ **The connotations:** *Accurate* has a positive connotation; *inaccurate* has a negative connotation.

- ⊙ **The derivations/word family members:** *accurate, inaccurate, accuracy, inaccuracy, accurately, inaccurately*

Feldman and Kinsella (2008) outline an explicit routine for teaching vocabulary:
(1) read and pronounce the word,
(2) explain,
(3) deepen understanding, and
(4) coach use.

This instructional routine for teaching critical lesson terms is an adaptation of the protocol outlined by Beck and colleagues (2002), with vital enhancements for second-language learners, namely multiple repetitions of the word, use of cognates, clapping out syllables, visual representations of the word, and a structured oral and written task. The following steps can certainly be elaborated or modified, depending on the relative importance of the words in the lesson and students' background knowledge. However, given the goal of accomplishing ELD standards and laying a linguistic foundation for meeting content standards, teachers of secondary English learners cannot afford to shortchange the process.

Read and Pronounce (I/We do it)

Step 1: Direct students' attention to the written word (on the board, overhead, or handout) and pronounce the word a few times.

Students need to look carefully at the target word as the teacher pronounces it. They point to the word, cued by the teacher, if it is written in a text or notetaking scaffold. (See the sample notetaking scaffold on page 193). Consider having students take a moment to copy on a notetaking scaffold or on a sheet of paper the word directly underneath the written word. Otherwise, some are apt to engage in "linguistic approximations," guessing what the teacher is saying rather than building a strong visual and auditory imprint. Although the teacher is clearly pronouncing *analyze,* students may be hearing "animal eyes" and become perplexed by the subsequent clarification of meaning.

Step 2: Guide students in correctly pronouncing the word at least twice.

Students must repeat the word with correct pronunciation and stress a few times to develop an accurate phonological representation of the word (Nation 2001). Despite expert modeling, many will not initially repeat the word correctly, particularly a polysyllabic word. Guiding students in correctly pronouncing the word supports learners in decoding the word competently while also building auditory and muscle memory (Shaywitz 2003).

Step 3: Break longer, polysyllabic words into discrete syllables.

Have students pronounce each syllable chorally while tapping out the syllables of the word. Tactile involvement helps to ensure students actually hear and pronounce each syllable. To help students hear the stressed syllable in a word, consider humming the word after saying it and then having the students hum the word with you. After they have said it slowly in discrete syllables, have them repeat it again quickly.

Explain (I do it)

Step 4: Provide a primary language cognate (if there is an appropriate one).

Cognates are words in two or more languages that sound quite similar or are spelled the same. Students whose first language shares cognates with English benefit from having parallel words called out, such as the Spanish and English cognates *prediction/predicción* that share a common Latin root (Bravo, Hiebert, and Pearson 2005; August, Calderón, and Carlo 2002). These students can take advantage of their cognate knowledge to help them process the unfamiliar English word. Many high-frequency academic words in English have a direct Spanish cognate. Teachers who serve Spanish speakers but lack proficiency in Spanish can seek assistance with identifying cognates from a colleague or bilingual dictionary. They can write the cognates on the board and assign a student "cognate helper" to pronounce the cognate during this instructional step. Students can also suggest words they think may be cognates, and they or the teacher can verify them by consulting a dictionary or a bilingual adult.

Step 5: Explain the meaning clearly and efficiently rather than exhaustively.

To understand a new term, students require a relatively brief explanation framed in everyday language, including common synonyms and the part of speech (Stahl 1999; Nation 2001). Teachers of English learners should consider what is most essential for students to come away with from their first encounter with the word. A learner dictionary, specially designed for adolescent English learners, is an invaluable lesson planning tool. The term *learner dictionary* is used to distinguish those developed specifically for second-language learners versus conventional desktop dictionaries. These resources provide clearly worded definitions, example sentences, and grammar information that can make lesson preparation more efficient and effective.

Deepen Understanding (I do it)

Step 6: Provide a quick visual representation of the word, if possible.

Pictures, simple drawings, and other forms of tangible realia can help students engage in deep processing and formulate a mental model of the word meaning (Gersten and Baker 2000; Marzano, Pickering, and Pollock 2001; Mazano 2004; Schmitt 2000), but academic vocabulary is often quite abstract and difficult to portray in a single, convenient image. If supplying an appropriate visual aid is challenging, make sure to provide engaging, relevant example sentences that help students create vibrant and memorable mental images.

Step 7: Provide at least two examples, drawing from familiar contexts, not only the one to be addressed in the lesson material.

A variety of examples helps students conceptually grasp a new word while building in a range of associations that assist them with recall of the word meaning in appropriate contexts (Baker, Simmons, and Kame'enui 1998; Nation 2001). In other words, offering diverse examples helps to ensure that every student receives at least one reliable form to make the word meaning stick, an image that will come easily to mind the next time he or she encounters the word.

Coach Use (We/You)

Step 8: Engage students in a structured oral and written task.

Students need structured and guided practice to be able to use a newly taught word appropriately in speaking and writing. Once English learners have begun to develop a semantic grasp of a word, they need form-focused instruction that directs their attention to how the word operates in a sentence (Ellis 2005a; Norris and Ortega 2006). Assign an oral task to the class by using a response frame that engages pairs of students in effectively applying the new word in a familiar context and in a syntactically and grammatically correct sentence. Sentence-starters that frame

correct usage help students develop expressive word knowledge. Make sure that the sentence frame is appropriate for your students' English proficiency level and direct their attention to specific grammatical features necessary for accurate usage. Simply listening to the teacher use the target word appropriately will not ensure students' grammatical competence. Once students have shared their response with a partner, call on a few individuals to share with the entire class. To bolster expressive word knowledge, close by assigning a sentence-completion task that requires application of the correct form of the word in addition to relevant content that illustrates comprehension of the word in this new context.

> **Simply listening to the teacher use the target word appropriately will not ensure students' grammatical competence.**

Here is an illustration of how explicit instruction of the word *convenient* might appear following the eight-step routine:

⊙ Our first important lesson term is *convenient*. Point to the word *convenient* in your notetaking guide. We'll see the word *convenient* in our article on the effect of plastic bags on the *environment*.

⊙ Let's say *convenient* together twice: *Convenient. Convenient.*

⊙ Now let's pronounce it slowly by syllables: *con•ven•ient.* One more time (clapping out the syllables). Say it again quickly: *convenient.*

⊙ The English word *convenient* has a Spanish cognate. Will my cognate helper help us with pronunciation? c*onveniente.*

⊙ *Convenient* is an adjective, a "describing" word. The adjective *convenient* means useful to you because it makes something easier or saves you time.

⊙ Let's look at some examples (pointing at the classroom microwave oven).

The microwave oven in my classroom is a *convenient* way for me to heat up my lunch. Because I don't have to wait in a long line to use the microwave oven in the Teachers Lounge, my classroom microwave oven really saves me time. It is very what? Students respond: *convenient.* I live in a small town with no department stores, so online catalogs are a *convenient* way for me to shop for clothes. The nearest mall is 45 minutes away, and there aren't many choices so online catalogs make shopping a lot easier. Online shopping is much more_____. Students respond: *convenient.*

⊙ Now it's your turn to use the word. I'd like you to think about the most *convenient* way for you to get to school. Here is your sentence-starter: The most *convenient* way for me to get to school is _____ (verb + ing) because _____. I'll share my idea first. The most *convenient* way for me to get to school is riding my bike because I don't waste time in traffic. Notice that you need to complete the sentence using an action word, a verb ending in *-ing* just as I did with riding. Take a moment to think of your answer. Number one: please share your idea with your partner. Then number two: let's hear from a few of you. So it seems that riding a bicycle, taking the bus, and walking are all ways of getting to school that are very _____ (Students chime in: *convenient*). Here is your homework writing task. Complete this sentence using the correct word form and filling in content that makes sense: Sending e-mail is more _____ than _____ (verb + ing) friends who live far away because _____. After finishing the response frame, write one original "show you know" sentence that clearly demonstrates your understanding.

Notetaking Scaffolds for Vocabulary Instruction

English learners have a great deal to attend to during explicit instruction of important lesson terms. For second-language learners, academic listening is the skill that makes the heaviest processing demands. Unlike a face-to-face conversation about familiar content, English learners must store conceptually demanding new information in short-term memory at the same time as they are attempting to understand the information (Mendelsohn and Rubin 1995). To process the auditory and visual clues during vocabulary instruction more efficiently, English learners benefit from a consistent and familiar instructional routine and a complementary notetaking scaffold or guide (Mendelsohn 1994). Without a familiar process that enables them to anticipate specific content and intended student responses, English learners find notetaking extremely challenging, if not impossible. English learners must dedicate all of their attention to simply following along; if they stop to write, they risk missing critical content. If they do not have a written record, they have no tool for future review and study.

> **For second-language learners, academic listening is the skill that makes the heaviest processing demands.**

An important accommodation that teachers of adolescent English learners can make to support active listening and response during vocabulary instruction is to provide a notetaking scaffold for the most critical unit or lesson terms, particularly during the first few months of instruction. The notetaking scaffold should contain the most essential content but leave blanks for students to follow along and fill in key words.

In this way, they will have an active but manageable role. As students become familiar with the instructional process, teachers can gradually relinquish the notetaking scaffold or provide one for only a few high-priority words. A well-structured notetaking scaffold not only frames and facilitates students' listening and response, but it also models for them how effective language learners assume a dynamic and responsible role in the instructional process (Kinsella 1996). Table 3.5 displays an example.

Table 3.5. Vocabulary Notetaking Scaffold

Oral Language Development in Instructed ELD

Word	Meaning	Examples	Oral Task
convenient con•ven•ient (adjective) Spanish: *conveniente*	Useful to you because it makes something _____ or saves_____	A microwave oven in the classroom Online catalog shopping	The most **convenient** way for me to get to school is by _____ (verb + *ing*) because _____
Writing Task: Sending e-mail is more _____ than _____ (verb + *ing*) friends because _____ .			
My Sentence:			

Although all domains of language (listening, speaking, reading, writing) are important to develop during an instructed ELD period, students' oral competence with appropriate vocabulary and sentence structures merits high priority. This emphasis is needed in part because of the strong relationship between oral language proficiency and reading comprehension and writing skills. It is also needed because content instruction in secondary school is highly text-focused, providing scant opportunities for English learners to orally process new learning or to practice expressing their understanding.

A primary function of ELD course work is to ensure that English learners develop the oral English necessary to communicate effectively in social and academic settings. To develop communicative competence, English learners need daily supported opportunities to utilize their second language for diverse purposes. However, research in ELD classrooms and in the general education context illustrates that English learners are characteristically passive observers during critical lesson discussions and activities in both core content and dedicated ELD classes. Research also reveals that the only individual using any complex language is the teacher (Arreaga-Mayer and Perdomo-

Rivera 1996). Ramirez (1992) notes an equally low level of oral language engagement in all the various models of English learner education. Further, when English learners do contribute orally, their discourse is typically limited to brief casual utterances in response to teacher questions. Small-group and partnering activities also routinely fail to promote substantive oral language growth (see Foster and Ohta 2005). Merely increasing student interaction without explicit, coached language instruction and accountability for application can lead to discussions with minimal cognitive or linguistic challenge and negligible academic content (Jiménez and Gersten 1999; Lee and Fradd 1996; Saunders and O'Brien 2006). (See Saunders and Goldenberg in this publication for additional discussion of the pivotal role of oral language proficiency.)

Designing effective classroom interactions begins with a careful analysis of the cognitive and linguistic demands of lesson materials and optimal occasions for language production.

An emerging body of research points to the necessity for more conscientious structuring of second-language classroom interactions than has been the norm (see Guideline 3, Saunders and Goldenberg, in this publication). Gersten and Baker (2000) question the historical overemphasis in discussions of effective practices for English learners in K–12 contexts on "natural language use" when cognitive and linguistic growth is paramount. Pairing English learners for productive interactions decidedly involves more than a modified seating arrangement and unfettered opportunities to converse. To engage in competent and extended academic discourse, English learners benefit from form-focused explicit instruction in the language feature and teacher-mediated practice (Norris and Ortega 2006; Lightbown 1998). Moreover, subsequent interactive tasks with the intent of facilitating accurate production of the language feature must be carefully structured and clearly require, rather than merely encourage, correct application of the focal language (Keck et al. 2006). Interactive tasks that actually require English learners to attempt to produce a language feature for successful completion consistently yield stronger learning outcomes than those that do not establish clear expectations for application of specific language forms.

In this section, we illustrate some concrete ways in which secondary ELD teachers can structure dynamic and democratic oral language use for academic and real-life purposes. Designing effective classroom interactions begins with a careful analysis of the cognitive and linguistic demands of lesson materials and optimal occasions for language production. Ideally, students should have several opportunities for supported and accountable language production during a lesson and a wide array of mediated experiences over the course of a unit of study.

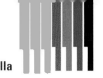

Effective partner interactions. Because of the compelling cognitive and social benefits of structured group work in linguistically and culturally diverse classrooms (e.g., Kagan and Kagan 1992; McGroarty 1992; Gersten and Baker 2000), peer collaboration has become an essential component of contemporary English learner instruction. In secondary school, students need multiple opportunities in a single ELD lesson to use the second language for varied purposes, whether it be providing an example of a new term in context by using a sentence frame or identifying a significant detail in a reading selection. When language application is the goal, student pairs are generally more efficient and effective than group activities. Partner activities maximize the amount of classroom language use because, theoretically, half the students are able to talk simultaneously and all students leave class with more "miles on the tongue."

ELD teachers can manageably integrate several strategies in their daily lessons to bolster students' oral language production. Two particularly effective partner "participation structures" are Think-Pair-Share and Think-Write-Pair-Share, initially designed by Kagan and Kagan (1992). Research supports their use in linguistically and culturally diverse classrooms. Although both structures are widely recognized strategies to democratize oral participation, they tend to be underused and poorly implemented (Fiechtner and Davis 1992; Lyman 1981). Simply telling a class of English learners to "share an idea with a partner" can easily devolve into a number of disappointing scenarios, ranging from no interaction whatsoever to students completing the task in the most efficient manner, investing minimal thought and using limited language (Jimenez and Gersten 1999; Lee and Fradd 1996). Student-to-student lesson interactions intended to accomplish academic tasks must be carefully conceived with target content and language goals, monitored well, and consistently implemented to reach full potential (Long and Porter 1985).

These interaction protocols are labeled as "classroom structures" because of the consistent scaffolding included to ensure that all English learners receive the instructional support necessary to thrive. A key reason they are referred to as *participation* structures is because they are intended to be implemented on a daily basis so routinely, in fact, that students can essentially move into "automatic pilot" once they are given the signal. In this way the *structure* and *process* of the task are so familiar and habitual that students can devote their complete attention to the *language demands* of the task. A final rationale for labeling these task-based discussion strategies as "structures" is to distinguish them from widely used activities such as a K-W-L chart or a graphic organizer. Such activities, while intended to tap into students' knowledge and experiences prior to reading or writing, typically lack specific language development, teacher modeling, peer rehearsal, and accountability necessary for less-proficient students to contribute in a mixed-ability classroom. In other words, they are often not structured well enough to elicit the interaction and learning intended.

Partner interaction with Think (Write)-Pair-Share. Think (Write)-Pair-Share, also discussed in Chapter 3, is a quick (one- to two-minute) interaction between partners. There are three distinct stages of student action:

⊙ **Thinking/Thinking and Writing:** Students independently compose a response to a question or task using a response frame or scaffold that guides them in successful use of target vocabulary, sentence structure, grammar, and register.

  Pairing: Partners take turns stating their composed response by using the frame and are held accountable for speaking and listening.

⊙ **Sharing:** Students present to the class (or another pair) individually or together the ideas they discussed.

This seemingly simple yet potent strategy has several critical features:

⊙ A focused and manageable task

⊙ Dual learning outcomes: concept attainment and language development

⊙ Scaffolded participation with posted vocabulary and sentence frames or signal words

⊙ Adequate time to reflect and prepare

⊙ Rehearsal time with a partner

⊙ Efficient participation by 100 percent of the class

To support all English learners in responding competently and efficiently, ELD teachers should faithfully follow these steps:

1. Clarify the purpose of the discussion task and how it relates to the lesson objectives.

2. Direct students' attention to any written instructions. Clarify the task components, expectations for completion, and the time frame.

3. Explain any potentially challenging vocabulary in the instructions.

4. Model an appropriate response using a response frame, both orally and in writing.

5. Assign two response frames if there is a range of ability and regular "fast finishers."

6. Point out any grammar necessary for effectively writing a sentence using the response frame.

7. Provide a small word bank to assist less-proficient students in writing a response.

8. Tell students to write quietly and read over their responses in preparation for the discussion. Remind students to write a second idea if they have finished the first.

9. Monitor students' writing and nominate one or two students to launch the discussion.

10. Partner students to share responses in preparation for the unified class discussion.

11. Assign an active listening and notetaking task for the unified class discussion (e.g., acknowledge similarities and differences in ideas, report a partner's idea).

12. Call on a few students to respond before answers are volunteered. Remind students to report using their "public voice" suitable for class discussions-two times slower than casual conversation and three times louder.

13. Summarize discussion contributions.

Designing appropriate response frames. In an explicit ELD lesson, a response frame functions as a crucial instructional scaffold to teach high-leverage language structures. Keep in mind that an instructional scaffold is a temporary lesson structure employed in a gradual release model (Figure 3.5) that conscientiously supports learners in performing a challenging academic task that could not otherwise be performed confidently and competently, much like training wheels for a bicycle or water wings in a swimming pool.

A response frame provides English learners with a scaffold for responding competently by explicitly clarifying the grammatical and lexical goals of an accurate response. A well-crafted response frame enables an ELD teacher to construct a model response, deconstruct the response, and guide students in reconstructing a unique but appropriate response.

Simple sentence-starters are not sufficient linguistic scaffolds. Equipped with only a response frame for linguistic support, English learners commonly launch a response in academic register that devolves into conversational register or grammatical chaos. For example, providing the response frame "I predict that" to make a prediction about character development in a story, students are likely to respond with statements such as, "I predict that, the brother, he win the race" or "I predict won't win."

We often underestimate the linguistic complexities of routine but deceptively complex language functions. Prediction requires use of the future tense, and justifying a prediction requires use of the simple past tense. English learners benefit from more explicit guidance using well-crafted response frames such as the following ones:

I predict that the character _____ will _____ (base verb: win, leave, . . .) or I predict that the character _____ will be _____ (adjective: upset, proud).

To provide a rationale for a prediction about a character's future actions, a student is typically called on to cite previous actions or developments in a narrative. Again, an English learner will benefit from explicit scaffolding in the form of a response frame to successfully engage in this complex language function:

I predicted this would happen because she/he _____ (past-tense verb: said, tried, practiced) or I made this prediction because she/he _____ (past-tense verb: wanted, left).

It is difficult to provide impromptu response frames for different English proficiency levels after assigning a discussion task. Therefore, effective lesson plans include identifying key points for partnering tasks and preparing response frames in advance. It is wise to prepare two response frames: one to appropriately stretch the least-proficient English learners and one for the more-proficient students. To accommodate the range of oral language ability that may exist in an ELD class, even when students are ostensibly already grouped by proficiency levels, teachers can reasonably assign the first starter to the entire class and require more adept language users (and/or fast finishers) to prepare an additional response using a second, more advanced starter.

Tables 3.6 and 3.7 demonstrate how ELD teachers in a secondary school might select appropriate response frames for students to apply newly taught language structures and vocabulary. Notice the progression in linguistic challenge evident in the sample response frames of:

(1) the discussion task to orient English learners to structured partnering and

(2) prereading brainstorming task.

Table 3.6
Discussion Task: What are the characteristics of an effective lesson partner?

Early Intermediate Level	A good partner is _____ (adjective: *helpful, polite, friendly, serious*).
Intermediate Level	An effective partner tries to _____ (verb: *help, finish, listen*).
Early Advanced	I work more effectively with a partner who _____ (verb + -s: *listens, participates, assists*)
Advanced Level	I tend to work more productively with a _____ (adjective) partner who _____ (verb + s).

Table 3.7

Brainstorm Task: Identify reasons people decide to immigrate to the U.S.

Beginning/ Early Intermediate	People immigrate for better _____ (noun: *jobs, education, lives, schools*).
Intermediate Level	Many people decide to immigrate because they want/need _____ (noun phrase: *a safer life, a better job, better schools*). Many immigrants come to the U.S. for _____ (noun phrase: *a better job, education, more opportunities*).
Early Advanced/ Advanced	People from many countries decide to immigrate because _____ (independent clause: *they are victims of war in their homeland; they want to join family members*). Some families immigrate to the U.S. in order to _____ (verb phrase: *escape war, make more money, attend school*).

In the preceding sections, we described how to determine and explicitly teach high-leverage vocabulary ("bricks") and the linguistic forms ("mortar language") to accomplish a range of cognitive tasks (functions) to illustrate the framework for explicit language instruction (Figure 3.3). Throughout the chapter, we also highlighted the necessity of structuring contextualized oral practice to build accurate fluency and provided examples across proficiency levels.

Conclusion

In this chapter we presented an ambitious approach for rethinking English language instruction for adolescent English learners based on current research and promising practices. We outlined a model for rigorous standards-aligned instructed ELD taught during a dedicated course of study and included illustrative examples and practical tools to inform ELD program design. Schools can design and implement a sustainable program of second-language instruction, one that responsibly prepares students for the demands of course work in secondary school. As an integral part of socially and academically vibrant schooling for language-minority students, an effective ELD program targets instruction at their English levels, prioritizes explicit teaching of vocabulary, provides syntactical structures for significant academic and social purposes, and allots consistent practice opportunities. Adolescents whose second-language learning needs are conscientiously met can and will make strides in their secondary schooling better equipped to realize their academic and real-life goals.

References

Alcón, Eva. 2004. Research on language and learning: Implications for language teaching. *International Journal of English Studies* 4(1): 173–96.

Arreaga-Mayer, Carmen, and Claudia Perdomo-Rivera. 1996. Ecobehavioral analysis of instruction for at-risk language-minority students. *The Elementary School Journal 96*(3) (January): 245–58.

August, Diane, and Timothy Shanahan, ed. 2006. *Developing literacy in second language learners: Report of the National Literacy Panel on Language-Minority Children and Youth.* Center for Applied Linguistics. Mahwah, NJ: Lawrence Erlbaum.

August, Diane, Margarita Calderón, and María Carlo. 2002. *Transfer of reading skills from Spanish to English: A study of young learners.* Report ED-98-CO-0071 to the Office of Bilingual Education and Minority Languages Affairs, U.S. Department of Education.

August, Diane, María Carlo, Cheryl Dressler, and Catherine Snow. 2005. The critical role of vocabulary development for English language learners. *Learning Disabilities Research & Practice* 20(1): 50–57.

Bailey, Alison, ed. 2007. *The language demands of school: Putting academic English to the test.* New Haven, CT: Yale University Press.

Baker, Scott K., Deborah C. Simmons, and Edward J. Kame'enui. 1998. Vocabulary acquisition: Instructional and curricular basics and implications. In *What reading research tells us about children with diverse learning needs,* ed. D. C. Simmons and E. J. Kame'enui, 219–38. Mahwah, NJ: Lawrence Erlbaum.

Batalova, Jeanne. *Spotlight on limited English proficient students in the United States.* 2006. http://www.migrationinformation.org/USfocus (accessed September 20, 2008.)

Beck, Isabel, Margaret G. McKeown, and Linda Kucan. 2002. *Bringing words to life: Robust vocabulary instruction.* New York: Guilford Press.

Boyson, Beverly A., and Deborah J. Short. 2003. *Secondary school newcomer programs in the United States.* Research Report #12. Santa Cruz, CA: Center for Research on Education, Diversity, and Excellence.

Bravo, Marco, Elfrieda Hiebert, and P. David Pearson. 2005. Tapping the linguistic resources of Spanish/English bilinguals: The role of cognates in science. In *Vocabulary development and its implications for reading comprehension,* ed. R. K. Wagner, A. Muse, and K. Tannenbaum. New York: Guilford.

Brown, Douglas H. 1994. *Principles of language learning and teaching.* 3rd ed. Englewood Cliffs, NJ: Prentice Hall Regents.

Byrd, Patricia. 2005. Instructed grammar. In *Handbook of research in second language teaching and learning,* ed. Eli Hinkel, 545–61. Mahwah, NJ: Erlbaum.

Calderón, Margarita. 2007. *Teaching reading to English language learners:* Grades 6–12. Thousand Oaks, CA: Corwin Press.

California Department of Education. 2007 Language Census. http://dq.cde.ca.gov/dataquest/ (accessed July 1, 2008.)

Canale, Michael, and Merrill Swain. 1980. Theoretical bases of communicative approaches to second language teaching and testing. *Applied Linguistic*s 1(1): 1–47.

Carlo, María, Diane August, Barry McLaughlin, Catherine Snow, Cheryl Dressler, David Lippman, Teresa Lively, and Claire White. 2004. Closing the gap: Addressing the vocabulary needs of English-language learners in bilingual and mainstream classrooms. *Reading Research Quarterly* 39(2): 188–215.

Carrell, Patricia L. 1992. Awareness of text structure: Effects on recall. *Language Learning* 42: 1–20.

Celce-Murcia, M., and Elizabeth Olshtain. 2005. Discourse-based approaches: A new framework for second language teaching and learning. *In Handbook of research in second language teaching and learning,* ed. Eli Hinkel, 729–41. Mahwah, NJ: Erlbaum.

Chamot, Anna. Uhl. 2005. Language learning strategy instruction: Current issues and research. *Annual Review of Applied Linguistics* 25: 112–30.

Coxhead, Avril. 2000. A new academic word list. *TESOL Quarterly* 2: 213–38.

Coxhead, Avril. 2006. *Essentials of teaching academic vocabulary.* Boston: Houghton Mifflin.

Darling-Hammond, Linda. 1997. Doing what matters most: Investing in quality. New York: National Commission on Teaching and America's Future.

Doughty, Catherine, and Jessica Williams, eds. 1998. *Focus on form in classroom second language acquisition.* New York: Cambridge University Press.

Dutro, Susana. 2005a. *Systematic English language development: A focused approach.* 2nd ed. San Marcos, CA: E.L.Achieve.

Dutro, Susana. 2005b. Courses of study for secondary English learners. *The California Reader* 39(1): 45–58.

Dutro, Susana. 2008. *Systematic English language development: A handbook for K–6 teachers.* 2nd ed. San Marcos, CA: E.L. Achieve.

Dutro, Susana, and Lori Helman. In press. Explicit language instruction: A key to constructing meaning. *In Literacy development with English learners: Research-based instruction in grades K–6,* ed. L. Helman. New York: Guilford Publications.

Dutro, Susana, and Ellen Levy. 2008. *A focused approach to constructing meaning: Explicit language for secondary content instruction.* San Marcos, CA: E. L. Achieve.

Dutro, Susana, and Carrol Moran. 2003. Rethinking English language instruction: An architectural approach. In *English learners: Reaching the highest level of English literacy,* ed. Gil Garcia. Newark, DE: International Reading Association.

Echevarria, Jana, Mary Ellen Vogt, and Deborah J. Short. 2000. *Making content comprehensible for English language learners: the SIOP model.* Needham Heights, MA: Allyn & Bacon.

Ellis, Rod. 2005a. Principles of instructed language learning. *System* 33: 209–24.

Ellis, Rod. 2005b. Instructed language learning and task-based teaching. In *Handbook of research in second language teaching and learning,* ed. Eli Hinkel, 713–28. London: Routledge.

English language development standards for California public schools: Kindergarten through grade twelve. 2002. Sacramento: California Department of Education.

Feldman, Kevin, and Kate Kinsella. 2008. Narrowing the language gap: The case for explicit vocabulary instruction in secondary classrooms. In *Effective practices for adolescents with reading and literacy challenges,* ed. L. Denti and G. Guerin. New York: Routledge.

Fiechtner, Susan Brown, and Elaine Actis Davis. 1992. Why some groups fail: A survey of students' experiences with learning groups. In *Collaborative learning: A sourcebook for higher education,* ed. A. Goodsell, M. Maher, and V. Tinto. University Park, PA: National Center on Postsecondary Teaching, Learning, and Assessment.

Fisher, Doug, Carol Rothenberg, and Nancy Frey. 2007. *Language learners in the English classroom.* Urbana, IL: National Council of Teachers of English.

Foster, Pauline, and Amy Snyder Ohta. 2005. Negotiation for meaning and peer assistance in second language classrooms. *Applied Linguistics* 26(3) (September): 402–30.

García-Vázquez, Enedina, Luis A. Vázquez, and Isabel C. López. 1997. Language proficiency and academic success: Relationships between proficiency in two languages and achievement among Mexican-American students. *Bilingual Research Journal* 21(4): 395–408.

Genesee, Fred, Kathryn Lindholm-Leary, William M. Saunders, and Donna Christian. 2006. *Educating English language learners: A synthesis of research evidence.* New York: Cambridge University Press.

Gersten, Russell, and Scott Baker. 2000. What we know about effective instructional practices for English-language learners. *Exceptional Children* 66(4): 454–70.

Gleason, Jean Berko. 2005. The development of language. In *The development of language.* 6th ed., ed. Jean Berko Gleason, 1–38. Boston: Pearson.

Gold, Norm, and Julie Maxwell-Jolly. 2006. *The high schools English learners need.* Policy Paper for University of California Language Minority Research Institute. http://www.lmri.ucsb.edu/publications/06_gold.pdf (accessed April 28, 2008).

Graves, Michael F. 2000. A vocabulary program to complement and bolster a middle grade comprehension program. In *Reading for meaning: Fostering comprehension in the middle grades,* ed. Barbara Taylor, Michael F. Graves, and P. Van Den Broek, 116–35. Newark, DE: International Reading Association.

Hakuta, Kenji, Yuko Goto Butler, and Daria Witt. 2000. *How long does it take English learners to attain proficiency?* University of California Linguistic Minority Research Institute. Policy Report 2000-1. ERIC Document Reproduction Service No. FL 026 180.

Halliday, Michael. 1973. *Explorations in the functions of language.* London: Edward Arnold.

Haycock, Kati. 1998. Good teaching matters: How well-qualified teachers can close the gap. *Thinking K–16* 3(2).

Heritage, Margaret, Norma Silva, and Mary Pierce. 2007. Academic language: A view from the classroom. In *The language demands of school: Putting academic language to the test,* ed. A. Bailey. New Haven, CT: Yale University Press.

Jimenez, Robert, and Russell Gersten. 1999. Lessons and dilemmas derived from the literacy instruction of two Latina/o teachers. *American Educational Research Journal* 36: 265–301.

Kagan, Spencer, and Miguel Kagan. 1992. *Kagan cooperative learning.* San Clemente, CA: Kagan Publishing.

Keck, Casey M., Gina Iberri-Shea, Nicole Tracy-Ventura, and Safary Wa-Mbaleka. 2006. Investigating the empirical link between task-based interaction and acquisition: A meta-analysis. In *Synthesizing research on language learning and teaching,* ed. J. M. Norris and L. Ortega, 91–131. Philadelphia: John Benjamins.

Kinsella, Kate. 2002. *Language strategies for active participation and learning: A rationale for systematically teaching classroom language functions.* New York: Scholastic Red.

Kinsella, Kate. 1997. Moving from, comprehensible input to "learning to learn" in content-based instruction. In *The content-based classroom: Perspectives on integrating language and content,* ed. M. A. Snow and D. B. Brinton, 46–68. White Plains, NY: Longman..

Kinsella, Kate. 1998. Developing ESL classroom collaboration to accommodate diverse work styles. In *Understanding learning styles in the second language classroom,* ed. Joy Reid. Old Tappan, NJ: Prentice Hall.

Kinsella, Kate. 1996. Designing group work that supports and enables diverse classroom work styles. *TESOL Journal* 6: 24–30.

Lee, Okee, and Sandra Fradd. 1996. Interactional patterns of linguistically diverse students and teachers: Insights for promoting science learning. *Linguistics and Education: An International Research Journal* 8: 269–97.

Lightbown, Patsy. 1998. The importance of timing in focus on form. In *Focus on form in classroom second language acquisition,* ed. Jessica Williams and Catherine Doherty, 77–196. Cambridge: Cambridge University Press.

Lightbown, Patsy, and Nina Spada. 2006. *How languages are learned.* 3rd ed. New York: Oxford University Press.

Long, Michael H. 1991. Focus on form: A design feature in language teaching methodology. In *Foreign language research in cross-cultural perspective,* ed. K. de Bot, D. Coste, R. Ginsberg, and C. Kramsch, 39–52. Amsterdam: John Benjamins.

Long, Michael H. 2007. *Problems in SLA.* Mahwah, NJ: Lawrence Erlbaum.

Long, Michael, and Patricia Porter. 1985. Group work, interlanguage talk, and second language acquisition. *TESOL Quarterly* 19: 207–28.

Lyman, Frank. 1981. The responsive class discussion. In *Mainstreaming digest,* ed. A. S. Anderson. College Park, MD: University of Maryland.

Lyster, Roy. 1987. Speaking immersion. *Canadian Modern Language Review* 43: 701–17.

Lyster, Roy. 2004. Research on form-focused instruction in immersion classrooms: Implications for theory and practice. *Journal of French Language Studies* 14: 321–41.

Lyster, Roy. 2007. *Learning and teaching languages through content: A counterbalanced approach*. Philadelphia: John Benjamins.

Marzano, Robert. 2004. *Building background knowledge for academic achievement: Research on what works in schools*. Alexandria, VA: Association for Supervision and Curriculum Development.

Marzano, Robert, Debra Pickering, and Jane E. Pollock. 2001. *Classroom instruction that works: Research-based strategies for increasing student achievement*. Alexandria, VA: Association for Supervision and Curriculum Development.

McGroarty, Mary. 1992. Cooperative learning: The benefits for content-area teaching. In *The multicultural classroom,* ed. Patricia Richard-Amato and Marguerite Ann Snow. White Plains, NY: Longman.

Mendelsohn, David J. 1994. *Learning to listen: A strategy-based approach for the second-language learner.* San Diego, CA: Dominie Press.

Mendelsohn, David J. and Joan Rubin, eds. 1995. *Guide for the teaching of second language listening.* San Diego, CA: Dominie Press.

Nassaji, Hossein, and Sandra Fotos. 2004. Current developments in research on the teaching of grammar. *Annual Review of Applied Linguistics* 24: 126–45.

Nation, I. S. P. 2001. *Learning vocabulary in another language.* Cambridge: Cambridge University Press.

Nation, I. S. P. 2005. Teaching and learning vocabulary. In *Handbook of research in second language teaching and learning,* ed. Eli Hinkel, 581–95. Mahwah, NJ: Erlbaum.

National Assessment of Educational Progress (NAEP). 2004. Group results for sex, region, and size of community. Washington, DC: U.S. Government Printing Office.

Norris, John M., and Lourdes Ortega. 2000. Effectiveness of L2 instruction: A research synthesis and quantitative meta-analysis. *Language Learning* 50(3): 417–528.

Norris, John M., and Lourdes Ortega, eds. 2006. *Synthesizing research on language learning and teaching.* Philadelphia: John Benjamins Pubs.

Nunan, David, ed. 1992. *Collaborative language learning and teaching.* Cambridge: Cambridge University Press.

Olsen, Lauri, Alicia Romero, and Norman Gold. 2006. *Meeting the needs of English learners in small schools and learning communities.* Oakland: California Tomorrow.

Ramirez, J. David. 1992. Executive summary: Longitudinal study of structured English immersion strategy, early-exit and late-exit transitional bilingual education programs for language-minority children. *Bilingual Research Journal* 16(1): 1–62.

Ruiz-de-Velasco, Jorge, and Michael Fix. 2000. *Overlooked and underserved: Immigrant students in U.S. secondary schools.* Washington, DC: Urban Institute.

Russell, Jane, and Nina Spada. 2006. The effectiveness of corrective feedback for the acquisition of L2 grammar: A meta-analysis of the research. In *Synthesizing research on language learning and teaching,* ed. J. M. Norris and L. Ortega, 133–62. Philadelphia: John Benjamins.

Saunders, William C., and Gisela O'Brien. 2006. Oral language. In *Educating English language learners: A synthesis of research evidence,* ed. Fred Genesee, Kathryn Lindholm-Leary, William C. Saunders, and Donna Christian, 14–63. Cambridge: Cambridge University Press.

Saunders, William, Barbara Foorman, and Coleen Carlson. 2006. Is a separate block of time for oral English language development in programs of English learners needed. *Elementary School Journal* 107(2): 181–98.

Saville-Troike, Muriel. 1984. What really matters in second language learning for academic achievement? *TESOL Quarterly* 18: 199–219.

Scarcella, Robin. 1996. Secondary education and second language research: Instructing ESL students in the 1990's. *The CATESOL Journal* 9: 129–52.

Scarcella, Robin C. 2003. *Accelerating academic English: A focus on the English learner.* Oakland: Regents of the University of California.

Schleppegrell, Mary. 2004. *The language of schooling: A functional linguistic perspective.* Mahwah, NJ: Lawrence Erlbaum.

Schmitt, Norbert. 2000. *Vocabulary in language teaching.* New York: Cambridge University Press.

Shaywitz, Sally. 2003. *Overcoming dyslexia: A new and complete science-based program for reading problems at any level.* New York: Knopf.

Short, Deborah, and Shannon Fitzsimmons. 2007. *Double the work: Challenges and solutions to acquiring language and academic literacy for adolescent English language learners.* Washington, DC: Alliance for Excellent Education.

Spada, Nina and Lightbown, Patsy. 2008. Form-focused instruction: Isolated or integrated? *TESOL Quarterly* 42(2) 181–207.

Stahl, Steven. 1999. *Vocabulary development*. Vol. 2 of *Reading research to practice*. Cambridge, MA: Brookline Books.

Stahl, Steven. A., and M. M. Fairbanks. 1986. The effects of vocabulary instruction: A model based meta-analysis. *Review of Educational Research* 56(1): 72–110.

Swain, Merrell. 1986. Communicative competence: Some roles of comprehensible input and comprehensible output in its development. In *Bilingualism in education,* ed. James Cummins and Merrell Swain, 116–37. New York: Longman.

Swain, Merrell. 1988. Manipulating and complementing content teaching to maximize second language learning. *TESL Canada Journal* 6(1): 68–83.

Swain, Merrell, and Sharon Lapkin. 1998. Interaction and second language learning: Two adolescent French immersion students working together. *Modern Language Journal* 83 (Autumn): 320-37.

Wong Fillmore, Lily, and Catherine Snow. 2000. *What teachers need to know about language.* (Contract No. ED-99-CO-0008). U.S. Department of Education's Office of Educational Research and Improvement, Center for Applied Linguistics.

Chapter 4

Effective English Literacy Instruction for English Learners

Diane August, Center for Applied Linguistics
Timothy Shanahan, University of Illinois, Chicago

This chapter presents eight basic guidelines for effective literacy instruction of English learners. It draws substantially from our previous work (August and Shanahan 2006).

The definitions for key terms used in this chapter have been adopted from August and Shanahan (2006). A *language-minority student* is a student who comes from a home where a language other than English is spoken. A language-minority student may be of limited second-language proficiency, bilingual, or essentially monolingual in the second language (August and Hakuta 1997). Individuals who come from language backgrounds other than the national language and whose second-language proficiency is not yet developed to the point where they can profit fully from instruction solely in the second language are called *second-language learners,* and when that second language is English, these students may be referred to as *English learners* (ELs).[1] The term *bilingual* refers to students who speak or use two languages and to programs that teach two languages (such as *bilingual education*).

Research on English Learner Instruction

This chapter is based heavily on the literature review reported by the National Literacy Panel for Language Minority Children and Youth (August and Shanahan 2006); therefore, the nature and methodology of that review are described so readers can better evaluate the information. The National

---

1. Outside California these students are referred to as English-language learners.

Literacy Panel was charged with the responsibility of conducting a comprehensive review of the research literature to determine what was known about teaching literacy to second-language learners and to help establish a future research agenda on this issue. This panel of experts conducted extensive searches of the relevant research literatures to identify all studies of the literacy learning of language-minority children ages three to eighteen.[2] Some of the questions the panel raised could best be answered by using studies of other national languages, but questions that were directly about instruction used data only on English learning. To be reviewed, the articles had to report research, which means that they had to report some systematic analysis of data. Opinion pieces or "think pieces," reports of personal experience, and the like were not included. Studies were reviewed for quality, and those with serious concerns that made them impossible to interpret unambiguously were set aside.

The National Literacy Panel reviewed studies that were reported during the period 1980 to 2002. For this chapter, a second review was conducted to update the database from 2003 to 2006. Although the panel included studies that appeared as dissertations and technical reports, the review of instructional methods includes only studies published in peer-reviewed journals. Experimental and quasi-experimental designs are essential to evaluate properly the effectiveness of determining what works. In the discussion below focused on instructional methods, only experimental and quasi-experimental research was used as a basis for generating the guidelines for effective practice. What this means is that the study had to evaluate the effectiveness of an instructional method or approach in comparison with conditions in which the method or approach was not used.[3] In all, 83 relevant studies were drawn from both reviews to inform this chapter. What this means is that this chapter is based on an up-to-date, comprehensive review of the best studies on teaching literacy to language-minority children who were trying to learn English. While the review of instructional methods relies on experimental and quasi-experimental studies, the background research and the research on professional development are drawn from studies using a broader range of methodologies, including single-subject designs, case studies, ethnographies, and correlations, as well as variants of these approaches.

Although this chapter focuses mainly on studies that examined effective instruction, the National Literacy Panel report was more extensive than this, and information

---

2. It should be noted that some chapters of the panel report also included studies that focused on the acquisition of English as a foreign language.

3. However, the panel also considered questions about the nature of literacy instruction, relationships among various instructional approaches, teacher and learner attributes, and the status of particular approaches in the education of language-minority students. These questions are better answered through correlational and qualitative studies. Such studies can help identify potentially important variables or determine why something worked.

from the report about development, cross-language influence, oral English proficiency, sociocultural factors, and academic language provides important context for interpreting and implementing the findings of the instructional studies.[4] For that reason, those other topics are briefly summarized first.

Background of Literacy Development

Literacy development requires the acquisition of word-level skills (those involved in word-reading and spelling) and text-level skills (those involved in comprehension and writing). An important finding from three studies (Fitzgerald and Noblit 2000; Neufeld and Fitzgerald 2001; Lesau and Siegel 2003) is that, although some second-language learners may progress at slower rates than native speakers, their growth in literacy generally follows similar developmental paths.

> **. . . although some second-language learners may progress at slower rates than native speakers, their growth in literacy generally follows similar developmental paths.**

Studies examining the development of word-reading and spelling among language-minority students have demonstrated that the development of these skills is similar to that of native speakers (Abu-Rabia and Siegel 2002; Chiappe and Siegel 1999; Chiappe, Siegel, and Wade-Woolley 2002; Da Fontoura and Siegel 1995; D'Angiulli, Siegel, and Serra 2001; Geva, Yaghoub-Zadeh, and Schuster 2000; Mumtaz and Humphreys 2001; Wade-Woolley and Siegel 1997). Skills such as phonological awareness and orthographic knowledge are implicated in the word-reading and spelling of both native speakers and second-language learners. Generally, the studies show that language-minority students are able to achieve similar levels of phonological awareness, decoding skills, and spelling skills as those attained by successful first-language learners with adequate instruction and sufficient time to acquire these skills.

Ultimately, the goal of literacy instruction is to build students' comprehension and writing skills. Unfortunately, the picture that emerges of the comprehension development of language-minority students is quite different. Most of the available studies that compared the comprehension development of language-minority students with their native-speaking peers have indicated that the reading comprehension performance of language-minority students falls well below that of their native-speaking peers (Aarts and Verhoeven 1999; Droop and Verhoeven 1998; Hacquebord 1994; Verhoeven 1990, 2000; Lindsey, Manis, and Bailey 2003; Hutchinson et al. 2003). These findings are consistent with the results of the intervention studies that examine

---

4. The methods used in these studies are both descriptive and experimental.

the effectiveness of various procedures for enhancing the comprehension of language-minority students (Shanahan and Beck 2006). The effect sizes from studies that measured the outcomes on comprehension were consistently lower than those for word-level skills, and all failures to gain significant learning benefits for these students were in reading comprehension rather than word-level skills.

The Role of First-Language Literacy

Students who have learned to read and write in their first language are likely to apply many of their skills to the process of literacy development in the second language. However, many factors influence the nature and degree of such cross-language relationships. In the development of second-language literacy, the similarities of the native and second languages matter, as does the experience students have had in developing first-language literacy (Dressler and Kamil 2006).[5] Many studies reveal a facilitating effect of first-language experiences. There are cross-language relationships in word-reading (Abu-Rabia 1997; Chitiri and Willows 1997; Da Fontoura and Siegel 1995; Durgunoglu, Nagy, and Hancin-Bhatt 1993; Gholamain and Geva 1999). Studies on spelling skills show that in some cases students carry over, sometimes erroneously, features of first-language spelling to their second language. However, most of the studies viewed the acquisition of second-language spelling as a stage in which reliance on the first language early in the process is helpful because in the studies reviewed many of the phoneme–grapheme mappings were applied in both the first language and English (Edelsky 1982; Fashola et al. 1996; Nathansen-Mejía 1989; Zutell and Allen 1988).

As to vocabulary, most studies show that there are relationships between a first and a second language in word knowledge (Garcia 1991, 1998; Hancin-Bhatt and Nagy 1994; James and Klein 1994; Jiménez, Garcia, and Pearson 1996; Nagy et al. 1993; Saville-Troike 1984 cited in Dressler 2006). These cross-language vocabulary relationships were mediated by developmental factors, proficiency levels, and the actual or perceived differences of writing systems between the languages. Although some languages such as English and Spanish are similar, speakers need to perceive the languages as close for transfer to occur (Kellerman 1977). In the process of inferring meaning for unknown words, transfer may also be negative, as when meaning is erroneously assigned to words on the basis of the influence of first-language syntax

---

5. The findings in this section are attributed to Cheryl A. Dressler and Michael Kamil, First and second language literacy. In *Developing literacy in second- language learners: Report of the National Literacy Panel on Language- Minority Children and Youth,* ed. Diane August and Timothy Shanahan, 197–239 (Mahwah, NJ: Erlbaum, 2006).

(Nagy, McClure, and Mir 1997), or the meaning associations of cognates are not differentiated in the two languages (Garcia 1991).[6] For example, the word *embarazar* in Spanish means to become pregnant, not to be embarrassed. Such cases of negative transfer are language-dependent and may be resolved through exposure to the second language, but negative transfer may persist even as students become more proficient in the second language.

For reading comprehension, most studies examined older students (above grade three). Reading comprehension in the first language was found to correlate significantly with reading

A comprehensive review of studies that compare English-only instruction to bilingual instruction demonstrate that language-minority students receiving instruction in both their native language and English did better on English reading measures than language-minority students instructed only in English.

comprehension in the second language under most conditions, including typological distance (i.e., the differences between the writing systems), language status, direction of transfer, age of learner, and tasks (Goldman, Reyes, and Varnhagen 1984; Nagy, McClure, and Mir 1997; Reese et al. 2000; Royer and Carlo 1991; Verhoeven 1994). The evidence also suggests that the processes underlying reading comprehension, when developed in one language, are predictive of reading comprehension in the other.

A similar relationship was found for reading strategies, again investigated primarily with older students. Most studies that addressed this component found that bilingual students who read strategically in one language also read strategically in their other language (subject to proficiency level and other influences). The effects tended to be facilitative, such as using strategies related to obtaining cognate knowledge (Calero-Breckheimer and Goetz 1993; Jiménez, Garcia, and Pearson 1996; Garcia 1998; Langer et al. 1990). In general, strategic reading skills do not need to be relearned as second-language acquisition proceeds because they are not language-specific.

For writing, several studies showed that writing skills that have been developed in one language can be tapped into for writing in the other (Edelsky 1982; Francis 2000). The skills assessed included emergent skills associated with the writing process (such as directionality of print) and also skills related to higher-order processes, including discourse elements in beginning writers and sense of story structure in older elementary students.

---

6. An example is when hypotheses formed about the meaning of verbs in the second language may be influenced by the relationships between the lexical meaning of verbs and their syntactic behavior in the first language.

A comprehensive review of studies that compare English-only instruction to bilingual instruction demonstrate that language-minority students receiving instruction in both their native language (usually Spanish in these studies) and English did better on English reading measures than language-minority students instructed only in English (Francis, Lesaux, and August 2006). This was true at both the elementary and secondary levels. The strongest evidence of this pattern came from studies that used randomized assignment of students to program types; these studies reported a moderate effect in favor of bilingual instruction. However, recent evaluations of scientifically based beginning reading programs that used only English to teach English-language learners to read in English are showing promising results, suggesting that if children receive good instruction with appropriate scaffolding, they can successfully master word-level reading skills in English, such as decoding (Lesaux and Siegel 2003; August et al. 2006). This is an important finding in that first-language instruction is not an option in many schools where children speak multiple languages or staff cannot provide first-language instruction.

The Role of English-Language Proficiency

Research examined the role of oral English proficiency in the acquisition of English word-reading skills (Arab-Moghaddam and Sénéchal 2001; Da Fontoura and Siegel 1995; Durgunoglu, Nagy, and Hancin-Bhatt 1993; Geva, Yaghoub-Zadeh, and Schuster 2000; Gottardo 2002; Gottardo et al. 2001; Jackson and Lu 1992; Muter and Diethelm 2001; Quiroga et al. 2002). Findings suggest that, in many of these studies, phonological processing skills in English, such as phonological awareness, rapid letter naming, and phonological memory, were much better predictors of word-reading skills than was oral language proficiency in either the native language or English. However, although oral language proficiency may not be a key predictor of word-reading skills, it is correlated to some extent with phonological processing skills, such as phonological awareness, rapid naming, and phonological memory—skills that underlie word-reading in language-minority students' learning to read in a second language. A small number of studies also indicate that oral English proficiencies, such as vocabulary and syntactic sensitivity, are not strongly related to English spelling skills (Everatt et al. 2000; Jackson and Lu 1992; Wade-Woolley and Siegel 1997), but phonological processing skills in English play a significant role in the spelling abilities of language-minority students.

In contrast, oral English proficiency plays a much greater role in reading comprehension development in English learners. English reading comprehension is related to diverse components of oral English proficiency, including oral vocabulary knowledge, awareness of cognates, listening comprehension, oral storytelling skills, syntactic skills, and the ability to handle decontextualized aspects of language, such as defining words (Beech and Keys 1997; Carlisle et al. 1999; Carlisle, Beeman, and Shah 1996; Dufva and Voeten 1999; Goldstein, Harris, and Klein 1993; Jiménez, Garcia, and Pearson 1996; Peregoy 1989; Peregoy and Boyle 1991; Royer and Carlo 1991; Lee and Schallert 1997). Unfortunately, most of these data were drawn from young school-age children, and not much is known about older school-age students.

> **. . . oral English proficiency and the skills that allow accurate and effortless recognition of printed words are essential factors in comprehension development.**

The point of these studies is not that oral language proficiency alone guarantees high levels of reading comprehension ability, but that oral English proficiency and the skills that allow accurate and effortless recognition of printed words are essential factors in comprehension development. Cognitive ability and memory play a role as well. Findings of the few available multivariate studies also suggest that the relationship between oral English proficiency and English reading comprehension is mediated by contextual factors, such as home language use and literacy practices and socioeconomic status, as well as by differences in instructional experiences.

Sociocultural Context

Use of language-minority students' native language in school is one important element of the sociocultural context in which these students are educated. A meta-analysis of studies that compared English-only instruction with instruction that used some native language found that bilingual programs were significantly better than English-only programs in developing English literacy skills. The average effect size in favor of native language instruction was moderate (Francis, Lesaux, and August 2006) suggesting that measurable benefits can be derived from programs that support learning in both the first and second languages.

Another aspect of sociocultural context is curriculum that is aligned with students' culture. Several studies found that programs incorporating culturally appropriate curriculum resulted in higher levels of engagement (Au and Mason 1981) or in positive literacy gains for Native American children in these programs (Tharpe 1982). For example, in their highly influential study, Au and Mason (1981) found that culturally compatible instruction had positive effects on native Hawaiian speakers' level of engagement and participation during reading lessons. The culturally compatible instruction used "informal participation structures containing overlapping speech, mutual participation of students and teacher, co-narration, volunteered speech, instant feedback and lack of penalty for wrong answers" (Tharp 1982, 519).

However, this study did not measure literacy achievement, so we do not know whether the higher engagement and participation noted by the researchers led to higher reading achievement.

A second study (Tharp 1982) was carried out in public schools in communities densely populated by Hawaiians and part Hawaiians. All children in the classrooms spoke Hawaiian Creole. The instructional program, KEEP, did produce positive, if modest, effects on student reading achievement. In addition to instruction accommodating the children's interactional styles, however, the KEEP program comprised other elements, such as small-group format, emphasis on comprehension, active direct instruction by teachers, systematic instructional objectives, frequent monitoring of teaching, and criterion-referenced assessment of student learning. Because this program had many elements, it is difficult to determine exactly what made it effective. It may be that improved methods of teaching reading and writing, as well as culturally appropriate curricula, enhanced students' literacy (Goldenberg, Rueda, and August 2006). Future research is clearly needed because of the importance of native languages and culture to the communities that have developed and implemented those programs and the promising effects on student engagement.

Social Versus Academic Language

Recently, there has been much emphasis on the importance of building academic language, which is usually contrasted with social language. Academic language has been defined by Scarcella (2003) as "a variety or register of English used in professional books and characterized by the specific linguistic features that are used in particular situational contexts" (pp. 10–11). (See also Saunders and Goldenberg, this publication, for an expanded definition.) However, we are in accord with Bailey (2007), who stressed the importance of guarding "against believing that there is something inherent in social language that makes it less sophisticated or less cognitively demanding than language used in an academic context." There are times when academic discourse does not demand complex linguistic responses, and there are times when social uses of language are complex and complicated. Thus, it is most accurate to characterize the difference between academic language and social language as differences in the *relative frequency* of complex grammatical structures, specialized vocabulary, and uncommon language functions.

> It is most accurate to characterize the difference between academic language and social language as differences in the *relative frequency* of complex grammatical structures, specialized vocabulary, and uncommon language functions.

In any event, the basic premise has been that some English learners may have special problems in developing academic language in a second language because those students have had poor or interrupted schooling in their first language as well as relatively less experience with the academic register. This complicates the teaching of English learners because teachers need to help such students learn the concepts as well as the labels associated with these concepts and students cannot draw on primary language cognate knowledge (where relevant) to help with academic vocabulary in the second language. In addition, teachers sometimes assume that students' academic language is more developed than it is because of their facility with discourse in more informal situations where context helps mediate language. No direct research was found on these issues, however.

Guidelines for Teaching Literacy to English Learners

Research on how best to teach literacy to English learners is not so thorough or specific that it would be possible to provide a detailed research-based plan for such instruction. Nevertheless, it is possible to derive some useful guidelines for the design of such instruction from the systematic analysis of the existing research.

Guideline 1: Effective instruction for English learners emphasizes essential components of literacy.

The National Reading Panel issued a report that provided an analysis of research on the teaching of reading to native speakers of English (NICHD 2000). That report examined five topics that focused largely on the usefulness of explicitly teaching particular aspects of literacy. Although that analysis dealt with some questions of instructional methodology, for the most part it focused on whether teaching students to know or do specific things helped them to learn to read. Specifically, that report indicated that it is helpful to explicitly teach young children:

- To hear the individual English sounds or phonemes within words (phonemic awareness)

- To use the letters and spelling patterns within words to decode the word's pronunciation (phonics)

- To read text aloud with appropriate speed, accuracy, and expression (oral reading fluency)

- To know the meanings of words and affixes (vocabulary)

- To think in particular ways during reading (reading comprehension)

Those five components appear to be essential to reading development because they are included in theoretical analyses of the reading process and because instruction in them helps at least some students to read more proficiently.

The issue here is whether these same components of reading are equally necessary for the reading development of English learners. The National Literacy Panel reviewed a comparable set of studies that experimentally attempted to improve the reading ability of English learners by providing explicit teaching of these same reading components, and we have updated that review with more recent research.

Nine studies examined the development of phonological awareness and word-reading in language-minority students (Gunn et al. 2000, 2002, 2005; Giambo and McKinney 2004; Kramer, Schell, and Rubison 1983; Stuart 1999; Swanson, Hodson, and Schommer-Aikins 2005; Troia 2004; Roberts and Neal 2004). The findings of those nine studies are generally consistent with the findings from the much more extensive first-language research (the National Reading Panel examined 52 studies of phonological awareness instruction and another 38 studies on phonics instruction). Teaching children to hear the sounds of language and to use these sounds in conjunction with letters in order to read text is valuable for those learning to read, whether they are native speakers of English or are English learners.

Likewise, teaching oral reading fluency appears to be beneficial for English learners, as well as for native speakers of English. "Fluency" (in reading) refers to the ability to read text accurately, with sufficient speed and proper expression (that is, with appropriate pausing or phrasing and intonation). The National Reading Panel reviewed 16 studies that demonstrated the benefits of teaching fluency to monolingual students. Here we located three studies that considered the impact of fluency instruction on English learners (Gunn et al. 2000, 2002, 2005). Fluency instruction was found to improve both fluency and, in some cases, reading comprehension for English learners.

Another important aspect of reading achievement is vocabulary knowledge. Students who know the meanings of many words are able to comprehend better than those who do not. The National Reading Panel found 45 studies that showed that teaching word meanings, word-learning strategies, and word consciousness improved student reading ability. For English learners, we were able to locate eight studies that focused on vocabulary, in most cases in conjunction with other constructs (Biemiller and Boote 2006; Carlo et al. 2004; Pérez 1983; Neuman and Koskinen 1992; Uchikoshi 2005; Giambo and McKinney 2004; Roberts and Neal 2004; and Ulanoff and Pucci 1999). The findings were generally consistent with vocabulary studies for native speakers of English in showing that explicitly focusing on vocabulary improved reading proficiency. In two cases, children were incidentally exposed to vocabulary through television (Neuman and Koskinen 1992; Uchikoshi 2005), and in one study, phonological awareness training improved English receptive vocabulary (Giambo and McKinney 2004).

Research has also demonstrated that it is possible to provide explicit instruction that improves reading comprehension. The

> **Explicit instruction in key aspects of literacy . . . provides clear learning benefits for students.**

National Reading Panel reviewed 205 studies that found that teaching comprehension strategies or ways of thinking during reading (e.g., how to summarize text, visualize, apply prior knowledge productively during reading) improves reading ability in native speakers of English. Studies on English learners have also reported that when explicit attention to reading comprehension was involved, it had a positive impact on reading achievement (Tharp 1982; Bean 1982: Cohen and Rodríguez 1980; Slavin and Madden 1999; Saunders and Goldenberg 1999; Fung, Wilkinson, and Moore 2003; Liang, Peterson, and Graves 2005)[A1]. Additionally, the second-language research includes two studies in which learning was incidental. In the first study, children were exposed to an extensive range of high-interest storybooks and encouraged to read and share them (Elley 1991), and in the other, children were encouraged to read freely from a range of graded readers and report orally on their reading (Tudor and Hafiz 1989).

Writing is another aspect of literacy that benefits from explicit instruction. Studies have revealed many effective approaches for improving the writing abilities of native English-speaking students (Graham and Perin 2007; Hillocks 1986). As with the other components of literacy already discussed, there were far fewer studies of writing conducted with English learners (Franken and Haslett 1999; Gomez et al. 1996; Prater and Bermudez, 1993; Sengupta 2000). Some of the same types of instructional routines seem to be beneficial for English learners as well. For example, structured writing was more effective than free writing (Gomez et al. 1996) in improving quality of writing, and writing with peer response groups led to greater amounts of writing, though it did not impact writing quality (Prater and Bermúdez 1993).

In summary, although there were many fewer studies of English learners, the general pattern found with English-proficient students seems to hold: explicit instruction in key aspects of literacy—phonemic awareness, phonics, oral reading fluency, vocabulary, reading comprehension, and writing—provides clear learning benefits for students. In order to be literate, students must be able to:

⊙ Decode words.

⊙ Understand word meanings.

⊙ Read text quickly and easily enough that cognitive resources can be devoted to interpretation.

⊙ Read text in a manner that reflects the syntactic and prosodic aspects of the language.

⊙ Understand text.

⊙ Use strategies that help them to think effectively about the text.

⊙ Engage in writing practice.

These skills and abilities have to be developed by any reader—no matter what the language status. Generally, this research suggests that a sound literacy curriculum for English learners will focus on the same components of literacy as a curriculum geared for English-proficient students. The following section further elaborates on this guideline.

Guideline 2: Effective instruction for English learners is similar to effective literacy instruction for native speakers.

From the first guiding principle, it is evident that English learners have to focus on the same components of literacy as monolingual students. What needs to be learned to read in English is largely the same whether one is a native speaker of English or an English learner. However, that does not necessarily mean that English learners benefit from the same types of instructional routines and programs that are effective with native speakers of English. The need to focus on the same components does not imply that exactly the same instructional approaches will be equally effective with both groups. However, analysis of research suggests that, indeed, many of the instructional approaches that have been successful with native speakers of English are effective with English learners, too.

Earlier it was noted that English learners can benefit from explicit instructional attention to phonemic awareness, phonics, and oral reading fluency. Many of the cited studies used commercial programs to guide the teaching of these skills, and were programs that have previously worked well with students who are proficient in English (Gunn et al. 2000, 2002, 2005; Giambo and McKinney 2004; Kramer, Schell, and Rubison 1983; Stuart 1999; Slavin and Madden 1999; Swanson, Hodson, and Schommer-Aikins 2005; Troia 2004). For example, the studies found programs such as *Success for All, Reading Mastery, Corrective Reading, Jolly Phonics, Fast ForWord Language,* and *Read Naturally* were effective for English learners. The studies provided instruction to English learners—often in small groups—that matched the explicit decoding instruction, use of leveled texts, or oral reading practice with repetition that has been effective in teaching native speakers of English.

Not only is this true of the commercial programs focused on phonemic awareness, phonics, and oral reading fluency, but it is also true for a range of other instructional routines that teachers use in their classrooms with students who are proficient in English. For example, adjustments to the structure and content of stories, such as deleting trivial story events that distract from a more predictable story structure or making pronoun referents more explicit, are helpful to both first- and second-language learners (Bean 1982). Studies of vocabulary development yielded findings consistent with those of vocabulary studies for proficient speakers of English (e.g., Graves 2006; Nagy and Stahl 2006). High-quality vocabulary instruction teaches individual words and word learning strategies, provides rich and varied language experiences, and promotes word consciousness. For example, in the Vocabulary Improvement Project (Carlo et al. 2004), words are selected from text and pretaught; but words are also taught in context, and word meanings are reinforced using engaging activities.

In designing successful lessons for English learners, teachers and instructional designers are advised to examine the kinds of instruction that work with native speakers of English as a starting point.

Writing studies with English learners have also demonstrated the effectiveness of instructional approaches and routines that have been successful with native speakers. For example, explicit instruction and practice in revision (Sengupta 2000) have been found to improve writing quality with both first- and second-language students. Such instruction reveals weaknesses in the students' writing to them and then provides explicit support and guidance to show students how to improve the communicative quality of what they write.

That the same types of instruction can improve the reading and writing performance of both first-language and second-language students who do not have reading difficulties is true for struggling readers as well. In some studies, students in mainstream classrooms who had learning difficulties were provided with supplemental reading instruction that improved their literacy outcomes (e.g., Gunn et al. 2000, 2002, 2005; Linan-Thompson et al. 2003; Vaughn et al. 2006; Swanson, Hodson, and Schommer-Aikins 2005). Invariably, this instruction was provided in small-group pullout sessions. Several of these studies found that explicit phonological awareness and phonics instruction was beneficial for older second-language learners (Gunn et al. 2000 [third- and fourth-graders]; Swanson, Hodson, and Schommer-Aikins 2005 [seventh- through ninth-graders]). Finally, in some studies, students worked on leveled materials at their own pace and had to meet criteria to move to the next level (e.g., Cohen and Rodriguez 1980), ensuring that all students mastered the curriculum.

221

These practices are consistent with effective instruction for struggling readers who are proficient in English.

To be literate in English, students must master a diverse set of skills. These skills must be mastered no matter what language background a student might come from. Not surprisingly, instruction that explicitly explains these features to students, models their uses, and provides sufficient scaffolded practice at appropriate levels supports the learning of students from different language backgrounds (August and Shanahan 2006). In designing successful lessons for English learners, teachers and instructional designers are advised to examine the kinds of instruction that work with native speakers of English as a starting point, as appropriate versions of such instruction have tended to be successful with English learners as well. However, teachers are also advised to examine the skills English learners have acquired in their first language because many of these skills will help students who are learning to read and write in a second language.

Guideline 3: Effective literacy curriculum and instruction for English learners must be adjusted to meet their needs.

Although there are important similarities between the kinds of teaching that best support first- and second-language learners in their literacy development, there are also important differences. Although instructional approaches that have worked with native speakers of English can be a good place to start, using these procedures slavishly with no adjustment despite the very real differences that often exist between first- and second-language learners is less effective. The reason that common instructional procedures would be effective with English learners too is probably due to the fact that students are similar no matter what their language background (similar in perceptual skills, memory capacity, ability to learn, etc.), so modeling, explanation, and practice in instruction probably do not differ very much from one group to another. However, as similar as learning mechanisms and capacities are, the role of background experience and prior knowledge in comprehension and learning has been well documented. Therefore, the differences in the language and background experiences of English learners must be reflected in the instruction designed for them.

> **Although there are important similarities between the kinds of teaching that best support first- and second-language learners in their literacy development, there are also important differences.**

In fact, although research has shown that procedures such as reciprocal teaching or the writing-conference method can work well with English learners, the procedures that were implemented in these studies appear to be versions of procedures that have

been carefully adapted to the needs of English learners (Shanahan and Beck 2006). Unfortunately, the extant research does not thoroughly document all of the adaptations that have been made when common instructional procedures are the focus of study, and no studies we reviewed explicitly compared an intervention developed for students proficient in English with the same intervention adapted for English learners. Often, even when adjustments were made, variations in approach were not detailed in the methods section of the studies; they are implicit in the description of the intervention and are mentioned in passing in the discussion sections. For that reason, it is impossible to thoroughly catalog the adaptations that make these instructional procedures work with English learners, but we can provide some insights based on studies, about the kinds of variations that may help.

Strategic use of the first language. One obvious variation that can be made is to use the home or the primary language for part of the instruction. This particular adjustment is separate from the idea that students should be taught bilingually; that topic is covered later in this publication by Lindholm-Leary and Genesee. In this chapter, we focus, rather, on the strategic use of the first language to make instruction in a second language comprehensible and effective. By providing necessary information and explanations in the language that students understand best, a teacher can increase student success. For example, in one study a modified reciprocal teaching method was used (Fung, Wilkinson, and Moore 2003). In the standard version of reciprocal teaching, after teacher modeling, students take turns assuming the role of teacher as they read and discuss segments of text, using four strategies to make the text more comprehensible—summarizing, question generating, clarifying, and predicting. In the adapted version, Chinese and English were used on alternate days during the reciprocal teaching lessons, with new information presented in Chinese first. On each day prior to the Chinese reciprocal teaching procedure (for the first 12 days), there was a 15-minute session of teacher-directed strategy instruction. The language used for the direct instruction was the same as the language used for reciprocal teaching on that day. Those adjustments both increased the amount of discussion that students engaged in during the lesson (a greater amount of talking about the text in their home language) and also improved their reading comprehension.

Similarly, in a study of vocabulary teaching, English passages—the source of the vocabulary words—were translated into the students' first language to ensure comprehension of the overall text; bilingual glossaries were provided for the targeted vocabulary; and, explicit instruction in the transfer of cognate and morphological knowledge from a first language to a second language was provided (Carlo et al. 2004). Another study used students' first language to build comprehension in English (Ulanoff and Pucci 1999). Otherwise, the instructional procedures used in these studies were quite similar to those that had been found to be successful in building vocabulary in a first language.

Enhanced instructional delivery routines. Earlier it was noted that phonics instruction—teaching English learners to use letters and sounds to decode English— is beneficial. Many methods for teaching phonics have been found to work with English-proficient students, though results vary under different instructional conditions (NICHD 2000). For example, phonics instruction works better when delivered in a small group rather than in whole-class settings. Small-group instructional delivery may increase the amount of practice individual students can engage in and clarifies confusion more immediately.

All of the English learner studies of phonics used enhanced procedures for teaching these skills. In seven of the studies, instruction was provided to small groups in pull-out sessions (Gunn et al. 2000, 2002, 2005; Giambo and McKinney 2004; Kramer, Schell, and Rubinson 1983; Swanson, Hodson, and Schommer-Aikins 2005; Troia 2004). In two studies, it was conducted with classrooms of English learners (Stuart 1999; Slavin and Madden 1999), although even in these studies whole-class instruction was supplemented by small-group instruction. English learners are more likely to have difficulty reading in a second language because of language differences, so enhanced instructional routines that provide extra amounts of teaching or, as in this example, more interactive and individualized instruction that allows difficulty with new material to be addressed immediately would be beneficial adjustments to regular instructional routines. Other alterations that have enhanced the delivery routines in the phonics studies included providing additional time for language-minority students to complete lessons so that the instructor could provide sufficient explanation of vocabulary and better support students' comprehension (Gunn et al. 2000, 2002).

Adjustments for differences in knowledge. The most obvious difference between first- and second-language learners is that second-language learners can draw upon a body of knowledge and skills that first-language learners may not yet have (e.g., decoding ability, conceptual knowledge). This means that sometimes it is not necessary to cover exactly the same content since the knowledge is already available to second-language learners (Dressler 2006). For example, phonemic awareness and decoding skills (in the case of orthographically similar languages) have been found to generalize well across languages—meaning that if students can hear and read the sounds in one language, they either do not need to master this skill in English or they only need to master it for those sounds and sound combinations that are different from or unique to English.

In one study of phonemic awareness instruction for English learners (Kramer, Schell, and Rubinson 1983), the intervention was aimed specifically at helping students hear sounds that could be confusing for Spanish-speaking students learning English. The sound pairs used for the intervention included *ch/sh, b/v, l/ld,* and *s/st.* Giambo and McKinney (2004) included 10 pairs of sounds that are difficult for Spanish-speaking students learning English. Studies of this type can be useful in helping to design approaches to phonological awareness and phonics that would be particularly effective with certain populations of language-minority students.

Similar adjustments may be beneficial in vocabulary instruction. In first-language learning, differences have been found in how thorough instruction needs to be depending on students' level of knowledge: students who need to learn only the word or label for an already-understood concept generally do not need as much instructional support as students who have to learn both the label and the meaning of the underlying concept (see discussion of vocabulary instruction in Snow and Katz, this publication). English learners often already have developed underlying concepts even though their language development in English lags behind their experiences and knowledge of the world. Instruction that builds on English learners' awareness of concepts in their home language and labels for these concepts (in the case of cognates) could be adjusted accordingly. On the other hand, English learners with poor or interrupted schooling in their first language may need additional instruction to help them learn the concepts associated with domain knowledge as well as the oral language associated with this knowledge.

More scaffolding. Another common strategy to increase the chances that students who are unfamiliar with English will understand lessons sufficiently is to provide scaffolding in the form of visual representations of language, as well as enhanced or more explicit modeling or explanation than they might normally get. This might include using pictures or gestures as a form of explanation (Carlo et al. 2004; Pérez 1983; Stuart 1999). Studies aimed at increasing comprehension used techniques such as identifying and clarifying difficult words and passages and consolidating text knowledge through carefully orchestrated discussion called instructional conversations (Saunders 1999; Saunders and Goldenberg 1999; Tharp 1982). Studies of writing instruction with English learners have shown that providing students with explicit explanations of argument structures and text features leads to better writing performance (Franken and Haslett 1999), as does more explicit instruction in text revision (Gomez et al. 1996). A fourth study (Echevarría and Short 2006) used the SIOP Model, a comprehensive model of professional development that focuses on concurrent attention to developing content and academic English, with teachers of adolescent language-minority students (see Echevarria and Short, this publication). They found improvements in students' academic literacy as measured through an expository writing assessment. One important characteristic of SIOP instruction is

225

explicit language instruction "targeted to and slightly beyond students' level of English proficiency also is presented in every lesson" (Echevarria and Short 2006, 207).

Additional time. Another alteration that has enhanced the delivery routines has included providing additional time for language-minority students to complete lessons so that the instructor could provide sufficient explanation of vocabulary and better support students' comprehension (Gunn et al. 2000, 2002).

Although the experimental research generally did not focus on time, evidence from longitudinal studies indicates that time is an important factor to consider with English learners. In thinking about the time required to become proficient in English, one must make a distinction between language needed to learn complex academic subjects and conversational language that is less cognitively demanding and embedded in context (Cummins 1981; Snow 1987; Collier 1995). For students to cope with the demands of mainstream class work, they need to attain mastery of academic English as well as conversational language. Recent work by Hakuta, Butler, and Witt (2000) indicates that it takes English learners from three to five years to acquire oral language proficiency and four to seven years to acquire academic language. Findings are based on large samples of students in four school districts, two in California and two in Canada. In three of the districts, the English learners were schooled entirely in English; in the district that provided a bilingual option, student outcomes in oral language proficiency and in academic language were equivalent to English-only instruction and bilingual instruction. Additionally, Collier (1987) and Collier and Thomas (1989) examined the development of content area knowledge in a group of 1,548 middle-class English learners with grade-level skills in their first language attending middle-class suburban schools and found that it took this group of students four to eight years of schooling to reach national norms in all subjects as measured by Science Research Associates (SRA) tests in reading, language arts, social studies, and science. Those students eventually did reach grade-level norms.

Other adaptations. Our purpose here is not to examine all possible variations to common instructional routines that can be effective with English learners, but to document the importance and value of such variations. Many other adaptations or adjustments to common instructional approaches have been evident in the research literature and have resulted in positive outcomes for English learners (Shanahan and Beck 2006): provision of written instructions and modeling as well as access to English-proficient peers (e.g., Franken and Haslett 1999); clarifying and simplifying text (Bean 1982); and introducing skills to students at different ages than they might be typically taught to monolingual English learners because they were lacking in these skills due to poor and interrupted schooling (Gunn 2000, 2002, 2005; Swanson et al. 2005). In the latter studies, older students who were recent immigrants were taught using explicit phonics techniques.

Guideline 4: Effective literacy instruction for English learners is comprehensive and multidimensional.

Examinations of research studies can sometimes be misleading. Often researchers investigate particular aspects of instruction, abstracted from the total constellation of efforts that they themselves would consider to be sound literacy teaching. For example, when researchers study the benefits of enhanced instructional routines that focus primarily on phonemic awareness, phonics, oral reading fluency, vocabulary, reading comprehension, or writing, they are not claiming that such instruction is all that

Research with English learners has shown the benefits of more comprehensive and complex instructional routines for teaching literacy to English learners.

students should receive. In fact, such investigations typically take place in the context of literacy instruction that also covers at least some of the aspects of literacy being ignored in the targeted instruction. Literacy instruction needs to be thorough and complete; that is, it should provide adequate instructional attention to all of the skills and knowledge that must be learned, and such instruction can include complex approaches that may address more than one skill simultaneously.

Research with English learners has shown the benefits of more comprehensive and complex instructional routines for teaching literacy to English learners. For example, in a study that was part of a series of related efforts, an extensive array of improvements to literacy and language arts lessons were explored (Saunders 1999). This study examined the literacy learning of language-minority students in grades two to five who were participating in a Spanish transitional bilingual program. The instructional approach that was examined included 12 instructional components aimed at providing a fairly comprehensive response to students' literacy and language learning needs:

- ⊙ Literature units that employed an experience-text relationship method of presentation
- ⊙ Literature logs
- ⊙ Instructional conversations
- ⊙ Writing as a process
- ⊙ Direct teaching of comprehension strategies
- ⊙ Assigned independent reading
- ⊙ Dictation

- Lessons in written conventions

- English-language development through literature

- Pleasure reading

- Teacher read-alouds

- Interactive journals

The experimenters report statistically significant differences at fifth grade, when most students were tested in English, in which the experimental students increasingly outperformed control students on both the Comprehensive Test of Basic Skills (CTBS) and a district assessment battery (a combination of measures of oral English proficiency, Spanish reading, and Spanish writing).

Another example of the benefits of more complete or more complex instructional responses to the needs of English learners is provided in a study by Tharp (1982) on instruction that included six elements:

- More time spent on reading comprehension and relatively less time on decoding

- More frequent criterion-referenced testing to monitor student progress

- Classes that relied entirely on small-group discussion during reading lessons in which the "dominant participation structure was highly informal, continuing overlapping speech, mutual participation by teacher and students, co-narration, volunteered speech, instant feedback, and lack of penalty for wrong answers" (p. 519)

- Child motivation maintained through high rates of praise and other forms of positive interpersonal reinforcement

- Individualized diagnostic prescriptive instruction

- A quality control system in which the program characteristics were measured, rated, and used to monitor program implementation

On the vocabulary subtest of the Gates-MacGinitie Reading Tests (a measure that focuses mainly on decoding skill despite its name), the experimental groups significantly outperformed the control groups despite a reduction in phonics instruction. On the comprehension subtest of the same battery, the differences favoring the experimental groups nearly reached the .05 significance level, but full-scale scores on the Metropolitan Reading Tests showed no differences.

A third example is the *Success for All* program (Slavin and Madden 1999). At the heart of the program is 90 minutes of uninterrupted daily reading instruction that emphasizes a balance between word-level (e.g., phonics and spelling) and text-level skills (e.g., reading comprehension and writing), using both phonetically regular

texts and children's literature. The highly structured curriculum provides extensive guidance for teachers, helping to ensure that all classroom instruction follows the same essential design and includes tutoring for students who need additional support. Students are regrouped for reading, and children with similar performance levels are placed in the same group. Students are assessed every eight weeks and regrouped as needed. There is variation in the results across sites and grade levels, but generally the results are positive.

Finally, positive results have been obtained with other complex instructional procedures, such as cooperative grouping (Calderón, Hertz-Lazarowitz, and Slavin 1998) This study found benefits for such procedures compared to basal reader instruction for Spanish-background students. The two groups used the same Spanish and English text materials. However, the experimental students were placed in groups of four in which they carried out cooperative work during the lessons, and they received specialized teaching in comprehension, vocabulary, oral reading fluency, and writing. The investigators found that, by the end of second grade, there was no difference in Spanish reading comprehension between the two groups, although the cooperative-grouping students did better in Spanish writing. By the end of third grade, there was no difference on a test of English writing, but the experimental subjects did significantly better in English reading.

These studies emphasize the importance of developing more substantial and comprehensive responses to English learners' needs, including attention to the amount of instruction, completeness of the curriculum, quality of the instructional interactions between teacher and student and among students, adequate assessment, and an emphasis on student motivation. Research also suggests the importance of parental involvement. Parents of English learners have successfully been taught to read to their children (Hancock 2002) and to help their children with skills learning (Gunn et al. 2000, 2002, 2005).

Guideline 5: Effective literacy instruction for English learners develops oral proficiency.

As has been noted, instructional interventions have generally had a greater impact on the decoding and spelling skills of English learners than on their reading comprehension. English learners often acquire basic skills as well as native speakers of English do (e.g., phonemic awareness, decoding, spelling), but they rarely match English-proficient students in reading comprehension. Although instruction in

Instructional interventions have generally had a greater impact on the decoding and spelling skills of English learners than on their reading comprehension.

229

various basic skills provides a clear benefit to English learners (as they do with the native speakers of English), the effect associated with such efforts are clearly smaller than when English-proficient students are the target population (Shanahan and Beck 2006). This pattern seems logical: teaching decoding, for instance, helps by allowing the reader to produce an appropriate oral language representation of written language. But this will only lead to better comprehension if the reader can understand the oral language. Thus, phonics would help readers of English up to the level of their oral proficiency; when text difficulty exceeds the students' oral proficiency, the beneficial effects of phonics would diminish. The same pattern is evident with older native speakers; that is, phonics instruction yields less payoff for comprehension as students proceed through school because the texts they confront are more likely to present language and concepts that they cannot understand and use orally. It seems clear that, in order to provide maximum benefit to language-minority students, instruction must do more than develop a complex array of basic literacy skills; it must also develop oral English proficiency along with basic reading skills.

There is some evidence for the benefits of vocabulary instruction on reading-comprehension outcomes, but this evidence is not consistent (Carlo et al. 2004; Biemiller and Boote 2006). Differences in students' initial levels of oral English proficiency may help explain this inconsistency. As an example, one study (Klingner and Vaughn 2000) examined the effects of collaborative strategic reading on the peer group participation and vocabulary development of fifth-grade Spanish-speaking students, some of whom were English learners. In collaborative strategic reading, students of various reading and achievement levels work in small, cooperative groups to assist one another in applying specific reading strategies to help them comprehend subject-matter texts. The assessments used in the study revealed that, overall, students made statistically significant gains in vocabulary. However, when the data were examined by subgroup (English learners; high-achieving, average-achieving, and low-achieving students who were not English learners), the high-achieving students demonstrated the greatest gains, and the English learners made the smallest.

The study suggests the importance of requisite levels of English proficiency for taking advantage of instruction in strategy use. In a second study (Neuman and Koskinen 1992) focused on developing vocabulary, all students were middle-grades English learners. The only students to benefit from the intervention, which consisted of providing students with access to high-quality captioned television as a supplement to reading, were students with sufficient oral English proficiency. In discussing the findings, the authors note that the more linguistic competence the students had, the more they acquired, supporting the need for substantial direct teacher intervention in building oral English proficiency for students who are below a threshold of linguistic competence in their new language. Moreover, teaching language-minority students strategies (for decoding or comprehension) can be effective, but it should be combined with concerted efforts to build students' facility in oral English; strategies of various types are unlikely to help students who do not have the requisite oral language proficiency to comprehend the text.

These examples highlight the idea that providing high-quality instruction in literacy skills alone may be insufficient to support equal academic success for language-minority students. Sound instruction in reading strategies (and instruction in other literacy basics) must be combined with efforts to increase the scope and sophistication of these students' oral language proficiency. Although this recommendation makes sense, research is needed that would directly test this hypothesis.

There are many examples of methods to build oral language proficiency in the context of literacy instruction. These examples include providing oral language activities intended to clarify specific concepts in the basal readers (Perez 1981); grouping second-language learners with speakers of fluent English in peer response and conferencing groups and thus providing rich opportunities for students to interact with native speakers of English (Carlo et al. 2004); providing additional time after school to read books in English with adult support, as needed (Tudor and Hafiz 1989); using instructional conversations (Saunders 1999; Saunders and Goldenberg 1999), and shared interactive reading (Liang, Peterson, and Graves 2005; Biemiller and Boote 2006; Elley 1991).

Although English proficiency is important, we cannot underestimate the importance of domain knowledge (Hirsch 2003). The continual, systematic, and everyday ways in which we engage children in learning new knowledge and information, starting in the early years, plays an important role in building conceptual knowledge (Glaser 1984; Neuman 2001). As previously mentioned, students who have only to learn the English labels for concepts they have in their first language enjoy much more of an advantage than students who must learn both the English label and the concept. Thus, while students are acquiring English proficiency it is essential to give them access to domain knowledge through their first language or through course content in English that has been carefully scaffolded to ensure it is comprehensible.

Guideline 6: Effective literacy instruction for English learners is differentiated.

English learners are a heterogeneous group (e.g., age of arrival in a new country, educational history, socioeconomic status, cognitive capacity, English proficiency, reading ability, interests), and instruction, if it is to be maximally effective, has to be differentiated to address their diverse learning needs. Often English learners, because of their relatively lower levels of achievement, are compared with special education students. Such comparisons are misleading, however. Students with learning problems represent a narrow range of performance and learning capacities, and such students often have difficulty progressing even with enhanced instruction. In fact, in a review of research that compared the development of native speakers of English to the development of English learners, Lesaux and Siegel (2003) documented the differential progress of average readers and readers with disabilities across these groups, noting similar proportions of readers with disabilities in both groups and similar learning profiles for English learners with disabilities and the English-proficient students with disabilities. "Reading disability in both groups was characterized by low scores on all measures of phonological processing as well as on syntax and working memory" (p. 1017).

> **English learners as a group include students with learning disabilities, of course, but most English learners have no special learning problems.**

English learners, however, are much more diverse in their learning ability than special education students. English learners as a group include students with learning disabilities, of course, but most English learners have no special learning problems. This means that most English learners are likely to make appropriate progress if provided with access to sound instruction (see studies cited above) and sufficient time (Lesaux, Rupp, and Siegel 2007) to acquire English proficiency and domain knowledge. Some of the instruction described above that has been effective has provided supplemental small-group instruction to English learners (e.g., Gunn et al. 2000, 2002, 2005) where instruction can be provided at the appropriate instructional level. Additionally, *Success for All* uses a Joplin plan where students are grouped across classrooms for literacy instruction according to their reading level so that they can maximally benefit from instruction (Slavin and Madden 1999). Unlike traditional ability grouping, however, students are assessed every eight weeks and moved to a different instructional group when it was appropriate to do so.

Despite the diverse needs of these students, there is relatively little research that can provide guidance on how to accommodate their diverse needs in the classroom. For example, while most teachers have classrooms composed of students with very different levels of early reading skills, in most studies reviewed in this chapter, teachers provided phonics and phonological awareness instruction to students in small groups outside the regular classroom who were at the same level of reading proficiency.

English learners benefit from teaching that attends to their individual learning needs and ensures that they are instructed to the same high standards as their peers. Teaching that provides a variety of reading activities and resources matched to students' levels of second-language proficiency and domain knowledge (through maintaining high expectations), and individual attention during instruction can benefit all these students, as can increased amounts or intensity of instruction. In some studies, students worked on leveled materials at their own pace and had to reach criteria before moving to the next level (e.g., Cohen et al. 1980), ensuring that all students mastered the curriculum. For example, in this study first-grade English learners in the treatment group were pretested and placed at their appropriate point of entry along the continuum of lessons and used instructional cassettes and a self-directing workbook to master each objective. Following mastery for each competency, students read silently from the reader or read orally in a small teacher-led group. The control group was taught as a full class or in a traditional three-group mode using the same curricular materials. After 90 lessons, the authors found the individualized approach was more effective than the group approach as measured by a silent-reading comprehension test.

English proficiency. An important difference among English learners is their level of English proficiency. As noted earlier, results of several studies indicate that language-minority children with low levels of oral English proficiency do not benefit from some instructional methods as much as those with greater English proficiency (Klingner and Vaughn 2000; Neuman and Koskinen 1992).

Older recently arrived immigrants. In successful instructional programs, students learn foundational skills and use them as building blocks for acquiring later, more complex skills. In learning to decode, for example, children first learn simple spelling patterns for single-syllable words and then apply their knowledge of these patterns to decoding multisyllable words. Likewise, in the case of instruction targeting specific skills, researchers have made an obvious, although often unstated, assumption about the appropriate developmental level for their subjects. However, some language-minority students may begin acquiring literacy for the first time in the upper grades because of poor and interrupted schooling in their home country; others who immigrate when they are older may have acquired first-language literacy in their home country but begin acquiring second-language literacy skills in the upper grades. Few studies have focused on older second-language learners who are recent immigrants. As one example, a study by Swanson and others (2005) found that older students without first-language reading skills who were given phonological awareness training, followed by instruction in decoding, writing, and reading high-interest decodable books, showed significant improvement in phonological awareness, word attack, word identification, word comprehension, and reading comprehension.

English learners with special educational needs. All English learners face the challenge of trying to learn to read in a language different from the one they know how to speak. That is a difficult task, and it is no surprise that most English learners accomplish it at a pace somewhat slower than their native-speaking counterparts. If these students were being schooled in their home languages rather than in English, it seems likely that they would progress more quickly. Teachers sometimes confuse the learning challenges of English learners (challenges that primarily are due to language differences) with learning disabilities. Likewise, there are English learners who not only are challenged by language differences, but who also suffer from learning disabilities. Such students not only have difficulty learning to read in English, they would likely have trouble learning to read in their home language as well.

For English learners identified with special education needs who are taught in special settings, there have been a variety of successful approaches (Bos, Allen, and Scanlon 1989; Echevarria 1996; Klingner and Vaughn 1996; Perozzi 1985; Rohena, Jidentra, and Browder 2002; Rousseau, Tam, and Ramnarain 1993; VanWagenen, Williams, and McLaughlin 1994). Some approaches are based on behaviorist principles of learning, and others employ so-called cognitive or holistic-interactive approaches. Because of the small sample sizes and lack of controls in some of the studies, however, more research is needed to explore their effectiveness.

In some studies, students in mainstream classrooms with learning difficulties were provided with supplemental reading instruction, which improved their literacy outcomes (Gunn et al. 2000, 2002, 2005; Linan-Thompson et al. 2003; Swanson et al. 2005; Vaughn et al. 2006). Invariably this instruction was provided in small-group pullout sessions. Of note is that several of the studies found that explicit phonological awareness and phonics instruction was beneficial for older second-language learners (Gunn et al. 2000 [third- and fourth-graders]; Swanson et al. 2005 [seventh- to ninth-graders]).

Guideline 7: Effective literacy instruction for English learners requires well-prepared teachers.

Quality of teaching plays an important role in students' success or failure (Au and Carroll 1997; Haager and Windmueller 2001; Kucer 1999). The value of increased teacher knowledge and skills; support for teacher learning and development; and teacher-support systems that are intensive, elaborate, and enduring has been documented. For example, in the KEEP program (Au and Carroll 1997), there was intensive

The value of increased teacher knowledge and skills; support for teacher learning and development; and teacher-support systems that are intensive, elaborate, and enduring has been documented.

mentoring by the KEEP consultants; each consultant worked with only one to three project teachers and observed and mentored in classrooms twice a week. This level of support is considerably more than occurs in most schools. The authors advocate providing teachers with sustained coaching so they can develop the practices necessary to succeed, including organizing the classroom to support a constructivist approach, creating opportunities for student-centered learning, employing appropriate instructional practices, and developing an assessment system tied to instruction. Two critical tools in supporting teacher change were a classroom implementation checklist that tracked fidelity of implementation of the KEEP program and grade-appropriate benchmarks used to assess student progress.

The studies indicate that, consistent with previous findings, teachers found professional development to be most helpful when it provided opportunities for hands-on practice, with teaching techniques readily applicable to their classroom, in-class demonstrations with their own or a colleague's students, or more personalized coaching. Other means to improve the quality of teaching for students experiencing learning difficulties included the collaboration between special education teachers and resource specialists (Haager and Windmuller 2001).

Research has indicated that teachers align instructional approaches with their expectations for students who exhibit differing levels of English proficiency. (Neufeld and Fitzgerald 2001), but their expectations are not always aligned with students' actual capabilities. Thus, it may be important to focus on changing teachers' beliefs and values as well as practices.

Guideline 8: Effective literacy instruction for English learners is respectful of the home language.

The most obvious difference between English learners and their monolingual counterparts is that English learners already know a language and have to learn English along with the rest of the school curriculum and not just the school curriculum alone. For that reason it is not surprising that there is so much interest in the role of students' home or primary language in learning. Both naïve and scholarly theories abound as to how children should best be introduced to a second language, and these views range from the idea that use of the home language must be avoided, discouraged, or prohibited so that students will gain maximum experience with English to those in which the home language is to be developed, preserved, used, and respected so as to facilitate the transition to English.

Although the rationale for English-only views is somewhat more intuitive (e.g., maximize time on task), research using meta-analytic techniques (Francis, Lesaux, and August 2006; Rolstad, Mahoney, and Glass 2005; Greene 1997; Willig 1985) confirms that approaches that use the first language as well as the second do better at helping students become literate in a second language. (Also see Lindholm-Leary and Genesee, this publication.). That bilingual instruction is more effective may be related in part to research evidence that there is a relationship between many literacy skills and knowledge acquired in a student's first language and the acquisition of those skills in a second language (Dressler 2006).

> **Research using meta-analytic techniques ... confirms that approaches that use the first language as well as the second do better at helping students become literate in a second language.**

The reviews that found bilingual approaches to be relatively more effective indicated that the effects were moderate in size. August and Hakuta (1997) concluded that the quality of the instruction provided and the context in which it was provided were important issues regardless of the language used for instruction.

The point here is not that only bilingual approaches should be used, as such approaches would be difficult or impossible to implement in some situations. This would be the case when many different languages are represented in a school or when teachers proficient in the home language are not available. Such instruction might be problematic because of lack of community support. Nevertheless, it should be clear from these reviews that instruction in the home language may be an effective way to support more successful English acquisition, especially when a program of instruction is high in quality in other regards as well.

There are other ways of showing respect for the home language as well. Research suggests the benefit of instructional routines that, although focused on the teaching of English, exploit students' native language. Examples of ways to show respect are as follows:

⊙ Provide books in students' first language during school reading time (Fung et al. 2003).

⊙ Preview and review storybook reading in students' first language (Ulanoff and Pucci 1999).

⊙ Allow students to write and converse in either their first or second language and provide bilingual teachers (Gomez et al. 1996).

⊙ Conduct instructional conversations that permit and encourage some interpretation to take place in the home language (Saunders and Goldenberg 1999).

⊙ Translate into students' first language the passages from which the vocabulary words were selected to ensure comprehension of the overall context (Carlo et al. 2004).

⊙ Use bilingual glossaries for the targeted vocabulary (Carlo et al. 2004) and instruction in the transfer of cognate knowledge from a first language to a second (Carlo et al. 2004).

From this evidence, we conclude that literacy instruction is likely to be most successful when the home language is respected, used, and—when possible—developed in the classroom.

Conclusion

In the previous sections we examined research on basic programs and intervention strategies focused on developing second-language literacy in English learners. The research is heterogeneous, covering children ages three to eighteen with diverse family, language, and literacy backgrounds and schooling experiences. Additionally, the intervention research was varied in terms of both methods used and intended outcomes. For instance, some of the methods involved practices as simple as having students spend a few minutes a day for several weeks reading or listening to someone read; others were as involved as requiring an elaborate multiyear agenda of professional development, revision of the school reading curriculum, replacement of instructional materials, establishment of intervention support for struggling readers, and reorganization of instruction in an entire school. Although many studies examined approaches to teaching one or two essential parts of literacy such as word recognition or comprehension, others focused more broadly on student outcomes. As previously mentioned, the samples of students were also very diverse.

When sufficient numbers of studies on a particular literacy component do exist, it is possible to examine correlates to the variations in the development of that component construct, which can give researchers and practitioners valuable insights into aspects of the instruction that may be leading to the differences. When few studies are available on any particular component, as in this case, these correlations can be misleading because they will be confused with the individual studies themselves. Nevertheless, we believe the research provides several generalizations that can constitute a broad basis for evidence-based practice. We have expressed these in terms of eight guidelines for developing English learners' literacy. We hope the guidelines will be useful to practitioners as they grapple with the everyday challenge of educating English learners, to policymakers as they endeavor to create contexts in which effective instruction can occur, and to researchers attempting to build on previous research.

References

Aarts, Rian, and Ludo Verhoeven. 1999. Literacy attainment in a second language submersion context. *Applied Psycholinguistics* 20(3) (September): 377–93.

Abu-Rabia, Salim. 1997. Verbal and working-memory skills of bilingual Hebrew-English speaking children. *International Journal of Psycholinguistics* 13(1) (January): 25–40.

Abu-Rabia, Salim, and Linda S. Siegel. 2002. Reading, syntactic, orthographic, and working memory skills of bilingual Arabic-English speaking Canadian children. *Journal of Psycholinguistic Research* 31(6) (November): 661–78.

Arab-Moghaddam, Narges, and Monique S n chal. 2001. Orthographic and phono-logical processing skills in reading and spelling in Persian/English bilinguals. *International Journal of Behavioral Development* 25(2) (March): 140–47.

Au, Kathryn Hui-Pei, and Jana M. Mason. 1981. Social organizational factors in learning to read: The balance of rights hypothesis. *Reading Research Quarterly* 17(1) (January–March): 115–52.

Au, Kathryn Hui-Pei, and Jaquelin H. Carroll. 1997. Improving literacy achievement through a constructivist approach: The KEEP demonstration classroom project. *Elementary School Journal* 97(3) (January): 203–21.

August, Diane, and Kenji Hakuta. 1997. *Improving schooling for language-minority children: A research agenda.* Washington, DC: National Research Council.

August, Diane, and Timothy Shanahan, eds. 2006. *Developing literacy in second-language learners: Report of the National Literacy Panel on Language-Minority Children and Youth.* Mahwah, NJ: Lawrence-Erlbaum.

August, Diane, and others. 2006. Developing literacy in English-language learners: An examination of the impact of English-only versus bilingual instruction. In *Childhood bilingualism: Research on infancy through school age,* ed. Peggy D. McCardle and Erika Hoff. Clevedon, England: Multilingual Matters.

Bailey, Allison L., ed. 2007. *Language demands of school: Putting academic English to the test.* New Haven CT: Yale University Press.

Baker, Keith A. and Adriana A. de Kanter. 1981. *Effectiveness of bilingual education: A review of the literature.* (Final draft report). Washington, DC: U.S. Department of Education, Office of Technical and Analytic System.

Bean, Thomas W. 1982. Second language learners' comprehension of an ESL prose selection. *Journal of the Linguistic Association of the Southwest* 4(4): 376–86.

Beech, John. R., and Allison Keys. 1997. Reading, vocabulary and language preference in 7- to 8-year-old bilingual Asian children. *British Journal of Educational Psychology* 67(4): 405–14.

Biemiller, Andrew and Catherine A. Boote. 2006. An effective method for building meaning vocabulary in primary grades. *Journal of Educational Psychology* 98(1): 44–62.

Bos, Candace S., Adela Artola Allen, and David J. Scanlon. 1989. Vocabulary instruction and reading comprehension with bilingual learning disabled students. *Yearbook of the National Reading Conference* 38: 173–79.

Calderon, Margarita, Rachel Hertz-Lazarowitz, and Robert E. Slavin. 1998. Effects of bilingual cooperative integrated reading and composition on students making the transition from Spanish to English reading. *Elementary School Journal* 99(2) (November): 153–65.

Calero-Breckheimer, Ayxa, and Earnest T. Goetz. 1993. Reading strategies of biliterate children for English and Spanish texts. *Reading Psychology* 14(3): 177–204.

Carlisle, Joanne F., Margaret M. Beeman, Davis, Lyle Hull, and Galila Spharim. 1999. Relationship of meta-linguistic capabilities and reading achievement for children who are becoming bilingual. *Applied Psycholinguistics* 20(4): 459–78.

Carlisle, Joanne F., Margaret Beeman, and Priti P. Shan. 1996. The metalinguistic capabilities and English literacy of Hispanic high school students: an exploratory study. *Yearbook of the National Reading Conference* 45: 306–16.

Carlo, María S., Diane August, Barry McLaughlin, Catherine Snow, Cheryl Dressler, David Lippman, Teresa Lively, and Claire White. 2004. Closing the gap: Addressing the vocabulary needs of English language learners in bilingual and mainstream classrooms. *Reading Research Quarterly* 39(2): 188–215.

Cohen, S. Alan, and Samuel Rodriguez. 1980. Experimental results that question the Ramirez-Castaneda model for teaching reading to first-grade Mexican Americans. *Reading Teacher* 34(1): 12–18.

Collins, Molly Fuller. 2005. ESL preschoolers' English vocabulary acquisition from storybook reading. *Reading Research Quarterly* 40(4): 406–08.

Chiappe, Penny, and Linda S. Siegel. 1999. Phonological awareness and reading acquisition in English- and Punjabi-speaking Canadian children. *Journal of Educational Psychology* 91(1): 20–28.

Chiappe, Penny, Linda S. Siegel, and Lesly Wade-Woolley. 2002. Linguistic diversity and the development of reading skills: A longitudinal study. *Scientific Studies of Reading* 6(4): 369–400.

Chitri, Helena-Fivi, and Dale M. Willows. 1997. Bilingual word recognition in English and Greek. *Applied Psycholinguistics* 18(2): 139–56.

Collier, Virginia P. 1987. Age and rate of acquisition of second language for academic purposes. *TESOL Quarterly* 21(4): 617–41.

Collier, Virginia P. 1995. Acquiring a second language for school. *Directions in Language and Education* 1(4): 3–13.

Collier, Virginia P., and W. P. Thomas. 1989. How quickly can immigrants become proficient in English? *Journal of Educational Issues of Language Minority Students* 5: 26–38.

Cummins, James. 1981. The role of primary language development in promoting educational success for language minority students. In *Schooling and language-minority students: A theoretical framework,* 3–49. Sacramento: California State Department of Education.

Da Fontoura, Helena A., and Linda S. Siegel. 1995. Reading, syntactic, and working memory skills of bilingual Portuguese-English Canadian children. *Reading and Writing* 7(1): 139–53.

D'Angiulli, Amedeo, Linda S. Siegel, and Emily Serra. 2001. The development of reading in English and Italian in bilingual children. *Applied Psycholinguistics* 22: 479–507.

De la Colina, Maria Guadalupe, and others. 2001. Intensive intervention in reading fluency for at-risk beginning Spanish readers. *Bilingual Research Journal* 25(4): 503–38.

Dressler, Cheryl A. 2006. First and second language literacy. In *Developing literacy in second-language learners: Report of the National Literacy Panel for Language-Minority Children and Youth,* ed. Diane L. August and Timothy Shanahan, 197–23. Mahwah, NJ: Lawrence Erlbaum.

Dressler, Cheryl A., and Michael Kamil. 2006. First and second language literacy. In *Developing literacy in second- language learners: Report of the National Literacy Panel on Language- Minority Children and Youth,* ed. Diane August and Timothy Shanahan, 197–239. Mahwah, NJ: Erlbaum.

Droop, Mienke, and Ludo T. Verhoeven. 1998. Background knowledge, linguistic complexity, and second-language reading comprehension. *Journal of Literacy Research* 30(2): 253–71.

Dufva, Mia, and Marinus J. M. Voeten. 1999. Native language literacy and phonological memory as prerequisites for learning English as a foreign language. *Applied Psycholinguistics* 20(3): 329–48.

Durgunoglu, Aydin Y., William E. Nagy, and Barbara J. Hancin-Bhatt. 1993. Cross-language transfer of phonological awareness. *Journal of Educational Psychology* 85(3): 453–65.

Echevarría, Jana. 1996. The effects of instructional conversations on the language and concept development of Latino students with learning disabilities. *Bilingual Research Journal* 20(2): 339–63.

Echevarria, Jana, and Deborah Short. 2006. School reform and standards-based education: A model for English language learners. *The Journal of Educational Research* 99(4): 195–210.

Edelsky, Carole. 1982. Writing in a bilingual program: The relation of L1 and L2 texts. *TESOL Quarterly* 16(2): 211–28.

Elley, Warwick B. 1991. Acquiring literacy in a second language: The effect of book-based programs. *Language Learning* 41(3): 375–411.

Escamilla, Kathy. 1994. Descubriendo la lectura: An early intervention literacy program in Spanish. *Literacy Teaching and Learning* 1(1): 57–70.

Everatt, John, Ian Smythe, Evan Adams, and Dina Ocampo. 2000. Dyslexia screening measures and bilingualism. *Dyslexia* 6(1): 42–56.

Fashola, Olatokunbo S., Priscilla A. Drum, Richard E. Mayer, and Sang-Jin Kang. 1996. A cognitive theory of orthographic transitioning: Predictable errors in how Spanish-speaking children spell English words. *American Educational Research Journal* 33(4): 825–43.

Fawcett, Angela J., and Lisa Lynch. 2000. Systematic identification and approach for reading difficulty: Case studies of children with EAL. *Dyslexia* 6(1): 57–71.

Fitzgerald, Jill, and George Noblit. 2000. Balance in the making: Learning to read in an ethnically diverse first-grade classroom. *Journal of Educational Psychology* 92(1): 3–22.

Francis, David J., Nonie K. Lesaux, and Diane L. August. 2006. Language of instruction for language minority learners. In *Developing literacy in second-language learners: Report of the National Literacy Panel for Language-Minority Children and Youth,* ed. Diane L. August and Timothy Shanahan, 365–414. Mahwah, NJ: Lawrence Erlbaum.

Francis, Norbert. 2000. The shared conceptual system and language processing in bilingual children: Findings from literacy assessment in Spanish and Náhuatl. *Applied Linguistics* 21(2): 170–204.

Franken, Margaret, and Stephen J. Haslett. 1999. Quantifying the effect of peer interaction on second language students' written argument texts. *New Zealand Journal of Educational Studies* 34(2); 281–93.

Fung, Irene, Y. Y., Ian A. G. Wilkinson, and Dennis W. Moore. 2003. L1-assisted reciprocal teaching to improve ESL students' comprehension of English expository text. *Learning and Instruction* 13: 1–31.

Garcia, Eugene. 1991. *Education of linguistically and culturally diverse students: Effective instruction practices.* Washington, DC: Center for Applied Linguistics.

Garcia, Georgia E. 1998. Mexican-American bilingual students' metacognitive reading strategies: What's transferred, unique, problematic? *National Reading Conference Yearbook* 47: 253–64.

Geva, Esther. 2006. Second-language oral proficiency and second-language literacy. In *Developing literacy in second-language learners: Report of the National Literacy Panel on Language-Minority Children and Youth,* ed. D. L. August and T. Shanahan, 123–39. Mahwah, NJ: Lawrence Erlbaum.

Geva, Esther, Zhoreh Yaghoub-Zadeh, and Barbara Schuster. 2000. Part IV: Reading and foreign language learning: Understanding individual differences in word recognition skills of ESL children. *Annals of Dyslexia* 50: 121–54.

Gholamain, Mitra, and Esther Geva. 1999. Orthographic and cognitive factors in the concurrent development of basic reading skills in English and Persian. *Language Learning* 49(2): 183–217.

Giambo, Debra A., and James D. McKinney. 2004. [LTA2]The effects of a phonological awareness intervention on the oral English proficiency of Spanish-speaking kindergarten children. *TESOL Quarterly* 38(1): 95–117.

Glaser, Robert. 1984. Education and thinking: The role of knowledge. *American Psychologist* 39(2): 93–104.

Goldenberg, Claude, Robert Rueda, and Diane August. 2006. Sociocultural influences on the literacy attainment of language minority children and youth. In *Developing literacy in second-language learners: Report of the National Literacy Panel on Language-Minority Children and Youth,* ed. D. L. August and T. Shanahan. Mahwah, NJ: Lawrence-Erlbaum.

Goldman, Susan R., Maria Reyes, and Connie K. Varnhagen. 1984. Understanding fables in first and second languages. *NABE Journal* 8: 835–66.

Goldstein, Barbara Comoe, Kathleen C. Harris, and M. Diane Klein. 1993. Assessment of oral storytelling abilities of Latino junior high school students with learning handicaps. *Journal of Learning Disabilities* 26(2): 138–32.

Gomez, Richard, Jr., Richard Parker, Rafael Lara-Alecio, and Leo Gomez. 1996. Process versus product writing with limited English proficiency students. *Bilingual Research Journal* 20(2): 209–33.

Gottardo, Alexandra. 2002. The relationship between language and reading skills in bilingual Spanish-English speakers. *Topics in Language Disorders* 22(5): 46–70.

Gottardo, Alexandra, Bernice Yan, Linda S. Siegel, and Lesly Wade-Woolley. 2001. Factors related to English reading performance in children with Chinese as a first language: More evidence of cross-language transfer of phonological processing. *Journal of Educational Psychology* 93(3): 530–42.

Graham, Steve, and Delores Perin. 2007. *Writing next: Effective strategies to improve writing of adolescents in middle and high schools.* Washington, DC: Alliance for Excellent Education.

Graves, Anne W., Eugene C. Valles, and Robert Rueda. 2000. Variations in inter-active writing instruction: A study in four bilingual special education settings. *Learning Disabilities Research & Practice* 15(1): 1–9.

Greene, Jay P. 1997. A meta-analysis of the Rossell and Baker review of bilingual education research. *Bilingual Research Journal* 21(2/3): 1–22.

Gunn, Barbara, Anthony Biglan, Keith Smolkowski, and Dennis Ary. 2000. The efficacy of supplemental instruction in decoding skills for Hispanic and non-Hispanic students in early elementary school. *Journal of Special Education* 34(2): 90–103.

Gunn, Barbara, Keith Smolkowski, Anthony Biglan, and Carol Black. 2002. Supplemental instruction in decoding skills for Hispanic and non-Hispanic students in early elementary school: A follow-up. *The Journal of Special Education* 36(2): 69–79.

Gunn, Barbara, Keith Smolkowski, Anthony Biglan, Carol Black, and Jason Blair. 2005. Fostering the development of reading skill through supplemental instruc-tion: Results for Hispanic and non-Hispanic students. *The Journal of Special Education* 39(2): 66–85.

Haager, Diane, and Michelle P. Windmueller. 2001. Early reading approach for English language learners at-risk for learning disabilities: Student and teacher outcomes in an urban school. *Learning Disability Quarterly* 24(4): 235–49.

Hacquebord, Hilde. 1994. L2-reading in the content areas: Text comprehension in secondary education in the Netherlands. *Journal of Research in Reading* 17(2): 83–98.

Hakuta, Kenji, Yuko Goto Butler, and Daria Witt. 2000. *How long does it take English learners to attain proficiency?* University of California Linguistic Minority Research Institute Policy Report 2000-1.

Hancin-Bhatt, Barbara, and William E. Nagy. 1994. Lexical transfer and second language morphological development. *Applied Psycholinguistics* 15(3): 289–310.

Hancock, Dawson R. 2002. The effects of native language books on the pre-literacy skill development of language minority kindergartens. *Journal of Research in Childhood Education* 17(1): 62–68.

Hillocks, George. 1986. *Research on written composition.* Urbana, IL: National Council of Teachers of English.

Hirsch, E. D. 2003. Reading comprehension requires knowledge—of words and the world. *American Educator* 27(1): 10–49.

Hutchinson, Jane M., Helen E. Whitely, Chris D. Smith, and Liz Connors. 2003. The developmental progression of comprehension-related skills in children learning EAL. *Journal of Research in Reading* 26: 19–32.

Institute for Education Sciences. *Intervention: Reading recovery.* March 19, 2007. http://ies.ed.gov/ncee/wwc/reports/beginning_reading/reading_recovery.

Jackson, Nancy Ewald, and Wen-Hui Lu. 1992. Bilingual precocious readers of English. *Roeper Review* 14(3): 115–19.

James, Carl, and Kerstin Klein.1994. Foreign language learners' spelling and proof-reading strategies. *Papers and Studies in Contrasting Linguistics* 29: 31–46.

Jiménez, Robert T., Georgia Earnest Garcia, and P. David Pearson. 1996. The reading strategies of bilingual Latina/o students who are successful English readers: Opportunities and obstacles. *Reading Research Quarterly* 31(1): 90–112.

Kellerman, Eric. 1977. Toward a characterization of the strategies of transfer in second language learning. *Interlanguage Studies Bulletin* 2: 58–145.

Klingner, Janette K., and Sarah Vaughn. 1996. Reciprocal teaching of reading comprehension strategies for students with learning disabilities who use English as a second language. *Elementary School Journal* 96(3): 275–93.

Klingner, Janette K., and Sarah Vaughn. 2000.The helping behaviors of fifth graders while using collaborative strategic reading during ESL content classes. *TESOL Quarterly* 34(1): 69–98.

Kramer, Virginia R., Leo M. Schell, and R. Michael Rubison. 1983.Auditory discrimination training in English of Spanish-speaking children. *Reading Improvement* 20(3): 162–68.

Kucer, S. G. 1999. Two students' responses to, and literacy growth in, a whole language curriculum. *Reading Research and Instruction* 38(3): 233–53.

Langer, Judith A., Lilia Bartolome, Olga Vasquez, and Tamara Lucas. 1990. Meaning construction in school literacy tasks: A study of bilingual students. *American Educational Research Journal* 27(3): 427-71.

Lee, Jeong-Wong, and Diane Lemonnier Schallert. 1997. The relative contribution of L2 language proficiency and L1 reading ability to L2 reading performance: A test of the threshold hypothesis in an EFL context. *TESOL Quarterly* 3(4): 713–39.

Leseaux, Nonie K. and Linda S. Siegel. 2003. The development of reading in children who speak English as a second language. *Developmental Psychology* 39(6): 1005–19.

Lesaux, Noni, K., Andre A. Rupp, and Linda S. Siegel. 2007. Growth in reading skills of children from diverse linguistic backgrounds: Findings from a 5-year longitudinal study. *Journal of Educational Psychology* 99: 821–34.

Liang, L. A., C. Peterson, and Michael F. Graves. 2005. Investigating two approaches to fostering children's comprehension of literature. *Reading Psychology* 26: 387–400.

Linan-Thompson, Sylvia, Sharon Vaughn, Peggy Hickman-Davis, and Kamiar Kouzehanani. 2003. Effectiveness of supplemental reading instruction for second-grade English language learners with reading difficulties. *The Elementary School Journal* 103(3): 221–312.

Lindsey, Kim A., Franklin R. Manis, and Caroline E. Bailey. 2003. Prediction of first-grade reading in Spanish-speaking English-language learners. *Journal of Educational Psychology* 95: 482–94.

Mumtaz, Shazia, and Glyn W. Humphreys. 2001. The effects of bilingualism on learning to read English: Evidence from the contrast between Urdu-English bilingual and English monolingual children. *Journal of Research in Reading* 24(2): 113–34.

Muter, Valerie, and Kay Diethelm. 2001. The contribution of phonological skills and letter knowledge to early reading development in a multilingual population. *Language Learning* 51(2): 187–219.

Nagy, William E., Georgia Earnest Garcia, Aydin Y. Durgunoglu, and Barbara Hancin-Bhatt. 1993. Spanish-English bilingual students' use of cognates in English reading. *Journal of Reading Behavior* 25(3): 241–59.

Nagy, William E., Erika F. McClure, and Montserrat Mir. 1997. Linguistic transfer and the use of context by Spanish-English bilinguals. *Applied Psycholinguistics* 18(4): 431–52.

Nathanson-Meija, Sally. 1989. Writing in a second language: Negotiating meaning through invented spelling. *Language Arts* 66(5): 516–26.

National Institute of Child Health and Human Development. 2000. *Report of the National Reading Panel. Teaching children to read: An evidence-based assessment of the scientific research literature on reading and its implications for reading instruction.* NIH Publication No. 00-4769. Washington, DC: U.S. Government Printing Office.

Neufeld, Paul, and Jill Fitzgerald. 2001. Early English reading development: Latino English learners in the "low" reading group. *Research in the Teaching of English* 36: 64–109.

Neuman, Susan, B. 2001. The role of knowledge in early literacy. *Reading Research Quarterly* 36(4): 468–475.

Neuman, Susan B., and Patricia Koskinen. 1992. Captioned television as comprehensible input: Effects of incidental word learning from context for language minority students. *Reading Research Quarterly* 27(1): 94–106.

Peregoy, Suzanne F. 1989. Relationships between second language oral proficiency and reading comprehension of bilingual fifth grade students. *The Journal of the National Association for Bilingual Education* 13(3): 217–34.

Peregoy, Suzanne F., and Owen F. Boyle. 1991. Second language oral proficiency characteristics of low, intermediate and high second language readers. *Hispanic Journal of Behavioral Sciences* 13(1): 35–47.

Perez, Eustolia. 1983. Oral language competence improves reading skills of Mexican-American third graders. *Reading Teacher* 35(1): 24–27.

Perozzi, Joseph A. 1985. A pilot study of language facilitation for bilingual, language-handicapped children: Theoretical and approach implications. *Journal of Speech & Hearing Disorders* 50(4): 403–06.

Prater, Doris L., and Andrea B. Bermúdez. 1993. Using peer response groups with limited English proficient writers. *Bilingual Research Journal* 17(1–2): 99–116.

Quiroga, Teresa, Zenia Lemos-Britten, Elizabeth Mostafapour, Robert D. Abbott, and Virginia W. Berminger. 2002. Phonological awareness and beginning reading in Spanish-speaking ESL first graders: Research into practice. *Journal of School Psychology* 40(1): 85–111.

Reese, Leslie, Helen Garnier, Ronald Gallimore, and Claude Goldenberg. 2000. Longitudinal analysis of the antecedents of emergent Spanish literacy and middle-school English reading achievement of Spanish-speaking students. *American Educational Research Journal* 37(3): 633–62.

Roberts, Teresa, and Harriet Neal. 2004. Relationships among preschool English language learner's oral proficiency in English, instructional experience and literacy development. *Contemporary Educational Psychology* 29: 283–311.

Rohena, Elba I., Asha K. Jitendra, and Diane M. Browder. 2002. Comparison of the effects of Spanish and English constant time delay instruction on sight word-reading by Hispanic learners with mental retardation. *Journal of Special Education* 36(3): 169–84.

Rolstad, Kellie, Kate Mahoney, and Gene Glass. 2005. The big picture: A meta-analysis of program effectiveness research on English language learners. *Educational Policy* 19(4): 572–94.

Rossell, Christine H., and Keith Baker. 1996. The educational effectiveness of bilingual education. *Research in the Teaching of English* 30(1): 7–69.

Rousseau, Marilyn K., Brian Kai Yung Tam, and Rajdai Ramnarain. 1993. Increasing reading proficiency of language-minority students with speech and language impairments. *Education and Treatment of Children* 16(3): 254–71.

Royer, James M., and Maria S. Carlo. 1991. Transfer of comprehension skills from native to second language. *Journal of Reading* 34(6): 450–55.

Saunders, William M. 1999. Improving literacy achievement for English learners in transitional bilingual programs. *Educational Research & Evaluation* 5(4): 345–81.

Saunders, William M., and Claude Goldenberg. 1999. Effects of instructional conversations and literature logs on limited- and fluent-English proficient students' story comprehension and thematic understanding. *Elementary School Journal* 99(4): 277–301.

Saville-Troike, Muriel. 1984. What really matters in second language learning for academic achievement? *TESOL Quarterly* 18(2): 199–219.

Scarcella, Robin. 2003. *Academic English: A conceptual framework*. Technical Report 2003–1. Irvine: The University of California Linguistic Minority Research Institute.

Schon, Isabel, Kenneth D. Hopkins, and Carol Vojir. 1985. The effects of special reading time in Spanish on the reading abilities and attitudes of Hispanic junior high school students. *Journal of Psycholinguistic Research* 14(1): 57–65.

Sengupta, Sima. 2000. An investigation into the effects of revision strategy instruction on L2 secondary school learners. *System* 28(1): 97–113.

Shanahan, Timothy, and Isabel Beck. 2006. Effective literacy teaching for second-language learners. In *Developing literacy in second-language learners: Report of the*

National Literacy Panel for Language-Minority Children and Youth, ed. D. L. August and T. Shanahan, 415–88. Mahwah, NJ: Lawrence Erlbaum.

Slavin, Robert E., and Alan Cheung. 2004. A synthesis of research on language of reading instruction for English language learners. Baltimore, MD: Johns Hopkins University.

Slavin, Robert E. and Nancy A. Madden. 1999. Effects of bilingual and English as a second language adaptations of Success for All on the reading achievement of students acquiring English. *Journal of Education for Students Placed at Risk* 4(4): 393–416.

Snow, Catherine E. 1987. Beyond conversation: Second language learners' acquisition of description and explanation. In *Research in second language learning: Focus on the classroom,* ed. J. Lantolf and A. Labarca, 3–16. Norwood, NJ: Ablex.

Stuart, Morag. 1999. Getting ready for reading: Early phoneme awareness and phonics teaching improves reading and spelling in inner-city second language learners. *British Journal of Educational Psychology* 69(4): 587–605.

Swanson, Teri. J., Barbara W. Hodson, and Marlene Schommer-Aikins. 2005. An examination of phonological awareness treatment outcomes for seventh-grade poor readers from a bilingual community. *Language, Speech, and Hearing Services in Schools* 36: 336–45.

Syvanen, C. 1997. English as a second language students as cross-age tutors. *ORTESOL Journal* 18: 33–41.

Tharp, Roland G. 1982. The effective instruction of comprehension: Results and descriptions of the Kamehameha early education program. *Reading Research Quarterly* 17: 503–27.

Troia, Gary A. 2004. Migrant students with limited English proficiency: Can Fast ForWord Language™ make a difference in their language skills and academic achievement? *Remedial and Special Education* 25(6): 353–66.

Tudor, Ian, and Fateh Hafiz. 1989. Extensive reading as a means of input to L2 learning. *Journal of Research in Reading* 12(2): 164–78.

Uchikoshi, Yuuko. 2005. Narrative development in bilingual kindergarteners: Can Arthur help? *Developmental Psychology* 41(3): 464–78.

Ulanoff, Sharon H., and Sandra L. Pucci. 1999. Learning words from books: The effects of read-aloud on second language vocabulary acquisition. *Bilingual Research Journal* 23(4): 409–22.

VanWagenen, Margaret A., Randy Lee Williams, and T. F. McLaughlin. 1994. Use of assisted reading to improve reading rate, word accuracy, and comprehension with ESL Spanish-speaking students. *Perceptual and Motor Skills* 79: 227–30.

Vaughn, Sharon, Sylvia Linan-Thompson, Patricia. G. Mathes, Paul T. Cirino, Colleen D. Carlson, Sharolyn D. Pollard-Durodola, Elsa Cardenas-Hagan, and David J. Francis. 2006. Effectiveness of Spanish intervention for first-grade English language learners at risk for reading difficulties. *Journal of Learning Disabilities* 39(1): 56–73.

Verhoeven, Ludo T. 1994. Transfer in bilingual development: The linguistic interdependence hypothesis revisited. *Language Learning* 44(3): 381–415.

Verhoeven, Ludo T. 1990. Acquisition of reading in a second language. *Reading Research Quarterly* 25(2): 90–114.

Verhoeven, Ludo T. 2000. Components in early second language reading and spelling. *Scientific Studies of Reading* 4(4): 313–30.

Wade-Woolley, Lesly, and Linda S. Siegel. 1997. The spelling performance of ESL and native speakers of English as a function of reading skill. *Reading & Writing: An Interdisciplinary Journal* 9(506): 387–406.

Willig, Ann. 1985. A meta-analysis of selected studies on the effectiveness of bilingual education. *Review of Educational Research* 55(3): 269–317.

Zutell, Jerry, and Virginia Allen. 1988. The English spelling strategies of Spanish-speaking bilingual children. *TESOL Quarterly* 22(2): 333–40.

Chapter 5

Programs and Practices for Effective Sheltered Content Instruction

Jana Echevarria, California State University, Long Beach
Deborah Short, Center for Applied Linguistics

Overview

This chapter describes effective sheltered content instruction[1] that teachers and programs can use to provide English learners with access to the core curriculum and concurrently develop their proficiency in academic English.

Many approaches and combinations of techniques can be applied to the delivery of sheltered content instruction. Currently, however, the Sheltered Instruction Observation Protocol (SIOP) Model[TR] is the only scientifically validated model of sheltered instruction for English learners (Short and Echevarria 2007) and has a growing research base. The SIOP Model[TR] is distinct in that it offers a field-tested protocol

> **Many approaches and combinations of techniques can be applied to the delivery of sheltered content instruction.**

for systematic lesson planning, delivery, and assessment, making its application for teaching English learners transparent for both preservice candidates preparing to be teachers and for practicing teachers engaged in staff development. Further, it provides a framework for organizing the instructional practices essential for sound sheltered content instruction.

According to the California *Education Code,* students are to be provided with access to the core curriculum through a methodology known as SDAIE (specially designed academic instruction in English). However, the SDAIE

---

1. See Saunders and Goldenberg, this publication, for a definition and discussion of sheltered instruction.

approach does not have a comprehensive operational definition, and the result has been inconsistent and sometimes ineffective practice. Without an agreed-upon model of instruction, teachers do not teach SDAIE classes in the same way across the state nor in the same way sometimes in the same school. No empirical research has been published to demonstrate that any particular model of the SDAIE approach improves the academic performance of English learners. Therefore, we present the SIOP Model[TR] as a comprehensive model of sheltered content instruction for teachers and programs in California because empirical research shows that when teachers implement it well, they provide consistent, high-quality teaching to English learners that results in gains in student academic literacy (Echevarria, Short, and Powers 2006).

The SIOP Model[TR] incorporates and systematizes many techniques that teachers use in SDAIE classes to provide students with access to core content and adds features that develop students' academic English skills. Current SDAIE teachers will thus find that they already have a strong foundation in the SIOP Model[TR], but they need to offer comprehensive instruction that focuses explicitly and consistently on both content knowledge and academic language development. And when done well, the SIOP Model[TR] ensures a shift from knowing to doing: from understanding the principles of instruction for English learners to rigorously implementing specific instructional features in an organized fashion.

The SIOP Model[TR] incorporates and systematizes many techniques that teachers use in SDAIE classes to provide students with access to core content and adds features that develop students' academic English skills.

We recognize that, for various reasons, some schools may wish to modify aspects of the model. However, this should be done with caution. We would suggest that the model not be changed unless there is a sufficiently strong research-based or theoretically based rationale that has been tested. Even in those circumstances, the changes to the SIOP Model[TR] should be monitored carefully to determine the effects on student performance.

Besides describing the features of effective sheltered content instruction, this chapter also discusses some educational program models for English learners that can help them succeed in school. A number of models are discussed in other chapters of this book, so we focus on those program designs that typically include content area courses where instruction is delivered in English and the educators use sheltered content instruction as the pedagogical approach.

Giving English Learners Access to the Core Content

The educational reform movement has had a direct impact on English learners, as states have moved to implement high-stakes testing and standards-based instruction for all students. Classroom instruction is guided by standards for core subjects such as social studies, mathematics, science, and language arts. In many mainstream classes, little or no accommodation is made for the specific language needs of English learners, which poses a significant barrier to success because they are expected to achieve high academic standards in English. Moreover, under many state-level accountability measures, all students are expected to pass end-of-grade tests in order to be promoted or exit examinations in order to graduate, although some states offer an exemption for English learners for one to three years.

English learners have experienced persistent underachievement that has become highlighted by high-stakes testing and accountability measures enacted through the No Child Left Behind legislation. On nearly every measure of state and national assessments, English learners lag behind their native English-speaking peers and demonstrate significant achievement gaps (California Department of Education 2008; Grigg et al. 2003; Kindler 2002; Olsen 2003; Snow and Biancarosa 2003). The Introduction in this publication clearly delineates the academic underachievement of English learners in California schools. Despite major school reform efforts of the past decade, the performance of English learners on state accountability measures has not improved substantially. This situation is not unique to California. Consider the following statistics:

⊙ Only 4 percent of eighth-grade English learners scored at the proficient or advanced levels on the reading portion of the 2005 National Assessment for Educational Progress (National Center for Education Statistics 2005). This means that 96 percent of the eighth-grade limited-English-proficient students scored at or **below** the Basic level. This is particularly noteworthy because NAEP examinations often exempt students at the beginning level of English as a second language (Grigg et al. 2003).

⊙ A five-year, statewide evaluation study (Parrish et al. 2006) in California found that English learners with 10 years of schooling in the state had a less than 40 percent chance of meeting the criteria to be redesignated as fluent English proficient.

⊙ According to the 2000 U.S. census, only 10 percent of young adults who speak English at home fail to complete high school, but the percentage is 31 percent for young adult English learners. If English learners reported on the census speaking English very well, their likelihood of graduating was 51 percent; however, if they reported speaking English with difficulty, their likelihood of completing high school dropped to 18 percent (National Center for Education Statistics 2004).

⊙ In Texas, a recent study (McNeil et al. 2008) revealed that 60 percent of African American students, 75 percent of Hispanic students, and 80 percent of English learners did not graduate high school within five years. The researchers concluded that state accountability measures enacted after 2001 led to the significant increase in the number of students failing to graduate. These measures rated schools and rewarded or punished administrators according to the performance of all student subgroups. When low-achieving students left school, the system recorded an appearance of rising test scores and a narrowing of the achievement gap between white and minority students, which increased the schools' ratings.

⊙ The Center for Education Policy (Kober et al. 2006) reported that English learners have lower pass rates on high school exit examinations and lower graduation rates than native speakers, even with test accommodations, such as directions provided in their native language and use of bilingual dictionaries or glossaries.

But these results should not surprise anyone. If students are designated English learners, they are by definition not proficient in English, yet we test them primarily through that language. Second-language acquisition is a long-term process. Research has shown that beginning English learners need four to seven years of instruction in order to reach the average performance level of their English-speaking peers (Collier 1987, Cummins 2006; Lindholm-Leary and Borsato 2006; Thomas and Collier 2002). Furthermore, the relationship between literacy proficiency and academic achievement grows stronger as grade levels rise—regardless of individual student characteristics.

When we examine the performance of former English learners, however, the outcomes are better. For example, recent analyses from New York City, New Jersey, Washington, and California revealed that former English learners outperformed students as a whole on state tests, exit exams, and graduation rates (DeLeeuw 2008; New York City Department of Education 2004; New Jersey Department of Education 2006; Sullivan et al. 2005). So, when students are given time to develop academic English proficiency in their programs and are exited (and redesignated) with criteria that measure their ability to be successful in mainstream classes, they perform on average as well or better than the state average on achievement tests.

What we have learned is that the difficulties English learners experience in school are often caused by inappropriate modes of instruction that do not consider their linguistic and sociocultural needs (Garcia 2003; McField 2006; Nieto 1999). Methods that teachers have typically used, especially in the upper elementary and secondary schools, do not facilitate learning or literacy instruction for English learners (Tharp et al. 2000). Reliance on lecture and oral discussion can hinder an English learner's comprehension of new information, and completing work sheets and reports without scaffolded instruction is challenging. Many students come from educational backgrounds in foreign countries where rote learning is the norm. In contrast, U.S. classrooms often want student participation and critical thinking, but teachers do not always show students how to participate nor guide them to think critically and express their thoughts in English. Textbook features intended to aid student understanding may have the opposite result for students who have not been taught how to use such features as bolded words, headings, sidebars, and graphs. Instead, many English learners have difficulty tracking the flow of information on cluttered pages. Moreover, preteaching a few vocabulary words before asking students to read a text is not sufficient to help them employ reading-comprehension strategies.

> **What we have learned is that the difficulties English learners experience in school are often caused by inappropriate modes of instruction that do not consider their linguistic and sociocultural needs.**

Furthermore, students who arrive in the U.S. beyond the initial age for literacy instruction and are not literate in their native language find teachers underprepared to teach basic literacy skills (Fillmore and Snow 2002; Rueda and Garcia 2001). In addition, as explained in the chapter by Saunders and Goldenberg (this publication), developing students' academic English proficiency across the curriculum has been overlooked. Participation in informal conversation demands less from an individual than joining in an academic discussion (Cummins 2000), which may require students to summarize information, evaluate perspectives, and draw conclusions in their new language. Certainly, one may converse in a cognitively demanding way—such as debating a current event that requires significant knowledge of both sides of the topic and use of high level academic language—but that is not the typical social conversation. In many instances, English learners appear to speak English well—in hallways, on playing fields, in small talk before a lesson begins—but struggle to use English well in classroom lessons. In those situations, some teachers believe students are not putting forth the effort necessary for completing academic tasks because they "speak English." These teachers mistakenly viewed students' academic limitations in English as a motivational issue rather than a linguistic or language-acquisition one.

The Evolution of Sheltered Content Instruction

Efforts to provide English learners with access to core content and thereby offer them equal educational opportunities have had a relatively long history in the United States, illustrated in Figure 5.1. Programs and instructional methods for these students have evolved over the past century (Short 2006; Stoller 2004). In the first half of the twentieth century, language instruction for immigrant students was primarily a grammar translation approach—the students' native language was used in instruction with English grammar lessons that consisted of drills and translation of words. Later, the direct method of instruction that did not use the native language emerged. It used conversational dialogues and questions in English for developing the language. By the 1950s, the audiolingual method reflected changing ideas about learning. Based on principles of behavioral psychology, the audiolingual method sought to develop "habits" of language use by having students memorize set phrases and use language labs and audiotapes.

Figure 5.1. History of Sheltered Instruction

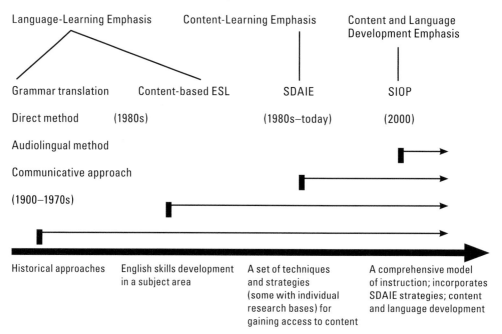

In the 1970s, the increasing number of English learners in U.S. schools and adult education programs led to the design of English as a second language (ESL, or English language development—ELD—the term used in California) classes that used the communicative method for teaching English. School districts implemented communicative curricula through which students were given opportunities to discuss material of high interest and topicality. Students were encouraged to experiment with language and assume greater responsibility for their learning. Yet communication was primarily about social or survival topics, not topics related to school subjects,

so this method was not sufficient for students in K–12 schools who, upon exiting the ESL programs, struggled in the regular, English-medium classrooms.

Realizing that grade-level curricula provided relevant, meaningful content for learning English, second-language educators in the 1980s began developing content-based English language curricula and instructional strategies to better prepare English learners for their transition to regular classes taught through English. In content-based English classes, as still implemented today, all the students are English learners and are taught by language educators. The main goal of the class is English language development, but by incorporating the texts and vocabulary of school subjects for topics and tasks, a secondary goal of preparing the students for the regular, English-medium classroom can be met (Cantoni-Harvey 1987; Crandall 1993; Mohan 1986; Short 1994).

In the mid- to late 1980s, it became clear that content-based English classes alone were not sufficient to help all English learners develop the academic language skills and knowledge needed for success in school. ESL professionals began to develop the sheltered content instruction approach in conjunction with content teachers. The need for such an instructional approach was accelerated by the educational reform movement. Through sheltered instruction, English learners would participate in a grade-level content course delivered through modified instruction that made the information comprehensible to the students (Northcutt et al. 1986; Sanchez 1989). Sheltered content instruction would not be a watered-down version of grade-level instruction but rather a means for making rigorous lessons comprehensible to English learners by incorporating specialized strategies and techniques that accommodate the second language acquisition process (Genesee 1999). In later years, these courses would be standards-based as well.

The California Context

As noted in the Introduction, several federal and state court cases had an impact on the educational programs for English learners in California. The decision in the 1974 *Lau v. Nichols* lawsuit, along with a series of state statutes requiring bilingual education under some circumstances, brought about access to the core curriculum through students' primary languages. There was tremendous growth in the number of bilingual education programs offered in schools, and teacher-preparation institutions began offering bilingual teacher credentialing programs. The state statutes also permitted alternatives to bilingual education under labels such as "planned variation." In many instances, school districts began to apply sheltered content approaches in the educational program for English learners and also in transition programs to bridge primary-language instruction and English-medium instruction.

Unfortunately, the programs that offered bilingual and sheltered instruction for English learners tended to be generally inconsistent in design, quality, and effectiveness. In some cases, those programs were stigmatized and viewed as remedial or second-track programs. In 1987, the California law providing for bilingual education was allowed to "sunset." At that time, the state needed a way to certify nonbilingual teachers to deliver core content to English learners. In response, a group of language educators in California coined the term SDAIE (specially designed academic instruction in English) as a replacement for *sheltered instruction*. The term SDAIE exists in the California *Education Code* as a legal construct, but the practices that are typically incorporated into SDAIE content classes have been based on theoretical models (Diaz-Rico and Weed 2006; Walqui 2006). Teachers are trained in numerous techniques that might be applied in SDAIE classes, but which combination of techniques should be used to yield the greatest student achievement has not been determined. In fact, no empirical research has shown that any particular model of SDAIE has a positive effect on student academic achievement.

Language education policy continues to be adjusted in California. In 1998, voters passed Proposition 227 instituting structured English immersion (SEI) (known as an "English-only" program) as the new term for a program type that was intended to give students access to the core curriculum. The California *Education Code* defines SEI as "an English language acquisition process for young children in which nearly all classroom instruction is in English but with a curriculum and presentation designed for children who are learning the language" (EC 306[d]). Similar to the term SDAIE—although a program label rather than a classroom-based instructional approach—SEI is not operationally defined. As a result, there has been wide variation in implementation with numerous program types operating under the label of SEI (McField 2006). With the passage of Proposition 227, bilingual programs also became less prevalent. Whereas approximately 29 percent of the English learner population received primary-language instruction for most of the 1990s, less than 10 percent did so after 1998 (California Department of Education 2008) [For a discussion of high-quality bilingual programs, see Krashen 1996; Krashen and McField 2005; Lindholm-Leary and Genesee, this publication; and McField 2006.]

Current Practice

In 2001, the No Child Left Behind Act (NCLB) was passed and led to significant changes to programs and accountability systems in schools with Title I and Title III funding. NCLB increased the focus of states and school districts on providing English learners with programs that have a scientific research base and on assessing the students' English proficiency and their achievement in core content areas in

order to demonstrate effectiveness. By requiring such accountability measures, NCLB strives to provide English learners with access to the core content and to equal educational opportunities.

One positive outcome of the student performance measures put into place in response to the NCLB legislation is that schools have started to focus on the development of academic language among English learners and have revised the instructional practices and educational programs being offered to them. Content-based English language development and sheltered instruction are currently favored methods for developing academic English and providing access to core content across the U.S. Ideally, these two approaches work in tandem: one foregrounding language development; the other, content knowledge (see Table 5.1). Students may have content-based instruction as the delivery model for their English language development (ELD) classes and sheltered instruction for their content area classes.

Table 5.1. Goals of Content-Based ELD and Sheltered Content Instruction

Content-based ELD	Primary goal	English language development, meeting ELD standards, addressing some English-language arts standards
	Secondary goal	Introduction to content topics, vocabulary, reading and writing genres
	High school credit	Language/elective credit
	Student grouping	English learners
Sheltered content	Primary goal	Grade-level, standards-based content knowledge
	Secondary goal	Academic language development as pertains to each specific content area
	High school credit	Content credit
	Student grouping	English learners, or English learners and fluent-English-proficient and/or English-only students

In California, the preferred program for English learners would offer a combination of ELD, sheltered content instruction, and targeted instruction and support through the first language to prepare students for mainstream instruction in the general education program. As noted in the chapters by Saunders and Goldenberg, Snow and Katz, and Kinsella and Dutro in this publication, the purpose of ELD instruction is to develop students' English skills so they can fully participate in school and beyond as well as meet the ELD standards and be successful on the state assessment, known as the CELDT (California English Language Development Test). Instruction should be tailored to each student's level of language proficiency to promote the acquisition of speaking, listening, reading, and writing in English. Although the California ELD standards do not focus specifically on acquisition of content, a content-based ELD curriculum may be implemented.

Academic Language Proficiency

For students to have full access to the core curriculum, they need to be proficient in the language of schooling. This understanding is reflected in the national ESL (English as a second language) standards developed by the Teachers of English to Speakers of Other Languages (TESOL) Association. Four of the five standards in the *Pre-K–12 English Language Proficiency Standards* (2006) are specifically geared to the academic language of the core subject areas.[2] Most states have established ESL standards that include attention to academic English. In fact, 19 states have adopted a common set of English language development standards similar to TESOL's and formed the WIDA (World-Class Instructional Design and Assessment) Consortium. They use the same English proficiency assessment, *Access for ELLs,* for NCLB accountability and thus monitor student development of academic English.

Some states with large populations of English learners, such as California, Florida, New York, and Arizona, have teacher-preparation programs that include some course work on effective teaching practices for English learners. However, despite increasing numbers of English learners in California schools and NCLB's accountability system, most teacher-preparation programs still do not provide teacher candidates with sufficient information and strategies for teaching culturally and linguistically diverse students, including a solid understanding of second-language development (Bailey and Butler 2007; Crawford 2003; Fillmore and Snow 2000). New York state, for example, which serves a large percentage of those students, requires only six credit hours of course work to prepare new teachers for working with these students. Therefore, vast numbers of English learners in mainstream classes across the United States have teachers who are not well prepared to teach them in appropriate ways that facilitate their acquisition of academic English and the subject matter required for school.

The bottom line is that the development of academic English is a complicated endeavor that involves more than simply additional vocabulary development and grammar practice. Academic language is used in different ways in different content areas. (See Saunders and Goldenberg, Snow and Katz, and Dutro and Kinsella, this publication.) The writing of a scientific lab report is not the same as the writing of

---

2. See Saunders and Goldenberg, this publication, for a definition of academic language.

a persuasive speech or an essay comparing historical perspectives. Students need semantic and syntactic knowledge and facility with language functions. In their various classes, English learners must join their emerging understanding of the English language with the content knowledge they are studying in order to complete the academic tasks associated with the content area. They must also learn *how* to do these tasks, such as generate an outline, negotiate roles in cooperative learning groups, and interpret charts and graphs. Figure 5.2 shows how the knowledge of language, content, and tasks intersect and identifies the type of academic language practice that can occur, using activities in lessons from a middle school social studies unit on the American Revolution as an example (Short 2000).

Figure 5.2. The Language-Content-Task Framework Applied to Middle School Social Studies Lessons

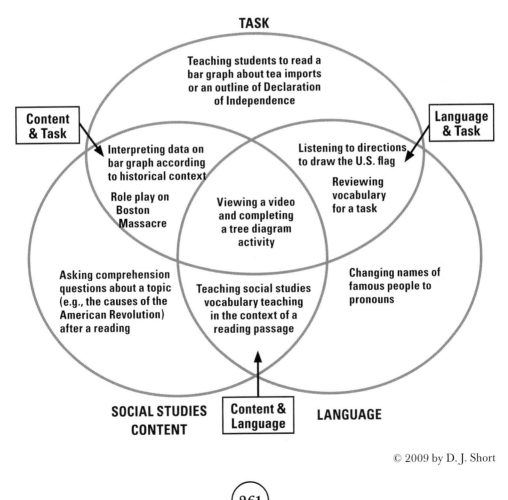

© 2009 by D. J. Short

261

Meeting the academic language needs of students is challenging for teachers. To ensure that English learners develop reading, writing, listening, and speaking skills in a variety of academic subjects, teachers need to have a sufficient grasp of students' language knowledge (primary language and English) and content knowledge coupled with the skills for differentiating instruction to meet the instructional objectives (Echevarria and Graves 2007; Heritage, Silva, and Pierce 2007). When teachers take into consideration English learners' unique second-language acquisition needs, they are better able to design and deliver lessons that are meaningful and appropriate. Effective sheltered content instruction is one way to do this.

Pedagogical Models of Sheltered Content Instruction

As described in the previous section, sheltered content instruction has evolved over the years as understanding of English learners and their educational needs has increased. This approach has also changed in response to shifting educational policies and trends. Research conducted in the mid-1990s found that there was no explicit model for effectively delivering sheltered lessons and that it was implemented unevenly across districts and schools (Sheppard 1995). Currently in California, some "sheltered content" approaches are alternatively referred to as *sheltered English immersion* or *structured English immersion (SEI)* and *specially designed academic instruction in English (SDAIE)*. State policy recognizes sheltered instruction both as a program and as an instructional approach. Although the terms have unique statutory contexts, the underlying legal premise of all types of sheltered content approaches is to provide English learners with meaningful access to the core curriculum.

Sheltered content instruction has evolved over the years as understanding of English learners and their educational needs has increased.

The following approaches to instruction for English learners are variations of sheltered instruction that have been used broadly in the United States.

Cognitive Academic Language Learning Approach

In the mid-1980s, the cognitive academic language learning approach (CALLA) was developed and teacher-training materials prepared (e.g., Chamot and O'Malley 1987, 1994). This model focused on helping students develop academic English skills through explicit instruction in the use of learning strategies, categorized by Chamot and O'Malley as metacognitive, cognitive, and social/affective strategies. Early CALLA research sought to determine the type of learning strategies students used. Using a small-group interview process, researchers found students used more cognitive strategies than metacognitive ones (O'Malley et al. 1985b). In a subsequent,

small-scale study, 75 English learners in three high schools were randomly assigned to one of three groups: metacognitive and cognitive, cognitive alone, and control. The first two groups received an eight-day intervention to learn to use CALLA strategies. All groups were assessed with a researcher-developed listening comprehension test and an oral-presentation task. No significant differences were found across the groups for the listening task, but the metacognitive and cognitive group did perform significantly better on the oral-presentation task in comparison with the other two groups (O'Malley et al. 1985a).

Originally CALLA was used in ESL and sheltered language arts classrooms, but in the 1990s its use in school districts expanded to other content areas. Another small-scale study was conducted in 1993 in elementary, middle, and high school mathematics classrooms (Chamot et al. 1992). Thirty-two students of low or intermediate levels of English proficiency participated and were classified as having high (13), average (8), or low (11) math ability. They were asked to solve a researcher-developed word problem using a think-aloud protocol and retrospective interview as the data collection instruments. Teachers were also observed and determined to be high or low implementers of the CALLA method. The findings showed that only students with high math ability solved the problem correctly, although not all—only seven of the 13 students in that category—did. Further, students in classrooms with teachers who were high implementers used the correct sequence of problem-solving steps and more metacognitive strategies than students in low-implementation classes and more than students with average or low math ability.

In another study (Waxman et al. 1994), the CALLA approach was one of four treatments in a quasi-experimental design with 325 Spanish-speaking students in grades one through five. Each treatment group participated in 15 three-hour instructional sessions delivered by specially trained teachers. The Iowa Test of Basic Skills was used for pre- and post-testing of students. The results for students in the CALLA group ($n = 52$) did not indicate a statistically significant difference in mean scores.

The inclusion of CALLA in professional development programs was fairly widespread in the 1990s, but it is not as prevalent now. Apart from a few small-scale studies with researcher-developed outcome measures that showed students could be taught to utilize the learning strategies, the model has not been part of a rigorous, empirical study to determine its effect on student achievement.

Specially Designed Academic Instruction in English

The California Commission on Teacher Credentialing (CTC) has defined SDAIE as "a component of a comprehensive program for English learners, consisting of a variety of strategies, techniques, and materials specially designed to provide students at an intermediate or advanced level of English proficiency access to grade-level core curriculum in English" (http://www.ctc.ca.gov). The CTC further clarified SDAIE instruction as a variety of techniques to be used to provide access to the core curriculum, such as slower, enunciated speech; use of visuals and realia; sufficient repetition; hands-on learning tasks; providing authentic language experiences; and so forth.

Although SDAIE teaching involves some techniques and strategies that individually have a separate research base showing the technique or strategy has had some effectiveness with English learners as a small-scale targeted intervention, SDAIE models are only theoretical (Diaz-Rico and Weed 2006; Walqui 2006). In other words, teachers (and administrators) may be able to articulate SDAIE techniques, but there is no consensus as to what specifically constitutes an effective SDAIE lesson, nor agreement on how one should organize the wide variety of techniques into a coherent model. Generally, there has been a lack of concrete guidance for teachers to implement it consistently, systematically, and effectively in ways that meet English learners' needs. Teachers receive training in SDAIE techniques through preservice and in-service opportunities (Diaz-Rico and Weed 2006; Walqui 2006), but in practice, teachers tend to pick and choose their favorite SDAIE techniques without significantly changing their teaching. More important, in light of current efforts for educational accountability, SDAIE has not been operationally defined and therefore cannot be scientifically validated. No experimental or quasi-experimental studies have been undertaken to determine whether the SDAIE techniques improve student performance on language or content assessments.

There is growing awareness that most SDAIE techniques and strategies, while valuable, are not sufficient to ensure success with grade-level content for English learners. As discussed in the Introduction of this publication, English learners are not closing the achievement gap. Most SDAIE techniques focus on making the content accessible to students, not necessarily on academic language development. Moreover, some schools limit enrollment in SDAIE classes to students with intermediate or advanced proficiency levels, a remnant of bilingual programs where students were taught core content in their primary language until they reached higher proficiency levels in English. Students at the beginner level need access to content too. When bilingual classes are not offered or available, SDAIE is the preferred instructional approach rather than mainstream classes in English.

The Sheltered Instruction Observation Protocol Model

The Sheltered Instruction Observation Protocol (SIOP) Model[TR] is another type of sheltered instruction and has a research base stretching for more than 10 years. It

was developed to better meet the needs of English learners and their content teachers. Because academic language is so critically important for English learners, it cannot be addressed solely during a specified ELD period; it must be developed throughout the day in all subject areas. In order for students to be successful and reach redesignation status (known as fluent English

The Sheltered Instruction Observation Protocol (SIOP) Model[TR] is another type of sheltered instruction and has a research base stretching for more than 10 years.

proficient, or FEP)—which involves more than simply passing the CELDT in California—academic language needs to be integrated throughout content teaching. However, because few content teachers had the skills to teach content and promote language development at the same time, consistent academic language instruction across the curriculum was relatively rare. Consequently, the effect was poor performance by English learners on state assessments and other measures. Therefore, we set out to design a model that would be applicable for all subject areas, all grade levels, and all English levels and would offer a concrete, explicit framework for instruction that incorporates best instructional practice for teaching both language and content. This intervention would help English learners acquire content knowledge while they develop and improve academic English language skills.

The SIOP Model[TR] began as an observation instrument—a sheltered instruction observation protocol—used by researchers to measure teachers' implementation of sheltered instruction lessons. The protocol evolved into a lesson planning and delivery approach, known as the SIOP Model[TR] (Echevarria, Vogt, and Short 2000, 2004, 2008; Echevarria and Short 2004; Short and Echevarria 1999) through a seven-year research study, "The Effects of Sheltered Instruction on the Achievement of Limited English Proficient Students," which was sponsored by the Center for Research on Education, Diversity & Excellence (CREDE) and funded by the U.S. Department of Education. It began in 1996 and involved collaborating teacher-researchers. As a team, we reviewed the professional literature on best practices and found many techniques and strategies that showed promise but did not have student outcome results or were not part of a comprehensive lesson model (use of advance organizers, for example, helped build schema for students before reading but did not teach other reading-comprehension strategies). We needed to test combinations of these techniques and so built an initial model of sheltered instruction, grounded in more than two decades of classroom-based research and the experiences of competent teachers. During four years of field testing, we analyzed teacher implementation and student effects as teachers tried out variations of the model in their classrooms. In 2000, we finalized its format—30 features of instruction grouped into eight components essential for making content comprehensible for English learners—Lesson Preparation,

Building Background, Comprehensible Input, Strategies, Interaction, Practice & Application, Lesson Delivery, and Review & Assessment (see Figure 5.3).

Figure 5.3. The Sheltered Instruction Observation Protocol (SIOP) Model™

Lesson Preparation

1. **Content objectives** clearly defined, displayed and reviewed with students
2. **Language objectives** clearly defined, displayed and reviewed with students
3. **Content concepts** appropriate for age and educational background level of students
4. **Supplementary materials** used to a high degree, making the lesson clear and meaningful (e.g., computer programs, graphs, models, visual aids)
5. **Adaptation of content** (e.g., text, assignment) to all levels of student proficiency
6. **Meaningful activities** that integrate lesson concepts (e.g., interviews, letter writing, simulations, models) with language practice opportunities for reading, writing, listening, and/or speaking

Building Background

7. **Concepts explicitly linked** to students' background experiences
8. **Links explicitly made** between past learning and new concepts
9. **Key vocabulary emphasized** (e.g., introduced, written, repeated, and highlighted for students to see)

Comprehensible Input

10. **Speech** appropriate for students' proficiency levels (e.g., slower rate, enunciation, and simple sentence structure for beginners)
11. **Clear explanation** of academic tasks
12. **A variety of techniques** used to make content concepts clear (e.g., modeling, visual aids, hands-on activities, demonstrations, gestures, body language)

Strategies

13. Ample opportunities provided for students to use **learning strategies**
14. **Scaffolding techniques** consistently used, assisting and supporting student understanding (e.g., think-alouds)
15. A variety of **questions or tasks that promote higher-order thinking skills** (e.g., literal, analytical, and interpretive questions)

Figure 5.3. *(continued)*

Interaction

16. Frequent opportunities for **interaction** and discussion between teacher/ student and among students, which encourage elaborated responses about lesson concepts

17. **Grouping configurations** support language and content objectives of the lesson

18. Sufficient **wait time for student responses** consistently provided

19. Ample opportunities for students to **clarify key concepts in Ll** as needed with aide, peer, or L1 text

Practice & Application

20. **Hands-on materials and/or manipulatives** provided for students to practice using new content knowledge

21. Activities provided for students to **apply content and language knowledge** in the classroom

22. Activities integrate all **language skills** (i.e., reading, writing, listening, and speaking)

Lesson Delivery

23. **Content objectives** clearly supported by lesson delivery

24. **Language objectives** clearly supported by lesson delivery

25. **Students engaged** approximately 90 to 100 percent of the period

26. **Pacing** of the lesson appropriate to students' ability levels

Review & Assessment

27. Comprehensive review of key vocabulary

28. Comprehensive review of key content concepts

29. Regular feedback provided to students on their output (e.g., language, content, work)

30. Assessment of student comprehension and learning of all lesson objectives (e.g., spot checking, group response) throughout the lesson

Comments:

We also created a scale for each feature of the observation protocol so we could measure the level of implementation in any given lesson (4 being closest to recommended practice, 0 being no evidence of the use of the practice). By scoring their lessons over time, we could also provide feedback to the teachers and thus coach them to implement the model more closely. See Figure 5.4 for an example of a feature.

Figure 5.4. SIOP Feature Rating Scale

Building Background (feature #7)

4	3	2	1	0	N/A
Concepts explicitly linked to students' background experiences	Concepts loosely linked to students' background experiences		Concepts not linked to students' background experiences		

The SIOP Model[TR] offers a framework for teachers to present curricular content concepts to English learners through strategies and techniques that make new information comprehensible to the students. While doing so, teachers develop student language skills across the four domains: reading, writing, listening, and speaking. They may accomplish this in multiple ways suited to the particular lesson, asking students, for example, to engage in peer discussions or a class debate, read textbook chapters or supplementary materials, complete a graphic organizer, write in a journal, or compose an essay. Some teachers might implement readers or writers workshops or a teacher-directed reading lesson. As such, the SIOP Model[TR] shares many features recommended for high-quality instruction for all students, such as linking lesson objectives to content standards, but adds key features for the academic success of students learning through a second language, such as the inclusion of language objectives in every content lesson and the development of background knowledge for students.

Although the SIOP Model[TR] has eight components, it is not a step-by-step approach. Rather, it is a system for lesson planning and teaching that ensures critical features of instruction for English learners in research-supported combinations are present in every lesson. As a framework, it allows for some natural variation in teaching styles and lesson delivery. In other words, there is more than one way to deliver a SIOP lesson. Teachers can use their creativity and knowledge to implement the components in a meaningful manner for their particular students. However, teachers need to follow the whole model for effectiveness. The SIOP Model[TR] identifies the features that we know are beneficial to students. The features need to be practiced daily in a systematic way, not selectively and occasionally. We have moved from a pick-and-choose approach to a tested model that improves student achievement (Echevarria, Short, and Powers 2006).

Components of the SIOP Model^TR

The SIOP Model^TR consists of eight components and 30 features. The following provides a brief overview of this model of sheltered instruction.

Lesson Preparation. SIOP lessons need to have both language and content objectives linked to curriculum standards. In this way, students gain important experience with key grade-level content and skills as they progress toward fluency in the second language. Teachers discuss the daily objectives with students so that they know what they are expected to learn and can take an active part in assessing their own progress. The lessons need to prepare second-language learners for content area classes by giving them practice with the academic language, tasks, and topics they will encounter in those classes, such as interpreting fiction and nonfiction texts, tracking the chronology of an historical event, and writing science lab reports. Because grade-level textbooks are difficult for many English learners to comprehend, the SIOP Model^TR also encourages teachers to use supplementary materials (e.g., visual aids, multimedia, adapted text, related literature at lower reading levels).

Building Background. SIOP lessons connect new concepts with the students' personal experiences and past learning. To prepare English learners for reading, writing, and oral language tasks, SIOP lessons build background and/or activate the students' prior knowledge. Teachers are sensitive to sociocultural factors that may influence student learning and make appropriate accommodations, such as when texts exhibit cultural biases or curricula expect students to have learned certain concepts through prior schooling in the U.S.

The SIOP Model^TR underscores the importance of building a broad vocabulary base for students to be effective readers, writers, speakers, and listeners. In the SIOP Model^TR, teachers directly teach key vocabulary and word structures, word families, cognates, and word relationships. Lesson activities provide further opportunities for students to use this vocabulary orally and in writing. Teachers can begin with everyday expressions to describe concepts but must introduce academic and technical terms to the students (Gibbons 2002). Key vocabulary needs reinforcement through different learning modes to put the knowledge of the words into the students' expressive vocabulary tool set.

Comprehensible Input. SIOP teachers use sheltered techniques to make content comprehensible. These techniques include, among others:

⊙ Demonstrations and modeling

⊙ Gestures, pantomime, and role play

- Pictures, real objects, graphs and charts, graphic organizers

- Restating, repeating, and reducing the speed of the teacher's presentation

- Previewing important information

- Hands-on, experiential activities

Teachers need to modulate their speech (rate, word choice, sentence complexity, use of idioms, etc.) according to student proficiency level. The academic tasks must be explained clearly, both orally and in writing, with models and examples of good work so students know the steps they should take and can envision the desired result.

Teachers may also boost the comprehensibility of the content material through primary language support. Supplementary materials (e.g., text, audiotapes, the Internet) in a student's primary language may be used to introduce a new topic. Instructional supports such as preview/review and tutoring in the primary language can help students with difficult and abstract concepts.

Strategies. To equip students for learning outside the sheltered classroom, the SIOP Model[TR] calls for explicit instruction and practice in learning strategies. Good strategies for reading comprehension, for example, need to be modeled and practiced, one at a time, with authentic text. SIOP teachers must scaffold instruction so students can be successful, beginning at the students' performance level and providing support to move them to a higher level of understanding and achievement. This gradual release of responsibility (see Figure 3.5) leads students to be able to complete independent work successfully. Teachers have to ask critical thinking questions as well, so that students apply their language skills while developing a deeper understanding of the subject matter.

SIOP teachers should also capitalize on the cognitive and metacognitive strategies students already use in their first language. Research on literacy acquisition has revealed that primary language strategies will transfer to a new language (August and Shanahan 2006). Riches and Genesee (2006) found that students will use more effective strategies and more metacognitive ones as they become more proficient in their second language.

Interaction. Students learn through interaction with one another and with their teachers. They need oral language practice to help develop content knowledge and second-language literacy. Teachers can provide language models of appropriate speech, word choice, intonation, and fluency. But student–student interaction is also important and needs to occur regularly so English learners can develop oral language proficiency by practicing important language functions, such as confirming information, elaborating on one's own or another's idea, and evaluating opinions.

Increasing English learners' oral language proficiency is essential for literacy development (Shanahan and Beck 2006). However, sometimes the interaction patterns expected in an American classroom differ from students' cultural norms. SIOP teachers are sensitive to sociocultural differences among students and work with the students to become competent in the classroom culture while respecting their values.

It is also important for students to interact with text in substantive ways. Interactive journals, for example, can help students make sense of what they read and inspire students to see themselves as writers.

Practice & Application. Practice and application of new material is important for all learners. The SIOP Model[TR] research found that lessons with hands-on, visual, and other kinesthetic tasks benefit English learners because learners practice the language and content knowledge through multiple modalities. SIOP lessons include a variety of activities that encourage students to practice and apply the content they are learning, *and* practice and apply their language skills, too. It is important to build and reinforce reading, writing, listening, and speaking skills together in SIOP lessons, not solely one at a time. (Although in some ELD lessons, one skill may be the object of primary emphasis. See Saunders and Goldenberg, Guideline 4, this publication.)

Lesson Delivery. Successful delivery of a SIOP lesson means that the content and language objectives were met, the pacing was appropriate, and the students had a high level of engagement. The art of teaching and classroom management skills play roles in effective lesson delivery. Having routines, making sure students know the lesson objectives so they can stay on track, and designing meaningful activities that appeal to students is helpful. Time should not be wasted, yet a lesson should not move so swiftly that the English learners do not understand the key information.

Review & Assessment. Each SIOP lesson should wrap up with time allocated for review and assessment. English learners need to revisit key vocabulary and concepts, and teachers need to use frequent comprehension checks and other informal assessments to measure how well students retain the information. Ideally, SIOP teachers also offer multiple pathways for students to demonstrate their understanding of the content. Assessments should look at the range of language and content development, including measures of vocabulary, grammar, comprehension skills, and content concepts.

Because the SIOP Model[TR] is an approach for delivering sheltered lessons, it does not address large-scale assessments directly. It provides an excellent opportunity for English learners to learn requisite information and language structures through rich, integrated, standards-based lessons. If students have repeated opportunities to learn and use academic English through meaningful, relevant content tasks, they are likely to perform better on large-scale assessments, demonstrating their acquisition of both

271

language and content knowledge (Francis et al. 2006; Gersten et al. 2007; Torgesen et al. 2007).

The SIOP Model™ in Action

The following two lessons, drawn from our research and coaching observations, describe how the SIOP Model™ is applied in sheltered classes. The first lesson was designed and taught by a third-grade teacher at Lela Alston Elementary School in Phoenix, Arizona. The class was composed of 25 students: 20 were English learners at various levels of proficiency; three were learning-disabled; one student used a wheelchair; and four students received speech services. The observation was conducted during the spring semester. The second lesson was designed and taught by a sheltered biology teacher at Central Falls High School in Central Falls, Rhode Island. His school had semester-long courses and used block scheduling. This biology class was 90 minutes long. Fifteen English learners of mixed proficiency levels were present on the day of the observation, which occurred near the end of the semester. (See both these lessons at the end of this chapter.)

Third-Grade General Education: Geography

Students were seated in teams, at individual desks arranged in groups of three. Throughout the lesson, students were asked to talk to or work with their teammates.

The lesson began with the teacher telling the students they would continue with their study of landforms. She asked them to take their landform cards out of their desks and arrange them on top so that they could see each of the five cards. She reminded them that on the previous day, they had used laptop computers to use the "Google" search engine to learn about landforms. They had talked about each one, had drawn a picture of each landform on a card, and had written a definition on the back. The teacher then said, "Thumbs up if you think, 'Yes, I remember this' and thumbs down if you don't." All students showed their thumbs up. Then the teacher wrote the word *mountain* on the board and said, "I'm going to count to 3 and I want you to read the word aloud." The students chorally read the word. Next the teacher selected a student and asked her to read the definition she had written on her card. This process was continued with the other terms for landforms: *island, peninsula, river, and plains.*

The next part of the review involved students reading something they had written the previous day: *If I lived on a landform, what would it be like?* Students selected a landform and wrote a short paragraph about what job they would have and what they would do for fun. The teacher asked for volunteers to read their paragraphs to the class.

Once the review was completed, the teacher drew students' attention to the board and asked them to read the content objectives:

"Students will be able to generate five words that belong together. Students will be able to create a country and use those five words to label landforms."

They read the language objective:

"Students will be able to discuss categories of words with their teams." Students were told that they would begin only the second content objective and finish the following day.

Referring to a chart generated the previous day that displayed ideas of things to do and to eat, the teacher modeled what students would do next. She said, "Let me think of something I like to do. I like to read. What would be a picture of something that has to do with reading?" Students called out various answers, eager to participate. The teacher selected *book.* She drew a large picture of an open book (see the lesson plan at the end of this chapter). Then above it she drew a circle with five lines extending out, as a semantic web. She said, "I'm going to draw an island that has to do with a book. I'm thinking to myself, 'Hmmm, these are categories, things that go together. For example, red, blue, yellow green are . . . (students answered in unison, 'colors') or triangle, hexagon, circle . . . (students answered, 'shapes'). What words would go together with book? Talk with your teams."

Immediately students turned to their teams and began talking. After a couple of minutes, the teacher asked for teams to report words they had generated. She completed the graphic by writing the words *pages, words, title, illustrator,* and *author* that had been reported by the students above each of the five lines. Then she wrote a landform under each line. Throughout this part of the lesson, when a student was unsure of an answer or hesitated, the teacher provided assistance by using prompts such as, *Would you like some help? Sayed, can you help Eduardo?*

Next, students practiced generating five words associated with the word *pizza,* then *computer.* Students worked efficiently in their groups, and it appeared that all groups had generated words to report. When it was clear students understood the idea of categorizing words, the teacher drew two landforms on the book and labeled them. She said, "Thumbs up if you see what we're doing, thumbs down if you need more clarification." Several students had thumbs down so she gave further explanation.

After passing out white construction paper, she told the students that they should pick an idea, something they like to do or eat, then draw that word in their graphic organizer. She instructed them to tell their team the word and to help each other generate the five words in that category. A student asked if one of his team members could write his list in Spanish and the teacher replied, "You bet!" (The student used the word *taco* and wrote *carne, salsa, pollo, queso,* and *cebolla.*) The teacher announced that students could generate their own word or use words from the chart.

A buzzer sounded to let students know it was time to stop after 10 minutes. The teacher asked the students to meet her at the back carpet. Students immediately picked up their papers and went to sit on the carpet. As the class sat together, they played several rounds of a guessing game related to the assignment. One student said the five words (*mouse, monitor, cpu, keyboard, game*); and the class guessed what the topic word was. From the five clues, students guessed, *computer.* Finally, the teacher asked if there were students who had not finished, so that the class could help them. Three students had fewer than five words on their graphic organizer, and the other students assisted in suggesting words for them.

After dismissing students back to their seats, the teacher counted backwards from 5 to give them time to put their landform cards and paper away. Then the class reviewed the objectives together, and the teacher reminded them that they would complete their poster of Country with Landforms the next day.

An analysis of this lesson revealed a high level of SIOP implementation. The lesson was driven by the content and language objectives that were introduced and posted at the start of the lesson and then reviewed at the end. There were multiple opportunities to check for understanding throughout the lesson, accommodating varying levels of English proficiency. For example, if a student struggled to answer a question, the teacher scaffolded participation by asking questions such as *Would you like some help? Sayed, can you help Eduardo?* Perhaps most significant were the frequent opportunities for interaction between teacher and students and among the students. They allowed English learners to practice oral language skills, develop and expand their vocabularies, and use academic language. Working in teams also provided the necessary support for completing the assignment, with students assisting one another and jointly constructing answers. Providing a model of the completed product helped students to comprehend and participate as did the teacher's use of think-alouds. The lesson was well organized and well paced, flowing efficiently from activity to activity. The expectations for students were clear. Overall, the students were engaged and productive, and all students met the objectives.

High School ESL Biology: Evolution and Natural Selection

(See the lesson plan at the end of this chapter.)

The language objectives (Students will be able to listen to and summarize key concepts) and content objectives (Students will be able to define evolution by natural selection) were written on the board and on the lesson plan. These objectives were reviewed orally with the students. The first assignment was a carousel activity with four stations. Four pieces of chart paper with the following headings were posted around the room: Evolution Vocabulary, Synonyms, Examples of Adaptations, and Why Organisms Evolve. The teacher presented written instructions for the task and reviewed them with the class. Students were then divided into four groups and recorded their ideas for each topic on the chart paper as they moved clockwise around the room. The teacher kept time carefully so each group spent only two minutes at each poster.

After the students returned to their seats, the teacher reviewed the chart with the class. The students drew a four-square organizer in their notebooks and recorded the information from the charts along with additional information provided by the teacher and elicited from the students through teacher questioning.

The next activity involved the presentation of new information to the class about three types of natural selection. To help the students with notetaking, the teacher distributed a three-circle Venn diagram and, using the overhead projector to write notes, taught about stabilizing, directional, and disruptive selection. The discussion included examples of how types of evolution had affected real animal and plant species. After the teacher shared a few examples, he asked students to describe ones they were familiar with, including examples from their native countries. The students asked some good questions during this time, such as "How does an animal become extinct?" Before moving on to the next activity, the teacher incorporated a one-minute reflection: "Turn to a partner and share one thing you learned about each type of selection."

The final major activity was a teacher read-aloud of a supplementary text, *How Whales Walked Into the Sea* (McNulty 1999). The high schoolers were fascinated with the book and listened actively. They showed their curiosity through their questions. The teacher had given the students a notetaking sheet, but most were so engrossed that they did not take notes at first. The teacher realized this and stopped his reading aloud from time to time. He encouraged the students to record the information and gave clues to help them respond to the questions on the sheet.

Five minutes before the end of the period, the teacher conducted a wrap-up and review. Students were asked to complete two outcome sentences using starters such as "I won-der . . . ," "I learned . . . ," "I didn't know that . . ." and then to write a brief summary of the key concepts. The teacher called students' attention to the key words on the Evolution Vocabulary chart so they could include them, as needed, in their summaries.

Upon analysis, this lesson demonstrated excellent SIOP implementation. The objectives were posted and reviewed; activities were meaningful but chunked well for student understanding; key vocabulary was discussed, written out, and used by the students in notetaking and review; connections to the students' lives and prior lessons were made; input was comprehensible; language skills were practiced (especially listening comprehension, which often gets overlooked with the book reading); students had to interact and do a hands-on carousel; the pacing was good; and the class reviewed and summarized information. Overall, the lesson was cohesive, and the transitions between the activities were smooth. Having the different notetaking sheets was efficient and purposeful. Students did not waste time drawing charts, and each sheet was geared to an appropriate learning goal—the four-square chart for recording and organizing notes and the three-circle Venn diagram for showing comparison and contrast. Supplying written directions for each task and reviewing them with the students was beneficial to the management of the different activities. Further, the four carousel stations offered a nice combination of science academic language and content practice.

Research Syntheses

In recent years, two major syntheses with meta-analyses have been conducted of empirical research on the education of English learners, examining language and literacy development as well as academic achievement. *Developing Literacy in Second-Language Learners: A Report of the National Literacy Panel on Language-Minority Children and Youth* (August and Shanahan 2006) presents the findings of a 13-member expert panel that looked at the reading and writing skills needed for successful schooling. The panel considered second-language literacy development, cross-linguistic influences and transfer, sociocultural contexts, instruction and professional development, and student assessment.

The second major review was conducted by researchers from the National Center for Research on Education, Diversity & Excellence (CREDE) who also examined best practices for developing English language skills in English learners. Their focus was on oral language development, literacy development (from instructional and cross-linguistic perspectives) and academic achievement. Their findings are found in *Educating English Language Learners: A Synthesis of the Research Evidence* (Genesee et al. 2006).

Both of these syntheses reached similar conclusions and are discussed in more depth elsewhere in the chapters on ELD research (this publication) by Saunders and Goldenberg, the acquisition of literacy skills by August and Shanahan, and alternative educational programs for English learners by Lindholm-Leary and Genesee. These findings are also supported by other recent publications of a smaller scale (e.g., Goldenberg 2004; Norris and Ortega 2006). For the purpose of this chapter, which seeks to provide guidance on helping English learners gain access to the core curriculum, we highlight some of the key findings that have implications for developing academic literacy:

- Processes of second-language (L2) literacy development are influenced by a number of variables that interact with each other in complex ways (e.g., L1 literacy, L2 oralcy, socioeconomic status, and more). If, for example, students have literacy in their primary language or strong oral English skills, they can use these resources to gain access to the content curriculum while developing academic L2 literacy skills.

- Certain primary language (L1) skills and abilities transfer to English literacy: phonemic awareness, comprehension and language-learning strategies, and L1 and L2 oral knowledge. When teachers tap into the skills and knowledge students already have and explicitly show students how to make use of these skills, academic literacy development can be enhanced. For students of Latin and Greek language backgrounds, many vocabulary words have cognates in academic English.

- Teaching the five major components of reading (NICHD 2000) to English learners is necessary but not sufficient for developing academic literacy. Whereas phonemic awareness, phonics, fluency, comprehension strategies, and vocabulary are essential elements for English literacy, English learners also need support in oral language development. Unlike English-only students, English learners rarely begin schooling with grade-level oral proficiency in English.

- Academic literacy in the native language facilitates the development of academic literacy in English. If students learn content concepts through their primary language, they will know those concepts. Teachers need not re-teach the *concepts* but need to teach students how to read, write, speak, and listen to information about them in English.

- High-quality instruction for English learners is similar to high-quality instruction for other English-speaking students, but English learners who are not yet at advanced levels of proficiency in English need instructional accommodations and supports.

- English learners need enhanced, explicit vocabulary development. Although English learners certainly need instruction in many aspects of academic English, recent research on vocabulary development (with English-only and English learners) emphasizes the need for more robust vocabulary knowledge among students (Biemiller 2001; Carlo et al. 2004; Nagy 1997; Nagy and Scott 2000).

Findings of the National Literacy Panel and the CREDE syntheses are entirely consistent with the features of the SIOP Model[TR]. English learners benefit from practices such as having:

(1) clear goals and objectives,

(2) opportunities to extend oral language skills,

(3) explicit attention to vocabulary development,

(4) use of their home language as appropriate, and

(5) active engagement and participatory tasks.

These practices, along with others to promote metacognitive and cognitive strategies and combine oral and literacy development, align the features of the SIOP Model[TR] directly with research recommendations (Echevarria, Short, and Vogt 2008; Goldenberg 2006, 2008).

SIOP Model[TR] Research

As we mentioned at the outset of this chapter, we have focused on the SIOP Model[TR] as an effective example of sheltered content instruction because it has a sustained and expanding research base. Since 1996, we have been investigating its effects on teachers and students. At that time during the development phase, we knew it would be important to make sure that implementation of the SIOP Model[TR] led to positive academic gains for English learners. We undertook an instrument validation study and a quasi-experimental research and design study during the original CREDE project. First, we sought to ensure the observation protocol was valid and reliable, and then we examined student achievement through a study of treatment and comparison classes. In recent years, as we describe below, we have been conducting additional empirical investigations on the SIOP Model[TR], which focus on its sustainability as a model of instruction as well as its impact on student achievement.

> **We have focused on the SIOP Model[TR] as an effective example of sheltered content instruction because it has a sustained and expanding research base.**

After the development of the model, a study was conducted to establish the validity and reliability of the SIOP rating instrument. Four experienced professors of sheltered instruction from three major universities in the Southwest used the protocol and its rating scale to observe six videotapes of teachers engaged in sheltered instruction and rate their performance. Three of the videos were deemed by specialists to be highly representative of the tenets of sheltered instruction, while the other three

were not. A statistical analysis revealed an interrater agreement of .99. Additional analyses indicated that the SIOP instrument is a highly reliable and valid measure of sheltered instruction (Guarino et al. 2001).

Student Writing Assessment Study

After finalizing the SIOP Model[TR] as a lesson delivery system and ensuring teachers could teach it with high fidelity, we investigated whether the model yielded positive results in terms of student achievement. Because the CREDE study preceded the NCLB legislation, most English learners in the research districts were exempted from the standardized testing process. So we used the writing assessment from the Illinois Measurement of Annual Growth in English (IMAGE) test as an outcome measure of academic literacy. The IMAGE was the standardized test of reading and writing that Illinois districts used to measure the annual growth of these skills for English learners in grades three and higher. The test was valid and reliable and had correlational and predictive value for achievement scores on the IGAP (the former standardized state assessment of achievement in subject areas such as reading and mathematics). It provided subscores for five dimensions of writing—language production, focus, support/elaboration, organization, and mechanics—as well as an overall score for each student.

During the 1998-99 school year, we gave the IMAGE writing exam to middle school English learners in our study. A pretest was given in the fall, a post-test in the spring. Two groups of English learners in sheltered classes participated: students whose teachers were trained in implementing the SIOP Model[TR] (the treatment group), and a similar group of English learners in the same district programs whose teachers had no exposure to the SIOP Model[TR] (the comparison group). The students in both groups were in grades six through eight, represented mixed English proficiency levels, and spoke a variety of first languages.

Results showed that English learners in sheltered classes with teachers who had been trained in the SIOP Model[TR] improved their writing and outperformed the students in comparison classes by receiving higher overall scores for the spring assessment (Echevarria, Short, and Powers 2006). The results for the SIOP treatment group were statistically significant when analyzed with the comparison group for the total writing score and on three of the five subtests (language production, organization, and mechanics). The SIOP group also made gains over the comparison group in the focus and support/elaboration subtests, but the gains were not statistically significant. A secondary analysis of the data revealed that special education students in the SIOP group who constituted a subset of the English learners made significant improvement overall in their writing as well. These results indicated that the SIOP Model[TR]

offered a promising approach for helping English learners develop academic literacy skills needed for success in school.

Since we conducted the original SIOP research for CREDE, additional investigations are taking place. As with any study, the merits of the CREDE study increase when results are replicated in subsequent research. Some school districts have implemented the SIOP Model[TR] and have evaluated the results for their programs. In addition, some large-scale quasi-experimental and experimental studies have taken place or are in progress. We describe three of these studies here.

Evaluation Research

Lela Alston Elementary School in the Isaac School District in Phoenix, Arizona, initiated a SIOP professional development program schoolwide in 2001. It was a new school in one of the lowest performing regions of the district. The SIOP staff development initially took place over two years (2002-03 and 2003-04) and was led by a training team—a lead SIOP teacher, the principal, and a coach. Besides conducting training of the entire staff, the SIOP coach and lead teacher worked with the individual teachers (e.g., observing and modeling lessons in their classrooms, helping with lesson plans) and with grade-level teams (e.g., developing a bank of language objectives for grade-level units).

The concerted effort to train and coach all the teachers and work on grade-level lessons yielded positive results with gains in student achievement after three years. In 2002, the average score for the grade three students was below 50 percent on the reading, mathematics, and writing tests of the state standardized assessment, the Arizona Instrument to Measure Standards (AIMS). However, two years later, in 2004, the grade three students' average score reached close to 60 percent or higher on all three tests.

In comparison with schools in the Isaac School District with similar socioeconomic status and performance levels, Alston was more successful. At the start of SIOP implementation, Alston students performed on par with or below students in similar schools. By the end of three years, Alston outperformed the other schools on the state standardized assessment.

Quasi-Experimental Research

A project called Academic Literacy Through Sheltered Instruction for Secondary English Language Learners was a quasi-experimental research study conducted in two school districts in northern New Jersey and funded by the Carnegie Corporation

of New York and the Rockefeller Foundation from 2004 to 2007. Its purpose was to replicate the CREDE research, scale it up to include high school students in addition to middle school English learners, and measure student gains on state assessments. Both New Jersey districts had two middle schools and one high school with similar multilingual English learner populations and followed an ESL program design in grades six through twelve with some designated sheltered courses. More than 500 English learners were in the treatment district (Clifton Public Schools), approximately 225 in the comparison site.

Researchers from the Center for Applied Linguistics (CAL) provided professional development in the SIOP Model[TR] at the treatment site to math, science, social studies, language arts, ESL, and technology teachers. Approximately 35 teachers formed Cohort 1 in August 2004 and received intensive, ongoing training and occasional coaching in 2004-05 with follow-up training and more coaching in 2005-06. An additional 23 teachers formed Cohort 2 in the 2005-06 school year and participated in the intensive training program and some coaching for one year. The district supported three part-time, on-site coaches in the first year and added two more in the second year to accommodate the increased size of the teacher group. The teachers in the comparison site did not receive any SIOP Model[TR] training but continued with their regular district staff development. A total of 19 teachers participated at the comparison site for the two years.

CAL researchers collected teacher implementation data (two classroom observations each year—in the fall and in the spring) using the SIOP protocol at both sites to assess the teachers' level of sheltered instruction. Teachers' lessons were scored according to the protocol's rubric, and teachers were identified as high, medium, or low implementers.[3] Findings showed that the number of high implementers of the SIOP Model[TR] increased to a greater extent in the treatment district than in the comparison district. After one year of SIOP professional development, 56 percent of Cohort 1 and 74 percent of Cohort 2 teachers in the treatment district implemented the model to a high degree. After two years, 71 percent of Cohort 1 reached a high level. In contrast, only 5 percent of the teachers reached a high level of implementation after one year at the comparison site and only 17 percent after two years (Center for Applied Linguistics 2007).

The researchers collected and analyzed student results on the state-approved English language proficiency assessment, the IPT (IDEA Language Proficiency Test), for all English learners in grades six through twelve who were in ESL programs. Analyses

---

3. High implementation was defined as a score of 75 percent or higher on the SIOP protocol. Low implementation was defined to be 50 percent or below.

showed that on average, students with SIOP-trained teachers (in the treatment district) outperformed students without SIOP-trained teachers (in the comparison district) to a statistically significant level (p < .05) when mean scores were compared on the IPT oral, writing, and total proficiency tests in the second year of the intervention (2005-06). There was no significant difference in the first year. However, SIOP students in the treatment district made greater gains in mean scores on all IPTs from baseline year (2003-04) to final year (2005-06) than the students in the comparison district did. (See Table 5.2.) Moreover, upon examining student performance within the treatment district (to determine if there might be district factors influencing the results), researchers found that on average, SIOP students outperformed non-SIOP students to a statistically significant level ($p < .05$) in both years when comparing mean scores on the IPT oral, reading, writing, and total proficiency tests (Center for Applied Linguistics 2007).

Table 5.2. New Jersey SIOP Study: IDEA Language Proficiency Test Comparison Group Versus Treatment Group Mean Scores, 2003-04 to 2005-06

IDEA Language Proficiency Test	Group	2003-04		2004-05		2005-06		Change from 2003-04 to 2005-06
		Number	Mean	Number	Mean	Number	Mean	
Oral proficiency level	Comparison	192	3.66 (1.28)	169	3.64 (1.32)	168	3.66 (1.33)	0.00
	SIOP	387	3.67 (1.37)	278	3.76 (1.27)	268	4.00** (1.06)	+0.33
Reading proficiency level	Comparison	190	3.95 (.92)	169	3.98 (1.02)	168	3.97 (.92)	+0.02
	SIOP	387	3.82 (.93)	278	3.91 (.88)	268	4.10 (.83)	+0.28
Writing proficiency level	Comparison	178	4.14 (.96)	169	4.04 (1.16)	168	4.02 (1.13)	-0.12
	SIOP	386	4.06 (1.08)	278	4.15 (.94)	267	4.32** (.83)	+0.26
Total proficiency level	Comparison	193	3.69* (1.04)	166	3.61 (1.22)	168	3.65 (1.21)	-0.04
	SIOP	386	3.11 (1.06)	283	3.69 (1.00)	267	3.88** (.93)	+0.77

Note: Standard deviations are given in parentheses.

* Statistically significant in favor of comparison group ($p < .05$)
** Statistically significant in favor of treatment SIOP group ($p < .05$)
© 2007, Center for Applied Linguistics. Used with permission.

The researchers also collected and analyzed student content area achievement data from New Jersey state tests in reading, math, social studies, and science for grades six and seven;[4] reading, math, and science for grade eight; and reading and math for grade eleven (or grade twelve for some English learners). The students in the treatment and comparison districts took these tests only once for the most part. The results showed a significant difference $(p < .05)$ in mean scores in favor of SIOP students in the treatment district on six state content tests:

2004-05	2005-06
⊙ TerraNova test in reading for grade six	⊙ New Jersey Assessment of Skills and Knowledge in language for grade six
⊙ TerraNova test in language for grade six	⊙ New Jersey Assessment of Skills and Knowledge language for grade seven
⊙ TerraNova tests total score for grade six	⊙ High School Proficiency Assessment in mathematics for grade eleven

There was a significant difference $(p < .05)$ in mean scores in favor of students in the comparison district on one state content test in the first year:

2004-05

⊙ TerraNova test in social studies for grade seven

There were no significant differences between groups on the other 19 content tests (Center for Applied Linguistics 2007). The content achievement results indicate some promise for the SIOP Model™, but the number of student subjects was very small for each test and therefore the results are not generalizable. In addition, students took different tests each year as they were promoted to a higher grade level and so growth on any one test could not be determined.

Experimental SIOP Research

The Impact of the SIOP Model[TR] on Middle School Science and Language Learning is a five-year study (2005-10) funded by the U.S. Department of Education for the National Center for Research on the Educational Achievement and Teaching of English Language Learners (CREATE). This SIOP research is conducted by researchers at California State University, Long Beach, the Center for Applied Linguistics, and

---

4. New Jersey changed tests during the study. In the second year, on the New Jersey Assessment of Skills and Knowledge examination, students in grades six and seven were tested only in reading and mathematics.

the University of Houston, Texas. The study uses a randomized experimental design to investigate the impact of the SIOP Model[TR] on student academic achievement in middle school science. The purpose of the study is to test the SIOP Model[TR] in a randomized manner with a focus on a single content area and to test alternative delivery systems of SIOP professional development to the teachers. Researchers developed science curriculum units with SIOP lesson plans and science language assessments that focused on the acquisition of science concepts and language development among English learners.

The study is being conducted in phases. Phase 1 was a pilot study designed to develop and refine science curriculum lessons that incorporate components and features of the SIOP Model[TR] and to field-test academic science language assessments. Phases 2 and 3 each involve one-year studies.

In 2006-07, eight schools were randomly assigned as treatment or control sites. Science teachers in both conditions had English learner authorization; however, science teachers at the treatment sites were trained in the SIOP Model[TR] and provided with SIOP science curriculum units so that they would implement the lesson plans effectively. Over a period of nine weeks, teachers taught four science units: Cell Structure and Function, Photosynthesis and Respiration, Cell Division, and Genetics. Control teachers taught the same science curriculum in their usual manner. Then we tested intervention and control student performance on the assessments and compared the results of students in the SIOP classes with those of control students. There were 649 students in the SIOP classes and 372 students in control classes. The sample included students who were native English-speaking students, also called English-only students (EOs), students who had been redesignated as fluent English proficient (FEP) for three months or longer, those who had been recently redesignated as FEP (three months or less), and English learners. (See Table 5.3.) Since previous research indicated that English learners benefit from the SIOP Model[TR], one of the goals of this study was to investigate its impact on other students.

Table 5.3. CREATE Study Year 2 Student Participants

Composition of Classes	SIOP Classes	Control Classes	Totals
EL	105	112	217
FEP ≤ 3 yrs redesignated	212	121	333
FEP ≥ 3 yrs redesignated	89	20	119
English only	243	109	352
Totals	649	372	1,021

Data collection and analyses included teacher implementation ratings using the SIOP protocol and student science language assessments. There were four pre- and post-tests administered to students and each assessment included multiple-choice items and one or two essay questions. Results indicated that students in the SIOP condition—regardless of language proficiency classification—outperformed, on average, those in the control, although not to a statistically significant degree. Perhaps most important, the analyses showed that, based on lesson ratings, when teachers implemented the SIOP Model[TR] to a high degree, students performed significantly better on the assessments than did control students, indicating that teacher implementation matters (Short and Richards 2008).

Phase 3 of the study is ongoing as of the time of this publication (the 2008-09 school year). One goal of this phase is to test ways to improve the professional development program so teachers implement the SIOP Model[TR] faster and to a higher degree, leading students to perform better on science language assessments.

Future Research on Sheltered Instruction

The National Literacy Panel report and the CREDE synthesis revealed the existing knowledge base for how to best educate English learners. It also illuminated the need for much more empirical research in this important area. The following topics are offered as potential research questions. Additional research questions can be found in Goldenberg (2008).

⊙ **Placement of English learners in sheltered courses.** In our work around the U.S., one of the most frequently asked questions is whether all English learners (ELs) should be placed together in one class or dispersed among classes so that they are mixed with fluent English-proficient (FEP) students and English-only students (EOs). Common sense suggests that if, for example, there are only five Spanish-speaking ELs in the third grade, they would benefit from being placed in one class together to support one another. Further, a teacher would be able to work more intensively with them in small-group instruction than if they were split among several classes with one or two students per class. In schools where the number of ELs is much greater, the decision becomes more complicated. When there are 29 ELs in third grade, should they all be placed in one class? Would they gain more exposure to academic English by being integrated into classes with EO students? In secondary schools, what is the most effective schedule for ELs? Would separate classes composed of only ELs make content learning better than classes where a variety of proficiency levels are represented, including EOs, if both used sheltered techniques? Would such grouping work better for lower proficiency levels than for higher ones? These are empirical

285

questions that are ripe for future research. (See Saunders and Goldenberg, this publication, for discussion of this topic compared with ELD instruction.)

> **When bilingual instruction is not offered or available, high-quality sheltered instruction is the most effective way for helping English learners gain access to the core curriculum while developing their academic English.**

⊙ **Instructional grouping configurations.** A related question is, what is the most effective way to group English learners for instructional purposes within one class? This issue has yet to be resolved through research studies. Both homogeneous and heterogeneous arrangements of English learners for small-group instruction or cooperative learning tasks have merit. When all students in a group are English learners, it may be easier for the teacher to differentiate instruction, move at the students' pace, and use students' native language for clarification. However, a mix of EOs and ELs provides the latter with exposure to rich language learning opportunities, among other benefits.

⊙ **Empirical research on other models of sheltered instruction.** Which approaches to sheltered instruction improve student academic performance? Some instructional approaches for sheltered classes may hold promise but lack evidence for their efficacy. Particularly for those theoretical or well-articulated models mentioned previously in this chapter, evidence of enhanced student achievement outcomes is needed to continue promoting their models of professional development and classroom implementation.

⊙ **Most effective instructional features.** There is fairly wide consensus that certain instructional features are effective for teaching English learners, such as having content and language objectives, focusing on vocabulary teaching, providing opportunities for oral language development, and so forth. But is there a combination of features that has a more powerful impact on student achievement than others? What are the most critical features of effective instruction and which are of secondary importance? These questions have yet to be addressed empirically, but such a study might yield important findings.

⊙ **Instruction for beginning speakers and underschooled students.** When bilingual instruction is not offered or available, high-quality sheltered instruction is the most effective way for helping English learners gain access to the core curriculum while developing their academic English. But is sheltered instruction (coupled with ELD instruction) sufficient for students at the beginning stages of English proficiency and those students with significant gaps in their schooling? If there is a need for more, how do we best augment their instructional programs?

286

Program Models and Contexts Using Sheltered Instruction

As mentioned earlier, the term *sheltered instruction* can be considered as both a classroom pedagogy and a program designed for educating English learners. In this section, we offer an overview of common program models for English learners where sheltered content instruction is often offered in addition to English language development services. Sheltered instruction programs, newcomer programs, dual-language and transitional bilingual programs, and general education programs with sheltered support are alternatives that can be effective for providing English learners with access to the core content. Choosing and implementing a successful program for these learners requires an understanding of the available alternatives and a careful consideration of a district's goals, resources, and the needs and characteristics of its students.

Although these programs are discussed here as separate options, a school district can implement more than one in order to better meet the diverse needs of its student population, and, in fact, many in California do. A variety of programs may also be offered at the school level. For example, a bilingual alternative, such as dual language instruction, may be one program in a school while an English-medium program, such as structured English immersion, may be another option for students (see http://www.cde.ca.gov/sp/el/er/). To accompany explanations of these program types, we include descriptions of actual school sites located in California and other states. The cases are illustrative only and are drawn from data collected over a range of years. Because of personnel changes and other factors, not all the program descriptions may be current, nor the results sustained.

Within the program models, English learners may take a combination of courses as they make progress in their academic language and content development. For example, most models offer ELD instruction organized around the English proficiency levels of the students. However, students may also spend part of their day in mainstream subject area classes (e.g., algebra taught in English), in sheltered content subjects (e.g., sheltered biology), and/or in bilingual subject area classes (e.g., world history taught through Spanish). If students are struggling with literacy and not making expected progress in the second language, then each of these program models should be augmented with specialized intervention courses, such as one focused on reading across the content areas.

How to assign English learners within these programs and courses is still a question that most districts and schools answer according to the needs of their students, their program goals, and resources. We do not yet have empirical evidence as to whether English learners should be grouped homogeneously in sheltered courses or whether

287

they should be mixed with former ELs and/or EOs. Sheltered instruction has been used in both of these types of settings. We acknowledge that each option for grouping students within courses is associated with advantages and disadvantages that seem to be related to pedagogical, linguistic, and sociocultural aspects of learning. We have anecdotal evidence that a wide range of proficiency levels in an English-medium course (e.g., beginners, intermediate, and advanced English learners plus native speakers of English) is not conducive to effective teaching and learning.

When a program is being implemented, several steps should be considered or in place (Short and Fitzsimmons 2007). A key area to address at the start is the course scheduling for students, particularly at the secondary level. While sheltered instruction provides access to core curriculum, we must ensure students are eligible for the credits needed to graduate from high school by having content-certified teachers and receiving standards-based curricula. It is critical to involve the guidance counselors in the process so they schedule English learners appropriately, with teachers trained in sheltered strategies, not just with teachers whose classes have fewer students and thus more available desk space.

The more-successful programs for English learners provide flexible pathways for students, through the program and into regular curriculum (Short and Fitzsimmons 2007). The key is to make sure that the program articulates smoothly with the mainstream program to maximize its effectiveness and ease the students' transition when they exit the language support program and have a full schedule in the mainstream classes. Moreover, making explicit a clear timeline and set of courses that will lead to graduation may help reduce the dropout rate of older English learners.

Another consideration is how to extend the students' time for learning. Adolescent English learners have more to learn in less time than younger English learners or native English-speaking adolescents. One effective strategy to address this situation is to provide more instructional time either through an extended school year calendar or extended hours of the school day. Use of Saturday and after-school programs as well as summer courses can help speed the acquisition of academic English and content knowledge.

Sheltered content instruction can be an effective approach for beginning English learners, but they may need additional support to complete a grade-level curriculum in one school year. In some instances, schools have created two-year courses for beginners who are grouped heterogeneously, especially for subjects such as U.S. history that have a heavy language load and for which many students have little background knowledge. In other cases, beginners participate in an adjunct course as part of their regular schedule, which acts like a tutorial and helps them with the course work in

the core content classes. For students with literacy in their primary language, primary language support may be utilized, as is the case with the California A–G courses (which refers to University of California and California State University subject-area admission requirements) that are available online in Spanish at http://www.universityofcalifornia.edu/collegeprep/future.pdf.

Sheltered Instruction Programs

Sheltered instruction programs are designed to prepare language-minority students to achieve high standards in core content courses. Teachers of sheltered instruction use English as the medium of instruction to teach academic subjects. Sheltered instruction is grounded in the understanding that learners can acquire content knowledge, concepts, and skills at the same time that they improve their English language skills. In a sheltered program, students generally have a schedule with a set of sheltered courses (e.g., sheltered algebra, sheltered earth science, sheltered U.S. history) in addition to ELD classes (http://www.cde.ca.gov/sp/el/er/). The content area teachers are trained in sheltered instruction and/or have an authorization to teach English learners in addition to their content area certification. These teachers use a variety of ESL techniques and pay close attention to language as used in the content area in order to teach the subject matter to the students. They promote oral interaction and meaningful activities. Each sheltered course (e.g., sheltered biology) should have specially developed curricula that identify the language goals of the subject area as well as strategies and techniques to help students develop appropriate academic literacy skills while covering state standards of learning. In strong programs, sheltered content courses are complemented by content-based ESL classes where content vocabulary and academic tasks are taught and practiced in a complementary fashion (Echevarria, Short, and Vogt 2008).

> **Sheltered instruction is grounded in the understanding that learners can acquire content knowledge, concepts, and skills at the same time that they improve their English language skills.**

Sheltered programs designed for students who are learning English as a new language would also include language-minority students with disabilities who are English learners. Theoretically, these learners would be represented in school at the same rate as native English-speaking students with disabilities. It is estimated that between 5 and 10 percent of school-age children have learning disabilities (http://www.cec.sped.org). However, in some schools, the characteristics of the normal second-language acquisition process are mistaken for more serious learning problems (Klingner, Artiles, and Barletta 2006). To do well in class, English learners with disabilities require the type of effective instruction described previously. When they do not understand the teacher's instruction or what is expected in order complete an assignment, or they do not yet have the English proficiency to complete work, they cannot demonstrate their knowledge or perform to their ability.

Students with learning disabilities benefit from inclusion in general education classes so that they are exposed to the same core curriculum and standards as their grade-level peers (Smith 2005). Individual accommodations may be necessary for these students to meet academic standards and do well on tests but, like most students, they respond best to high-quality instruction (Bryant, Smith, and Bryant 2007). We should not lose sight of that reality: solid instruction that is understandable and meaningful to students is highly effective. When the components of effective instruction are implemented to a high degree, all students achieve better academically, including students with disabilities, English learners, and typically developing speakers of English (Echevarria 1995; Short and Echevarria 2007).

Lela Alston Elementary School, Phoenix, Arizona

One school that has made effective instruction for English learners a priority is Lela Alston Elementary School in Phoenix, Arizona. The teachers at Alston Elementary School provide high-quality instruction to their students, with impressive results. In 2002, the principal agreed to implement a schoolwide sheltered program and used a Title III grant to fund SIOP Model[TR] training for every teacher at the school. Of the 450 K-3 students, 97 percent qualified for free/reduced lunch, 75 percent were categorized as LEP, and 10 percent were identified for special education services. All students—English learners and those with disabilities—are included in general education classes.

To ensure a high-quality program, several features were put into practice. First, the principal and staff committed to ongoing professional development for two years (2002-03, 2003-04) focusing on approximately one SIOP component per quarter. Second, coaches worked with grade-level teacher teams and modeled lessons in teachers' classrooms. Training sessions were augmented with administrative support. For example, the principal conducted classroom walk-throughs every day and checked that content and language objectives were posted; each staff meeting dedicated a few minutes to some SIOP-related presentation; and the formal observations included feedback on the SIOP protocol.

Since the special education teachers were also trained to use the SIOP Model[TR], team teaching was facilitated. The special education teachers at Alston team-teach with the general education teachers for certain subject areas. For example, in a first-grade class, the special education teacher would team-teach during reading and math each day, making sure that students with disabilities receive the individual attention needed to meet the goals designated on their IEPs. In every class, students with disabilities, including those who are English learners, are a part of the class fabric. To quote the special education teacher, "The hands-on, the small-group interaction—all of the components really lend themselves to making sure all the special education students are active. So I don't need to be there [in the class] to know that they are engaged, to know that they are a part of the classroom. A lot of times when you go into a classroom you can't tell who the special education students are because they are always in a group with other students who can help. It's been really neat to see. I don't think some of our special education students know that they are in special education because they're so involved in everything."

The Arizona Instrument for Measuring Standards (AIMS) is the statewide standardized assessment in Arizona. Since implementation of the SIOP Model[TR] at Alston School, students' scores improved steadily over three years and Alston students outperformed similar students at three neighboring elementary schools in reading, writing, and math. Perhaps most significant, of the third-grade students who had been in SIOP classes since kindergarten, 86 percent performed at or above grade level on the AIMS assessment. (See Table 5.4.)

Table 5.4. AIMS Scores on Spring 2005 Assessment of Third-Grade Students Who Began Kindergarten at Alston School in 2001

Above Grade Level	36%
At Grade Level	50%
Below Grade Level	14%

Hoover High School, San Diego, California

In the late 1990s, Hoover High School was ranked as the lowest-performing school in San Diego by the state's accountability measures. Like many large, urban Title I high schools with significant numbers of language-minority students (over 70 percent of the student population), Hoover struggled with high teacher turnover, low student graduation rates, and poor student performance on state tests. In 1999, the school embarked on its Literacy Staff Development Plan as a member of San Diego State University/City Heights Education Collaborative Partnership and focused on school reform. Hoover's score on the California Academic Performance Index (API) in 1999 was 444 out of 1000. In 2005, it was 578. It had improved 134 points on the state scale and had exceeded state growth benchmarks for several years in a row. Although the API score had not yet reached the recommended level for high schools, which is 800, Hoover demonstrated strong advancement.

The Hoover community accomplished this improvement through a sustained, mandatory, multiyear, and consistent professional development program. Seven strategies for literacy development and a strong support system were in place for the students. Hoover staff and San Diego State University partners designed and implemented the staff development and student assessment practices to guide and increase academic literacy among their adolescent English learners. The SIOP Model[TR] was incorporated into content area instruction for them.

The program for English learners at Hoover consisted of academic literacy-focused ESL and sheltered content classes. Hoover operated on a quarter system for its block schedule so that each student took four classes per quarter, resulting in 16 classes a year. Six levels of ESL classes offered at Hoover could be completed in three years (ESL 1–2, 3–4, 5–6). Students progressed through beginning ESL 1–2 reading, writing, and social studies courses, plus a mathematics course, to advanced ESL 5–6 language arts, literature, and sheltered science and history courses. Four quarters of ESL social studies were offered in the first four levels of language development (ESL Social Studies 1–4). Sheltered history and science were offered when students were in the last two levels of ESL (5–6). All of the classes were aligned to the *English-Language Arts Content Standards* (1998) and *English Language DevelopmentStandards* (2002). Four classes were offered for each level: one reading class, one writing class, one ESL class, and one literature class. Two classes for each of the three ESL levels were offered per quarter. Thus, students were able to take at least two of their four class periods each day in ESL programming. The course schedules were designed so that ELs at the same level had at least two of four courses with the same classmates per day. This practice provided a support system for these students and helped teachers to know and monitor the students better.

The seven literacy development instructional strategies (Fisher and Frey 2004) used across the curriculum were:

- ⊙ Anticipatory activities
- ⊙ Read-aloud/shared reading
- ⊙ Structured notetaking and note making
- ⊙ Reciprocal teaching
- ⊙ Graphic organizers
- ⊙ Vocabulary instruction
- ⊙ Writing-to-learn prompts

By introducing students to those strategies in ninth grade and using them across the curriculum and up the grade levels, all teachers established a common language and set of strategies for all students. This joint understanding enhanced the implementation process and contributed to successful reforms that took place at Hoover.

Newcomer Programs

Newcomer programs educate recent immigrant students—who have no or very limited English and who often have had limited formal education in their native countries—in a special academic environment for a limited period of time (Short and Boyson 2004). They are more typically found at middle and high school levels because older English learners who are recent immigrants are often at risk of educational failure or early dropout because of underdeveloped primary language literacy skills, limited English skills, and/or weak academic skills. Thus their needs often surpass the resources in ESL or bilingual programs (Francis et al. 2006; Short and Boyson 2004). Specifically they need academic skill development in the core curriculum so they can participate in mainstream classes. Most newcomer programs provide a welcoming environment to immigrant students and their families and help them acculturate to their new school and community.

Common features among newcomer programs include:

(1) distinct, intensive courses to integrate students into American life and accelerate or fill gaps in their educational backgrounds;

(2) specialized instructional strategies to address literacy because many students become literate for the first time in these programs, yet they are beyond the normal age for initial literacy instruction;

(3) enrollment lengths determined by individual students' needs, usually one to three semesters; and

(4) hand-picked staff members who have ESL endorsements and/or long-term professional development in working with adolescent English learners (Short and Boyson 2004).

In 2000-01, there were over 195 middle and high school newcomer program sites in 29 states plus the District of Columbia (Boyson and Short 2003). The newcomer sites may be located as a program-within-a-school or at a separate site. Almost 75 percent of those programs were established since 1990, reflecting changing demographics and the needs of the newcomer students. The accountability system of NCLB has had a dampening effect on self-contained newcomer *schools*, however, because as the sole student population within such a school, it is difficult for the newcomer students to reach the Adequate Yearly Progress (AYP) benchmarks, given their student-level characteristics when they enter the program. Nonetheless, some newcomer schools enroll students for all four years of high school, leading students to graduation and a high school diploma. An example of such a school is the International Schools Network (Short and Boyson 2004).

Newcomer sites may offer one program or a combination of language-support programs: English as a second language, bilingual, or sheltered instruction. Some provide native-language literacy classes as well. The Short and Boyson (2004) study found that 100 percent of the programs offered ELD courses, 89 percent offered at least one sheltered content course, and 55 percent offered at least one course in the students' primary language. Some content courses were designed to fill in gaps in the newcomer English learners' educational background (e.g., a sheltered U.S. history course, a Spanish pre-algebra course), and others were designed to give these students at the lowest levels of English proficiency more time to master grade-level content. Approximately 25 percent of the programs operated for the equivalent of a half day or less and limited the number and type of course offerings available to newcomer English learners.

The International Academy—LEAP, St. Paul, Minnesota

For many years, a school district in St. Paul, Minnesota, enrolled a large number of older, limited-English-proficient immigrant and refugee students. In 1994, the district decided to develop a specialized program to serve students who entered school after age fifteen (Dufresne and Hall 1997). Many of those students failed to meet graduation requirements and dropped out or became too old to remain in school. There was also little socialization between those students and native speakers of English. Consequently, the LEAP English Academy was established as a four-year, ungraded high school program that operated primarily with state funds. (It is now known as The International Academy—LEAP High School.)

The LEAP Academy is open to older students (ages sixteen through twenty-six) who have been in the U.S. for two years or less and who are unlikely to graduate from a traditional high school. The majority of students have been eighteen, nineteen, and twenty years old. The program serves more than 200 students who represent 15 or more countries and speak 15–19 different languages.

The program aims to help the students acquire a high school diploma; prepare for vocational training, college, or work; and improve English-language proficiency. The program is designed as an ESL program with native-language support and offers the courses necessary for a diploma, adapting the content to the language needs of the students. The course schedule offers classes for different levels of English and sheltered content classes in the core content areas. These sheltered courses are coupled with bilingual tutoring and support in Somali, Hmong, Russian, Spanish, Arabic, Lao, and

Vietnamese. Teachers devote considerable instructional time to developing students' academic vocabulary skills and background knowledge in the content areas. The program also includes cultural orientation activities.

The program prepares students for work by developing their computer and vocational skills and providing career exploration. The process is facilitated by the program's location—in the same building as the Center for Employment Training and the Gateway program for chemically dependent youth. The two programs help newcomer students find jobs or internships and allowed LEAP staff to set up tutoring situations: volunteer peer tutors from these two programs, who are native speakers of English but not necessarily bilingual, participate in structured conversations with the newcomers to help improve their English skills.

The LEAP Academy provides a flexible schedule. Mature, highly able students may earn more credits over a shorter period of time than they could in ordinary high schools because of independent study options, extended schedules, and cooperative arrangements with adult education programs, the St. Paul Technical College, and nearby community colleges. Those students are usually college-bound and need to accelerate their English proficiency. Many students remain at the school for their high school career and graduate with a high school diploma when they pass the Minnesota basic standards test. Some of the younger students make a transition to a traditional high school, while some older students may make a transition directly to a vocational program.

General Education Classes

A growing number of schools have large numbers of English learners as well as students who have been redesignated as fluent-English-proficient (FEP) and often enroll them in general education classes with teachers who have professional preparation for teaching culturally and linguistically diverse students. In California, the law requires these teachers to hold a specialized authorization to instruct English learners. Typically, classes consist of a mix of student who are native speakers of English, students who have been redesignated as FEP for many months or years, students who have been recently redesignated as FEP, and those students who are labeled English learners. Students in each of theses categories may have a range of academic proficiency levels.

It is important in these settings that teachers receive information such as English learners' date of arrival in the U.S., language proficiency level, and literacy level. In general education classes, teachers differentiate instruction for the various levels of English and literacy represented (Gibson and Hasbrouck 2008). Students are grouped strategically: sometimes students with similar abilities work together, and other times students proficient in English are used as language models for English learners (Tompkins 2006). Partner and group work also facilitate differentiation as students work at their own level with more-proficient students assisting by articulating their peers' ideas (Gibson and Hasbrouck 2008). Effective differentiation, as described here, is a challenge for teachers; in practice, many teachers make minimal attempts at differentiating lessons by using graphic organizers or reinforcing a few vocabulary words (Tomlinson 2001). As well intended as they may be, these efforts are not sufficient to meet the individual academic needs of English learners.

Hill Classical Middle School, Long Beach, California

At Hill Classical Middle School in Long Beach, California, each teacher is authorized to teach English learners. Although only about 7 percent of the 1,100 students are English learners, over 50 percent have been redesignated as FEP. Many FEP students continue to require language support and instructional scaffolds even though they have met the criteria for being considered fluent in English. Table 5.5 shows the school's demographics, illustrating its diversity.

Table 5.5. Hill Classical Middle School Demographics

Subgroup	Total Enrollment (percent)	Subgroup	Total Enrollment (percent)
African American	13.5	White	12.0
Native American or Alaskan Native	0.2		
Asian	14.1	Socioeconomically disadvantaged	73.7
Filipino	1.7	Students with disabilities	7.0
Hispanic or Latino	57.9	English learners	8.2
Pacific Islander	0.5	Redesignated FEP	52.4

The distinction "classical" is given to the school because of the rigorous academic requirements: students maintain a 2.0 grade point average, taking a minimum of one year of foreign language and/or fine arts and one semester of technology. Hill has met AYP benchmarks each year since 2000-01. Several factors contribute to the school's success:

⊙ *Student information.* Teachers at Hill receive information about students' language designation directly on their class lists. In this way, teachers are aware of each student's proficiency level at a glance and can form groups or differentiate instruction accordingly.

- ⊙ *Professional development.* It is ongoing and based on needs of the staff. Topics have included the matching of content with curriculum standards, test data analysis, and writing skills. Staff members at Hill have participated in intensive SIOP professional development as part of two research projects.

- ⊙ *Emphasis on language.* Development of academic language is a priority in all content areas.

- ⊙ *Data-driven decisions.* The entire school faculty studies student achievement in the area of expository writing during faculty meeting time, and departments analyze their content area's common assessments to continuously improve their instruction during department meetings. After students take certain exams, teachers review how the students performed by looking closely at item-analysis reports.

- ⊙ *Shared understanding.* Site-based professional development encourages teachers to post objectives for students to see. In addition, class work and homework assignments are also posted. In this way, classes have similar routines so students are familiar with procedures.

Professional Development

Professional development is a critical component of any program design or instructional practice that seeks to provide English learners with access to the core curriculum. The importance of ongoing professional development for educators—teachers and administrators alike—is widely recognized as a way to improve the quality of instructional programs. The teacher—student instructional relationship is paramount in terms of students' academic achievement (Schmoker 2006), and effective teaching rarely happens in isolation. Through professional development teachers expand their repertoire of skills and practices, hone their existing skills, and remain current on educational topics and issues. For administrators, ongoing professional development about best practices in teaching improves their ability to provide instructional leadership and support to teachers.

> **Although teacher development may begin at the collegiate level, it is an ongoing process and should include opportunities for learning throughout the span of a teacher's career.**

Further, there is a growing awareness that the development of a skilled, effective teacher is a process that occurs over time rather than as the result of having completed specific college or university course work. Although teacher development may begin at the collegiate level, it is an ongoing process and should include opportunities

297

for learning throughout the span of a teacher's career (Darling-Hammond 2000; Darling-Hammond et al. 2005).

The process of ongoing skill development for teachers has become acute for educating English learners. Being held accountable for student achievement has spurred a tremendous increase in professional development around best practices for teaching English learners. The troubling academic performance of English learners, delineated earlier, requires that we shift from what we have been offering these students to an improved model of instruction. This necessary shift needs to take place across the entire teacher-preparation process, starting with teacher-education courses (preservice) and continuing with induction and staff development (in-service) programs (Darling-Hammond 2006).

Preservice Programs

As the number of English learners in schools has continued to grow, many universities across the U.S. have responded by adding to their programs course work that specifically addresses issues surrounding the education of English learners. However, as mentioned earlier in this chapter, only four states require some degree of course work for preservice teachers to receive teaching certification.

In California, where approximately 25 percent of all children enrolled in school are designated as English learners, priority is placed on preparing teachers to work effectively with these students. Since 1976, teachers of English learners have been required to have English learner authorization and at present, all California multiple- and single-subject teacher-preparation programs are required to include an authorization for every prospective teacher to teach English learners (Diaz-Rico and Weed 2006). Most recently, these requirements were extended to include experienced teachers and out-of-state teachers who now must attain English learner authorization through the California Teachers of English Learners program course work or by examination. Those programs and requirements show consideration for English learners' needs.

The specific content of courses that meet English learner authorization standards varies; however, for the instructional component of authorization, the SIOP Model[TR] provides concrete examples of ways that teachers can make content accessible for English learners. It also emphasizes the importance of English language development in every lesson.

Although teacher-education programs are to be commended for responding to the changing face of education, a concern remains that many faculty members have not had sufficient professional preparation or experience in working with culturally and

linguistically diverse populations. A deep understanding of second-language acquisition, cultural diversity, and other issues associated with English learners is necessary for faculty to be most effective in teacher preparation.

In-service Staff Development

As mentioned previously, continual professional development of teachers is needed for improved teacher practice and student achievement. Although some professional development may take the form of in-service or workshops given by external experts, teachers are far more likely to implement new instructional approaches when there are follow-up activities and collaboration around issues of implementation at their school sites. Considerable research (Cushman 1998; Hord 1997; Riel and Fulton 2001; Stigler and Hiebert 1999; Weiss and Pasley 2006) shows that professional learning communities provide teachers with an opportunity to engage in a variety of important collaborative activities that extend learning and improve practice in the shared context of their school setting.

Effective professional development incorporates essential elements that are based on research (Joyce and Showers 1996; National Staff Development Council 2001; Newmann, King, and Youngs 2001; Valli and Hawley 2002). We have adapted them to focus on teachers of English learners and to illustrate how the SIOP Model[TR] can facilitate implementation of these essential elements.

1. *Theoretical knowledge.* Effective professional development provides opportunities for participants to develop an understanding of the theoretical underpinnings of instruction for English learners, including why various techniques, strategies, and practices are important for them. In addition, a theoretical understanding of the second-language acquisition process expands teachers' knowledge base as they work with students who are acquiring English while they are learning content. By understanding the theoretical base of the SIOP Model[TR], teachers become aware that it is more than "just good teaching"—it addresses the unique second-language needs of English learners.

2. *Specific strategies.* Valli and Hawley (2002) suggest that "professional development should focus on the specific content that students are expected to learn, problems students might confront in learning the content, and instructional strategies that address anticipated problems or issues" (p. 87). It is essential that a teacher anticipate which aspects of a lesson will be difficult for English learners and consistently use those strategies that have been shown to make instruction more understandable for them. The SIOP Model[TR] offers a set of specific, well-defined features that can be used consistently by all teachers at

a school site. The success of using a set of agreed-upon strategies schoolwide has been documented (Echevarria, Short, and Vogt 2008; Fisher, Frey, and Williams 2002) When students are familiar with teachers' practices and lesson routines, they can concentrate more on learning the content (Fisher and Frey 2007).

3. *Lesson planning.* Effective professional development is primarily school-based, providing teachers with opportunities to plan lessons or instructional units collaboratively. Through those planning sessions, teachers engage in inquiry around their practice and students' needs, assessing the impact of lessons on student learning. When lessons are planned collaboratively, then implemented, analyzed, and revised, the quality of the lessons improves, including more higher-level thinking and application skills (Chrispeels 2003).

4. *Modeling.* Teachers benefit from opportunities to observe classrooms that are organized for effective teaching of English learners. Demonstration lessons by teachers or coaches show how to implement the features of high-quality teaching. Initially, video examples of how the SIOP Model[TR] looks in a classroom setting may be used as a school begins the process of enhancing instruction for English learners.

5. *Practice.* Participants practice implementing the features of effective instruction with guidance and support. Typically, after teachers understand the SIOP Model[TR], they plan SIOP lessons collaboratively with peers and a more experienced teacher, coach, or administrator. Also, teachers may practice by modeling SIOP lessons for one another and receive constructive feedback on the lesson.

6. *Feedback and in-class coaching.* Lessons are observed by coaches or teachers who are provided with constructive feedback on the delivery. The SIOP protocol is especially useful for this part of the professional development process. Teachers may learn one component at a time, plan lessons focused on that component, and practice implementing its features. The protocol becomes a feedback form for assisting and supporting high-quality implementation of the SIOP features.

7. *Independent application and analysis.* After the initial process of implementation, teachers begin to use these practices, usually through independent lesson planning and teaching. In collaborative groups with colleagues, teachers evaluate their lessons and analyze the features, adjusting and refining as needed. They may revisit and relearn a feature if necessary.

8. *Program coherence.* Program coherence means "speaking the same language,"

having consistency in the message and practices and agreed-upon under-standing (Garet et al. 2001; Goldenberg 2004). Teachers and administrators reported that program coherence facilitated schoolwide implementation (Echevarria, Short, and Vogt 2008). In the case of the SIOP Model[TR], it is critical that those responsible for delivering professional development emphasize the importance of fidelity to the model. Exposing teachers only to certain components or features renders the model ineffective. The research demonstrating the model's effectiveness, reliability, and validity was based on the eight components and 30 features in combination, not just preferred components or features.

In a study of SIOP implementation, we found that many of these essential elements were part of SIOP professional development efforts around the U.S. and had a positive effect on student achievement (Echevarria, Short, and Vogt 2008). In these settings teachers engaged in activities such as analyzing their lessons by:

(1) reflecting on specific SIOP components or by videotaping the lesson and using the SIOP protocol for analysis;

(2) discussing SIOP features that needed more focused attention; and

(3) refining lesson plans.

High-quality SIOP professional development was influenced by some factors, including how well the trainer understood the SIOP Model[TR] and issues of second-language acquisition; the quality and duration of follow-up support; the level of collaboration teachers had with other teachers and leaders; the level of administrative support; the level of resources allocated for SIOP implementation (e.g., release time, materials, and coaching); and the level of classroom management (Echevarria, Short, and Vogt 2008).

Conclusion

The underachievement of English learners on state and national assessments indicates it is not enough for teachers to rely on theoretical models of best practice or to implement a few strategies from ESL methodologies, such as showing visual aids or slowing down the rate of speech, if academic success is the goal. In this chapter, we have made the case that those strategies may help students gain access to some content concepts, but it is clear that teachers need a comprehensive model of instruction for lesson planning, delivery, and reflection. Further, without systematic language development, students never develop the requisite academic literacy skills needed for success in mainstream classes, for meeting content standards, and for passing standardized assessments in their second language.

One of the strengths of the SIOP Model[TR] is that it provides a way for teachers to organize their instructional practices so that features of effective instruction are present in every lesson. The comprehensive nature of the model allows for teachers to include favored practices from their own repertoire but also reminds them of important features that may be overlooked. By following the model, lessons will include the features of instruction that we know benefit students, and teachers will implement the features systematically, providing high-quality instruction to their students.

The main points of this chapter are as follows:

- ⊙ In current practice, the goals of sheltered instruction are twofold:

    (1) to provide access to the core curriculum by teaching in a way that is meaningful and understandable for English learners, and

    (2) to develop English language proficiency, especially academic English, through sheltered lessons. Teachers experienced in sheltered instruction recognize that these students are learning a new language while learning new concepts, information, and skills; and the teachers make accommodations for the students' learning.

- ⊙ To develop English at a level that will help English learners be successful in school, teachers need to pay attention to language development throughout the day in all content classes (Echevarria, Vogt, and Short 2008), not only during a designated period of ELD.

- ⊙ The SIOP Model[TR] is presented as an approach to sheltered content instruction that teachers of English learners can use in California. It has an extensive research base and offers a comprehensive model of instruction that allows for systematic, consistent implementation of the instructional features that improve achievement for English learners. The SIOP protocol bridges the knowing–doing gap by providing a concrete description of each instructional feature.

- ⊙ Many program options are available for English learners. All of them should incorporate sheltered content instruction whenever English learners are studying content through a language they are learning at the same time.

- ⊙ English learners at all proficiency levels can participate in sheltered content instruction. Some newcomer and beginning-level students may need extended time for mastering grade-level curricula (e.g., through a two-year course, through an adjunct period during the day).

- ⊙ We do not yet have empirical evidence as to whether English learners should be grouped homogeneously in sheltered courses or whether they should be mixed

with former English learners and/or English-only students. However, teachers report that a wide range of proficiency levels in a course (e.g., beginners, intermediate, and advanced English learners together with native speakers of English) is not conducive to effective teaching and learning.

⊙ High-quality professional development can lead to instruction for English learners that boosts their achievement when teachers learn how to make content accessible for these students and how to promote the English learners' academic language development.

In conclusion, we submit that a comprehensive model of sheltered instruction is the most practical solution to teaching grade-level, standards-based, core content lessons to English learners when they are instructed through their new language.

References

August, Diane, and Kenji Hakuta, eds. 1997. *Improving schooling for language minority children: A research agenda.* Washington, DC: National Academy Press.

August, Diane, and Tim Shanahan, eds. 2006. *Developing literacy in second-language learners: A report of the National Literacy Panel on Language-Minority Children and Youth.* Mahwah, NJ: Erlbaum.

Bailey, Alison, ed. 2007. *The language demands of school: Putting academic English to the test.* New Haven, CT: Yale University Press.

Bailey, Alison, and Frances Butler. 2007. A conceptual framework of academic English language for broad application to education. In *The language demands of school: Putting academic English to the test,* ed. Alison Bailey. New Haven, CT: Yale University Press.

Biancarosa, Gina, and Catherine Snow. 2004. *Reading next: A vision for action and research in middle and high school literacy.* Report to the Carnegie Corporation of New York. Washington, DC: Alliance for Excellent Education.

Biemiller, Andrew. 2001. Teaching vocabulary: Early, direct, and sequential. *American Educator* 25(1) (Spring): 24–28.

Boyson, Beverly A., and Deborah Short. 2003. *Secondary school newcomer programs in the United States.* Research Report No. 12. Santa Cruz: Center for Research in Education, Diversity, and Excellence (CREDE), University of California.

Bryant, D., D. Smith, and B. Bryant. 2007. *Teaching students with special needs in inclusive classrooms.* Boston: Allyn & Bacon.

California Department of Education. 2008. Language census on student demographics, English learners. http://dq.cde.ca.gov/dataquest (accessed on July 1, 2008.)

Cantoni-Harvey, Gina. 1987. *Content-area language instruction: Approaches and strategies.* Reading, MA: Addison-Wesley.

Carlo, Maria, Diane August, Barry McLaughlin, Catherine Snow, Cindy Dressler, David Lippman, Teresa Lively, and Claire White. 2004. Closing the gap: Addressing the vocabulary needs of English language learners in bilingual and mainstream classrooms. *Reading Research Quarterly* 39(2): 188–215.

Center for Applied Linguistics. 2007. *Academic literacy through sheltered instruction for secondary English language learners.* Final Report to the Carnegie Corporation of New York. Washington, DC: Center for Applied Linguistics.

Chamot, Anna Uhl, Marsha Dale, J. Michael O'Malley, and George Spanos. 1992. Learning and problem-solving strategies of ESL students. *Bilingual Research Journal* 16(3&4): 1–34.

Chamot, Anna Uhl, and J. Michael O'Malley. 1987. The cognitive academic language learning approach: A bridge to the mainstream. *TESOL Quarterly* 21(2): 227–49.

Chamot, Anna Uhl. and J. Michael O'Malley. 1994. *The CALLA handbook.* 2nd ed. Reading, MA: Addison-Wesley.

Chrispeels, Janet. 2003. Improving instruction through teacher collaboration in grade-level meetings. *University of California Linguistic Minority Research Institute Newsletter* 12(2): 1–2.

The class of 2000 final longitudinal report: A three year follow-up study. 2004. New York: New York City Department of Education, Division of Assessment and Accountability.

Collier, Virginia P. 1987. Age and rate of acquisition of second language for academic purposes. *TESOL Quarterly* 21(4): 617–41.

Commission on Teacher Credentialing. Glossary of Credential Terms. http://www.ctc.ca.gov/glossary/glossary.html (accessed October 9, 2007.)

Crandall, JoAnn. 1993. Content-centered learning in the United States. *Annual Review of Applied Linguistics* 13: 111–26.

Crawford, Alan N. 2003. Communicative approaches to second language acquisition: The bridge to second-language literacy. In *English learners: Reaching the highest level of English literacy,* ed. Gilbert Garcia. Newark, DE: International Reading Association.

Cummins, James. 2006. How long does it take an English learner to become proficient in a second language? *In English language learners at school: A guide for administrators,* ed. E. Hamayan and R. Freeman, 59–61. Philadelphia: Caslon Publishing.

Cummins, Jim. 2000. *Language, power and pedagogy.* Clevedon, England: Multilingual Matters.

Cushman, Kathleen. 1998. *How friends can be critical as schools make essential changes.* Oxon Hill, MD: Coalition of Essential Schools.

Darling-Hammond, Linda. 2006. Securing the right to learn: Policy and practice for powerful teaching and learning. *Educational Researcher* 35(7): 13–24.

Darling-Hammond, Linda. 2000. Teacher quality and student achievement. *Educational Policy Analysis Archives* 8(1).

Darling-Hammond, Linda, D. Holtzman, S. J. Gatlin, and J. Vasquez Heilig. 2005. *Does teacher preparation matter? Evidence about teacher certification, teach for America, and teacher effectiveness.* Palo Alto: Stanford University.

DeLeeuw, Howard. 2008. *English language learners in Washington State.* Executive Summary. Report to the Washington State Board of Education, Olympia, Washington.

Diaz-Rico, Lynne, and Kathryn Weed. 2006. *The crosscultural, language, and academic development handbook.* Boston, MA: Allyn & Bacon.

Dufresne, J., and S. Hall. 1997. LEAP English Academy: An alternative high school for newcomers to the United States. *MINNE-WI TESOL Journal* 14: 1–17.

Dutro, Susana, and Carrol Moran. 2003. Rethinking English language instruction: An architectural approach. In *English learners: Reaching the highest level of English literacy,* ed. Gilbert Garcia, 227–58. Newark, DE: International Reading Association.

Echevarria, Jana. 1998. *A model of sheltered instruction for English language learners.* Paper presented at the conference for the Division on Diversity of the Council for Exceptional Children, Washington, DC.

Echevarria, Jana. 1995. Interactive reading instruction: A comparison of proximal and distal effects of instructional conversations. *Exceptional Children* 61(6): 536–52.

Echevarria, Jana, and Anne Graves. 2007. *Sheltered content instruction: Teaching English language learners with diverse abilities.* 3rd ed. Boston: Allyn & Bacon.

Echevarria, Jana, and Deborah Short. 2004. Using multiple perspectives in observations of diverse classrooms: The sheltered instruction observation protocol (SIOP). In *Observational research in U.S. classrooms: New approaches for understanding cultural and linguistic diversity,* ed. Hersh Waxman, Roland Tharp, and R. Soleste Hilberg. Boston: Cambridge University Press.

Echevarria, Jana, Deborah Short, and Kristen Powers. 2006. School reform and standards-based education: An instructional model for English language learners. *Journal of Educational Research* 99(4): 195–211.

Echevarria, Jana, Deborah Short, and MaryEllen Vogt. 2008. *Implementing the SIOP model through effective professional development and coaching.* Boston: Pearson Allyn & Bacon.

Echevarria, Jana, MaryEllen Vogt, and Deborah Short. 2007. *Making content comprehensible for English learners: The SIOP model.* 3rd ed. Boston: Pearson Allyn & Bacon.

Echevarria, Jana, MaryEllen Vogt, and Deborah Short. 2004. *Making content comprehensible for English learners: The SIOP model.* 2nd ed. Boston: Pearson Allyn & Bacon.

Echevarria, Jana, MaryEllen Vogt, and Deborah Short. 2000. *Making content comprehensible for English language learners: The SIOP model.* Needham Heights, MA: Allyn & Bacon.

English language arts content standards for California public schools, kindergarten through grade twelve. 1998. Sacramento: California Department of Education.

English language development standards for California public schools, kindergarten through grade twelve. 2002. Sacramento: California Department of Education.

ESL standards for preK–12 students. 1997. Alexandria, VA: Teachers of English to Speakers of Other Languages.

Faltis, Christian, and Maria Arias. 1993. Speakers of languages other than English in the secondary school: Accomplishments and struggles. *Peabody Journal of Education* 69(1): 6–27.

Fillmore, Lily Wong, and Catherine Snow. 2002. What teachers need to know about language. In *What teachers need to know about language,* ed. Carolyn T. Adger, Catherine E. Snow, and Donna Christian, 7–53. McHenry, IL: Delta Systems and Center for Applied Linguistics.

Fisher, Douglas, and Nancy Frey. 2004. *Improving adolescent literacy: Strategies at work.* Upper Saddle River, NJ: Pearson/Merrill/Prentice Hall.

Fisher, Douglas, Nancy Frey, and Douglas Williams. 2002. Seven literacy strategies that work. *Educational Leadership* 60(3): 69–73.

Francis, David, Mabel Rivera, Nonie Lesaux, Michael Kieffer, and Hector Rivera. 2006. *Research-based recommendations for serving adolescent newcomers.* Portsmouth, NH: RMC Research Corporation, Center on Instruction.

Garcia, Gilbert, ed. 2003. *English learners: Reaching the highest level of English literacy,* 2–33. Newark, DE: International Reading Association.

Gandara, Patricia, Rachel Moran, and Eugene Garcia. 2004. Legacy of Brown: Lau and language policy in the United States. In *Review of Research in Education* 28: 27–46.

Garet, Michael. S., Andrew Porter, Laura Desimone, Beatrice. F. Birman, and Kwang S. Yoon. 2001. What makes professional development effective? Results from a national sample of teachers. *American Educational Research Journal* 38: 915–45.

Genesee, Fred, ed. 1999. Program alternatives for linguistically diverse students. *Educational Practice Report* No. 1. Santa Cruz, CA, and Washington, DC: Center for Research on Education, Diversity & Excellence.

Genesee, Fred, Kathryn Lindholm-Leary, William Saunders, and Donna Christian. 2006. *Educating English language learners: A synthesis of research evidence.* New York: Cambridge University Press.

Gersten, Russell, Scott Baker, Timothy Shanahan, Sylvia Linan-Thompson, Penny Collins, and Robin Scarcella. 2007. *Effective literacy and English language instruction for English learners in the elementary grades: A practice guide.* (NCEE 2007-4011). Washington, DC: National Center for Education Evaluation and Regional Assistance, Institute of Education Sciences, U.S. Department of Education. http://ies.ed.gov/ncee.

Gibbons, Paula. 2002. *Scaffolding language, scaffolding learning.* Portsmouth, NH: Heinemann.

Gibson, V., and Jan Hasbrouck. 2008. Differentiated instruction: Grouping for success. New York: McGraw-Hill.

Goldenberg, Claude. 2008. Teaching English language learners: What research does—and does not—say. *American Educator* 32(2): 8–23, 42–44.

Goldenberg, Claude. 2006. Improving achievement for English learners: What research tells us. *Education Week* (July 26).

Goldenberg, Claude. 2004. *Successful school change: Creating settings to improve teaching and learning.* New York: Teachers College Press.

Grigg, Wendy S., Mary C. Daane, Ying Jin, and Jay R. Campbell. 2003. *The nation's report card: Reading 2002.* Jessup, MD: Education Publications Center.

Guarino, A. J., Jana Echevarria, Deborah Short, J. E. Schick, S. Forbes, and Robert Rueda. 2001. The sheltered instruction observation protocol. *Journal of Research in Education* 11(1): 138–40.Hawley, Willis. 2002. *The keys to effective schools.* Thousand Oaks, CA: Corwin Press.

Heritage, Margaret, Norma Silva, and Mary Pierce. 2007. Academic language: A view from the classroom. In *The language demands of school: Putting academic English to the test,* ed. Alison Bailey. New Haven, CT: Yale University Press.

Hord, Shirley M. 1997. *Professional learning communities: Communities of continuous inquiry and improvement.* Austin, TX: Southwest Educational Development Laboratory.

Joyce, Bruce, and Beverly Showers. 2002. *Student achievement through staff development.* 3rd ed. Alexandria, VA: Association for Supervision and Curriculum Development.

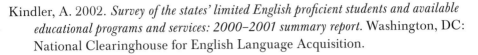
Kindler, A. 2002. *Survey of the states' limited English proficient students and available educational programs and services: 2000–2001 summary report.* Washington, DC: National Clearinghouse for English Language Acquisition.

Klingner, J., A. Artiles, and Laura Méndez Barletta. 2006. English language learners who struggle with reading: language acquisition or LD? *Journal of Learning Disabilities* 39(2): 108–28.

Kober, Nancy, Dalia Zabala, Naomi Chudowsky, Victor Chudowsky, Keith Gayler, and Jennifer McMurrer. 2006. *State high school exit exams: A challenging year.* Washington, DC: Center on Education Policy.

Krashen, Stephen. 1996. *Under attack: The case against bilingual education.* Culver City, CA: Language Education Associates.

Krashen, Stephen, and Grace McField. 2005. What works? Reviewing the latest evidence on bilingual education. *Language Learner* 1(2): 7–10, 34.

Lindholm-Leary, Kathryn, and Graciela Borsato. 2006. Academic achievement. In *Educating English language learners: A synthesis of research evidence,* ed. Fred Genesee, Kathryn Lindholm-Leary, William Saunders, and Donna Christian, 176–221. New York: Cambridge University Press.

Lucas, Sam R. 1999. *Tracking inequality: Stratification and mobility in American high schools.* New York: Teachers College Press.

McField, Grace. P. 2006. The many faces of structured English immersion. *International Journal of Foreign Language Teaching* X(X): 16–24.

McField, Grace. P. 2007. What is structured English immersion? Variations on a theme. *International Journal of Foreign Language Teaching* 3(3): 2–22.

McNeil, Linda M., Eileen Coppola, Judy Radigan, and Julian Vasquez Heilig. 2008. Avoidable losses: High-stakes accountability and the dropout crisis. *Education Policy Analysis Archives* 16(3): http://epaa.asu.edu/epaa/v16n3/ (accessed February 24, 2008.)

McNulty, Faith. 1999. *How whales walked into the sea.* New York: Scholastic.

Mohan, Bernard. A. 1986. *Language and content.* Reading, MA: Addison-Wesley.

Nagy, William. 1997. On the role of context in first- and second-language vocabulary learning. In *Vocabulary: Description, acquisition and pedagogy,* ed. N. Schmitt and M. McCarthy, 64–83. Cambridge: Cambridge University Press.

Nagy, William. E., and Judith A. Scott. 2000. Vocabulary processes. In *Handbook of reading research, Vol. III,* ed. Michael L. Kamil, Peter Mosenthal, P. David Pearson, and Rebecca Barr, 269–84. New York: Longman.

National Center for Education Statistics. 2002. *Schools and staffing survey, 1999–2000: Overview of the data for public, private, public charter, and Bureau of Indian Affairs elementary and secondary schools.* (NCES 2002-313). Washington, DC: U.S. Department of Education, National Center for Education Statistics.

National Institute of Child Health and Human Development. 2000. *Report of the National Reading Panel. Teaching children to read: An evidence-based assessment of the scientific research on reading and its implications for reading instruction.* NIH Publication No. 00-4769. Washington, DC: U.S. Government Printing Office.

National Staff Development Council. *NSDC standards for staff development.* 2001. http://www.nsdc.org/standards/index.cfm (accessed July 17, 2008.)

New Jersey State Department of Education. 2006. *Preliminary analysis of former limited English proficient students' scores on the New Jersey language arts and literacy exam, 2005–2006.* Trenton, NJ: State of New Jersey Department of Education, New Jersey State Assessment Office of Title I.

Newmann, Fred M., M. Bruce King, and Peter Youngs. 2001. Professional development that addresses school capacity: Lessons from urban elementary schools. *American Journal of Education* 108: 259–99.

Nieto, Sonia. 1999. *The light in their eyes: Creating multicultural learning communities.* New York: Teachers College Press.

Northcutt, Linda, and Daniel Watson. 1986. *Sheltered English teaching handbook.* Palm Springs, CA: Northcutt, Watson, Gonzales.

Olsen, Laurie. 2003. State debate exam polices for diplomas. *Education Week* XXII(36): 1, 22.

O'Malley, J. Michael, Anna Uhl Chamot, Gloria Stewner-Manzanares, Rocco Russo, and Lisa Kupper. 1985a. Learning strategy applications with students of English as a second language. *TESOL Quarterly* 19(3): 557–84.

O'Malley, J. Michael, Anna Uhl Chamot, Gloria Stewner-Manzanares, Rocco Russo, and Lisa Kupper. 1985b. Learning strategies used by beginning and intermediate ESL students. *Language Learning* 35(1): 21–46.

PreK–12 English language proficiency standards. 2006. Alexandria, VA: Teachers of English to Speakers of Other Languages, Inc.

Riches, Caroline, and Fred Genesee. 2006. Crosslinguistic and crossmodal issues. In *Educating English language learners: A synthesis of research evidence,* ed. Fred Genesee, Kathryn Lindholm-Leary, William Saunders, and Donna Christian, 64–108. New York: Cambridge University Press.

Riel, Margaret, and Kathleen Fulton. 2001. The role of technology in supporting learning communities. *Phi Delta Kappan* 82(7): 518–23.

Rueda, Robert, and Georgia Garcia. 2001. How do I teach reading to ELLs? *Teaching Every Child to Read.* Ann Arbor, MI: Center for the Improvement of Early Reading Achievement.

Sanchez, Francisca. 1989. *What is sheltered instruction?* Hayward, CA: Alameda County Office of Education.

Schleppegrell, Mary. 2004. *The language of schooling: A functional linguistic perspective.* Mahwah, NJ: Erlbaum.

Schmoker, Michael. 2006. *Results now.* 2nd ed. Alexandria, VA: Association for Supervision and Curriculum Development.

Shanahan, Timothy, and Isabel Beck. 2006. Effective literacy teaching for English-language learners. In *Developing literacy in second-language learners: A report of the National Literacy Panel on Language-Minority Children and Youth,* ed. Diane August and Timothy Shanahan. Mahwah, NJ: Erlbaum.

Sheppard, Ken. 1995. *Content-ESL across the USA* (Volume I, Technical Report). Washington, DC: National Clearinghouse for Bilingual Education.

Short, Deborah. 2006. Language and content learning and teaching, In *Encyclopedia of Language and Linguistics,* 2nd ed., ed. B. Spolsky. Oxford: Elsevier.

Short, Deborah. 2000. Teacher discourse in social studies classrooms: How teachers promote academic literacy for English language learners. PhD diss., George Mason University.

Short, Deborah. 1999. Integrating language and content for effective sheltered instruction programs. In *So much to say: Adolescents, bilingualism, and ESL in the secondary school,* ed. Christian Faltis and Paula Wolfe, 105–37. New York: Teachers College Press.

Short, Deborah. 1994. Expanding middle-school horizons: Integrating language, culture and social studies. *TESOL Quarterly* 28(3): 581–608.

Short, Deborah, and Beverly Boyson. 2004. *Creating access: Language and academic programs for secondary newcomers.* McHenry, IL: Delta Systems.

Short, Deborah, and Jana Echevarria. 1999. The sheltered instruction observation protocol: A tool for teacher-researcher collaboration and professional development. *Educational Practice Report* No. 3. Santa Cruz, CA and Washington, DC: Center for Research on Education, Diversity & Excellence.

Short, Deborah, and Jana Echevarria. 2007. *Academic uses of English: A focus on science.* Paper presented at the Center for Research on the Educational Achievement and Teaching of English Language Learners (CREATE) Conference, Chicago, IL, October 1, 2007.

Short, Deborah, and Shannon Fitzsimmons. 2007. *Double the work: Challenges and solutions to acquiring language and academic literacy for adolescent English language learners.* Washington, DC: Alliance for Excellent Education.

Short, Deborah, and Catherine Richards. 2008. *Linking science and academic English: Teacher development and student achievement.* Paper presented at the Center for Research on the Educational Achievement and Teaching of English Language Learners (CREATE) Conference, October 6. Minneapolis, MN.

Snow, Catherine, and Gina Biancarosa. 2003. *Adolescent literacy and the achievement gap: What do we know and where do we go from here?* New York: Carnegie Corporation of New York.

Stigler, Jim, and James Hiebert. 1999. *The teaching gap: Best ideas from the world's teachers for improving education in the classroom.* New York: The Free Press.

Stoller, Fredricka. 2004. Content-based instruction: Perspectives on curriculum planning. *Annual Review of Applied Linguistics* 24: 261–83.

Sullivan, Patricia, Margery Yeager, Eileen O'Brien, Nancy Kober, Keith Gayler, Naomi Chudowsky, Victor Chudowsky, Jana Wooden, Jack Jennings, and Diane Stark Rentner. 2005. *States try harder, but gaps persist: High school exit exams 2005.* Washington, DC: Center on Education Policy.

Tharp, Roland, Peggy Estrada, Stephanie Dalton, and Lois Yamauchi. 2000. *Teaching transformed: Achieving excellence, fairness, inclusion and harmony.* Boulder, CO: Westview Press.

Thomas, Wayne, and Virginia Collier. 2002. *A national study of school effectiveness for language minority students' long-term academic achievement.* Final report. Santa Cruz and Washington, DC: Center for Research on Education, Diversity & Excellence.

Tomlinson, Carol. 2001. *How to differentiate instruction in mixed-ability classrooms.* 2nd ed. Alexandria, VA: Association for Supervision and Curriculum Development.

Tompkins, G. E. 2006. *Literacy for the 21st century: A balanced approach.* 4th ed. Upper Saddle River, NJ: Merrill Prentice Hall.

Torgesen, Joseph, Debra Houston, Lila Rissman, Susan Decker, Greg Roberts, Sharon Vaughn, Jade Wexler, David Francis, Mabel Rivera, and Nonie Lesaux. 2007.

Academic literacy instruction for adolescents: A guidance document from the Center on Instruction. Portsmouth, NH: RMC Research Corporation, Center on Instruction.

Valli, Linda, and Willis Hawley. 2002. Designing and implementing school-based professional development. In *The keys to effective schools,* ed. Willis. Hawley. Thousands Oaks, CA: Corwin Press, Inc.

Walqui, Aida. 2006. Scaffolding instruction for English language learners: A conceptual framework. *The International Journal of Bilingual Education and Bilingualism* 9(2): 159–80.

Waxman, Hersh, Judith Walker de Felix, Alicia Martinez, Stephanie Knight, and Yolanda Padron.1994. Effects of implementing classroom instructional models on English language learners' cognitive and affective outcomes. *Bilingual Research Journal* 18(3 & 4): 1–22.

Weiss, Iris. R., and Joan D. Pasley. 2006. Scaling up instructional improvement through teacher professional development: Insights from the local systemic change initiative. Philadelphia, PA: Consortium for Policy Research in Education (CPRE) Policy Briefs. http://www.cpre.org/images/stories/cpre_pdfs/rb44.pdf

Sample Lesson Plan on Landforms, Elementary Grade Levels

Teacher: Deb Painter

Class: Grade 3

Unit: Geography

Topic: Landforms

Content Objectives: Students will be able to generate five words that belong together; students will be able to create a country and use those five words to label landforms.

Language Objectives: Students will be able to discuss categories of words with teams.

Key Concepts/Vocabulary: *Mountain, island, peninsula, river, category, landforms*

Supplementary Materials:

1. Teaching supplies: chart paper
2. Student supplies: white construction paper, landform cards

Motivation and Building Background

1. Review each of the five landforms introduced yesterday.

   ⊙ Have students place landform cards on desks.

   ⊙ Write each landform on the board and have students point to the corresponding card.

   ⊙ Students read aloud each landform word.

   ⊙ Students read the definition of each landform individually from their cards.

   ⊙ Randomly select sentences about landforms and ask individual students to read the sentences aloud.

   ⊙ Review the Ideas poster generated yesterday (Things to Do, Things to Eat).

Presentation

1. After reviewing things to do or eat, teacher selects something she likes to do and models making a graphic organizer of the idea.

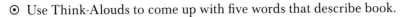
⊙ Use Think-Alouds to come up with five words that describe book.

⊙ Write the words on the chart (the graphic organizer).

2. Practice with teams to come up with five words about another topic suggested by teacher (e.g., pizza).

Practice/Application

1. Tell students to each come up with their own thing they like to do or eat.

⊙ Teams work together to generate five words for each student's topic (each one is different).

⊙ Students may think of their own topic or select one from the list.

Review/Assessment

1. Students bring their papers to the carpet and share with the group.

⊙ Have a student say his or her five descriptor words and students guess the topic word.

⊙ Group assists those who did not complete their graphic organizer (five words).

⊙ Read objectives aloud and ask students if they met the objectives.

Ideas	
Do	**Eat**
basketball	pizza
swim	hamburgers
read	tacos
draw	salad
computer games	apples
baseball	chips
soccer	tamales
paint	hot dogs

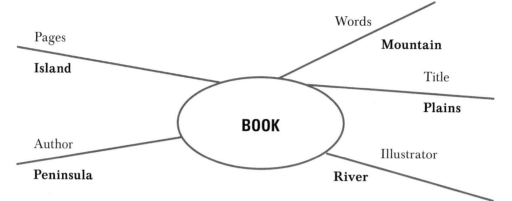

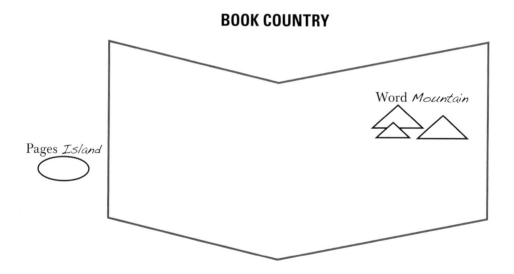

Sample Lesson Plan in Biology Secondary School

Teacher: Joshua LaPlante   **Date:** 1/10/08

Class: ESL Biology

Unit: Evolution

Topic: Natural Selection

Language Objectives: Students will be able to listen to and summarize key concepts about natural selection.

Content Objectives: Students will be able to define evolution by natural selection.

Key Concepts/Vocabulary: *Evolution, natural selection, adaptation, survival, reproduction, traits*

Supplementary Materials: Venn diagram for identifying types of selection; paper; markers; *How Whales Walked into the Sea* by Faith McNulty; notetaking sheet for book activity; and instructions for tasks posted in class

---

Motivation and Building Background

1. Post instructions for student groups to do a Carousel activity and review them together. Each group chooses from the following topics and displays one on chart paper:

    ⊙ Examples of adaptations

    ⊙ Reasons for adaptations

    ⊙ Key vocabulary for *evolution*

    ⊙ Synonyms for *evolve*

    Notetaking strategy: After the Carousel, have students draw a 2x2 chart on notebook paper and label each box with the titles of the charts. Review the information written on the charts with class and have students take notes on their 2x2 chart. Prompt students to explain, clarify, and add to the charts as needed. Add additional information students may not have recorded. Check student comprehension of key vocabulary when it comes up in this discussion.

Presentation

1. Ask students to try to define *natural selection* and to share knowledge or experiences related to it. Discuss types of *natural selection* with students and provide examples.

   ⊙ Stabilizing selection

   ⊙ Directional selection

   ⊙ Disruptive selection

   Introduce new key vocabulary by writing terms on the board and discussing them (e.g., *reproduction, traits*).

2. Review the task instructions to have students complete the three-ring Venn diagram in pairs or small groups. When students have finished, discuss as a class. Ask students questions: *How do disruptive selection and stabilizing selection differ? Which type of selection might happen if a new predator is introduced in an ecosystem? Why?*

Practice/Application

1. Book Activity. Preview the book *How Whales Walked Into the Sea* with the students and discuss the notetaking and summary sheet. Read the book aloud, pausing occasionally to discuss the information and show the pictures. Ask students to actively listen by taking notes and then complete two outcome statements.

Review/Assessment

1. Students write two- or three-sentence summary of the key concepts of the lesson and give it to the teacher.

Extension

1. Students compare animal characteristics and identify how each characteristic helps the organisms survive in their respective environments.

Carousel Instructions

1. Work with a team to complete each task (making a list of ideas on a chart).

2. Your team has two minutes for each task.

3. Move in a circle (clockwise) around the room.

4. Complete each task.

Venn Diagram Instructions

1. Draw a graph to illustrate each form of natural selection.

2. Define each type of selection.

3. Identify what all three forms of selection have in common.

4. Examine how pairs of selection relate to each other.

Natural Selection

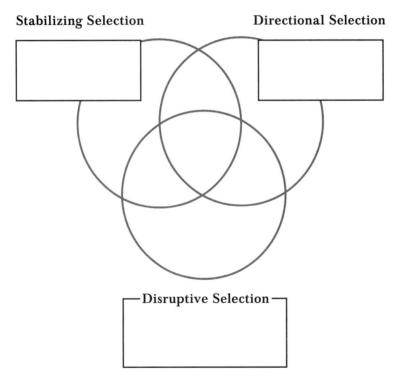

Stabilizing Selection   **Directional Selection**

─Disruptive Selection─

Book Activity Instructions

1. Listen to the story read by the teacher and pay attention to the pictures.

2. Take notes as the story is being read.

3. Complete two outcome statements.

4. Summarize key concepts using appropriate vocabulary.

How Whales Walked Into the Sea

by Faith McNulty

Notes:

Outcome Statements

1. I think it is important to remember _____

_____

_____

_____

_____

2. I was surprised that _____

_____

_____

_____

_____

Summary

Chapter 6

Alternative Educational Programs for English Learners

Kathryn Lindholm-Leary, San Jose State University
Fred Genesee, McGill University

Currently, several alternative school programs exist in California for educating English learners (ELs) that differ from English-only programs in the use of two languages (English and another language) for language, literacy, and academic instruction. These programs comprise (a) transitional bilingual, (b) developmental bilingual, and (c) two-way immersion. Those programs are the focus of this chapter. There is some discussion elsewhere in this publication on how English learners' home language is used in other program models, such as newcomer programs and sheltered instruction in the chapter by Echevarria and Short. We outline the rationale for and advantages of a dual language approach to education for English learners in California and across the country. The primary characteristics of those alternative program are described. We go on to review research that has investigated the language, literacy, academic, and other outcomes of students who have participated in dual language programs.

Finally, we briefly present research pertinent to program effectiveness, implementation issues, and learner needs in dual language programs. Some of these topics (e.g., student outcomes) have been the subject of extensive systematic research. In those cases, our discussion, conclusions, and recommendations are closely based on empirical evidence. In other cases (e.g., students with special needs), the research base is less extensive or indirect and, as a result, our discussion is necessarily more circumspect and suggestive. However, because educational professionals need to make informed decisions about program alternatives now, with or without extensive research evidence, we have included suggestions and recommendations even for issues that lack extensive empirical investigation in order to provide as much professional guidance as we can.

Rationale and Advantages of Dual Language Education

As noted, the three program alternatives reviewed in this chapter use two languages to educate language-minority students (and language-majority students in the case of two-way immersion). Before proceeding with descriptions of these program alternatives, we discuss arguments for the use of two languages for teaching English learners. These arguments pertain to globalization, neurocognitive advantages, the home language advantage, and cultural competence.

Globalization

Few would deny that the world is experiencing unprecedented globalization. It is evident in multiple spheres of activity: economy and business, communications, travel, culture, and immigration. Globalization has brought opportunities, advantages, and challenges. One challenge is how best to prepare present-day students in U.S. schools for life in the global village. Linguistic and cultural competence play key roles in affording students the tools they need to take advantage of the opportunities of globalization. Although English is widely recognized as the most important world language (Crystal 2003), students who speak English and other languages will have the competitive edge in the global marketplace. As well, knowing other languages in addition to English will afford California students the full range of benefits that globalization offers, including personal benefits related to international travel or communication through the Internet. In short, educational programs that afford students opportunities to acquire English and other languages and to become familiar with other cultures are better suited to offering graduates a premium in the global village (Barker 2000; *Foreign Language Framework* 2003; Committee for Economic Development 2007).

> **Linguistic and cultural competence play key roles in affording students the tools they need to take advantage of the opportunities of globalization.**

Neurocognitive Advantages

Research conducted during the past two decades has found that advanced levels of bilingual competence are associated with several significant cognitive advantages (e.g., Bialystok 2001, 2008). A bilingual advantage has been demonstrated consistently by individuals competent in completing tasks or solving problems when competing information is available. Technically speaking, these advantages include cognitive abilities related to attention, inhibition, monitoring, and switching focus of attention. Collectively these cognitive skills comprise what are referred to as *executive control processes* and are located in the frontal lobe regions of the brain. Executive control processes permit the problem solver to focus attention when there is potentially conflicting information to be considered, to select relevant over irrelevant information, and to switch strategies when a solution is not forthcoming.

Bialystok and Martin (2004) have argued that the experience of controlling attention to two languages in order to keep them separate and use them appropriately is what enhances the development of executive control processes in bilingual people. These advantages in executive control functions are evident in childhood and in later adulthood as well. The bilingual advantage found by Bialystok is most evident in bilingual people who acquire relatively advanced levels of proficiency in two languages and use their two languages actively on a regular basis. A bilingual advantage is unlikely to occur in individuals who have taken a high school foreign-language course and have little competence in another language (e.g., Bialystok 2001; Cummins 1976, 1981).

These findings have significant implications for educators—implications that complement the economic and personal advantages that are associated with bilingual competence in a globalized world. In brief, these findings argue for bilingual forms of education as cognitive enrichment and, at the same time, argue for programs that provide substantive and continuous opportunities for students to develop bilingual competence in school so that they enjoy the cognitive advantages that high levels of bilingualism confer.

> **The bilingual advantage found by Bialystok is most evident in bilingual people who acquire relatively advanced levels of proficiency in two languages and use their two languages actively on a regular basis.**

The Home Language Advantage

Recent systematic reviews of research on the language, literacy and academic development of English learners by August and Shanahan (2006) and Genesee and others (2006), among others, have revealed that there are important developmental relationships between English learners' home language competencies and their academic and literacy development in English (see also Greene 1998; MacSwan et al. 2007; Rolstad, Mahoney, and Glass 2005; Slavin and Cheung 2005; Willig 1985). More specifically, English learners with advanced levels of competence in certain aspects of the home language demonstrate superior achievement in English literacy compared with English learners who lack or have lower levels of competence in these home language abilities. Moreover, English learners with more advanced levels of bilingual competence (in English and the home language) attain significantly higher levels of academic achievement than do English learners with lower levels of bilingual competence (Lindholm-Leary and Borsato 2006).

Phonological awareness can be used as an example. It has been reported in numerous studies that English learners who possess good phonological awareness skills in the home language acquire phonological awareness skills in English more easily and faster and, in turn, acquire superior word decoding skills in English in comparison to English learners with less-developed phonological awareness skills in the home language (see Geva and Genesee 2006 and Riches and Genesee 2006 for reviews of this research). These first- and second-language relationships have been found for language-related skills (such as depth and breadth of vocabulary), literacy-related skills (such as knowledge of the alphabet and phonological awareness), and language-processing strategies (such as inferring the meaning of new words or the use of reading-comprehension strategies). These findings are evident in English learners who are instructed in English-only classrooms as well as in English learners in bilingual programs, indicating that these linguistic interdependencies operate independently of the language of instruction. Moreover, these effects are most pronounced when English learners acquire competence in English reading and writing—fundamental skills for educational success.

> **In short, English learners use their existing home language skills to "bootstrap" into English literacy.**

These findings are important educationally because they indicate that English learners, like all students, are resourceful and use all their existing language and cognitive resources when learning to read, write, and learn new academic skills in English. Whereas monolingual English-speaking students have resources only in English, English learners have resources linked to the home language as well as those they are acquiring in English. In short, English learners use their existing home language skills to "bootstrap" into English literacy. As their knowledge of English grows, English learners have less need to draw on home language skills to fill the gaps. Dual language programs have the educational advantage in that they systematically use English learners' home language to scaffold the acquisition of English literacy and thus take advantage of English learners' existing language abilities. To ignore these cross-linguistic relationships risks squandering young English learners' most valuable learning assets as they face the challenges of learning literacy and other academic skills in English.

Schooling and Cultural Competence

Schooling involves more than reading, writing, and arithmetic, as important as these are. Schools are also important for socializing students to broader sociocultural values and norms. Among the sociocultural goals of public education in California

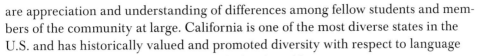

are appreciation and understanding of differences among fellow students and members of the community at large. California is one of the most diverse states in the U.S. and has historically valued and promoted diversity with respect to language and culture in its population. In the globalized world that we live in, the acculturation role of schooling takes on added significance because the range of diversity that California students face is itself global, extending beyond their immediate neighborhood to include peoples from all corners of the world. Likewise, the consequences of intolerance and ignorance of diversity are equally global in magnitude.

> **Dual language programs, in which students are instructed through two languages and sometimes with members of both language groups working together, provide many conditions that are essential for the reduction of prejudice and discrimination.**

Dual language programs, in which students are instructed through two languages and sometimes with members of both language groups working together (e.g., two-way immersion), provide many conditions that are essential for the reduction of prejudice and discrimination. These programs also provide students with communication skills and cultural awareness that facilitate intergroup contact and appreciation (see Genesee and Gándara 1999 for a detailed discussion). These possibilities are most likely in two-way immersion programs that include students from both language groups since they provide opportunities for sustained, personalized contact with members of the other group in a supportive, structured environment. Also, direct contact outside school with members of the other group (e.g., Spanish-speaking in the case of English-speaking students in two-way immersion) is afforded once students' language proficiency is sufficiently functional to engage in such contact.

Dual language programs offer another cultural advantage to language-minority students in California. For children from the majority language group, there is, generally speaking, a good match between the cultural norms of the home and of the school. However, for children from minority-language groups, there is often a poor match because what is considered appropriate in minority-language homes may be inappropriate or awkward in school (Greenfield, Quiroz, and Raeff 2000). A good example of this difference in American homes is the norms surrounding children's talk with adults. In mainstream middle-class American families, children are encouraged and expected to initiate conversations with adults and to demonstrate individually what they know and want (cf. Rogoff 2003). Moreover, teachers take those kinds of behaviors as signs that students are engaged and focused. This expectation contrasts sharply with the cultural norms of some groups that are not

European in origin. Children from many other cultures are socialized to not initiate conversations with adults (Greenfield, Quiroz, and Raeff 2000), to not look directly at adults when they talk to them (Whatley 1981), and to work together with their peers rather than as individuals (Au and Jordan 1981; Philips 1983). Those kinds of behaviors could be interpreted as signs of reticence, indifference, or even of learning problems by classroom teachers working with a mainstream point of view because they run counter to cultural expectations associated with mainstream socialization patterns. Such misattributions may be less likely to happen in dual language programs where teachers are sensitive to the cultural norms of their minority-language students.

Finally, all students possess what Luis Moll has referred to as "funds of knowledge" that shape their behavior and learning in school (Gonzalez, Moll, and Amanti 2005). Funds of knowledge are acquired in the home and community before children come to school and include the skills, knowledge, expectations, and understandings that children have about the world and their place in it. The funds of knowledge that mainstream students possess are used by mainstream classroom teachers as resources for linking new knowledge and skills to students' prior learning and life experiences (e.g., Snow, Burns, and Griffin 1998). This is done, for example, when teachers preview new learning objectives with their students by encouraging students to discuss and think about prior knowledge and experiences that are related to the new learning objectives. Students from different cultural backgrounds have different funds of knowledge that have grown out of their unique cultural experiences. Dual language programs that teach through students' home language as well as English are better prepared to accommodate students with diverse sociocultural back-grounds because dual language teachers usually have had appropriate training about the importance of these issues (Howard et al. 2007; Lindholm-Leary 2001). More-over, dual language programs usually include explicit objectives to enhance students' understanding and appreciation of cultural diversity since this is an integral part of acquiring bilingual competence.

Program Characteristics

Each type of dual language program, including the primary goals, theoretical rationale, and intended student populations, is described in this section. For more detailed descriptions of these models, along with other dual language program models, see Genesee 1999. This information is also summarized in Table 6.1, along with information about grade levels served, appropriate teacher qualifications, the role of mainstream teachers, and the nature of instructional materials used in each type of program.

Table 6.1. Summary of Alternative Educational Programs for English Learners

Components	Transitional Bilingual	Developmental Bilingual	Two-Way Immersion
Language goals	Transition to English only	Bilingualism	Bilingualism
Cultural goals	Integrate into mainstream American culture	Integrate into mainstream American culture and maintain home/heritage culture	Maintain/integrate into mainstream American culture and appreciate other culture
Academic goals	District goals and standards	District goals and standards	District goals and standards
Student characteristics	⊙ No/limited English ⊙ Same home language ⊙ Mixed cultural background	⊙ No/limited English ⊙ Same home language ⊙ Mixed culture background	Both native speakers of English and students with no/limited English; different cultural backgrounds
Grade levels served	Primary and elementary	Elementary	K–8; preferably K–12
Entry levels	K, 1, 2	K, 1, 2	K, 1
Length of student participation	2–4 years	• Usually 6 years (+K) • Preferably 12 years (+K)	• Usually 6 years (+K) • Preferably 12 years (+K)
Role of mainstream teachers	Mainstream teachers must have training in sheltered instruction.	Stand-alone program with its own specially trained teachers	Mainstream teachers with special training
Teacher qualifications	⊙ Bilingual certificate	⊙ Bilingual-multicultural certificate ⊙ Bilingual proficiency	⊙ Bilingual/immersion certification ⊙ Bilingual proficiency ⊙ Multicultural training
Instructional materials, texts, visual aids, etc.	In the home language of students and in English; English materials adapted to language levels	In the home language of students and in English; English materials adapted to language levels	In the minority language and in English, as required by curriculum of study

Transitional Bilingual Education

Transitional bilingual education (TBE), also sometimes referred to as early-exit bilingual education, has historically been a common form of dual language education for English learners in the United States (Genesee 1999).
TBE provides academic instruction in English learners' home language as they learn English. The typical TBE program begins in kindergarten or grade one and provides initial instruction in literacy and academic content areas through the student's home language along with instruction in oral English and nonacademic subjects, such as art, music, and physical education. Teaching English learners in all-English classes as soon as they begin schooling, it is argued, impedes their academic development because they cannot speak or understand English sufficiently to benefit from academic instruction through English. Thus, learners are put at academic risk. TBE is designed to avoid this pitfall. As students acquire proficiency in oral English, the language in which academic subjects are taught gradually shifts from the students' home language to English. Content instruction through English is often provided in individualized and specially designed units, often using sheltered instructional techniques (see Echevarria and Short, this publication). The transition to English instruction typically starts off with math, followed by reading and writing, then science, and finally social studies. Once they acquire sufficient English proficiency, TBE students make the transition to mainstream classes where all academic instruction is presented in English; often this occurs at grade three. In contrast to developmental bilingual education and two-way immersion programs, to be described shortly, TBE does not aim for full bilingualism. It uses the students' home language to ensure grade-level mastery of academic content but only until such time as students can make a full transition to all-English instruction, typically defined in California as one to two years (Genesee 1999).

> **As students acquire proficiency in oral English, the language in which academic subjects are taught gradually shifts from the students' home language to English.**

The primary goals of TBE are to:

- Ensure mastery of grade-appropriate academic skills and knowledge.
- Facilitate and speed up the process of learning English.

Early instruction in students' home language serves both goals. The fact that instruction through the home language supports the acquisition of English sounds counterintuitive to some, but the rationale is as follows. First, teaching academic content to English learners through their home language, while they are learning to speak and comprehend English, helps them to acquire academic knowledge at the same pace as their native English-speaking counterparts because they are learning in a

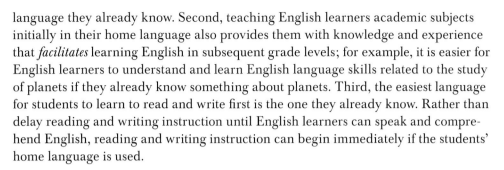

language they already know. Second, teaching English learners academic subjects initially in their home language also provides them with knowledge and experience that *facilitates* learning English in subsequent grade levels; for example, it is easier for English learners to understand and learn English language skills related to the study of planets if they already know something about planets. Third, the easiest language for students to learn to read and write first is the one they already know. Rather than delay reading and writing instruction until English learners can speak and comprehend English, reading and writing instruction can begin immediately if the students' home language is used.

Moreover, many literacy skills "transfer" from one language to another (August and Shanahan 2006; Genesee et al. 2006). Thus, if English learners learn to read and write reasonably well in their home language and learn to speak and comprehend English well, then it is relatively easy for them to learn to read and write in English. There is much evidence to support this approach (August and Shanahan 2006; Genesee et al. 2006), especially for languages that use the same script (e.g., Spanish and English). Fourth, it is argued that parents play a critical supporting role in their child's education. Teaching English learners in their home language increases the likelihood that their parents (who often speak little or no English) will be better able to support their children's academic development; for example, by reading with their children, supervising their homework, communicating with the teacher, and so on.

Developmental Bilingual Education

Developmental bilingual education (DBE), also referred to as *maintenance bilingual education* and *late-exit bilingual education,* is an enrichment form of dual language education that uses English learners' home language and English for literacy and academic instruction throughout the elementary grade levels and, wherever possible, high school as well. In comparison to two-way immersion programs (discussed next) in which students from language-minority backgrounds are schooled along with students from the majority-language group using both groups' languages, DBE is a kind of one-way program that includes only or primarily language-minority students. Although DBE programs are intended to serve speakers of one minority language in the same classroom, diversity among students is not uncommon; a single class or program might include Hispanic students who were born and raised in the U.S. but speak virtually no English when they first enroll, Hispanic students who are already proficiently bilingual, and recent Spanish-speaking immigrants from Mexico who are just beginning to acquire English.

Most current DBE programs begin in kindergarten or grade one and add one grade level each year. They teach regular academic subjects through English and the students' native language for as many grade levels as the school district can and will support, ideally until the end of high school. DBE programs are offered in a variety of minority languages, including Chinese, Vietnamese, Russian, Japanese, French, German, and Spanish. A listing of DBE programs is contained in the Center for Applied Linguistics Directory of Bilingual Programs. The vast majority of DBE programs include Spanish and English (Center for Applied Linguistics 2008).

DBE programs aim to promote high levels of academic achievement in all curricular areas and full proficiency in both the students' home language and English for academic purposes. They emphasize the cognitive and academic richness of exploring knowledge across academic domains from multiple cultural perspectives using both languages.

DBE programs aim to promote high levels of academic achievement in all curricular areas and full proficiency in both the students' home language and English for academic purposes.

DBE programs provide English learners with academic instruction in their home language as they learn English. Sheltered instructional techniques are the preferred method of delivering academic instruction (see Echevarria and Short, this publication). In this way, DBE aims for grade-level achievement in academic domains by the end of schooling. Indeed, well-implemented DBE leads to high academic achievement for English learners (Lindholm-Leary and Borsato 2006; Riches and Genesee 2006; Thomas and Collier 2002). DBE takes an enriched approach to educating English learners in that it promotes full proficiency in all aspects of the students' home language in addition to full proficiency in all aspects of English. As a result, it is viewed as an additive form of bilingual education (Cloud, Genesee, and Hamayan 2000).

The theoretical rationale for DBE is built on research in diverse domains, including linguistics, social sciences, and school effectiveness (e.g., Lindholm-Leary 2001). Accelerated learning, a concept from research on school effectiveness, is critical to understanding the learning situation of any group of potentially at-risk students. As a group, English learners generally score relatively low on tests related to all areas of the curriculum administered in English (cf. Abedi 2003). If they are to catch up to native English-speaking students who are advancing in achievement each year, they must make **more** academic progress per year than English-speaking students. Moreover, they must maintain such accelerated progress for several consecutive years in order to eventually close the achievement gap, which can be as much as 1.5 national standard deviation units. In a well-implemented DBE program, academic growth is accelerated through cognitively challenging academic work in the students' home language along with meaningful academic content taught through English. As students demonstrate that they have mastered grade-level curriculum material in their home language, they also close the achievement gap in English. With time (four to seven years), they are often able to demonstrate grade-level knowledge in English as well. DBE students in effective programs can outperform the average monolingual English-speaking group on standardized tests across the curriculum (Lindholm-Leary and Borsato 2006; Thomas and Collier 2002).

Research on language acquisition in school contexts also constitutes part of the theoretical base for DBE. It is widely believed that school programs that integrate second-language and content instruction are generally effective for promoting second-language proficiency (Genesee 1994) especially when accompanied by explicit and direct instruction of aspects of the second language that are difficult to acquire (Lyster 2007). Furthermore, developing students' home language so that it is commensurate with their cognitive development throughout the school years is crucial to academic success (Lindholm-Leary and Borsato 2006). Acquiring the second language in an additive context—in which the first language is not lost but promoted—leads to uninterrupted cognitive development and, thus, increased academic achievement (Lindholm-Leary and Borsato 2006).

Two-Way Immersion Education

Two-way immersion programs (also known as *two-way bilingual education* and *dual language immersion*) have been widely implemented in schools and districts that seek to provide educational opportunities for all students to become bilingual (Center for Applied Linguistics 2008; Howard and Christian 2002). Two-way immersion programs provide integrated language and academic instruction for native speakers of English and native speakers of another language with the goals of high academic achievement, first- and second-language proficiency, and cross-cultural understanding. In two-way immersion programs, language learning is integrated with content instruction, as in the other program alternatives reviewed in this chapter. Academic subjects are taught to all students through both English and the other language, although the same subject is usually not taught in both languages in the same year. As students and teachers interact socially and work together to perform academic tasks, the students' language abilities are developed along with their knowledge of academic subject matter. Most programs start in kindergarten or first grade and continue until the end of elementary school or into middle and high school. Although there is much variation with certain program features, there are also some important core similarities among programs (Genesee 1999).

⊙ There are usually approximately 50 percent English-only speakers and 50 percent native speakers of the other language (or no fewer than a third of either group).

- ⊙ By including students from both language groups, two-way immersion programs give students the opportunity to be both first-language models and second-language learners.

- ⊙ Academic instruction takes place through both languages, with the non-English language being used at least 50 percent of the time. There are two program alternatives, one (termed 50/50) in which both languages are used throughout the grades for 50 percent of the instructional day. In the other program alternative, called 90/10, the non-English language is used for 90 percent of the instructional day during kindergarten through grade one; after that, more English is added at each grade level until grade four or five, where the proportion is closer to 50/50.

- ⊙ Two-way immersion creates an additive bilingual environment for all students since the primary languages of both groups of students are developed at the same time as their second languages are developed.

The rationale for two-way immersion is based on theories and research findings concerning both first- and second-language acquisition. First, and as already noted, bilingual education research indicates that academic knowledge and skills acquired through one language pave the way for acquisition of related knowledge and skills taught through the medium of another language. When instruction through the home language is provided to language-minority students along with balanced second-language support, those students attain higher levels of academic achievement and literacy in English than if they had been taught only in English (August and Shanahan 2006; Lindholm-Leary and Borsato 2006).

Second, research indicates that English is best acquired by language-minority students with limited or no proficiency in English after home-language skills are fully established. Specifically, strong oral and literacy skills developed in the home language provide a solid basis for the acquisition of literacy and other academic language skills in English (August and Shanahan 2006; Genesee et al. 2006). Moreover, common literacy-related skills that underlie the acquisition and use of both languages transfer from the home language to the second language and, thereby, facilitate English language acquisition.

Third, immersion programs for language-majority students (those who are native speakers of English) enable them to develop advanced levels of proficiency in the second language without compromising their academic achievement or home-language development (Genesee 2004).

Finally, many researchers and educators believe that language is learned best by all students when it is the medium of instruction rather than the exclusive focus of instruction (e.g., Lyster 2007). In two-way immersion settings, students learn language while exploring and learning academic content because there is a real need to communicate.

More generally, the rationale for two-way immersion grows out of sociocultural theory that maintains that learning occurs through social interaction (Lantolf 2005; Vygotsky 1978). More specifically, the integration of native speakers of English and native speakers of another language facilitates second-language acquisition since it promotes authentic, meaningful interaction with native speakers. Because the students in two-way immersion programs are all native speakers of one of the two second languages being promoted, it follows that native-language models are available in the classroom for both groups of second-language learners.

Social science research also provides a strong theoretical rationale for two-way immersion programs in culturally and linguistically diverse settings. Students who study in socioculturally supportive classrooms that build on the knowledge base they bring from their homes and communities are able to accelerate their own academic growth (González, Moll, and Amanti 2005). The differential status enjoyed by language-minority and -majority students and particularly the low status of language-minority students can be transformed in a two-way immersion program where all students are respected and valued as equal partners in the learning process and where all are given access to the same resources as all other schools. Furthermore, in regions of the U.S. that provide economic rewards for graduates who are bilingual in English and another language, the economic advantages of bilingualism in the marketplace may serve to enhance the status and achievement of students who are bilingual.

> **... the integration of native speakers of English and native speakers of another language facilitates second-language acquisition since it promotes authentic, meaningful interaction with native speakers.**

Student Achievement and Program Outcomes

The achievement of English learners has been of considerable interest to educators, policymakers, and families. In this section, we examine the achievement of English learners in terms of oral language proficiency, content area achievement, and attitudes; we also review research that examines literacy outcomes of English learners in alternative programs. A more extensive and in-depth review of research on the acquisition of literacy skills in English by English learners is presented in the chapter by August and Shanahan, this

> **The achievement of English learners has been of considerable interest to educators, policymakers, and families.**

publication (see also August and Shanahan 2006 and Genesee et al. 2006 for recent comprehensive reviews). Along the way, we delve into some important educational and policy issues concerning the effectiveness of different program types for English learners, the question of the amount of English in the instructional day that is needed for learners to achieve grade-level norms, and how well students achieve in alternative dual language programs.

Oral Language Development

Oral language proficiency is critical for the general educational and academic success of English learners. The rate at which English learners achieve advanced levels of oral language proficiency in English is of interest to policymakers and lawmakers because it influences the amount of time English learners should receive federally funded services. Of course, the oral language development of English learners is of considerable interest to educators so that appropriate curriculum can be developed to facilitate their language and content learning and so that instruction can be tailored to the needs of English learners at different proficiency levels (see Snow and Katz as well as Dutro and Kinsella, this publication). Oral language development of English learners is important to parents, as parents want to be sure that their children become proficient in English; but many parents also want their children to maintain proficiency in the home language (Lindholm-Leary 2001; Ramos 2007; Shannon and Milian 2002).

Oral language proficiency is critical for the general educational and academic success of English learners.

Whereas in this book there has been a primary focus on the English language development of English learners, we address, to the extent possible, the development of both languages. It is important in these discussions to recognize that English learners may be at different stages of bilingualism, including full proficiency in two or more languages, full proficiency in the primary language and limited proficiency in English, limited proficiency in both the primary language and English, and even proficiency in English and limited proficiency in the primary language.

In this section, we address issues that are likely to be most critical to educators, researchers, and parents; that is, research on the development of proficiency in both the first and second languages and how long it takes for English learners to become proficient in English.

Research on the L1 and L2 development of English learners. To help readers better understand the English language development of English learners, we briefly review research on second-language learners in general and consider what it means to be proficient in English or a second language. First, it is important to distinguish the differences in the process of acquisition between monolingual students and that of second-language learners. We know that all normally developing children readily acquire their first language by the time they enter school (MacSwan 2000); that is, they have acquired the vocabulary, grammar, pronunciation, and speech styles that are appropriate for their speech community. However, even normally developing monolingual English speakers entering kindergarten continue to develop more complex vocabulary and syntactic skills in school, and they exhibit normal variations in their acquisition of various linguistic structures and sounds (Hoff and Shatz 2007; Maratsos 2000).

Children who grow up learning two languages simultaneously are called "simultaneous bilinguals" in the research literature; in California, they are referred to as I-FEPs (initially fluent English proficient). We know from research on these children that, given sufficient exposure in both languages, their language development in both languages is similar to that of monolinguals in that they typically follow the same stages in their acquisition of syntactic rules and structures as monolingual children do in each language (e.g., Baker 2006; Gathercole 2002a; Genesee, Paradis, and Crago 2004; Lindholm 1980, 1987). We also know that simultaneous bilingual children tend to mix languages, or code-switch, and that this is grammatical with respect to both languages and often serves social and communicative functions (e.g., to communicate with other bilinguals or to assert one's dual language identity) (Genesee 2002). In short, it is now well understood that bilingual code-switching is not evidence of either language or cognitive confusion (e.g.. Baker 2006; Genesee, Boivin, and Nicoladis 1996; Lindholm 1980; Romaine 1995).

> **It is now well understood that bilingual code-switching is not evidence of either language or cognitive confusion.**

Children who have acquired one language before school age and acquire an additional language in school are usually called *second-language learners* or *successive bilinguals* in the research literature (e.g., Baker 2006), although educators often refer to these students as English learners. They are even often referred to as *bilinguals* even though they may have minimal competence in their second language.

Research on second-language learners debunks the myth that children learn a second language easily and quickly (e.g., MacSwan and Pray 2005; Paradis 2005). Second-language learning is a challenging and lengthy process especially when it calls for the acquisition of academic language and not simply conversational language skills. In fact, research has shown that second-language learning in school contexts is not always easier for young children entering school than for adolescents or adults

(Genesee and Geva 2006). As MacSwan and Pray (2005) point out, second-language learners, unlike their school-age native peers, "have developed only partial knowledge of the structure of their target language [English], and exhibit substantial errors associated with tense, case, grammatical agreement, word order, pronunciation, and other aspects of language structure" (p. 656). However, Gathercole (2002a) has shown that while second-grade English learners in two-way programs may lag behind their monolingual English-speaking peers in developing certain grammatical structures such as mass/count distinctions, the gap disappears by fifth grade and there is no difference between the bilingual English learners and their monolingual English-speaking peers.

Saunders and O'Brien (2006) note, in a review of research on the oral language development of English learners, that with increased oral proficiency in English, English learners:

- ⊙ Use more English, which is associated, in turn, with subsequent gains in oral English proficiency.
- ⊙ Interact more frequently with English-only students, which provides more opportunity to use English.
- ⊙ Use more complex language-learning strategies, particularly strategies that enable them to interact with others and monitor their own and others' language use.
- ⊙ Display a wider range of language skills, including skills associated with academic uses of language, such as higher-level question forms and definitional skills.

There is very little research on English learners' proficiency in their native language since most research in the U.S. on the development of languages other than English has examined foreign language learning. The scant research that has been done on English learners' native-language proficiency pertains to Spanish and is mostly limited to teacher ratings and results on standardized language tests. Nonetheless, the available research shows that developmental bilingual and two-way programs promote relatively high levels of Spanish proficiency (August and Hakuta 1997; Escamilla and Medina 1993; Gathercole 2002b; Howard and Christian 1997; Howard, Christian, and Genesee 2004; Howard and Sugarman 2007; Lindholm-Leary 2001; Lindholm-Leary and Howard 2008; Ramirez 1992; Willig 1985). It has also been found that adolescent English learners who have participated in two-way programs for six to eight years think their Spanish skills are highly functional and, in particular, that they have the Spanish skills they need to participate in a variety of classroom and social exchanges (Lindholm-Leary 2003; Lindholm-Leary and Ferrante 2005).

Finally, Gathermore (2002b) has pointed out that by fifth grade, English learners in two-way programs show significantly greater proficiency in certain Spanish grammatical structures (e.g., gender distinctions) over English learners in English mainstream

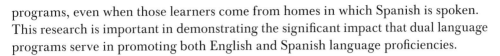
programs, even when those learners come from homes in which Spanish is spoken. This research is important in demonstrating the significant impact that dual language programs serve in promoting both English and Spanish language proficiencies.

Length of time to become proficient in English. A number of studies on the oral language development of English learners indicate that they typically require a minimum of two to five years to achieve advanced proficiency in oral English (Collier 1989; Hakuta, Butler, and Witt 2000; Saunders and O'Brien 2006; Thomas and Collier 2002), regardless of whether they participate in a bilingual, English mainstream, or structured English immersion program (Saunders and O'Brien 2006), although MacSwan and Pray (2005) found that students in bilingual programs acquired English as fast or faster than students in all-English programs. Those studies have examined proficiency in terms of students' speaking, listening comprehension, reading, and writing skills.

One way in which researchers have studied this issue is by examining reclassification rates of English learners; that is, how long it takes them to be reclassified "fully English proficient" if they had been previously designated "limited English proficient." The final report of the American Institutes for Research evaluation study of the implementation of Proposition 227 (Parrish et al. 2006) summarizes annual reclassification rates[1] of English learners from 1994-95 to 2004-05 in California. This study used data from the California English Language Development Test (CELDT), which includes measures of both oral (speaking, listening) and written (reading, writing) language skills. The authors report that "the overall redesignation rate has increased gradually over the past decade . . . with the most recent data showing a rate of 8.9 percent for 2004–2005" (p. I-19). The authors estimated the "current probability of an EL being redesignated to fluent English proficient status *after 10 years* in California to be less than 40 percent" (p. III-1). They go on to state: "we estimate that 75 percent of EL students are not redesignated [as fluent English proficient] *after five years of schooling"* (p. III-33). Their reclassification figure of only 25 percent is close to the figure reported by Grissom (2004), who found that only 30 percent of English learners were reclassified within five years.

Data from two-way programs are more optimistic. Lindholm-Leary (2008) reported that the percentage of students in two two-way 90/10 schools and one 60/40 dual language school that had been reclassified or met reclassification criteria[1] using the CELDT was 32 percent in grade five, 52 percent in grade six, and 72 percent in grade seven.

---

1. Reclassification usually occurs when an English learner reaches Early Advanced or Advanced on the CELDT and achieves at least Basic on the California Standards Test in English–language arts. There are other considerations as well, but these are the primary ones.

In a current review of research on students in two-way programs, Lindholm-Leary and Howard (2008) report that almost all English learners in two-way programs were rated as orally proficient in English, particularly by the upper elementary grade levels. Similar results were reported by Howard and Sugarman (2007) in their study of three two-way schools. In both 90/10 and 50/50 two-way programs, most English learners were rated by various oral proficiency measures as proficient in English by fourth grade. Those results were based on several large-scale studies of various two-way programs in different regions of the U.S. Moreover, these results were obtained whether they were based on cross-sectional or longitudinal studies and regardless of the language measures used (e.g., Language Assessment Scale, Bilingual Syntax Measure, Student Oral Language Observation Matrix, Student Oral Proficiency Assessment, Foreign Language Oral Skills Evaluation Matrix). However, most of these measures were limited to oral proficiency (speaking, listening) and not proficiency in written language (reading, writing).

Level of proficiency in English. Research that has examined the development of oral proficiency in a second language by English learner and foreign-language students has consistently shown that improvement from beginning to middle levels of proficiency is relatively rapid, but progress from middle to upper levels of proficiency is much slower (e.g., Hakuta, Butler, and Witt 2000; Howard, Christian, and Genesee 2004; Lindholm-Leary 2001; Medina and Escamilla 1992; Thomas and Collier 2002; Weslander and Stephany 1983; see Saunders and O'Brien 2006, for a review). The American Institutes for Research evaluation study of the implementation of Proposition 227 reports data that are consistent with this finding (Parrish et al. 2006). In 2003-04, only 11 percent of K–12 English learners were rated Advanced, 32 percent were rated Early Advanced, 36 percent Intermediate, and 22 percent as Beginning or Early Intermediate in oral proficiency on the CELDT. Even those data on students who were rated Early Advanced or Advanced may be artificially high because there was an overrepresentation of students in grades nine through twelve in the entire sample (Parrish et al. 2006; Rumberger and Gándara 2005).

> **Research . . . has consistently shown that improvement from beginning to middle levels of proficiency is relatively rapid, but progress from middle to upper levels of proficiency is much slower.**

Summary. Despite the obvious significance of proficiency in oral English in theory, practice, and policy, there is a scarcity of empirical research on this topic (see Saunders and O'Brien 2006). There is even less empirical evidence on the English learners' acquisition and use of specific linguistic structures (e.g., verbs, pronouns, causal connectors) and sociolinguistic skills, unlike the considerable documentation

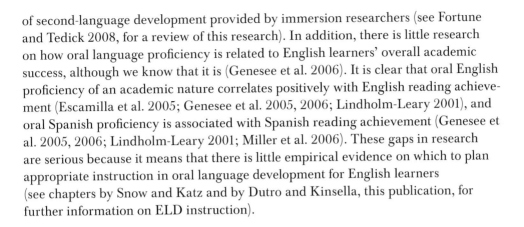

of second-language development provided by immersion researchers (see Fortune and Tedick 2008, for a review of this research). In addition, there is little research on how oral language proficiency is related to English learners' overall academic success, although we know that it is (Genesee et al. 2006). It is clear that oral English proficiency of an academic nature correlates positively with English reading achievement (Escamilla et al. 2005; Genesee et al. 2005, 2006; Lindholm-Leary 2001), and oral Spanish proficiency is associated with Spanish reading achievement (Genesee et al. 2005, 2006; Lindholm-Leary 2001; Miller et al. 2006). These gaps in research are serious because it means that there is little empirical evidence on which to plan appropriate instruction in oral language development for English learners (see chapters by Snow and Katz and by Dutro and Kinsella, this publication, for further information on ELD instruction).

Literacy Development

It is important to clarify what literacy development entails for English learners in English-only and dual language programs. English learners in English-only settings are exposed to literacy only in English, whereas English learner and English-proficient students in dual language settings are exposed to literacy in English and another language. This is an important distinction for two reasons. First, most curricula are developed for only one language and do not provide bridges between the two languages. Second, when students are tested in each language separately, the results may not reflect what they know in both languages, which, in fact, may be greater than the knowledge they possess in each language. This is, of course, true in relation to any academic testing (Solano-Flores and Trumbull 2003; Valdés and Figueroa 1994). Research on literacy development in English learners has typically focused on achievement outcomes assessed by tests of various literacy skills in English. There is also, fortunately, interesting research on the relationships between literacy development and oral proficiency and on literacy skills across languages, and that research is what we will examine next (see chapter by August and Shanahan, this publication, for a more complete discussion of English literacy development in English learners.)

Research on literacy and biliteracy development. Research on English literacy development in English learners indicates that it is similar in some important and fundamental respects to the acquisition of literacy skills in English for English-only students even though it is a first language for English-only students and a second language for English learners. More specifically, both types of literacy development are influenced by learners' oral language skills, by phonological processing abilities, and by metacognitive skills linked to reading (August and Shanahan, this publication; Garcia 1998). However, the acquisition of English literacy is more complex in

English learners than it is in native English-speaking students. A primary reason is the influence of English learners' first language on their acquisition of English reading and writing skills; this difference will be discussed shortly.

As in English literacy development for English-only students, some minimum level of oral proficiency in English is necessary for English literacy development in English learners, and students with well-developed oral English skills achieve greater success in English reading than students with less well-developed skills in oral English in the long run (Miller et al. 2006; Reese et al. 2000). Oral proficiency in English appears to play a minor role in the early stages of reading acquisition, when students are learning to decode. In this stage, it is skills that are directly related to word-reading that are important. Oral proficiency in English is much more important in later stages of English reading acquisition, when reading comprehension becomes important (August and Shanahan 2006). Diversity and depth of vocabulary knowledge in English (Miller et al. 2006; Perez 1981) and understanding of underlying story structure and strategies for constructing meaning from text are also important at this later stage (Goldstein, Harris, and Klein 1993; Miller et al. 2006). These processes and factors are similarly important in learning to read English whether as a first or second language.

At the same time, there are important differences between learning to read English as a first and as a second language (August and Shanahan 2006; Genesee et al. 2006). These differences are due primarily to cross-linguistic influences. For example, and in particular, English learners' phonological awareness skills in their native language correlate significantly and positively with their acquisition of phonological awareness skills in English, which, in turn, are significantly correlated with word-decoding skills in English. This means that students with well-developed phonological awareness and word-decoding skills in their first language acquire phonological awareness and decoding skills in English more readily than English learners with poorly developed skills in the native language. Cross-language influences are most evident during the early stages of second-language literacy development and become less evident, and arguably less necessary, later as English learners acquire more advanced skills in English. This makes sense since English learners who are in the early stages of literacy development and lack resources in English but have analogous skills in the first language can "bootstrap" themselves into English literacy by drawing on reading-related primary language skills (Riches and Genesee 2006).

Evidence of cross-language influences is also reported in studies that have examined the metacognitive strategies used by English learners during the performance of complex first- and second-language literacy tasks. These studies report that successful English learner readers/writers employ effective strategies (such as drawing inferences, the use of context and prior knowledge, and monitoring of comprehension) to comprehend text in English and that they use these strategies during both first- and second-language literacy tasks. The strategies resemble those used by successful English-only readers/writers (Padron and Waxman 1988; Jimenez, Garcia, and Pearson 1996). Successful English learner readers/writers also view reading and writing in English and the home language as similar activities with language-specific differences. At the same time, they are able to deploy a variety of effective bilingual strategies, such

Successful English learner readers/writers also view reading and writing in English and the home language as similar activities with language-specific differences.

as searching for first- and second-language cognates, judicious translation, or use of prior knowledge developed in the first language (Jiménez et al. 1996), suggesting that English learners have a unique bilingual reservoir of cross-language skills to draw on when engaged in second-language literacy tasks.

In contrast, less-successful English learner readers view reading in the first and second language as separate abilities and, in fact, see the first language as a source of confusion. That unsuccessful English learner readers/writers view first- and second-language reading in these ways suggests that they do not develop an understanding of the commonalities in first- and second-language literacy and, as a result, are unable to draw on useful connections between their two languages to acquire reading and writing skills in English. Jimenez (2000) suggests that unsuccessful English learner readers may need explicit instruction to learn about similarities between their languages (with respect to sound-letter correspondences or cognate vocabulary, for example) if they are to benefit from strategies based on the first language (see also Langer et al. 1990).

In most cases, cross-language influences are facilitative so that English learners with emergent first-language literacy skills, prior experiences with first-language literacy in the home, knowledge of cognate vocabulary, and well-developed metacognitive strategies for figuring out meaning from text in the first language, for example, acquire reading skills in English more readily than English learners who lack these first-language skills. In other cases, cross-linguistic influences may appear to have "negative" influences, for example, when Spanish-speaking English learners erroneously attribute the Spanish meaning to false cognates in English or pronounce words written in English using Spanish letter-sound correspondences. Even in these cases, however, it is important to keep in mind that these effects reflect an active and productive strategy on the part of English learners to draw on relevant, albeit sometimes inappropriate, knowledge about the first language when they are engaged in English reading and writing tasks.

343

In sum, research indicates that learning to read English as a second language is similar in some important respects to learning to read English as a first language (see August and Shanahan, this publication, for more details). At the same time, there are important differences, the primary one being influences from English learners' first language. English learners with limited competence in English, oral or written, draw on skills, knowledge, and experiences linked to the first language to fill gaps in their English reading skills until such time as they acquire the relevant English skills. Thus, contrary to claims that maintenance and continued development of English learners' first language impedes English literacy development because it diverts time that could be spent learning English, the empirical evidence indicates that continued use or development of the first language can facilitate English literacy development.

> **Empirical evidence indicates that continued use or development of the first language can facilitate English literacy development.**

Research on reading and writing development in dual language programs. Howard and her colleagues have conducted a number of studies on the reading and writing development of both English learners and English-only students in two-way programs (e.g., Howard 2003; Howard, Christian, and Genesee 2004; Serrano and Howard 2003, 2007; Howard and Sugarman 2007). This research is important because it goes beyond reporting scores on achievement tests and provides detailed descriptions of students' actual reading and writing performance in both English and Spanish. These studies found that English learners made good progress in both languages and developed high-level reading and writing skills in both languages, meeting or exceeding grade-level norms and narrowing achievement gaps in English with English-only students, at least by grade five (Howard and Christian 1997; Serrano and Howard 2003, 2007; Howard, Christian, and Genesee 2004; Howard and Sugarman 2007). In addition, the writing scores of English learners in English and Spanish were very similar at all time points.

English learners' English and Spanish writing skills were fairly sophisticated in all four domains of analysis (organization, topic development, mechanics, and language use), but particularly with regard to organization. The Spanish essays were usually comparable to the English essays in terms of organization and topic development, but they showed more mechanical errors, more linguistic/grammatical errors (e.g., word order, word choice, and subject-verb agreement), and some influences from English, mostly in borrowing English vocabulary, and also some influence from English grammar and mechanics. There was no code-switching in the English essays and only a few instances in the Spanish ones, and all were flagged with quotation marks, indicating that the students understood that they were mixing languages. The English writing samples of the English learners were generally comparable to those of the English-only students, especially among the fifth- and sixth-grade students.

In a longitudinal study of English learners in a dual language program, Lindholm-Leary (2005) found that English learners began kindergarten with fairly low vocabulary scores in Spanish (33rd percentile), but they made substantial gains to above average (61st percentile) by grade three. Their Spanish vocabulary scores were similar in grades three and six. In addition, their Spanish vocabulary scores in grade three, but not kindergarten, were highly correlated with reading achievement scores on norm-referenced achievement tests in both Spanish and English.

Together, these studies indicate that, given effective programs, English learners can acquire reading and writing skills in English that are virtually comparable to those of English-only students and, at the same time, they acquire strong reading and writing skills in Spanish.

Academic Achievement

Most researchers have examined the academic achievement of English learners in alternative educational programs in terms of outcomes on standardized achievement tests (cf. Lindholm-Leary and Borsato 2006), although some studies have used other measures, such as grade point average (GPA) (e.g., Curiel, Rosenthal, and Richek 1986; Lindholm-Leary and Borsato 2001), high school dropout rates (e.g., Curiel 1986; Thomas and Collier 2002), or even attitudes toward school and school-related topics (e.g., Cazabon et al. 1993; Gersten and Woodward 1995; Lambert and Cazabon 1994; Lindholm 1988; Lindholm-Leary and Borsato 2001). Although most studies have concentrated on students in elementary school, a few have focused on high school students to determine the influence of participation in a bilingual or dual language program during elementary school on later achievement levels. Studies at the secondary level have also often examined GPA, high school drop out or retention rates, and attitudes (Burnham-Massey and Piña 1990; Curiel, Rosenthal, and Richek 1986; Kirk Senesac 2002; Lindholm-Leary 2001; Medrano 1986; Thomas and Collier 2002). Only a few longitudinal studies have followed students from elementary into middle or high school (e.g., Lindholm-Leary and Borsato 2001; Thomas and Collier 2002). Finally, most studies on English learners during the past few years have focused on two-way programs (cf. Genesee et al. 2006), and this is reflected in the following review. Most of the studies also consist of comparative evaluations of outcomes in various program models. In general, these studies have been designed to answer one of three questions:

1. Which program is the best for English learners? This question has been addressed by studies that compare student outcomes on standardized tests of reading and/or mathematics achievement in different program types, usually bilingual versus something else (no program, structured English immersion [SEI], English as a second language [ESL], or two different bilingual models).

2. Does more English during the instructional day result in improved student outcomes? This question is often a secondary issue in research designed to address question #1 above.

3. How well do students achieve in dual language programs? This issue is addressed in studies that describe student achievement in particular programs with respect to norms on standardized achievement tests in mathematics, science, and social studies; GPA; high school completion/dropout rates; or various school-related attitudes. In other words, these studies seek to quantify the academic outcomes of English learners relative to some standard.

1. Which program is best for English learners?

Most large-scale studies as well as most systematic syntheses of relevant research indicate that there is a benefit from bilingual instruction over English-only instruction (for reviews, see August and Hakuta 1997; Francis, Lesaux, and August 2006; Genesee et al. 2005, 2006; Greene 1998; Rolstad, Mahoney, and Glass 2005; Slavin and Cheung 2005;[2] Willig 1985). A minority of studies report that bilingual instruction is equivalent to, or provides no benefit over, English-only instruction (Parrish et al. 2006) Interestingly, even the synthesis studies of Baker and his colleagues (Baker and de Kanter 1981; Rossell and Baker 1996) that have been used to support English-only approaches "do not state that English-only instruction is more effective, but merely that bilingual instruction should not be the only approach mandated by law" (Francis et al. 2006). This section provides a brief overview of relatively recent syntheses of research and does not report on the entire body of research because of space limitations; see the syntheses of studies mentioned earlier or specific studies for more detailed findings.

As part of the National Literacy Panel on Language-Minority Children and Youth, Francis and colleagues (2006) examined studies that compared programs that provided literacy instruction through a student's native language (bilingual program) with programs that provided literacy and other instruction through only English.

---

2. In Slavin and Cheung's (2005) analysis of 13 studies that examined whether bilingual or English-only approaches to reading instruction were more effective, nine studies favored a bilingual approach while four studies found no difference, for an overall positive effect favoring a bilingual approach.

Their conclusion was that:

> Overall, where differences between two instructional conditions were found in the studies reviewed, these differences typically favored the bilingual instruction condition. This is the case for studies conducted with students in both elementary and secondary schools, and with students possessing a range of abilities. (p. 398)

In their synthesis of available research on the achievement of English learners, Lindholm-Leary and Borsato (2006) found that there is strong convergent evidence that the academic achievement of English learners is positively related to sustained instruction that includes their first language, usually Spanish. They also reported that student achievement was related to length of participation in the program and the time of the assessment. More specifically, evaluations conducted in the early years of a program (kindergarten through grade three) typically revealed that students in bilingual programs scored below grade level (and sometimes very low), or either lower than or equivalent to comparison group peers (English learners or non-English learners in other types of programs). In contrast, almost all evaluations conducted at the end of elementary school or in middle and high school have found that the achievement of bilingually educated students, especially those in late-exit and two-way programs, was as good as and usually higher than that of comparison groups of students (e.g., Block 2007; Burnham-Massey and Piña 1990; Curiel, Rosenthal, and Richek 1986; Fulton-Scott and Calvin 1983; Lindholm-Leary 2001; Lindholm-Leary and Block in press; Lopez and Tashakkori 2006; Ramirez 1992). All studies of middle and high school students found that students who had received bilingual instruction in elementary school were as or more successful than comparison group students. In addition, most long-term studies report that the longer students stayed in the program, the more positive were their outcomes. These results were found for reading and mathematics achievement, GPA, attendance rates, high school completion rates, and attitudes toward school and self (e.g., Block 2007; Cazabon, Nicoladis, and Lambert 1998; Curiel, Rosenthal, and Richek 1986; Lambert and Cazabon 1994; Lindholm-Leary 2001; Lindholm-Leary and Borsato 2001, 2006; Lopez and Tashakkori 2006; Thomas and Collier 2002).

Rolstad, Mahoney, and Glass (2005) conducted a meta-analysis of studies on the effectiveness of bilingual education in Arizona, which like California, has an English-only mandate for English learners. Although the sample size was small (four studies), the results were consistent with other meta-analyses of studies based on national samples (Greene 1998; Willig 1985) and indicated a positive effect for bilingual instruction over English immersion (mainstream) instruction.

One limitation of this research concerns the definitions of program models under investigation (Francis et al. 2006; Lindholm-Leary and Borsato 2006). In some cases, bilingual education is clearly defined as to the amount of time devoted to instruction through each language and duration of the program (e.g., early-exit or transitional; late-exit or maintenance; see Ramirez 1992, for examples). In other cases, it is not clear what specialized instruction the students received in their "bilingual" classrooms (Burnham-Massey and Piña 1990; Curiel, Rosenthal, and Richek 1986; Medrano 1988; Saldate, Mishra, and Medina 1985). In studies that included nonbilingual programs, sometimes a mainstream English classroom was labeled "structured English immersion" and, in other cases, structured English immersion included specialized instruction for English learners, including instruction in the native language (Gersten and Woodward 1995; Ramirez 1992). As a result, it is difficult to pinpoint the specific features of bilingual programs that produced the positive effects reported in those studies (Francis et al. 2006).

Most studies of academic achievement in English learners are cross-sectional (single year); few are longitudinal. Thus, it is not always clear if students had been in the same program prior to the evaluation or whether they had changed programs (MacSwan et al. 2002; Parrish et al. 2006). This is important because students who belong to the English-only comparison group may have been formerly in a bilingual program, or students may have changed programs for various reasons. In fact, analyses of data from all students in grades three through nine in Arizona revealed that program placement was highly variable and erratic from year to year (MacSwan et al. 2002; MacSwan 2004). Changing programs can have important effects on program and student outcomes. More specifically, while Arizona reported that English immersion students scored higher than did students in bilingual education (Arizona Department of Education 2004, as reported in Rolstad, Mahoney, and Glass 2005), the state did not consider how many of the students in English immersion had formerly participated in bilingual programs. In other words, any positive effects that bilingual education might have had on these students' achievement would have been attributed to English immersion if the English learners had been reclassified. This is a recurrent problem in these studies and meta-analyses that report either no advantage or disadvantages of bilingual instruction.

Summary. The synthesis studies reviewed here provide evidence that English learners who participate in a bilingual program (receiving instruction through their primary language) may achieve at higher levels than English learners educated in English-only mainstream classrooms. These studies indicate further, and of particular importance, that English learners who participate in programs that provided extended instruction through the students' native language (i.e., two-way immersion and late-exit programs) outperform students who receive only short-term instruction through their native language (i.e., early-exit programs) (e.g., Cazabon, Nicoladis, and Lambert 1998; Fulton-Scott and Calvin 1983).

Several authors suggest that there is no one *best* model that will serve all English learners at all times (e.g., August and Hakuta 1997; Christian et al. 1997; Genesee 1999). Rather, they point out the importance of providing services for English learners that consider the community context, the needs of students to be served, and the resources that are available for implementing the program; we return to these issues in a later section.

2. Does more English lead to higher achievement in English?

An issue that underlies much of the debate and much of the research on educational alternatives for English learners concerns *time on task;* that is, the assumption that the more time English learners spend on studying English, the better their achievement in English will be. Next, we review three types of research that examine outcomes of students according to amount of instructional time in English.

Research Evidence 1. Findings from the studies on program type discussed in question #1 suggest that students who receive instruction through their primary language actually score higher than students who receive instruction only through English. Thus, this evidence suggests that, contrary to the time-on-task argument, maximizing time in English does not lead to higher achievement in English.

Research Evidence 2. Several studies in California have examined the impact of Proposition 227 on English learners' achievement, and these studies provide an indirect test of the time-on-task argument (Butler et al. 2000; Garcia and Curry-Rodriguez 2000; Gordon and Hoxby 2002; Grissom 2004; Parrish et al. 2006; Thompson et al. 2002). Overall, there is no evidence from this research that increasing the amount of exposure to English instruction has positive effects on English learners' achievement in English. Details from specific studies are provided below:

⊙ In their large-scale study of the impact of Proposition 227 on the achievement of students in California, Parrish and others (2006) reported that all subgroups, regardless of program placement (EL [English learners], RFEP [redesignated fluent English proficient], EO [English only]), demonstrated gains in academic achievement from 1997-98 to 2003-04, indicating that increasing English learners' exposure to English did not result in a differential advantage for English learners.

⊙ Gordon and Hoxby (2002) also studied the impact of Proposition 227 on the achievement of English learners in bilingual versus English immersion programs in California. They found that students who had been in a bilingual program and were immediately shifted to English immersion after Proposition 227 exhibited diminished results following the change in program. In fact, they reported a decrease in reading achievement of 12 percent for students in grades three to five, a decrease of 6 percent in grade six, and 4 percent in grades seven and eight. A more substantial negative effect occurred in math, where a decline of 27 percent was reported from grades three to five.

⊙ Grissom (2004) compared reclassification rates (from EL to RFEP) of Spanish-speaking English learners before and after the implementation of Proposition 227 in California. Despite greater exposure to English in the classroom after Proposition 227, Grissom concluded that there was not a correspondingly higher reclassification rate or higher test scores.

⊙ Thompson and others (2002) also examined whether the achievement of English learners improved after implementation of Proposition 227. Their careful analysis indicated that both English-only and English learners improved, but there was no reduction in the gap between English-only and English learner students. They interpreted the lack of gap reduction to indicate that English learners experienced the same increase that all students experienced and, thus, that there was no advantage of greater exposure to English in the classroom.

⊙ Garcia and Curry-Rodriguez (2000) and Butler and her collegues (2000), in analyses of student test outcomes, also reported no significant effects due to Proposition 227 on the English achievement of English learners; that is, more time spent in English did not result in higher achievement in English.

Research Evidence 3. Another way of examining the time-on-task issue is to compare the performance of English learners who have been in 50/50 versus 90/10 two-way immersion programs, since the former are exposed to almost twice as much English in the early years of the program as the latter. In a review of this research, Lindholm-Leary and Howard (2008) failed to find evidence to support the time-on-task argument; that is, English learners who had more instruction in English did not achieve at higher levels in English than English learners who spent considerably less time in English. More specifically, they found that:

⊙ English learners in both 50/50 and 90/10 programs developed high levels of oral English proficiency (Christian et al. 2004; Lindholm-Leary 2001);

⊙ Whereas English learners in 50/50 programs exhibited higher scores in English than English learners in 90/10 programs in the early grade levels, these differences disappeared by the upper elementary grade levels and the performance of both groups remained comparable throughout the secondary grade levels (Christian et al. 2004; Lindholm-Leary 2005). In short, there was no evidence that exposure to more English (50/50 program) resulted in higher achievement in English than less exposure to English (90:10) by late elementary school.

Summary. The results of these various types of studies do not provide evidence that spending more school time in English leads to higher achievement or proficiency in English. However, and in contrast, the research suggests that spending more time in the students' first language benefits students' first-language development. As Lindholm-Leary and Howard (2008) point out, the results show that more instructional time spent in Spanish positively impacts achievement in Spanish and has no negative effect on achievement measured in English. These results are consistent with findings reported in previous studies of dual language education (August and Hakuta 1997; Genesee et al. 2006; Lindholm-Leary and Borsato 2006).

> **More instructional time spent in Spanish positively impacts achievement in Spanish and has no negative effect on achievement measured in English.**

3. How well do students do in dual language programs?

A number of studies include results from standardized achievement tests in reading and math and, thus, allow us to determine the actual level of achievement of English learners in alternative programs (Block 2007; de Jong 2002; Gold 2006; Howard and Sugarman 2007; Kirk Senesac 2002; Lambert and Cazabon 1994; Lindholm-Leary 2001; Lindholm and Aclan 1991; Lindholm-Leary and Block in press; Lindholm-Leary and Howard 2008; Lopez and Tashakkori 2006; Thomas and Collier 2002). As noted previously, the program model that has been examined most often is two-way immersion. These studies all found that bilingual programs were effective in helping English learners achieve at or above grade level in their first language and progress toward grade-level achievement, or above, in English by middle school. On norm-referenced standardized tests and criterion-referenced state tests of reading and math achievement in English, English learners in late elementary or middle school scored not only significantly higher than English learners in general in the state, but they also performed on par with English-only students in English-only classrooms (Block 2007; Christian et al. 2004; Gold 2006; Gomez, Freeman, and Freeman 2005; Howard and Sugarman 2007; Lindholm-Leary 2005; Lindholm-Leary and Block in press; Lindholm-Leary and Borsato 2005, 2006; Thomas and Collier 2002). Those results extend to studies of Chinese and Korean dual language students as well (Garcia 2003; Ha 2001; Lindholm-Leary 2001, 2009). English learners in dual language programs also demonstrated above average or high levels of academic achievement in their first language according to standardized tests of achievement in Spanish (Gold 2006; Lindholm-Leary 2001; Lindholm-Leary and Borsato 2005, 2006).

Four studies included samples of high school students who had previously or were currently participating in a two-way program (Kirk Senesac 2002; Lindholm-Leary

2001; Lindholm-Leary and Borsato 2001; Thomas and Collier 2002). Both 90/10 and 50/50 models of two-way immersion were represented in these studies at both elementary and high school levels. These studies consistently found that students scored very low in English reading in the early grade levels and progressed toward grade-level performance by later elementary or high school. They also showed that students who had developed high levels of proficiency in both languages were more successful at closing the achievement gap in reading with the norming group by grade four than students with lower levels of bilingual proficiency (Kirk Senesac 2002; Lambert and Cazabon 1994; Lindholm-Leary 2001; Lindholm and Aclan 1991; Lindholm-Leary and Howard 2008).

> **English learners in dual language programs appear more likely to close the achievement gap by late elementary or middle school than their English learner peers in English main- stream programs.**

As to achievement in math, all studies showed that, although the students under evaluation had begun elementary school with low to below-average achieve- ment in math, they scored average to above average in math when assessed in English by grades four to six, depending on the study (Block 2007; de Jong 2002; Kirk Senesac 2002; Lindholm and Aclan 1991; Lindholm-Leary and Block in press). The participating students also typically met district or state proficiency standards (de Jong 2002; Gomez et al. 2005; Kirk Senesac 2002) and scored above district and state averages for English learners (de Jong 2002; Lindholm-Leary 2001).

Some studies have also been conducted with relatively small numbers of students in one or two schools in a single geographic location (e.g., Cazabon, Nicoladis, and Lambert 1998; de Jong 2002; Kirk Senesac 2002; Stipek, Ryan, and Alarcón 2001). On aggregate, these studies found that English learners in two-way immersion programs performed as well as or better than their peers educated in other types of programs, both on English-medium standardized achievement tests and Spanish- medium standardized achievement tests.

Summary. In summary, this body of research is consistent in demonstrating that English learners who participate in dual language programs demonstrate proficiency and achievement in English at comparable or higher levels than their peers in English mainstream programs. In addition, receiving more English in their instruc- tional day does not promote higher levels of English proficiency or achievement in reading/language arts. Rather, English learners in dual language programs appear more likely to close the achievement gap by late elementary or middle school than their English learner peers in English mainstream programs. This higher level of achievement for dual language English learners may be due to their ability to benefit from cross-language influences; that is, English learners who can use their first language to "bootstrap" into literacy in English are able to fill gaps in their reading skills in English until they have developed the array of relevant English literacy skills to become competent readers.

Identity and Attitudes

Several studies have examined students' attitudes toward bilingualism, other languages, the dual language program and school in general, and people who are different from themselves (Block 2007; Lambert and Cazabon 1994; Lindholm-Leary 2001; Lindholm-Leary and Borsato 2001; Lindholm-Leary and Ferrante 2005; Lopez and Tashakkori 2006; Potowski 2005). These studies found that English learners had positive perceptions of their academic competence, bilingualism, and two-way programs (Block 2007; Lambert and Cazabon 1994; Lindholm-Leary 2001; Lindholm-Leary and Borsato 2001; Lindholm-Leary and Ferrante 2005). Lindholm-Leary and Borsato (2001), for example, found that most English learners believed that they would not drop out of school; they wanted to go to college; they would go to college after high school; and they thought that getting good grades was important. Almost half of the students believed that the two-way program kept them from dropping out of school and that they were academically outperforming their peers who had also started school as English learners. Enrollment in two-way programs, compared with mainstream English-only classrooms, was also associated with greater participation in intergenerational family relationships, more positive attitudes toward bilingualism, and more acceptance toward students who differed in language background or physical appearance (Block 2007; Lopez and Tashakkori 2006).

Characteristics of Effective Dual Language Programs

In Chapter 1, the characteristics of effective English language development programs were presented according to research with English learners. In this section, we briefly present research on the characteristics of effective dual language programs. Not surprisingly, high-quality dual language programs share many of the same characteristics as high-quality mainstream programs (Lindholm-Leary and Borsato 2006).[3] However, there are other characteristics in dual language programs that need to be considered, and it is those characteristics that we discuss now.

---

3. Effective features are described in greater detail in a document entitled *Guiding Principles for Dual Language Education,* which provides a comprehensive literature review (Lindholm-Leary 2007) and a set of key indicators of program quality in two-way immersion (Howard et al. 2007).

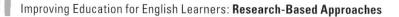

Program and School Structure

In a high-quality program, there is a vision of bilingualism and multiculturalism based on the concept of *additive bilingualism:* all students are given the opportunity to acquire English as a second language at no cost to their home language. Additive bilingual programs are associated with grade-level achievement in the content domains, high levels of proficiency in the second language without loss of the home language (Lindholm-Leary 2001; Ramirez 1992; Thomas and Collier 2002), and improved self-esteem and cross-cultural attitudes (Cazabon, Nicoladis, and Lambert 1998; Kirk Senesac 2002; Lindholm 1994; Lindholm-Leary 2001; Lindholm-Leary and Borsato 2001, 2006). Conversely, subtractive bilingual school contexts in which learners' second language replaces the native language have negative effects on the academic achievement of many English learners. In other words, loss of the native language is associated with lower levels of second-language attainment, scholastic underachievement, alienation from families and peers speaking the first language, and difficulties with identity (Hernandez-Chavez 1984; Lambert 1984; Tse 1998; Valenzuela 1999; Wong Fillmore 1991).

> **In a high-quality program, there is a vision of bilingualism and multiculturalism based on the concept of *additive bilingualism:* all students are given the opportunity to acquire English as a second language at no cost to their home language.**

An additive bilingual approach is critical if dual language education is to be successful because it ensures the implementation of high-level language and academic instruction. An additive bilingual approach helps to guarantee that decisions are made at program, curricular, and instructional levels that enrich English learners' and mainstream students' education. Fears that dual language learning is an unnecessary or unreasonable burden on students result in educational decisions that diminish or dilute the educational experience of students. For example, such fears often prompt educators to use bilingual modes of instruction (e.g., concurrent translation) to teach new or complex academic material when research shows consistently that such an approach is not only unnecessary but, furthermore, deleterious to dual language development if overused. Promoting additive bilingualism requires that school principals, and teachers as well, have some familiarity with and understanding of research on dual language education and its outcomes. A solid grounding in these domains empowers school principals to promote an attitude of additive bilingualism in the school, to encourage collegial and collaborative interaction among dual language and mainstream teachers in the school, and to advocate dual language programs. Knowledgeable and supportive school principals also ensure that teachers have access to the resources they need to implement an effective program, including adequate support personnel, instructional and material resources, and time for planning and development.

Successful dual language programs engage in extensive and high-level planning and, in particular, plan for articulation across grade levels and programs (Met and Lorenz 1997; Montecel and Cortez 2002). Regular and substantial ongoing time for planning during the school week and across the school year is critical if dual language education is to be successful. Collaborative planning that involves teachers

Successful dual language programs engage in extensive and high-level planning and, in particular, plan for articulation across grade levels and programs.

across grade levels and programs within a school is essential because dual language programs aim to accomplish all that mainstream programs aim for and, in addition, they seek to invest children with additional language and cultural competencies. Dual language programs represent value-added education and, as such, they demand careful planning. More specifically, schoolwide planning is critical to ensure:

(a) adequate and equitable distribution of school resources;

(b) collaboration among dual language and mainstream teachers in the creation of a coherent and integrated curriculum;

(c) the development and implementation of a schoolwide curriculum that integrates first- and second-language instruction with academic instruction at each grade level and across grade levels;

(d) language-minority and language-majority students are taught equitably and to high standards; and

(e) appropriate assessment protocols are developed and put in place to monitor program effectiveness (cf. Howard et al. 2007; Lindholm-Leary 2001).

In short, planning time ensures developmentally effective and efficient programs.

Supportive and knowledgeable leadership is also essential to guide decision making about critical issues in dual language schools (cf. Howard et al. 2007; Lindholm-Leary 2001). Chief among these is the allocation of time to each language and the sequencing of literacy instruction. The allocation of time entails decisions about how much time to devote to each language and when. As noted earlier, there are three prominent models of dual language education: developmental bilingual, two-way immersion, and transitional. Furthermore, developmental and two-way program models themselves can be differentiated by the allocation of time to each language—either 90/10 (90 percent of the time devoted to the minority language, 10 percent to the majority language) or 50/50. Each has its advantages and potential disadvantages. Proactive and informed leadership is essential to guide parents, teachers, and the public at large as to which model is optimal for their community. In the absence of effective leadership, decisions about program model and time allocation for each language are often made on the basis of hearsay, superstition, or simple ignorance, all of which risk jeopardizing the educational achievement of English learners.

If schools choose a 50/50 two-way immersion model, then a decision must be made about the sequencing of literacy instruction. Several options exist: each group receives instruction in its own language first, followed by literacy instruction in the other language; all students receive instruction in the minority language first; or all students receive literacy instruction in both English and the other language from the beginning. In determining which sequence to use, one should consider the English-language and literacy skills of the English learner population. Students with little or no oral language skills in English may be more academically successful if they are first provided with literacy skills in their native language; literacy in the first language can then be used to transfer to literacy skills in English.

Curriculum

Research has demonstrated clearly that a high-quality curriculum is critical for students' academic success. There are many components to a high-quality curriculum for English learners. In effective schools, the curriculum is meaningful, enriched, and academically challenging. It incorporates higher-order thinking and is thematically integrated (Berman et al. 1995; Cloud, Genesee, and Hamayan 2000; Doherty et al. 2003; Montecel and Cortez 2002; Ramirez 1992).

Research has demonstrated clearly that a high-quality curriculum is critical for students' academic success.

In addition, the curriculum is infused with language instruction at all times to meet the vision and goals associated with bilingualism and biliteracy (American Council on the Teaching of Foreign Languages 2006; Cloud, Genesee, and Hamayan 2000; Genesee 1987). Language objectives are considered in all aspects of curriculum planning (Lyster 2007), and language and literacy are developed across the curriculum (Doherty et al. 2003) to ensure that students learn required content as well as the academic language associated with that content.

Language objectives should be integrated with academic objectives. That is to say, language skills that are critical for the mastery of academic objectives should be identified and included along with relevant academic objectives. This also means that language objectives should be taught along with academic objectives so that students acquire the language skills needed to master academic subject matter. As

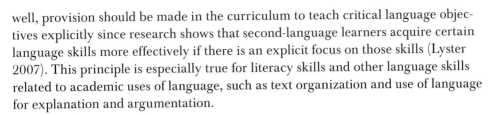

well, provision should be made in the curriculum to teach critical language objectives explicitly since research shows that second-language learners acquire certain language skills more effectively if there is an explicit focus on those skills (Lyster 2007). This principle is especially true for literacy skills and other language skills related to academic uses of language, such as text organization and use of language for explanation and argumentation.

Consequently, it is necessary for a balance between implicit and explicit language teaching that is integrated with academic instruction (Lyster 2007). The language arts portion of the curriculum should focus on explicit instruction of those language skills that are essential to the mastery of prescribed literacy and academic objectives. Language objectives should include functions, grammar, and vocabulary in alignment with academic demands of the curriculum and social demands of school and extracurricular activities. (See the chapters by Snow and Katz and by Dutro and Kinsella, this publication, for more information about providing effective ELD instruction.)

Instruction

Of course, good instruction is associated with higher student outcomes regardless of the type of educational model that is used. In dual language programs, good instruction includes the following characteristics:

> **Of course, good instruction is associated with higher student outcomes regardless of the type of educational model that is used.**

- ⊙ It has diverse instructional techniques that respond to different language proficiency levels (Berman et al. 1995; Echevarria, Short, and Powers 2006; Echevarria, Vogt, and Short 2008; Montecel and Cortez 2002).

- ⊙ Cooperative learning and other grouping strategies optimize student interactions and shared work experiences, especially in two-way programs that include both English learners and English-only students in the same classrooms (e.g., Calderon and Carreon 2001; Cohen 1994).

- ⊙ Optimal language input in turn calls for careful planning to integrate language and subject matter instruction to ensure access to the core curriculum (Berman et al. 1995; Echevarria et al. 2006, 2008). Sheltered instruction is one particularly useful way in which language teaching can be integrated with content instruction to ensure optimal language development at the same time as students master required content objectives (see Echevarria and Short, this publication).

- ⊙ Balanced use of both languages is required because there are two language populations, one of which is native speakers and one of which is language learners.

Both groups need support and enrichment. English learners need support to acquire academic language and intellectual stimulation to extend their native language skills. The risk in two-way immersion programs is that English learners are used as "props" to stimulate the language development of native speakers of English without getting sufficient language enrichment themselves (Kowal and Swain 1997; Valdés 1997). In addition, Gathercole (2002b) concludes that in the bilingual groups she studied (English learners in two-way, English learners in mainstream—both those with Spanish or English in the home) that performed the best had the greatest amount of input (considering both home and school), and those who performed the worst had the least. She argues that students need a "critical mass" of input that will enable them to understand the linguistic structures they are learning. Similarly, Tomasello (2000) points out that the frequency of input can be influential when overgeneralizations occur in children's language; that is, linguistic items that are heard more frequently can become entrenched and may be less likely to elicit errors than items that are heard less frequently.

- Students need explicit second-language instruction to promote second-language learning (Lyster 2007). It is important to base instruction on a curriculum that specifies which language skills (e.g., questioning, requesting information) and structures (e.g., conditional verb forms) should be mastered and how they should be integrated into academic content instruction (e.g., including preterit and imperfect forms of verbs in Spanish when teaching history; conditional, future, and subjunctive verb tenses when teaching mathematics and science).

- Monolingual lesson delivery (each language is used during different periods of time for instruction in specific domains) to ensure that students do not tune out when the nonnative language is being use (Dulay and Burt 1978; Legaretta 1979,1981).

Teachers also need to know how to use instructional strategies that draw on students' existing oral and written language skills and cultural resources; for example, instruction that draws on learners' background knowledge to preview new content and make links to the native language when teaching literacy (e.g., spelling, vocabulary, grammar). At the same time, dual language teachers should avoid using both languages simply to make teaching and learning easier (i.e., dual language instruction as a "crutch"). Language acquisition is facilitated when there is a focus on each language during specific instructional periods; otherwise, students who have recourse to the other language may fail to show growth in acquiring new language skills in their weaker language. Use of the home language is appropriate if done strategically; for example, at the upper grade levels to explicate similarities or differences between the home language and English or to preview new material that is particularly complex.

Appropriate Assessment and Accountability

Most research on effective schools, including effective dual language programs, high-lights the importance of assessment and accountability. Many studies have pointed out the benefits of using student achievement data to shape and/or monitor program effectiveness (August and Hakuta 1997; Berman et al. 1995; Slavin and Calderón 2001). Effective use of assessment data to improve program outcomes is most likely when schools use assessment measures that are aligned with the school's vision and goals, the curriculum, and district and state standards (Montecel and Cortez 2002). Dual language programs require the use of multiple measures in both languages to assess student progress toward meeting bilingual and biliteracy goals along with regular mandated curricular and content-related goals.

In light of evidence from the reviews conducted by the National Literacy Panel (August and Shanahan 2006) and the Center for Research on Education, Diversity and Excellence (Genesee et al. 2006), it is also important that classroom assessment take cross-language influences into account. For example, in the case of English learners being assessed in English, transfer from the home language that results in native language-like forms or usage in English should not simply be marked incorrect, but should be noted as instances of students' strategic use of the native language to acquire English. This kind of evidence can also be used for explicit instruction in how the native language and English differ (or are similar) so that students are better able to master the English forms.

Quality of Staff and Professional Development

The significance of highly qualified teachers has been demonstrated in many studies with English learners (e.g., August and Shanahan, this publication; Montecel and Cortez 2002). In dual language programs, research has identified several factors that are associated with effective teaching:

- ⊙ Appropriate teaching certificates or credentials, good content knowledge, and good classroom management skills (Cloud et al. 2000; Lindholm-Leary 2001; Met and Lorenz 1997; Montecel and Cortez 2002).

The significance of highly qualified teachers has been demonstrated in many studies with English learners.

- ⊙ Bilingual/BCLAD (Bilingual, Cross-cultural, Language, and Academic Development) and ESL/ELD credentials help provide teachers with a solid understanding of bilingual education theory, second-language development and theory, educational equity, appropriate instructional strategies for English learners, and other strategies that establish positive classroom environments for English learners. When teachers do not have appropriate understanding of bilingual theory and bilingual education, they risk making poor choices regarding program structure, curriculum, and instruction, which can lead, in turn, to lowered student performance and the perception that bilingual education does not work (Clark et al. 2002). However, one should not assume that all teachers who have a bilingual credential have current knowledge of or support for dual language education.

⊙ Native or native-like ability in the language(s) in which they teach (e.g., Clark et al. 2002; Doherty et al. 2003; Lindholm-Leary 2001; Montecel and Cortez 2002; Ramirez 1992).

Issues in Learner Needs

Academic performance is often related to characteristics of students and their backgrounds. In this section, we briefly review research evidence concerning the following learner and background characteristics and their influence on academic achievement and other school-related outcomes: socioeconomic status, length of residence or prior schooling, disability, language status, and demographic characteristics of the school's population.

Socioeconomic Status

There is an extensive body of research on the relationship between socioeconomic status (SES) and achievement among students from the mainstream population (Knapp and Woolverton 2003). In contrast, there are relatively few empirical studies of SES and its relationship to achievement in English learners. Moreover, most research on English learners includes Hispanic students from low-income families and, thus, there is insufficient variation in student SES to discern the true relationship between differences in SES and variations in achievement among English learners (Adams et al. 1994). Notwithstanding this limitation, the available evidence indicates that there is a positive relationship between SES and academic achievement in English learners, as has been found for mainstream students (Fernandez and Nielsen 1986; Hampton, Ekboir, and Rochin 1995; Lindholm-Leary 2001; Lindholm-Leary and Howard 2008; Nielsen and Lerner 1986). One measure of SES that has been used in research on mainstream and English learner students is parental level of education (Knapp and Woolverton 2004). The few research studies that have used parental education as a measure of SES have reported either no effect for parental education (Adams et al. 1994) or an effect but only for English and not Spanish

achievement (Lindholm-Leary 2001; Gatherole 2002b). The failure to find a link between SES and achievement should be interpreted with caution because there was little variation in parental education in the predominantly Hispanic and low-SES families that were included in these studies.

Length of Residence in United States and Prior Schooling

Studies on length of residence in the United States and prior schooling have found that the longer families reside in the United States, measured in terms of number of generations since immigration, the *lower* students' school achievement; in other words, recent immigrants tend to attain higher levels of achievement than do second- or third-generation Hispanic students (Adams et al. 1994; Fernandez and Nielsen 1986). Indeed, there is a growing evidence that recent immigrants in general, both Hispanic and Asian and not necessarily only English learners, have higher levels of achievement than second- and later-generation students (Kao and Tienda 1995; Olneck 2004; Rumbaut and Portes 2001). In one of the few studies to include English learners other than Spanish speakers, along with a wide range of SES levels, Collier (1987) examined 1,548 English learners with a variety of home languages who arrived in the United States at different ages to determine how long it took them to reach grade-level achievement in ESL classes. Collier reported that students who arrived between the ages of eight and eleven made the greatest achievement gains; those who arrived at ages five to six were projected to require at least two to three more years to reach the level of performance of the older students; and those who arrived between twelve and fifteen years of age were the lowest achievers and, in fact, had not reached the national average in any subject area, except math, even after four to five years of residence in the United States.

> **Recent immigrants tend to attain higher levels of achievement than do second- or third-generation Hispanic students.**

These results are important in highlighting the complex role of second-language literacy skills in the academic success of English learners at different grade levels. Arguably, since all students had no or limited proficiency in oral English, differences among these groups are attributable to the role of literacy in English in the face of a curriculum that becomes increasingly difficulty across grade levels. In particular, the youngest learners were at a disadvantage because of low levels of literacy in both English and their home language, and the oldest learners, although literate in their home language, were at a disadvantage because of a demanding academic curriculum that made it difficult for them to draw on native language literacy skills. In contrast, the eight- to eleven-year-olds were able to draw on native language literacy skills to cope with a curriculum of intermediate difficulty. This research suggests that English learners who arrive during the high school years with limited English language skills are at most risk for academic difficulty and struggle to catch up to grade-level expectations because of the high academic and literacy demands of the curriculum. Many districts have developed newcomer programs to address the specific needs of such students (see August and Shanahan, this publication, for further information on literacy development and Echevarria and Short, this publication, for more information on newcomer programs).

Students with Disabilities

Only a few studies of dual language programs have examined issues concerning English learners with special education needs (Lindholm-Leary and Howard 2008). Even these studies did not focus specifically on students with special education needs. Nevertheless, this are instructive for what they reveal about the achievement of special education students in dual language programs. Howard (2003) and Lindholm-Leary (2001, 2005) found that students with special education needs who participated in dual language programs experienced significant positive outcomes by the upper elementary grade levels. Students with special needs may be better served in dual language programs than in English-only programs because, although they may have less well-developed literacy skills in English than students without special needs, they are biliterate; in fact, some score average in Spanish reading achievement. Their peers in the English-only program who have special needs have low levels of literacy in the only language they know; they lack literacy skills in Spanish that they can draw on while learning English literacy skills. Dual language students with special needs who are bilingual and biliterate may have an advantage compared with English learner peers in English-only programs who are monolingual and have below-average literacy skills in their only language.

> **Students with special education needs who participated in dual language programs experienced significant positive outcomes by the upper elementary grade levels.**

In light of these findings, it would appear that English learners with special needs should be accepted into dual language programs and be kept in the program for its duration despite their special needs so that they acquire literacy skills in two languages to the level they are capable. Including such students in dual language programs confers advantages for English learners with special needs that would be lost if they were educated monolingually (e.g., Artiles and Ortiz 2002; Goldstein 2004; Kohnert and Derr 2004). Moreover, there is no evidence indicating that educating

English learners with special needs in English-only programs results in greater achievement in English.

Research on English learners with learning disabilities is also scant, and yet there is sufficient evidence at this time to argue that English learners with language-learning impairments can become bilingual to the extent that their impairment allows. There is no empirical justification for excluding such students from dual language programs on the grounds that restricting their language learning, in and outside school, to one language facilitates their language development and helps resolve their underlying impairment. To the contrary, research on English learners with language-learning difficulties indicates that such learners can acquire competence in two languages (de Valenzuela and Niccolai 2004) and can benefit from participation in dual language programs (Artiles and Ortiz 2002; Kohnert and Derr 2004).

In fact, it has been argued that English learners with language impairment are likely to attain higher educational outcomes in dual language programs than monolingual programs because the former take advantage of the considerable cross-linguistic transfer that has been observed to occur in the acquisition of literacy skills and the enhanced cognitive advantages that accompany bilingual proficiency (Bialystok 2001, 2008).

The research evidence that is available also indicates that the diagnosis of learning impairment involves assessment of both languages and that interventions for children with language-learning impairments be carried out using both languages. There is consensus among researchers who have studied bilingual students with special education needs that both languages should be considered in the planning and implementation of interventions for them (Artiles and Ortiz 2002; Baca and Cervantes 2004; Goldstein 2004; Kohnert 2004; Kohnert and Derr 2004; Restrepo and Gutierrez-Clellen 2004; see August and Shanahan, this publication).

Language Status

Most research is consistent in showing that bilingual proficiency and biliteracy are positively related to academic achievement in both languages (Lindholm-Leary and Borsato 2006). More specifically, several studies have shown that bilingual Hispanic students have higher achievement scores (Fernandez and Nielsen 1986; Lindholm-Leary 2001; Nielsen and Lerner 1986; Rumberger and Larson 1998), GPAs, and educational expectations (Fernandez and Nielsen 1986; Nielsen and

Most research is consistent in showing that bilingual proficiency and biliteracy are positively related to academic achievement in both languages.

Lerner 1986) than their monolingual English-speaking Hispanic peers. Consistent with these findings are results of studies of English learners who acquire both communicative and academic proficiency in English and, thus, are bilingual, indicating that they tend to achieve at even higher levels than do monolingual native English-speaking students in reading and math measured in English (Lindholm-Leary 2007).

Demographics of School Population

Lindholm-Leary and Block (Block 2007; Lindholm-Leary 2001; Lindholm-Leary and Block 2008) have examined the impact of school demographics on student achievement in dual language programs. Lindholm-Leary (2001) found higher levels of Spanish oral and reading proficiency in dual language schools with relatively high ethnic density and a high proportion of students from low SES backgrounds in comparison to schools with lower ethnic density and fewer low SES students. In contrast, students were more likely to attain higher levels of proficiency in English reading achievement when they attended schools with less ethnic density and with fewer low-SES students. In short, being schooled with a high proportion of Spanish speakers has a positive impact on Spanish achievement, while being schooled with a relatively high proportion of advantaged English speakers may confer a positive impact on English achievement. Block (2007) and Lindholm-Leary and Block (2008) reported that English learner and Hispanic English-speaking students in predominantly Hispanic, low-SES schools achieved similarly to or higher than their peers in mainstream English-only programs at the same or nearby schools.

Conclusions

We began this chapter with a discussion of various reasons for promoting bilingualism in English learners, including the cognitive and cultural advantages associated with high levels of bilingual proficiency and enhanced career opportunities that result from knowing two languages. Next we described various models of dual language education: transitional, developmental, and two-way immersion and explained that the only programs that could develop true bilingual, bilterate, and multicultural competencies are models that are additive in nature; namely, developmental bilingual and two-way immersion programs.

We then turned to research on the oral language development of English learners. Overall, the empirical evidence concerning the oral English and home language development of English learners is limited and fragmented and, thus, we have a weak empirical foundation for developing programs that promote oral English skills. Notwithstanding these limitations, some trends are discernible in the available evidence. First, contrary to much popular opinion, the acquisition of oral language skills in a second language is a complex process that takes time even for young second-language learners. More specifically, research on English learners in California and elsewhere in the U.S. indicates that it can take two years, or more, for English learners to acquire proficient oral language skills for general communicative purposes and even longer when it comes to acquiring oral academic language skills. Second, the available evidence also indicates that, despite the fact that most English learners in California are educated in English mainstream classrooms, the majority lack the academic language skills needed to be reclassified as English proficient *even after 10 years of English instruction.* Third, studies that have looked at the oral language development of English learners in a dual language program indicate that they attain the same or higher levels of oral proficiency in English as English learners in all-English programs and, at the same time, they achieve higher levels of proficiency in their native language than similar English learners in all-English programs.

The importance of oral language skills in the education of English learners is highlighted in research on literacy development. This research shows that literacy development in English as a second language is influenced by English learners' oral language skills, as it is in native English-speaking students. The relationship between English oral skills and English literacy is more complex in English learners than it is in native speakers of English because of cross-linguistic influences from English learners' first language on their acquisition of English reading and writing skills. English learners often call upon oral native language skills to "bootstrap" into English literacy prior to having acquired the necessary skills in English. In other words, skills in the native language support their literacy development in English. Thus, the development of oral proficiency in the native language, as well as in English, and the development of skills related to reading in their first language can facilitate the development of literacy skills in English among English learners.

Research that has looked at the relationship between literacy in the native language and English literacy development provides additional evidence of cross-language influences, most of which facilitate the development of literacy skills in English (see also August and Shanahan, this publication). Specifically, English learners with preliteracy skills in the native language progress more quickly and successfully in English literacy than English learners without these skills and related literacy experiences. In fact, it

Research that has looked at the relationship between literacy in the native language and English literacy development provides additional evidence of cross-language influences, most of which facilitate the development of literacy skills in English.

has been found that English learners who were identified as the best readers in their native language were able to transition to English reading instruction earlier than other students. Thus, contrary to claims that maintenance and continued development of English learners' native language impedes literacy development in the second language because it diverts time that could be spent learning English, there is little empirical evidence that continued use or development of the native language detracts from English literacy development. To the contrary, the available evidence argues for additive cross-language effects in those domains that are related to reading/writing and higher order academic and cognitive tasks.

We next examined research on the academic achievement of English learners in dual language programs. A common theme in this research is *time on task*—the assumption that the more time students spend in English in school, the higher will be their achievement in English. We have already seen that this is not true for the development of oral proficiency in English since the majority of English learners in English mainstream programs do not become proficient in English; nor do they necessarily outperform English learners in dual language programs in the long run. The time-on-task assumption does not hold up when it comes to academic achievement either. Research that has compared the achievement of English learners in dual language programs versus English mainstream programs has found that English learners in dual language programs attain the same or higher levels of achievement in academic domains as students in all-English programs. The same trend is evident in research that has examined alternative forms of dual language education. English learners who receive more instructional time in English (e.g., 50/50 two-way programs) do not achieve at higher levels than students who receive less instructional time in English (e.g., 90/10 two-way immersion programs). In contrast, spending more instructional time in Spanish improves English learners' achievement in Spanish. Once again, those studies highlight important additive cross-language facilitation effects when students are educated in two languages. Those additive bilingual effects are perhaps most evident in findings that indicate that English learners who develop high levels of proficiency in both languages are more successful at closing the achievement gap in reading with norming groups than students with lower levels of bilingual proficiency (e.g., students with higher levels of oral proficiency in English and lower levels of oral proficiency in Spanish).

We also examined research concerned with quality indicators of effective dual language programs. It is important to recognize that while some programs may call themselves dual language or two-way immersion, they may not actually conform to the program specifications outlined at the beginning of this chapter. Therefore, the research findings reported here may not apply to those programs. Research findings point to some characteristics of effective dual language programs, including an additive vision of bilingualism and multiculturalism; extensive planning time to ensure high-quality instruction and articulation and infusion of language instruction across all domains of the curriculum and across grade levels; professional development for all staff; and the use of assessment results to improve program delivery.

Finally, we noted that research has shown that certain learner or school characteristics (SES or parent education, special education, demographics of school population) can influence student outcomes. In this chapter we provide specific details about each of these variables and conclude that, overall, there is no research to suggest that any of those variables or combinations of variables impede the ability of any particular group of students from benefiting from instruction in a dual language program.

There is sufficient research to demonstrate the positive impact of high-quality dual language programs to promote bilingual, biliterate, content-area, and multicultural competencies.

In conclusion, while we and other researchers have pointed out the need for further research on the education of English learners, there is sufficient research to demonstrate the positive impact of high-quality dual language programs to promote bilingual, biliterate, content-area, and multicultural competencies.

References

Abedi, J. 2003. *Impact of students' language background on content-based performance: Analyses of extant data.* Executive Summary. CSE Technical Report No. 603. Los Angeles: University of California, Center for the Study of Evaluation/National Center for Research on Evaluation, Standards, and Student Testing.

Adams, D., B. Astone, E. M. Nunez-Wormack, and I. Smodlaka. 1994. Predicting the academic achievement of Puerto Rican and Mexican-American ninth-grade students. *Urban Review* 26(1): 1–14.

American Council on the Teaching of Foreign Languages. 2006 *Standards for foreign language learning in the 21st century.* 3rd ed. Lawrence, KS: Allen Press, Inc.

Artiles, A. J., and A. A. Ortiz, eds. 2002. *English language learners with special education needs: Identification, assessment, and instruction.* Washington, DC, and McHenry, IL: Center for Applied Linguistics and Delta Systems.

Au, K., and C. Jordan. 1981. Teaching reading to Hawaiian children: Analysis of a culturally appropriate instructional event. *Anthropology and Education Quarterly* 11: 91–115.

August, D., and K. Hakuta, eds. 1997. *Improving schooling for language minority children: A research agenda.* Washington, DC: National Academy Press.

August, D., and T. Shanahan, eds. 2006. *Developing literacy in second language learners. Report of the national literacy panel on minority-language children and youth.* Mahwah, NJ: Lawrence Erlbaum.

Baca, L., and H. Cervantes. 2004. *The bilingual special education interface.* 4th ed. Upper Saddle River, NJ: Pearson/Merrill/Prentice Hall.

Baker, C. 2006. *Foundations of bilingualism and bilingual education.* 4th ed. Clevedon: Multilingual Matters.

Baker, K. A., and A. A. de Kanter. 1981. *Effectiveness of bilingual education: A review of the literature.* Washington, DC: U.S. Department of Education, Office of Planning, Budget, and Evaluation.

Banks, J., ed., 2004. Immigrants and education in the United States. In *Handbook of research on multicultural education.* 2nd ed. New York: Macmillan.

Barker, C. M. 2000. *Education for international understanding and global competence.* Report of a Meeting Convened by Carnegie Corp of New York. http://www.carnegie.org/pdf/global.pdf (accessed March 11, 2007.)

Berman, P., C. Minicucci, B. McLaughlin, B. Nelson, and K. Woodworth. 1995. School reform and student diversity: *Case studies of exemplary practices for English language learner students.* Santa Cruz, CA: National Center for Research on Cultural Diversity and Second Language Learning, and B.W. Associates.

Bialystok, E. 2001. *Bilingualism in development: Language, literacy, and cognition.* New York: Cambridge University Press.

Bialystok, E. 2008. *Language processing in bilingual children.* New York: Cambridge University Press.

Bialystok, E., and M. Martin. 2004. Attention and inhibition in bilingual children: Evidence from the dimensional change card sort task. *Developmental Science* 7, 325–39.

Bikle, K., K. Hakuta, and E. S. Billings. 2004. Trends in two-way immersion research. In *Handbook of research on multicultural education.* 2nd ed., ed. J. A. Banks and C. A. McGee Banks, New York: Macmillan.

Block, N. 2007. Dual immersion programs in predominantly Latino schools. PhD diss., Claremont Graduate University, Claremont, CA.

Burnham-Massey, L., and M. Piña. 1990. Effects of bilingual instruction on English academic achievement of LEP students. *Reading Improvement* 27(2): 129–32.

Butler, Y., J. E. Orr, M. Bousquet Gutierrez, and K. Hakuta. 2000. Inadequate conclusions from an inadequate assessment: What can SAT-9 scores tell us about the impact of Proposition 227 in California? *Bilingual Research Journal* 24: 141–54.

Calderón, M., and A. Carreón. 2001. A two-way bilingual program: Promise, practice, and precautions. In *Effective programs for Latino students,* ed. R. Slavin and M. Calderon. Mahwah, NJ: Lawrence Erlbaum.

Cazabon, M., W. Lambert, and G. Hall. 1993. *Two-way bilingual education: A progress report on the amigos program.* Research Report No. 7. Santa Cruz, CA: National Center for Research on Cultural Diversity and Second Language Learning.

Cazabon, M., E. Nicoladis, and W. E. Lambert. 1998. *Becoming bilingual in the amigos two-way immersion program.* Research Report 3. http://www.cal.org/resources/pubs/becomebiling.html

Center for Applied Linguistics. 2008. Languages of instruction in TWI programs. http://www.cal.org/twi/directory/language.htm (accessed October 30, 2008.)

Christian, D., C. Montone, K. Lindholm, and I. Carranza. 1997. *Profiles in two-way immersion education.* Washington, DC: Delta Systems and ERIC Clearinghouse on Languages and Linguistics.

Christian, D., F. Genesee, K. Lindholm-Leary, and E. Howard. 2004. *Final progress report: CAL/CREDE study of two-way immersion education.* http://www.cal.org/twi/CREDEfinal.doc

Clark, E. R., B. B. Flores, M. Riojas Cortez, and H. R. Smith. 2002. You can't have a rainbow without a *tormenta:* A description of an IHE's response to a community need for a dual language school. *Bilingual Research Journal* 26(1): 123–48.

Cloud, N., F. Genesee, and E. Hamayan. 2000. *Dual language instruction: A handbook for enriched education.* Portsmouth, NH: Heinle & Heinle.

Cohen, Elizabeth G. 1994. *Designing groupwork: Strategies for the heterogeneous classroom.* New York: Teachers College Press.

Collier, V. P. 1987. Age and rate of acquisition of second language for academic purposes. *TESOL Quarterly* 21(4): 617–41.

Collier, V. P. 1989. How long? A synthesis of research on academic achievement in a second language. *TESOL Quarterly* 23(3): 509–31.

Committee for Economic Development. (2007). *Education for global leadership: The importance of international studies and foreign language education for U. S. economic and national security.* Washington, DC: Committee for Economic Development. http://www.ced.org/docs/report/report_foreignlanguages.pdf (accessed March 5, 2008.)

Crystal, D. 2003. *English as a global language.* New York: Cambridge University Press.

Cummins, J. 1976. The influence of bilingualism on cognitive growth: A synthesis of research findings and an explanatory hypothesis. *Working Papers on Bilingualism* 9: 1–43.

Cummins, J. 1981. The role of primary language development in promoting educational success for language minority students. In *Schooling and language minority students: An educational framework.* 1st ed., 3–49. Los Angeles: Evaluation, Dissemination and Assessment Center, California State University.

Curiel, H., J. A. Rosenthal, and H. G. Richek. 1986. Impacts of bilingual education on secondary school grades, attendance, retentions and drop-out. *Hispanic Journal of Behavioral Sciences* 8(4): 357–67.

De Jong, E. J. 2002. Effective bilingual education: From theory to academic achievement in a two-way bilingual program. *Bilingual Research Journal* 26(1): 65–84.

de Valenzuela, J. S., and S. L. Niccolai. 2004. Language development in culturally and linguistically diverse students with special education needs. In *The bilingual special education interface.* 4th ed., ed. L. Baca and H. Cervantes, 125–61. Upper Saddle River, NJ: Merrill.

Doherty, R. W., R. S. Hilberg, A. Pinal, and R. G. Tharp. 2003. Five standards and student achievement. *NABE Journal of Research and Practice* 1: 1–24.

Dulay, H., and M. Burt. 1978. From research to method in bilingual education. In *International dimensions in bilingual education,* ed. J. Alatis. Washington, DC: Georgetown University Press.

Echevarria, J., D. Short, and K. Powers. 2006. School reform and standards-based education: An instructional model for English language learners. *Journal of Educational Research* 99(4): 195–210.

Echevarria, J., M. E. Vogt, and D. Short. 2008. *Making content comprehensible for English language learners: The SIOP model.* 3rd ed. Boston: Allyn & Bacon.

Escamilla, K., and M. Medina. 1993. English and Spanish acquisition by limited-language proficient Mexican-Americans in a three-year maintenance bilingual program. *Hispanic Journal of Behavioral Sciences* 15(1): 108–20.

Escamilla, K., L. Baca, J. Hoover, and E. Almanza de Schonewise. 2005. *An analysis of limited English proficient student achievement on Colorado state reading, writing, and math performance standards* (Field Initiated Project No. T292B010005). Washington, DC: U.S. Department of Education, Office of English Language Acquisition.

Fernandez, R., and F. Nielsen. 1986. Bilingualism and Hispanic scholastic achievement: Some baseline results. *Social Science Research* 15: 43–70.

Foreign language framework for California public schools. 2003. Sacramento: California Department of Education.

Fortune, T., and D. Tedick, eds. 2008. *Pathways to bilingualism: Evolving perspectives on immersion education.* Avon, England: Multilingual Matters.

Francis, D. J., N. K. Lesaux, and D. L. August. 2006. Language of instruction for language minority learners. In *Developing literacy in a second language: Report of the National Literacy Panel,* ed. D. L. August and T. Shanahan, 365–414. Mahwah, NJ: Lawrence Erlbaum.

Fulton-Scott, M. J., and A. D. Calvin. 1983. Bilingual multicultural education vs. integrated and non-integrated ESL instruction. *NABE: The Journal for the National Association for Bilingual Education* 7(3): 1–12.

Garcia, G. E. 1998. Mexican-American bilingual students' metacognitive reading strategies: What's transferred, unique, problematic? *National Reading Conference Yearbook* 47: 253–64.

Garcia, Y. 2003. Korean/English two-way immersion at Cahuenga Elementary School. *NABE News* 26: 8–11, 25.

Garcia, E., and J. Curry-Rodriguez. 2000. The education of limited English proficient students in California schools: An assessment of the influence of Proposition 227 on selected districts and schools. *Bilingual Research Journal* 24(1 & 2): 15–35.

Gathercole, V. C. M. 2002a. Command of the mass/count distinction in bilingual and monolingual chidren: An English morphosyntactic distinction. In *Language and literacy in bilingual children* (Child Language and Child Development, 2), ed. D. K. Oller and R. E. Eilers. Avon, England: Multilingual Matters.

Gathercole, V. C. M. 2002b. Grammatical gender in bilingual and monolingual children: A Spanish morphosyntactic distinction. In *Language and literacy in bilingual children* (Child Language and Child Development, 2), ed. D. K. Oller and R. E. Eilers. Avon, England: Multilingual Matters.

Genesee, F. 1987. *Learning through two languages.* Cambridge: Newbury House Publishers.

Genesee, F. 1994. Integrating language and content: Lessons from immersion. *Educational Practice Report* 11: 1–15.

Genesee, F., ed. 1999. Program alternatives for linguistically diverse students. *Educational Practice Report* 1.

Genesee, F. 2002. Portrait of the bilingual child. In *Perspectives on the L2 user,* ed. V. Cook, 170–96. Clevedon, England: Multilingual Matters.

Genesee, F. 2004. What do we know about bilingual education for majority language students. In *Handbook of bilingualism and multiculturalism,* ed. T. K. Bhatia and W. Ritchie, 547–76. Malden, MA: Blackwell.

Genesee, F. 2007. The suitability of French immersion for students who are at-risk: A review of research evidence. *Canadian Modern Language Review* 63: 655–688.

Genesee, F., I. Boivin, and E. Nicoladis. 1996. Talking with strangers: A study of bilingual children's communicative competence. *Applied Psycholinguistics* 17: 427–42.

Genesee, F. and P. Gandara. 1999. Bilingual education programs: A cross-national perspective. *Journal of Social Issues* 55: 665–85.

Genesee, F., and E. Geva. 2006. Cross-linguistic relationships in working memory, phonological processes, and oral language. In *Developing literacy in second language learners. Report of the National Literacy Panel on Minority-Language Children and Youth*, ed. D. August and T. Shanahan, 175–84. Mahwah, NJ: Lawrence Erlbaum.

Genesee, F., K. Lindholm-Leary, W. Saunders, and D. Christian. 2005. English language learners in U.S. schools: An overview of research findings. *Journal of Education for Students Placed at Risk* 10(4): 363–85.

Genesee, F., K. Lindholm-Leary, W. Saunders, and D. Christian. 2006. *Educating English language learners: A synthesis of research evidence.* New York: Cambridge University Press.

Genesee, F., J. Paradis, and M. Crago. 2004. *Dual language development & disorders: A handbook on bilingualism and second language learning.* Baltimore: Brookes.

Gersten, R., and J. Woodward. 1995. A longitudinal study of transitional and immersion bilingual education programs in one district. *Elementary School Journal* 95(3): 223–39.

Geva, E., and F. Genesee. 2006. First-language oral proficiency and second-language literacy, Chapter 8. In *Report of the National Literacy Panel on K–12 Youth and Adolescents,* ed. D. August and T. Shanahan. Mahwah, NJ: Lawrence Erlbaum.

Glennen, Sharon, and M. Gay Masters. 2002. Typical and atypical development in infants and toddlers adopted in eastern Europe. *American Journal of Speech-Language Pathology* 11: 417–33.

Gold, N. 2006. *Successful bilingual schools: Six effective programs in California.* San Diego: San Diego County Office of Education.

Goldstein, B., ed. 2004. *Bilingual language development and disorders in Spanish-English speakers.* Baltimore: Brookes.

Goldstein, B., K. Harris, and M. Klein. 1993. Assessment of oral storytelling abilities of Latino junior high school students with learning handicaps. *Journal of Learning Disabilities* 26(2): 38–43.

Gomez, L., D. Freeman, and Y. Freeman. 2005. Dual language education: A promising 50-50 model. *Bilingual Research Journal* 29: 145–64.

Gonzalez, N., L. C. Moll, and C. Amanti. 2005. *Funds of knowledge: Theorizing practices in households, communities and classrooms.* Mahwah, NJ: Lawrence Erlbaum.

Gordon, N., and C. Hoxby. 2002. *Achievement effects of bilingual education vs. English vs. English immersion: Evidence from California's Proposition 227* (Working paper). Cambridge, MA: Harvard Institute for Economic Research.

Greene, J. P. 1998. *A meta-analysis of the effectiveness of bilingual education.* Claremont, CA: Tomas Rivera Policy Institute.

Greenfield, P. M., B. Quiroz, and C. Raeff. 2000. Cross-cultural conflict and harmony in the social construction of the child. In *The social construction of the child: Nature and sources of variability. New directions in child psychology,* ed. S. Harkness, C. Raeff, and C. M. Super, 93-108. San Francisco: Jossey-Bass.

Grissom, J. B. 2004. Reclassification of English learners. *Education policy analysis* archives 12(36): 1–38. http://epaa.asu.edu/epaa/v12n36/ (accessed August 3, 2007.)

Ha, J. H. 2001. Elementary students' written language development in a Korean/English two-way immersion program. Master's thesis, California State University, Long Beach.

Hakuta, K., Y. Butler, and D. Witt. 2000. *How long does it take English learners to attain proficiency?* University of California Linguistic Minority Research Institute Policy Report 2000–1.

Hampton, S., J. M. Ekboir, and R. I. Rochin. 1995. The performance of Latinos in rural public schools: A comparative analysis of test scores in grades 3, 6, and 12. *Hispanic Journal of Behavioral Sciences* 17(4): 480–98.

Hernández-Chavez, E. 1984. The inadequacy of English immersion education as an educational approach for language minority students in the United States. In *Studies on immersion education: A collection for United States educators.* Sacramento: California State Department of Education.

Hoff, E., and M. Shatz, ed. 2007. *Blackwell handbook of language development.* Malden, MA: Blackwell.

Howard, E. R. 2003. *Biliteracy development in two-way immersion education programs: A multilevel analysis of the effects of native language and home language use on the development of narrative writing ability in English and Spanish.* PhD diss., Harvard University.

Howard, E. R., and D. Christian. 1997. *The development of bilingualism and biliteracy in two-way immersion students.* Paper presented at the Annual Meeting of the American Educational Research Association, Chicago, IL (ERIC Document Reproduction Service No. ED 405741).

Howard, E. R., and D. Christian. 2002. Two-way immersion 101: Designing and implementing a two-way immersion education program at the elementary level. *Educational Practice Report* 9. http://www.cal.org/resources/pubs/twi_pubs.html#101

Howard, E. R., D. Christian, and F, Genesee. 2004. *The development of bilingualism and biliteracy from grades 3 to 5: A summary of findings from the CAL/CREDE study of two-way immersion education.* Santa Cruz, CA: Center for Research on Education, Diversity & Excellence and Center for Applied Linguistics.

Howard, E. R., and J. Sugarman. 2007. *Realizing the vision of two-way immersion: Fostering effective programs and classrooms.* Washington, DC: Delta Systems and ERIC Clearinghouse on Languages and Linguistics.

Howard, E. R., J. Sugarman, D. Christian, K. J. Lindholm-Leary, and D. Rogers. 2007 *Guiding principles for dual language education.* 2nd ed. Washington, DC: U.S. Department of Education and National Clearinghouse for English Language Acquisition. http://www.cal.org/twi/guidingprinciples.htm

Jiménez, R. T. 2000. Literacy and the identity development of Latina/o students. *American Educational Research Journal* 37(4): 971–1000.

Jimenez, R. T., G. E. Garcia, and P. D. Pearson. 1996. The reading strategies of bilingual Latina/o students who are successful English readers: Opportunities and obstacles. *Reading Research Quarterly* 31: 90–112.

Kao, G., and M. Tienda. 1995. Optimism and achievement: The educational performance of immigrant youth. *Social Science Quarterly* 76:1–19.

Kirk Senesac, B. V. 2002. Two-way immersion education: A portrait of quality schooling. *Bilingual Research Journal* 26(1): 85–101.

Knapp, M. S., and S. Woolverton. 2003. Social class and schooling. In *Handbook of research on multicultural education.* 2nd ed., ed. J. Banks and C. A. McGee Banks, 548–69. New York: Jossey Bass.

Kohnert, K. 2004. Children learning a second language: Processing skills in early sequential bilinguals. In *Bilingual language development and disorders in Spanish-English speakers,* ed. B. Goldstein 53–76. Baltimore: Brookes.

Kohnert, K., and A. Derr. 2004. Language intervention with bilingual children. In *Bilingual language development and disorders in Spanish-English speakers,* ed. B. Goldstein, 315–43. Baltimore: Brookes.

Kowal, M., and M. Swain. 1997. From semantic to syntactic processing: How can we promote it in the immersion classroom? In *Immersion education: International perspectives,* ed. R. K. Johnson and M. Swain. New York: Cambridge University Press.

Lambert, W. E. 1984. An overview of issues in immersion education. In *Studies in immersion education: A collection for United States educators,* 8–30. Sacramento: California State Department of Education.

Lambert, W. E., and M. Cazabon. 1994. *Students' view of the amigos program* (Research Report No. 11). Santa Cruz, CA: National Center for Research on Cultural Diversity and Second Language Learning.

Langer, J. A., L. Bartolome, O. Vasquez, and T. Lucas. 1990. Meaning construction in school literacy tasks: A study of bilingual students. *American Educational Research Journal* 27(3): 427–71.

Lantolf, J. P. 2005. Sociocultural and second language learning research: An exegesis. In *Handbook of research in second language teaching and learning.* ed. E. Hinkel, 335–53. Mahwah, NJ: Lawrence Erlbaum.

Legaretta, D. 1979. The effects of program models on language acquisition by Spanish-speaking children. *TESOL Quarterly* 8: 521–34.

Legaretta, D. 1981. Effective use of the primary language in the classroom. In *Schooling and language minority students: An educational framework,* 83–116. Los Angeles: Evaluation, Dissemination, and Assessment Center, California State University.

Lindholm, K. J. 1980. Bilingual children: Some interpretations of cognitive and linguistic development. In *Children's Language,* Volume II, ed. K. Nelson, New York: Gardner Press.

Lindholm, K. J. 1987. English question use in Spanish-speaking ESL children: Changes with English language proficiency. *Research in the Teaching of English* 21: 64–91.

Lindholm, K. J. 1988. *The Edison elementary school bilingual immersion program: Student progress after one year of implementation.* Technical Report No. 9. Los Angeles: Center for Language Education and Research, UCLA.

Lindholm, K. J. 1994. Promoting positive cross-cultural attitudes and perceived competence in culturally and linguistically diverse classrooms. In *Cultural diversity in schools: From rhetoric to practice,* ed. R. A. DeVillar, C. J. Faltis, and J. P. Cummins. Albany: State University of New York Press.

Lindholm-Leary, K. J. 2001. *Dual language education.* Avon, England: Multilingual Matters.

Lindholm-Leary, K. J. 2003. Dual language achievement, proficiency, and attitudes among current high school graduates of two-way programs. *NABE Journal* 26: 20–25.

Lindholm-Leary, K. J. 2005. The rich promise of two-way immersion. *Educational Leadership* 62: 56–59.

Lindholm-Leary, K. J. 2007. *Effective features of dual language education programs: A review of research and best practices.* 2nd ed. Washington, DC: Center for Applied Linguistics.

Lindholm-Leary, K. 2008. Dual language education: Hope or hype in the NCLB accountability era? Paper presented at the annual meeting of the California Association for Bilingual Education, San Jose, CA.

Lindholm-Leary, K. 2009. Language proficiency, achievement and attitudes in two-way Chinese immersion students. Paper presented at the National Association for Bilingual Education, Austin, TX, February 19.

Lindholm, K. J., and Z. Aclan. 1991. Bilingual proficiency as a bridge to academic achievement: Results from bilingual/immersion programs. *Journal of Education* 173: 99–113.

Lindholm-Leary, K. J., and N. Block. In press. Achievement in predominantly low-SES Hispanic dual language schools. *International Journal of Bilingual Education.*

Lindholm-Leary, K. J., and G. Borsato. 2001. Impact of two-way bilingual elementary programs on students' attitudes toward school and college. Research Report No. 10. University of California, Santa Cruz: Center for Research on Education, Diversity & Excellence.

Lindholm-Leary, K. J., and G. Borsato. 2005. Hispanic high schoolers and mathematics: Follow-up of students who had participated in two-way bilingual elementary programs. *Bilingual Research Journal* 29: 641–52.

Lindholm-Leary, K., and G. Borsato. 2006. Academic achievement. In *Educating English language learners: A synthesis of research evidence,* ed. F. Genesee, K. Lindholm-Leary, W. Saunders, and D. Christian, 176–221. New York: Cambridge University Press.

Lindholm-Leary, K. J. and A. Ferrante. 2005 Follow-up study of middle school two-way students: Language proficiency, achievement and attitudes. In *Language in multicultural education,* ed. R. Hoosain and F. Salili. Greenwich, CT: Information Age Publishing

Lindholm-Leary, K. J., and E. Howard. 2008. Language and academic achievement in two-way immersion programs. In *Pathways to bilingualism: Evolving perspectives on immersion education,* ed. T. Fortune and D. Tedick. Avon, England: Multilingual Matters.

Long, M. H. 1981. Input, interaction and second language acquisition. In *Native language and foreign language acquisition,* ed. H. Winitz, 379. New York: Annals of The New York Academy of Sciences.

Lopez, M., and A. Tashakkori. 2006. Differential outcomes of TWBE and TBE on ELLs at different entry levels. *Bilingual Research Journal* 30(1): 81–103.

Lyster, R. 2007. *Learning and teaching languages through content: A counterbalanced approach.* Philadelphia: John Benjamins.

MacSwan, J. 2000. The threshold hypothesis, semilingualism, and other contribution to a deficit view of linguistic minorities. *Hispanic Journal of Behavioral Sciences* 22(1): 3–45.

MacSwan, J. 2004. Bad data poison language study. *The Arizona Republic* (August 13): B9.

MacSwan, J, and L. Pray. 2005. Learning English bilingually: Age of onset of exposure and rate of acquisition among English language learners in a bilingual education program. *Bilingual Research Journal* 29(3): 653–78.

MacSwan, J., S. M. Stockford, K. Mahoney, M. S. Thompson, and K. E. DiCerbo. 2002. *Programs for English learners: A longitudinal exploration of program sequences and academic achievement in Arizona.* Tempe: Arizona State University and Arizona Department of Education.

MacSwan, J., M. S. Thompson, G. deKlerk, and K. McAlister. 2007. Theory, research, and theory-driven research: Explanations of academic achievement differences among English language learners. Paper presented at the University of California Linguistic Minority Research Institute, Arizona State University, Tempe, May 2–5, 2007.

Maratsos, M. 2000. More overregularizations after all. *Journal of Child Language* 28: 32–54.

Medina, M., and K. Escamilla. 1992. Evaluation of transitional and maintenance bilingual programs. *Urban Education* 27(3): 263–90.

Medrano, M. F. 1986. Evaluating the long-term effects of a bilingual education program: A study of Mexican-American students. *Journal of Educational Equity and Leadership* 6(2): 129–38.

Medrano, M. F. (1988). The effects of bilingual education on reading and mathematics achievement: A longitudinal case study. *Equity and Excellence* 23(4): 17–19.

Met, M., and E. B. Lorenz. 1997. Lessons from U.S. immersion programs: Two decades of experience. In *Immersion education: International perspectives,* ed. R. K. Johnson and M. Swain, 243–64. Cambridge: Cambridge University Press.

Miller, F., J. Heilmann, A. Nockerts, A. Iglesias, L. Fabiano, and D. J. Francis. 2006. Oral language and reading in bilingual children. *Learning Disabilities Research & Practice* 21(1): 30–43.

Montecel, M. R., and J. D. Cortez. 2002. Successful bilingual education programs: Development and the dissemination of criteria to identify promising and exemplary practices in bilingual education at the national level. *Bilingual Research Journal* 26: 1–21.

Nielsen, F., and S. Lerner. 1986. Language skills and school achievement of bilingual Hispanics. *Social Science Research* 15: 209–40.

Olneck. M. R. 2004. Immigrants and education. In *Handbook of research on multicultural education,* 2nd ed., ed. J. A. Banks and C. A. McGee Banks. New York: Macmillan.

Padrón, Y. N., and H. C. Waxman. 1988. The effect of ESL students' perceptions of their cognitive reading strategies on reading achievement. *TESOL Quarterly* 22: 146–50.

Paradis, J. 2005. Grammatical morphology in children learning English as a second language: Implications of similarities with specific language impairment. *Language, Speech, and Hearing Services in Schools* 36: 172–87.

Parrish, T., R. Linquanti, A. Merickel, H. Quick, J. Laird, and P. Esra. 2006. *Effects of the implementation of Proposition 227 on the education of English learners, K–12: Final report.* San Francisco: WestEd.

Perez, E. 1981. Oral language competence improves reading skills of Mexican American third graders. *Reading Teacher* 35: 24–27.

Philips, S. U. 1983. *The invisible culture: Communication in classroom and community on the Warm Springs Indian Reservation.* New York: Longman.

Potowski, K. 2007. *Language and identity in a dual immersion school.* Clevedon, England: Multilingual Matters.

Ramirez, J. D. 1992. Longitudinal study of structured English immersion strategy, early-exit and late-exit transitional bilingual education program for language-minority children (Executive Summary). *Bilingual Research Journal* 16(1-2): 1–62.

Ramos, F. 2007. What do parents think of two-way bilingual education? An analysis of responses. *Journal of Latinos and Education* 6(2): 139–50.

Reese, L., H. Garnier, R. Gallimore, and C. Goldenberg. 2000. A longitudinal analysis of the ecocultural antecedents of emergent Spanish literacy and subsequent English reading achievement of Spanish-speaking students. *American Educational Research Journal* 37(3): 633–62.

Restrepo, M. A., and V. F. Gutierrez-Clellen. 2004. Grammatical impairments in Spanish/English-speaking children. In *Language development: A focus on Spanish-English speakers,* ed. B. Goldstein. Baltimore: Brookes.

Riches, C., and F. Genesee. 2006. Cross-linguistic and cross-modal aspects of literacy development. In *Educating English language learners: A synthesis of research evidence,* ed. F. Genesee, K. Lindholm-Leary, W. Saunders, and D. Christian, 64–108. New York: Cambridge University Press.

Rogoff, B. 2003. *The cultural nature of human development.* Oxford: Oxford University Press.

Romaine, S. 1995. *Bilingualism.* 2nd ed. Oxford: Blackwell.

Rolstad, K., K. Mahoney, and G. V. Glass. 2005. The big picture: A meta-analysis of program effectiveness research on English language learners. *Educational Policy* 19: 572–94.

Rossell, C. H., and K. Baker. 1996. The educational effectiveness of bilingual education. *Research in the Teaching of English* 30(1): 7–74.

Rumbaut, R., and A. Portes. 2001. *Ethnicities: Children of immigrants in America.* Berkeley: University of California Press.

Rumberger, R. W., and P. Gándara. 2005. How well are California's English learners mastering English? *UC LMRI Newsletter* 14(2): 1–2.

Rumberger, R. W., and K. A. Larson. 1998. Toward explaining differences in educational achievement among Mexican-American language-minority students. *Sociology of Education* 71(1): 68–92.

Saldate, M., S. Mishra, IV, and M. Medina Jr. 1985. Bilingual instruction and academic achievement: A longitudinal study. *Journal of Instructional Psychology* 12(1): 24–30.

Saunders, W., and G. O'Brien. 2006. Oral language. In *Educating English language learners: A synthesis of research evidence,* ed. F. Genesee, K. Lindholm-Leary, W. Saunders, and D. Christian, D., 14–63. New York: Cambridge University Press.

Serrano, R., and E. R. Howard. 2003. Maintaining Spanish proficiency in the United States: The influence of English on the Spanish writing of native Spanish speakers in two-way immersion programs. In *Selected Proceedings of the First Workshop on Spanish Sociolinguistics,* ed. L. Sayahi, 77–88. Somerville, MA: Cascadilla Proceedings Project.

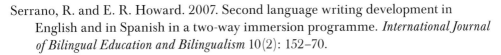
Serrano, R. and E. R. Howard. 2007. Second language writing development in English and in Spanish in a two-way immersion programme. *International Journal of Bilingual Education and Bilingualism* 10(2): 152–70.

Shannon, S. M., and M. Milian. 2002. Parents choose dual language programs in Colorado: A survey. *Bilingual Research Journal* 26(3): 681–96.

Slavin, R., and M. Calderon. 2001. *Effective programs for Latino learners.* Mahwah, NJ: Lawrence Erlbaum.

Slavin, R., and A. Cheung. 2005. A synthesis of research on reading instruction for English language learners. *Review of Educational Research* 75: 247–84.

Snow, C. E., M. S. Burns, and P. Griffin. eds. 1998. *Preventing reading difficulties in young children.* Committee on the Prevention of Reading Difficulties in Young Children, Commission on Behavioral and Social Sciences and Education, National Research Council. Washington, DC: National Academy Press.

Solano-Flores, G., and E. Trumbull. 2003. Examining language in context: The need for new research and practice paradigms in the testing of English language learners. *Educational Researcher* 32(2): 3–13.

Stipek, D., R. Ryan, and R. Alarcón. 2001. Bridging research and practice to develop a two-way bilingual program. *Early Childhood Research Quarterly* 16(1): 133–49.

Thomas, W., and B. Collier. 2002. *A national study of school effectiveness for language minority students' long-term academic achievement.* Santa Cruz, CA: Center for Research on Education, Diversity and Excellence.

Thompson, M., K. DiCerbo, K. Mahoney, and J. MacSwan. 2002. Exito en California? A validity critique of language program evaluations and analyses of English learner test scores. *Education Policy Analysis Archives* 10(7). http://epaa.asu.edu/epaa/v10n7/ (accessed August 3, 2007.)

Tomasello, M. 2000. Do young children have adult syntactic competence? *Cognition* 74: 209–53.

Tse, L. 1998. Ethnic identity formation and its implications for heritage language development. In *Heritage language development,* ed. S. D. Krashen, L. Tse, and J. McQuillan, 15–30. Culver City, CA: Language Education Associates.

Valdés, G. 1997. The teaching of Spanish to bilingual Spanish-speaking students: Outstanding issues and unanswered questions. In *La ensñnanza del espanol a hispanohablantes Praxis y teoria,* ed. M. C. Colombi and F. X. Alarcon, 93–101. Boston: Houghton Mifflin.

Valdés, G., and R. Figueroa. 1994. *Bilingualism and testing: A special case of bias.* Norwood, NJ: Ablex Publishing Company.

Valenzuela, A. 1999. *Subtractive schooling: U.S.-Mexican youth and the politics of caring.* Albany: State University of New York Press.

Vygotsky, L. 1978. *Mind in society: The development of higher psychological processes,* ed. M. Cole, V. John-Steiner, S. Scribner, and E. Souberman. Cambridge: Harvard University Press.

Weslander, D., and G. V. Stephany. 1983. Evaluation of English as a second language program for Southeast Asian students. *TESOL Quarterly* 17: 473–80.

Whatley, E. 1981. Language among black Americans. In *Language in the U.S.A.,* ed. C. A. Ferguson and S. B. Heath, 92-107. Cambridge: Cambridge University Press.

Willig, A. C. 1985. A meta-analysis of selected studies on the effectiveness of bilingual education. *Review of Educational Research* 55: 269–318.

Wong Fillmore, L. 1991. When learning a second language means losing the first. *Early Childhood Research Quarterly* 6: 323–34.

08-010 CN100253 10-10 11M